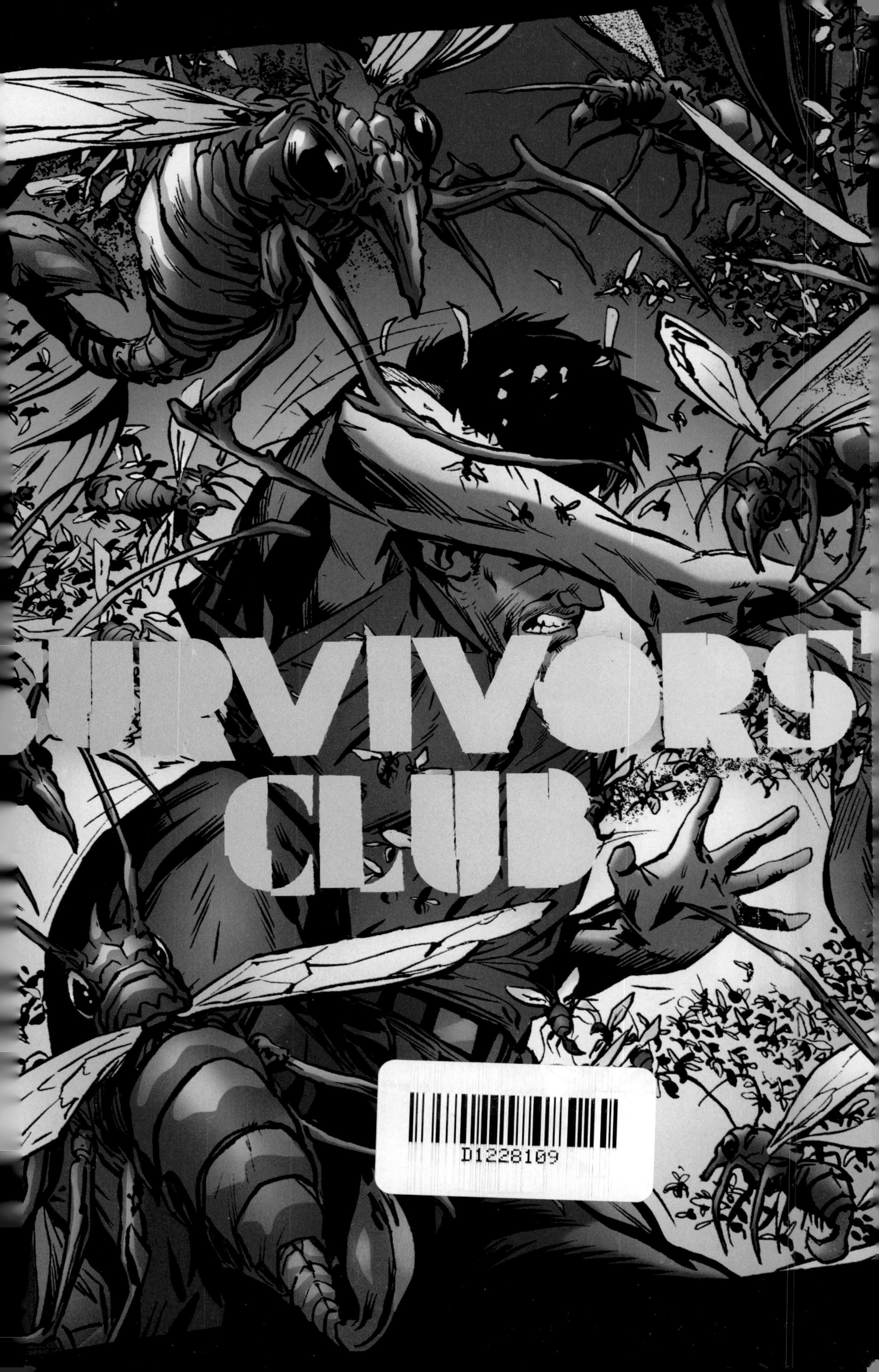

URVIVORS'
CLUB

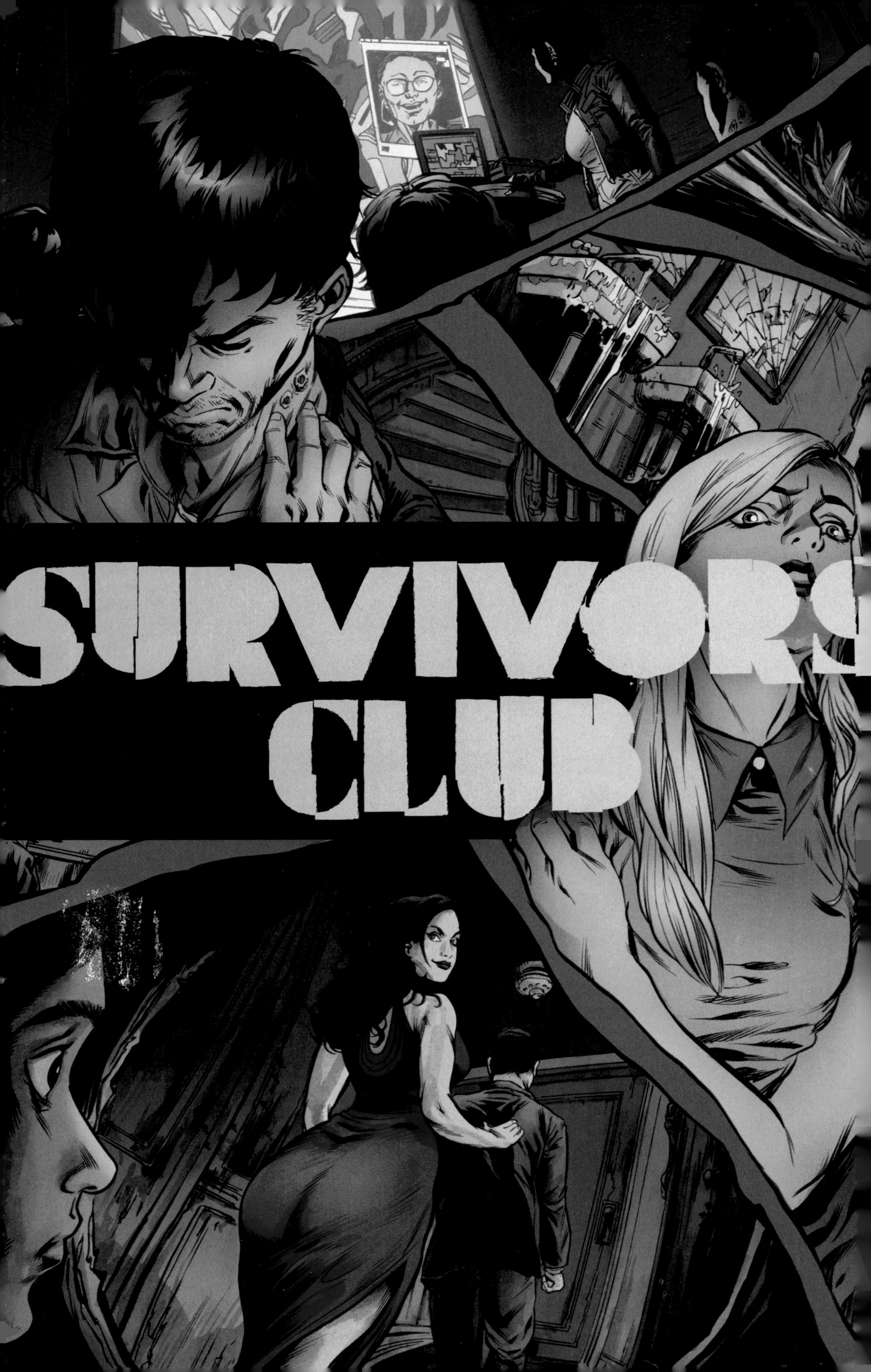
SURVIVORS
CLUB

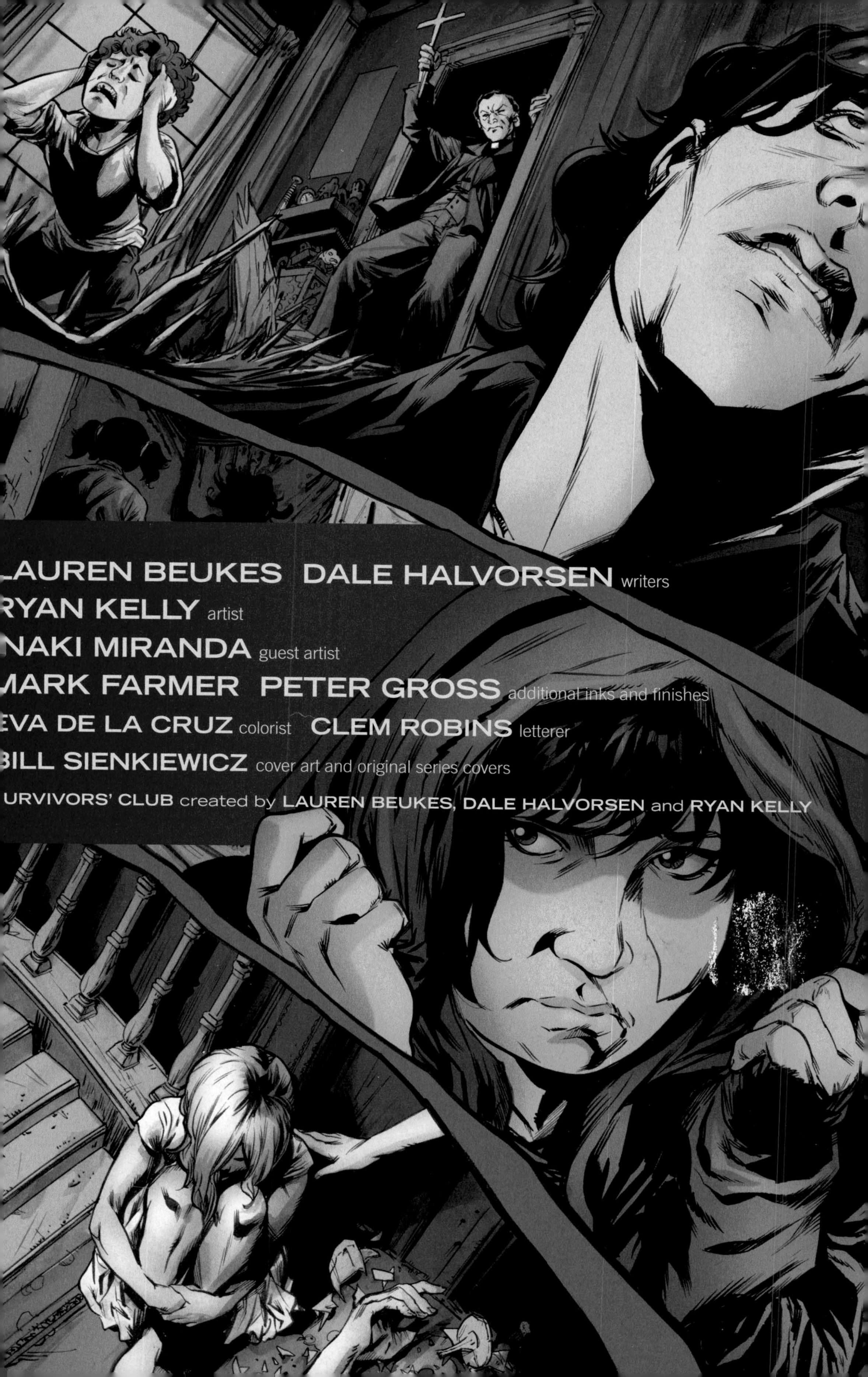

LAUREN BEUKES DALE HALVORSEN writers
RYAN KELLY artist
NAKI MIRANDA guest artist
MARK FARMER PETER GROSS additional inks and finishes
EVA DE LA CRUZ colorist CLEM ROBINS letterer
BILL SIENKIEWICZ cover art and original series covers
URVIVORS' CLUB created by LAUREN BEUKES, DALE HALVORSEN and RYAN KELLY

**SHELLY BOND**
Editor – Original Series

**ROWENA YOW  MOLLY MAHAN**
Associate Editors – Original Series

**JEB WOODARD**
Group Editor – Collected Editions

**SCOTT NYBAKKEN**
Editor – Collected Edition

**STEVE COOK**
Design Director – Books

**CURTIS KING JR.**
Publication Design

**SHELLY BOND**
VP & Executive Editor – Vertigo

**DIANE NELSON**
President

**DAN DIDIO** and **JIM LEE**
Co-Publishers

**GEOFF JOHNS**
Chief Creative Officer

**AMIT DESAI**
Senior VP – Marketing & Global Franchise Management

**NAIRI GARDINER**
Senior VP – Finance

**SAM ADES**
VP – Digital Marketing

**BOBBIE CHASE**
VP – Talent Development

**MARK CHIARELLO**
Senior VP – Art, Design & Collected Editions

**JOHN CUNNINGHAM**
VP – Content Strategy

**ANNE DEPIES**
VP – Strategy Planning & Reporting

**DON FALLETTI**
VP – Manufacturing Operations

**LAWRENCE GANEM**
VP – Editorial Administration & Talent Relations

**ALISON GILL**
Senior VP – Manufacturing & Operations

**HANK KANALZ**
Senior VP – Editorial Strategy & Administration

**JAY KOGAN**
VP – Legal Affairs

**DEREK MADDALENA**
Senior VP – Sales & Business Development

**JACK MAHAN**
VP – Business Affairs

**DAN MIRON**
VP – Sales Planning & Trade Development

**NICK NAPOLITANO**
VP – Manufacturing Administration

**CAROL ROEDER**
VP – Marketing

**EDDIE SCANNELL**
VP – Mass Account & Digital Sales

**COURTNEY SIMMONS**
Senior VP – Publicity & Communications

**JIM (SKI) SOKOLOWSKI**
VP – Comic Book Specialty & Newsstand Sales

**SANDY YI**
Senior VP – Global Franchise Management

**SURVIVORS' CLUB**

Published by DC Comics. Compilation and all new material Copyright © 2016
Lauren Beukes, Dale Halvorsen and Ryan Kelly. All Rights Reserved.

Originally published in single magazine form as SURVIVORS' CLUB 1-9. Copyright © 2015, 2016
Lauren Beukes, Dale Halvorsen and Ryan Kelly. All Rights Reserved. All characters, their distinctive
likenesses and related elements featured in this publication are trademarks of Lauren Beukes,
Dale Halvorsen and Ryan Kelly. VERTIGO is a trademark of DC Comics. The stories, characters and
incidents featured in this publication are entirely fictional. DC Comics does not read or accept
unsolicited submissions of ideas, stories or artwork.

PEFC Certified

Printed on paper from
sustainably managed
forests and controlled
sources

**PEFC**

PEFC/29-31-75   www.pefc.org

DC Comics
2900 West Alameda Avenue,
Burbank, CA 91505
Printed in the USA. First Printing.
ISBN: 978-1-4012-6554-0

Library of Congress Cataloging-in-Publication Data is available.

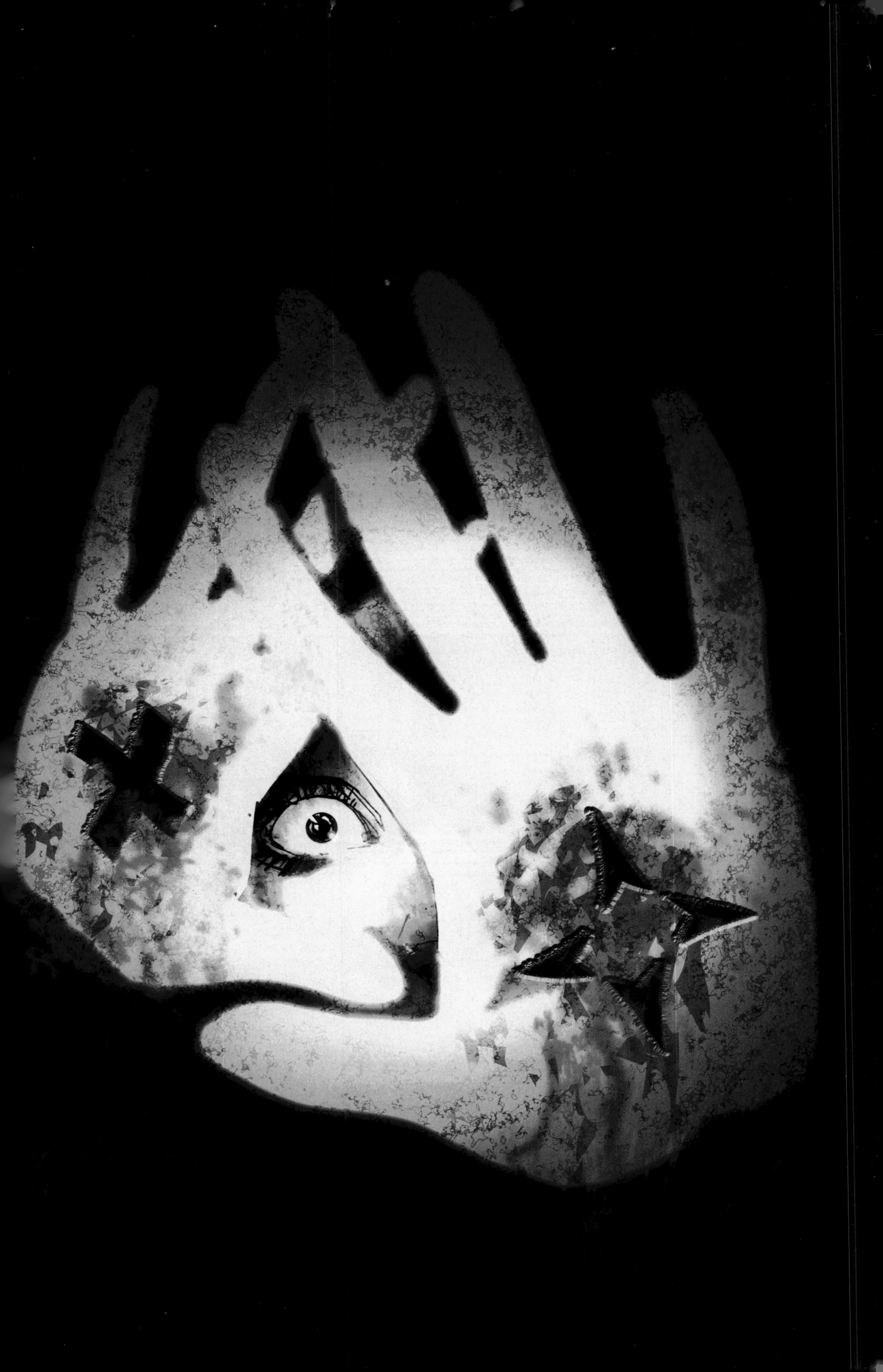

## Muskagee House

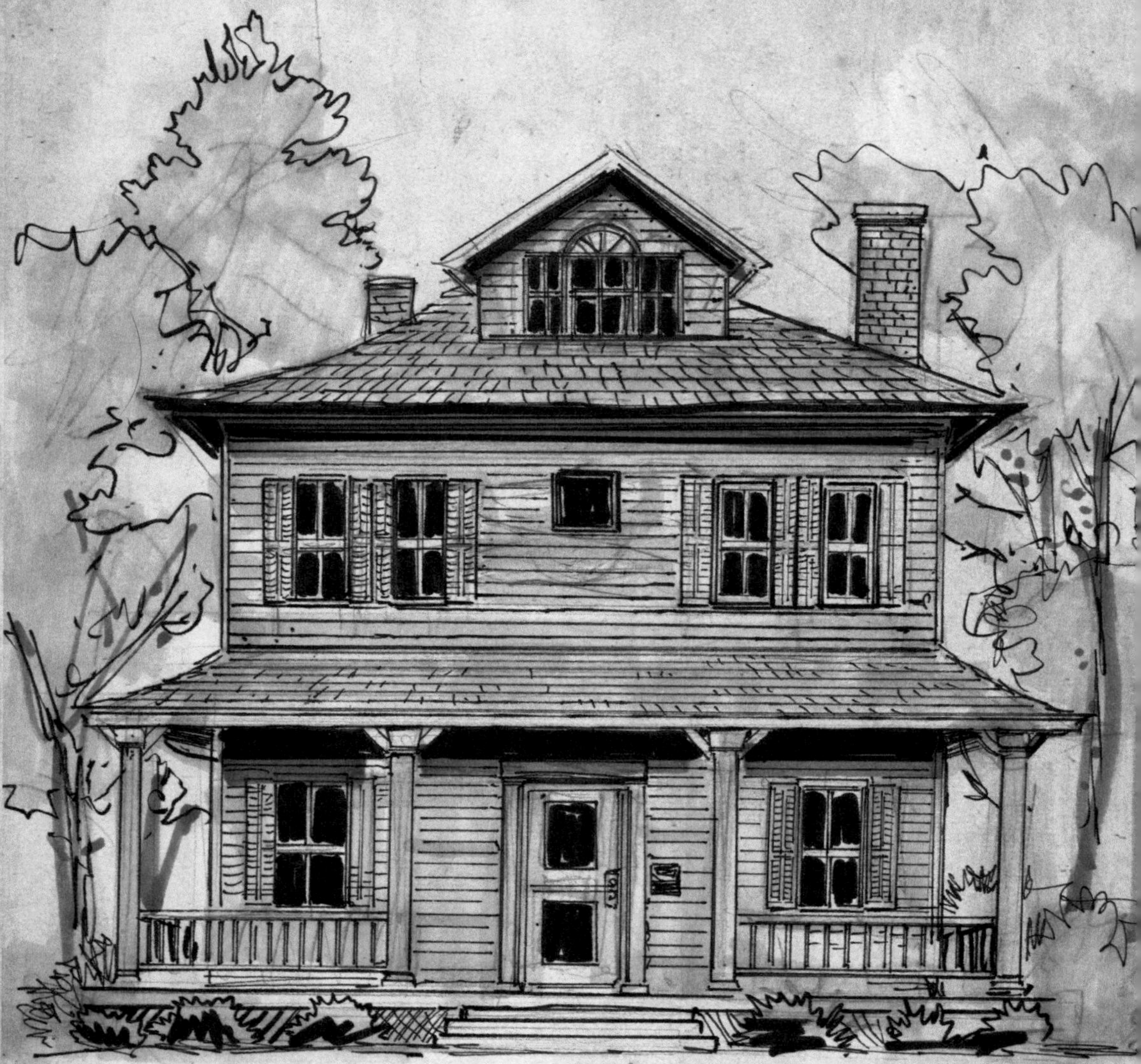

# SPECIAL THANKS

We believe in the power of research, but sometimes there's only so far research can get you and you have to ask the experts to make sure you're representing the real elements in your story in a way that's faithful and respectful.

We're grateful to the following people for taking the time to walk us through their various areas of expertise. Any mistakes are entirely ours.

Writer Daniel José Older shared his horrifying true-life paramedic experiences with us, talked us through Teo's scenes, slang and acronyms, and the setup for Teo's home lab, which, alas, never made it into the final story.

Akwasi Amo-Addae a.k.a. @afrocyberpunk, translated our Ghanian dialogue in the scene set in the Agbogbloshie dump. Thanks to Zukiswa Wanner for facilitating the introductions and to Pieter Hugo, whose striking photographs of the men and boys who sift through the dump to scavenge reclaimable materials inspired this scene.

Pablo Defendini advised us on appropriate (and inappropriate) Puerto Rican slang.

Johannesburg sangoma (traditional healer/diviner) Nokulinda Mkhize cast a professional eye over the sangoma consultation dream sequence and made very helpful suggestions for the sangoma's dialogue and important details. Please note that the inclusion of the troll doll was from Lauren's experience getting a reading from another sangoma at Mai Mai, when she was researching *Zoo City*.

Grant Hinds talked us through game demos, game culture, the harsh reality of game development, YouTube play-throughs (which he does on his YouTube channel) and a bunch of other stuff which made our brains hurt.

*Character designs and development sketches by Ryan Kelly are included here and throughout the volume.*

# SURVIVORS' CLUB
## CHAPTER ONE: KILL SCREEN

LAUREN BEUKES WRITER
DALE HALVORSEN WRITER
RYAN KELLY ARTIST

EVA DE LA CRUZ COLORIST CLEM ROBINS LETTERER
BILL SIENKIEWICZ COVER ARTIST
ROWENA YOW ASSOCIATE EDITOR SHELLY BOND EDITOR
SURVIVORS' CLUB CREATED BY BEUKES, HALVORSEN AND KELLY

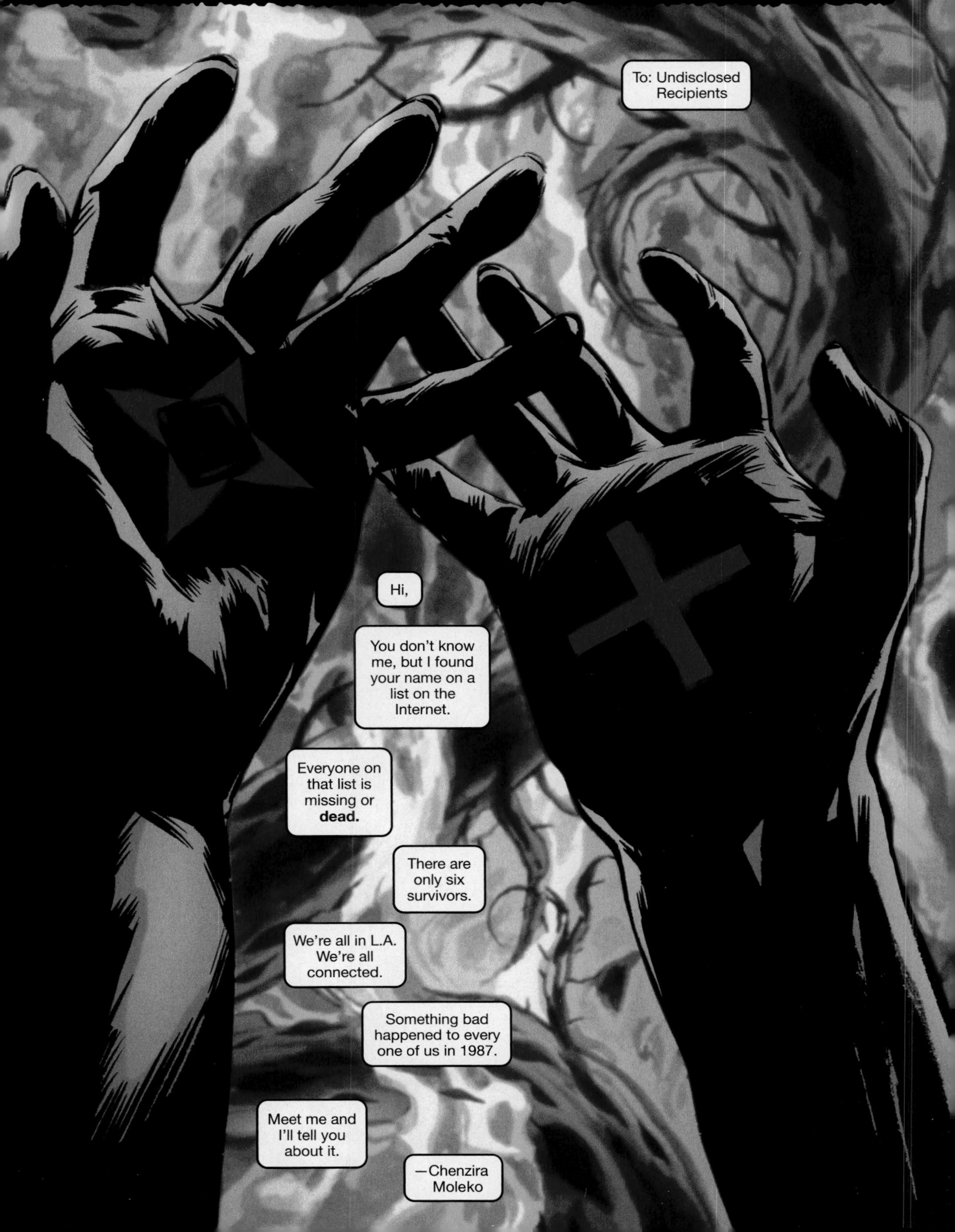
To: Undisclosed Recipients
Hi,
You don't know me, but I found your name on a list on the Internet.
Everyone on that list is missing or **dead.**
There are only six survivors.
We're all in L.A. We're all connected.
Something bad happened to every one of us in 1987.
Meet me and I'll tell you about it.
—Chenzira Moleko

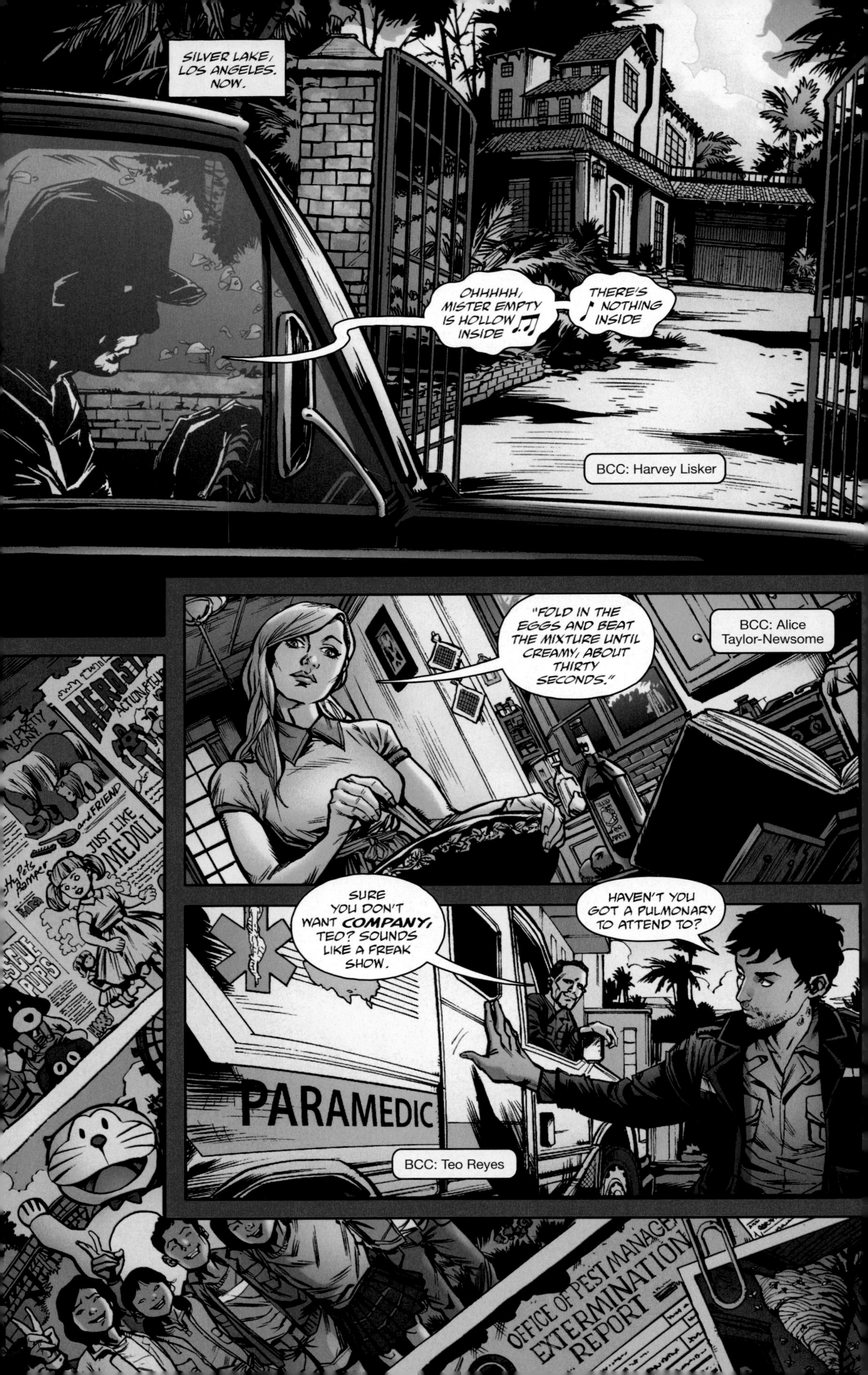
SILVER LAKE, LOS ANGELES. NOW.
OHHHHH, MISTER EMPTY IS HOLLOW INSIDE
THERE'S NOTHING INSIDE
BCC: Harvey Lisker
"FOLD IN THE EGGS AND BEAT THE MIXTURE UNTIL CREAMY, ABOUT THIRTY SECONDS."
BCC: Alice Taylor-Newsome
SURE YOU DON'T WANT COMPANY, TEO? SOUNDS LIKE A FREAK SHOW.
HAVEN'T YOU GOT A PULMONARY TO ATTEND TO?
PARAMEDIC
BCC: Teo Reyes
JUST LIKE MEDOLL
OFFICE OF PEST MANAGE
EXTERMINATION REPORT

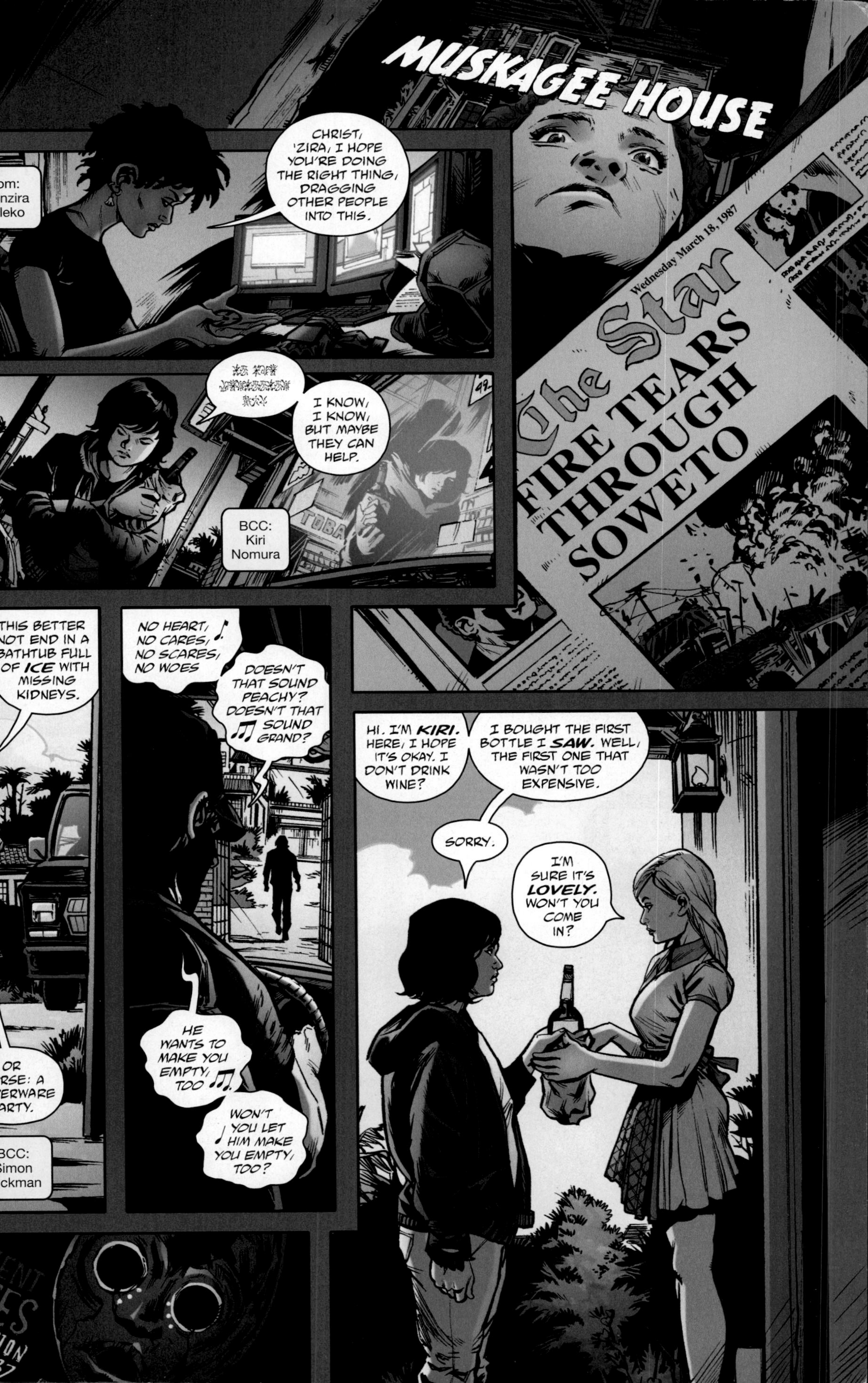
MUSKAGEE HOUSE
From:
Nzira
Uleko
CHRIST, 'ZIRA, I HOPE YOU'RE DOING THE RIGHT THING, DRAGGING OTHER PEOPLE INTO THIS.
I KNOW, I KNOW, BUT MAYBE THEY CAN HELP.
BCC:
Kiri
Nomura
Wednesday March 18, 1987
The Star
FIRE TEARS THROUGH SOWETO
THIS BETTER NOT END IN A BATHTUB FULL OF ICE WITH MISSING KIDNEYS.
OR ...RSE: A ...ERWARE ...ARTY.
BCC:
Simon
...ckman
NO HEART, NO CARES, NO SCARES, NO WOES
DOESN'T THAT SOUND PEACHY? DOESN'T THAT SOUND GRAND?
HE WANTS TO MAKE YOU EMPTY, TOO
WON'T YOU LET HIM MAKE YOU EMPTY, TOO?
HI. I'M KIRI. HERE, I HOPE IT'S OKAY. I DON'T DRINK WINE?
I BOUGHT THE FIRST BOTTLE I SAW. WELL, THE FIRST ONE THAT WASN'T TOO EXPENSIVE.
SORRY.
I'M SURE IT'S LOVELY. WON'T YOU COME IN?

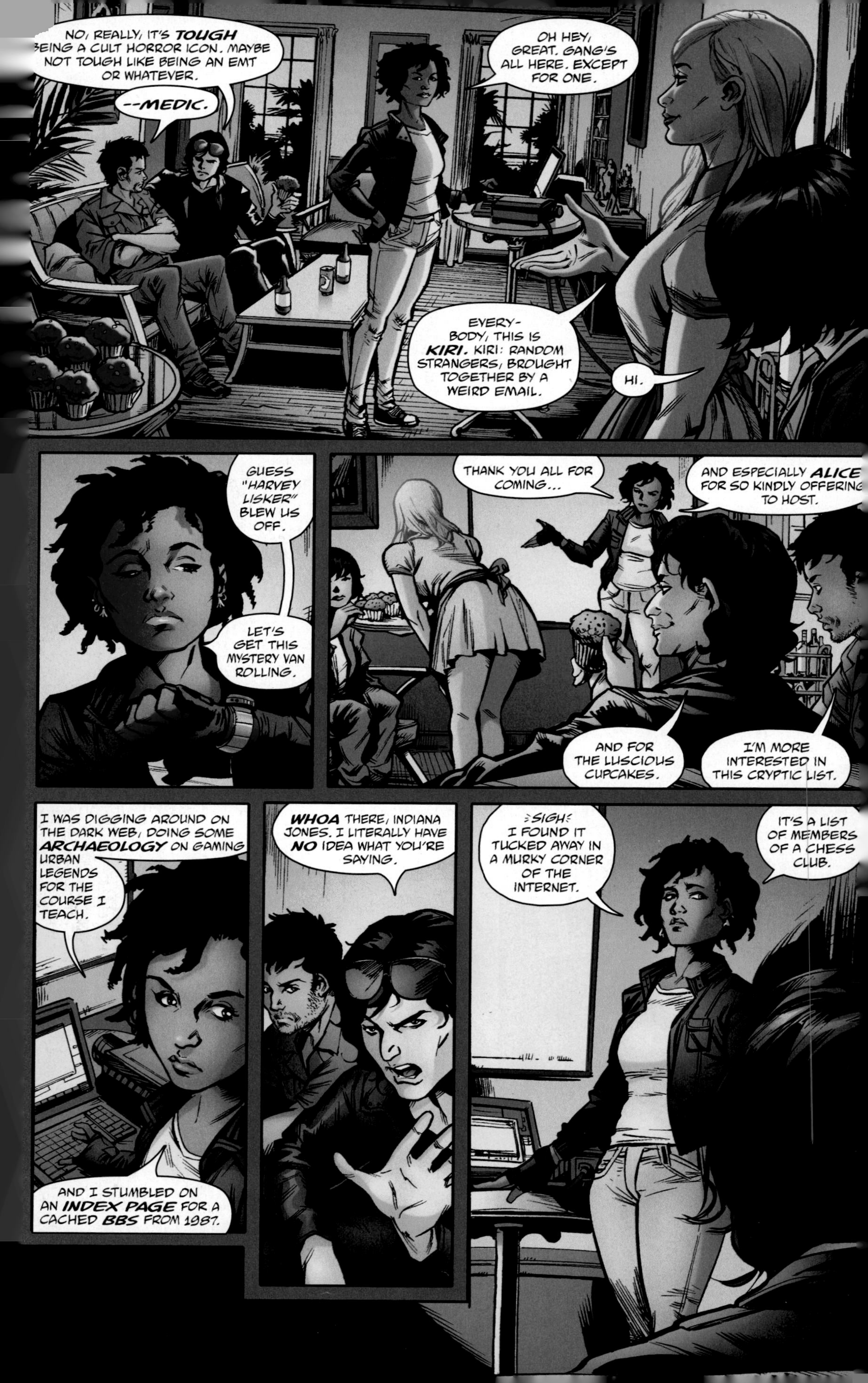
NO, REALLY, IT'S TOUGH BEING A CULT HORROR ICON. MAYBE NOT TOUGH LIKE BEING AN EMT OR WHATEVER.
--MEDIC.
OH HEY, GREAT. GANG'S ALL HERE. EXCEPT FOR ONE.
EVERYBODY, THIS IS KIRI. KIRI: RANDOM STRANGERS, BROUGHT TOGETHER BY A WEIRD EMAIL.
HI.
GUESS "HARVEY LISKER" BLEW US OFF.
LET'S GET THIS MYSTERY VAN ROLLING.
THANK YOU ALL FOR COMING...
AND ESPECIALLY ALICE FOR SO KINDLY OFFERING TO HOST.
AND FOR THE LUSCIOUS CUPCAKES.
I'M MORE INTERESTED IN THIS CRYPTIC LIST.
I WAS DIGGING AROUND ON THE DARK WEB, DOING SOME ARCHAEOLOGY ON GAMING URBAN LEGENDS FOR THE COURSE I TEACH.
AND I STUMBLED ON AN INDEX PAGE FOR A CACHED BBS FROM 1987.
WHOA THERE, INDIANA JONES. I LITERALLY HAVE NO IDEA WHAT YOU'RE SAYING.
SIGH I FOUND IT TUCKED AWAY IN A MURKY CORNER OF THE INTERNET.
IT'S A LIST OF MEMBERS OF A CHESS CLUB.

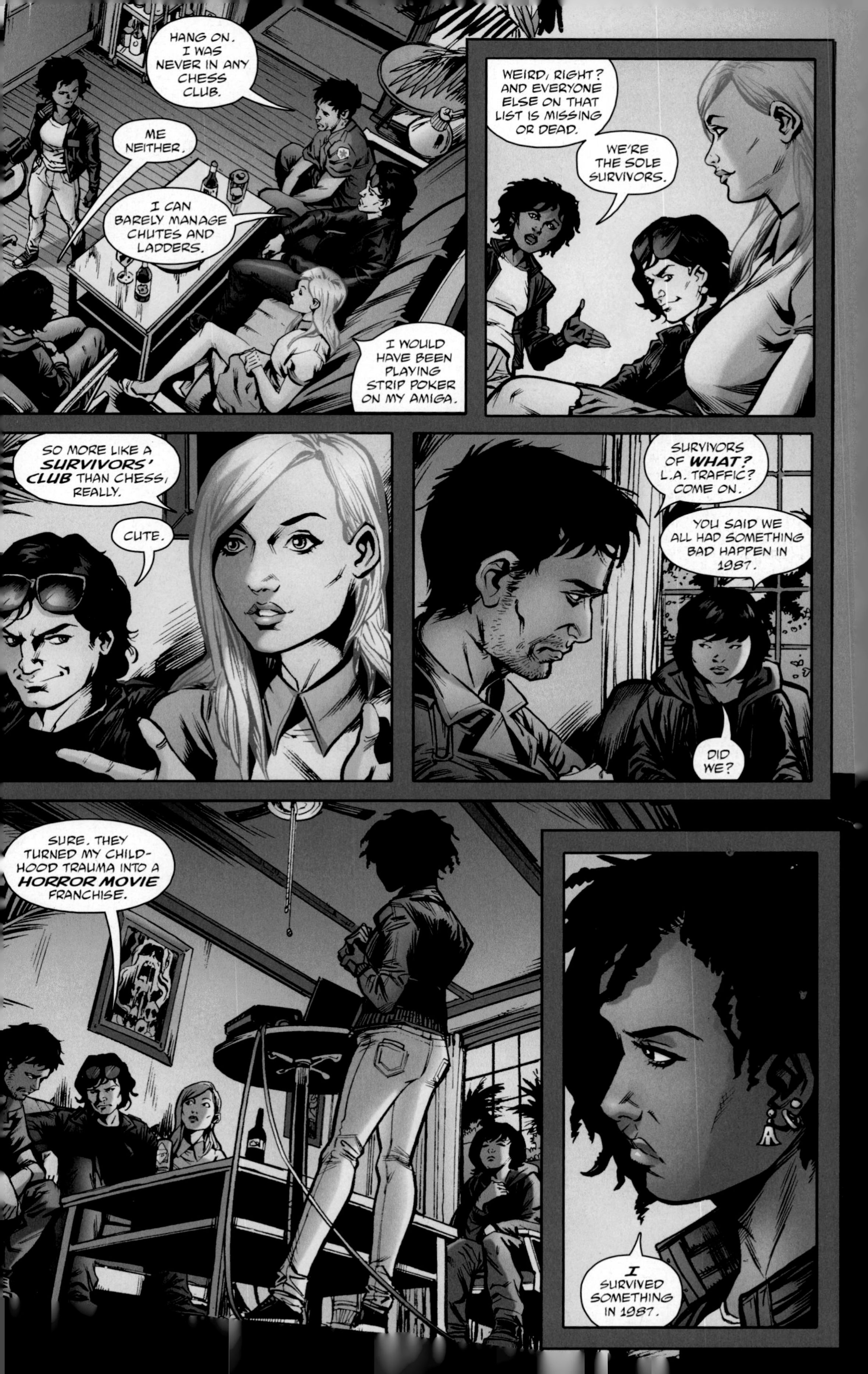
HANG ON. I WAS NEVER IN ANY CHESS CLUB.
ME NEITHER.
I CAN BARELY MANAGE CHUTES AND LADDERS.
I WOULD HAVE BEEN PLAYING STRIP POKER ON MY AMIGA.
WEIRD, RIGHT? AND EVERYONE ELSE ON THAT LIST IS MISSING OR DEAD.
WE'RE THE SOLE SURVIVORS.
SO MORE LIKE A SURVIVORS' CLUB THAN CHESS, REALLY.
CUTE.
SURVIVORS OF WHAT? L.A. TRAFFIC? COME ON.
YOU SAID WE ALL HAD SOMETHING BAD HAPPEN IN 1987.
DID WE?
SURE. THEY TURNED MY CHILDHOOD TRAUMA INTO A HORROR MOVIE FRANCHISE.
I SURVIVED SOMETHING IN 1987.

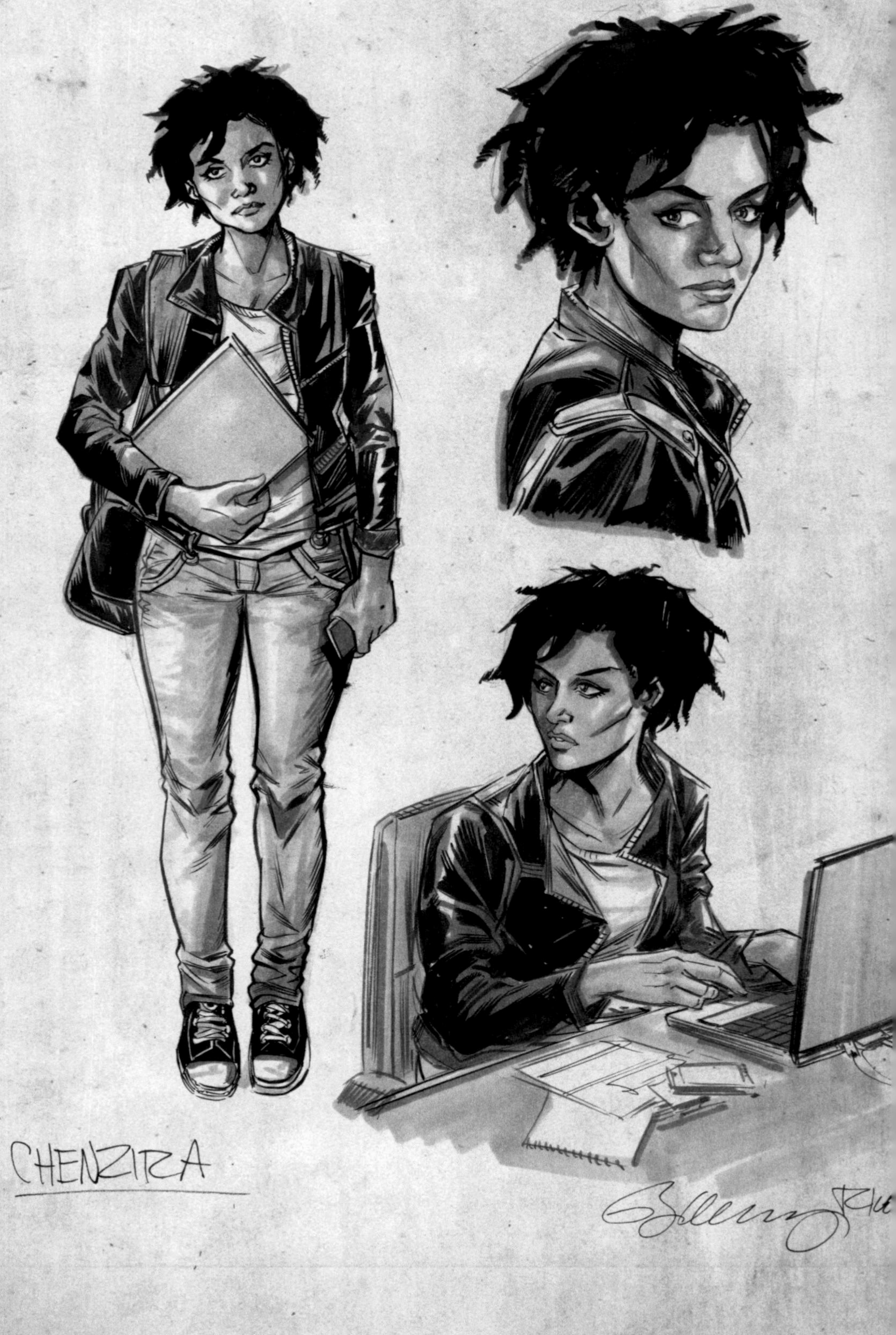
CHENZIRA

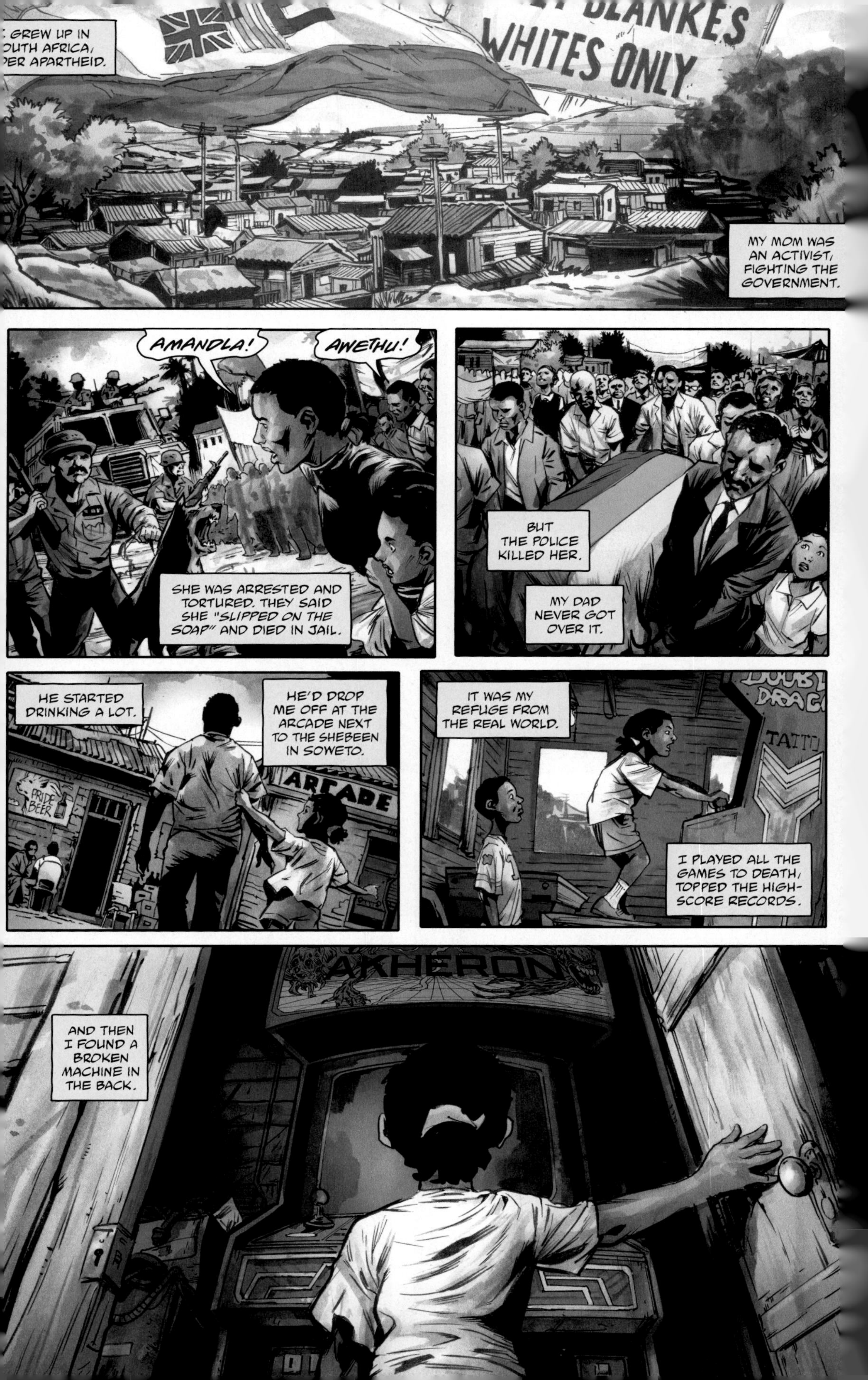

WHITES ONLY
MY MOM WAS AN ACTIVIST, FIGHTING THE GOVERNMENT.
AMANDLA!
AWETHU!
SHE WAS ARRESTED AND TORTURED. THEY SAID SHE "SLIPPED ON THE SOAP" AND DIED IN JAIL.
BUT THE POLICE KILLED HER.
MY DAD NEVER GOT OVER IT.
HE STARTED DRINKING A LOT.
HE'D DROP ME OFF AT THE ARCADE NEXT TO THE SHEBEEN IN SOWETO.
PRIDE BEER
ARCADE
IT WAS MY REFUGE FROM THE REAL WORLD.
I PLAYED ALL THE GAMES TO DEATH, TOPPED THE HIGH-SCORE RECORDS.
AND THEN I FOUND A BROKEN MACHINE IN THE BACK.
AKHERON

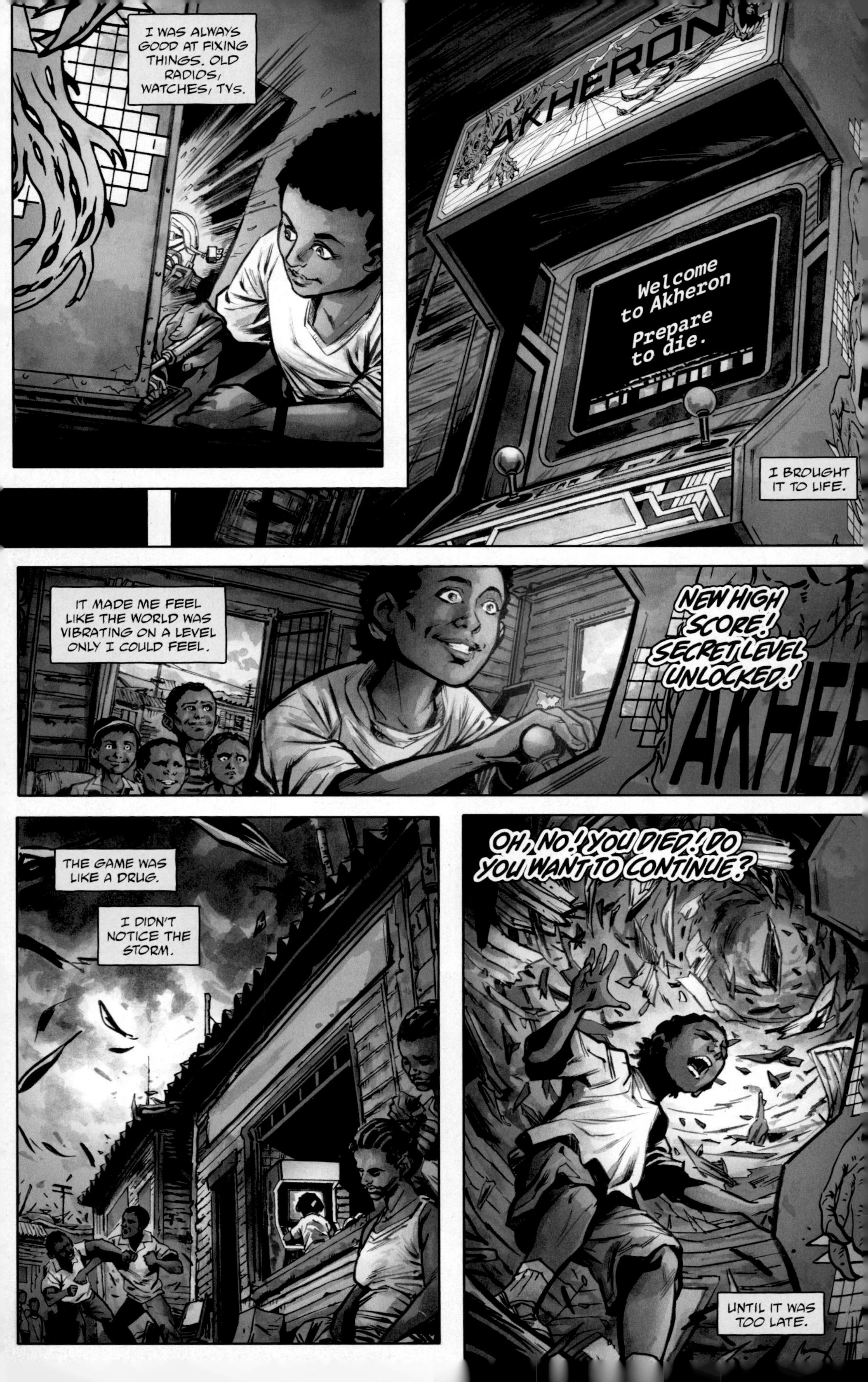
I WAS ALWAYS GOOD AT FIXING THINGS. OLD RADIOS, WATCHES, TVS.
AKHERON
Welcome to Akheron
Prepare to die.
I BROUGHT IT TO LIFE.
IT MADE ME FEEL LIKE THE WORLD WAS VIBRATING ON A LEVEL ONLY I COULD FEEL.
NEW HIGH SCORE! SECRET LEVEL UNLOCKED!
AKHER
THE GAME WAS LIKE A DRUG.
I DIDN'T NOTICE THE STORM.
OH, NO! YOU DIED! DO YOU WANT TO CONTINUE?
UNTIL IT WAS TOO LATE.

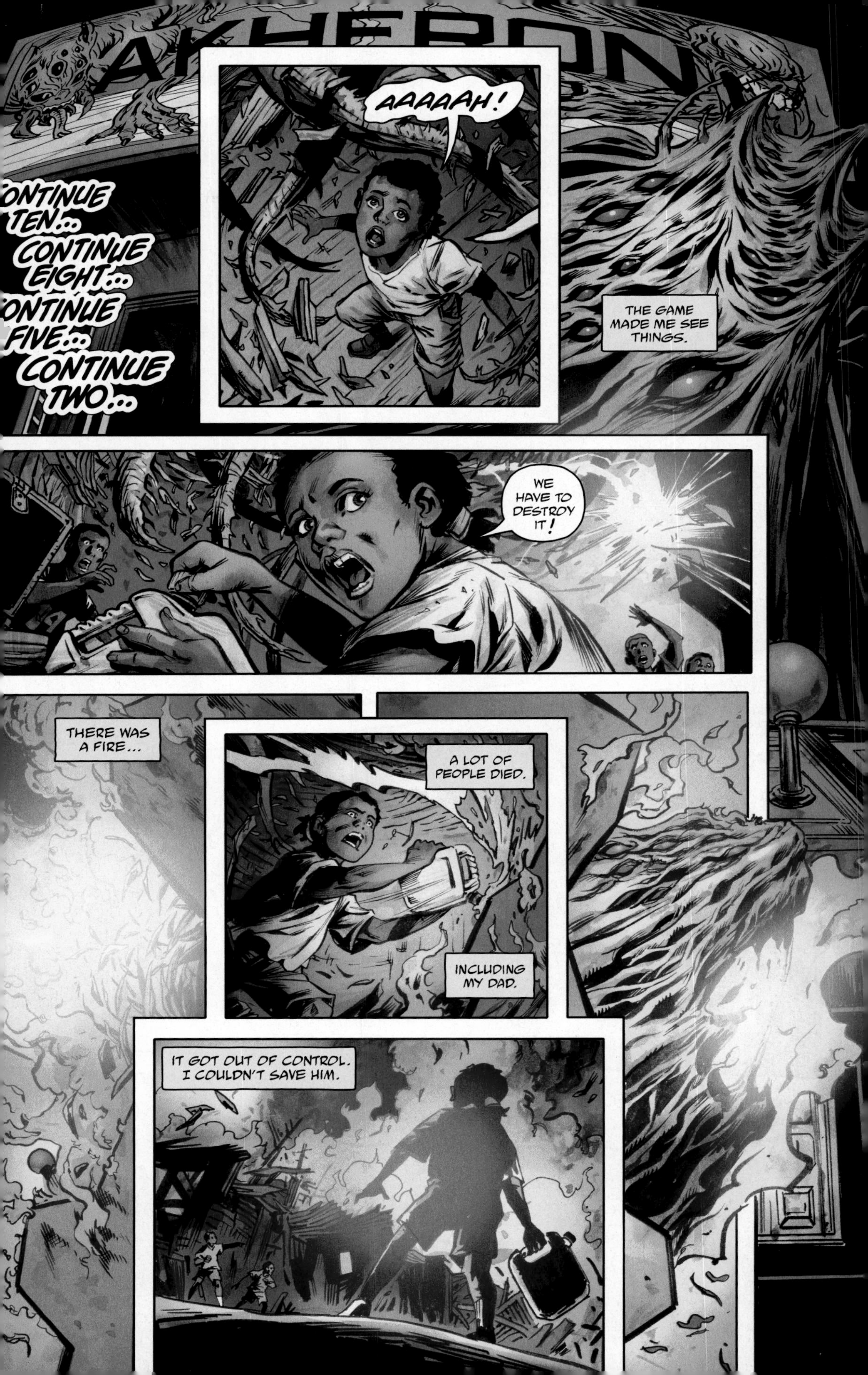
AKHERON
CONTINUE TEN... CONTINUE EIGHT... CONTINUE FIVE... CONTINUE TWO...
AAAAAH!
THE GAME MADE ME SEE THINGS.
WE HAVE TO DESTROY IT!
THERE WAS A FIRE...
A LOT OF PEOPLE DIED.
INCLUDING MY DAD.
IT GOT OUT OF CONTROL. I COULDN'T SAVE HIM.

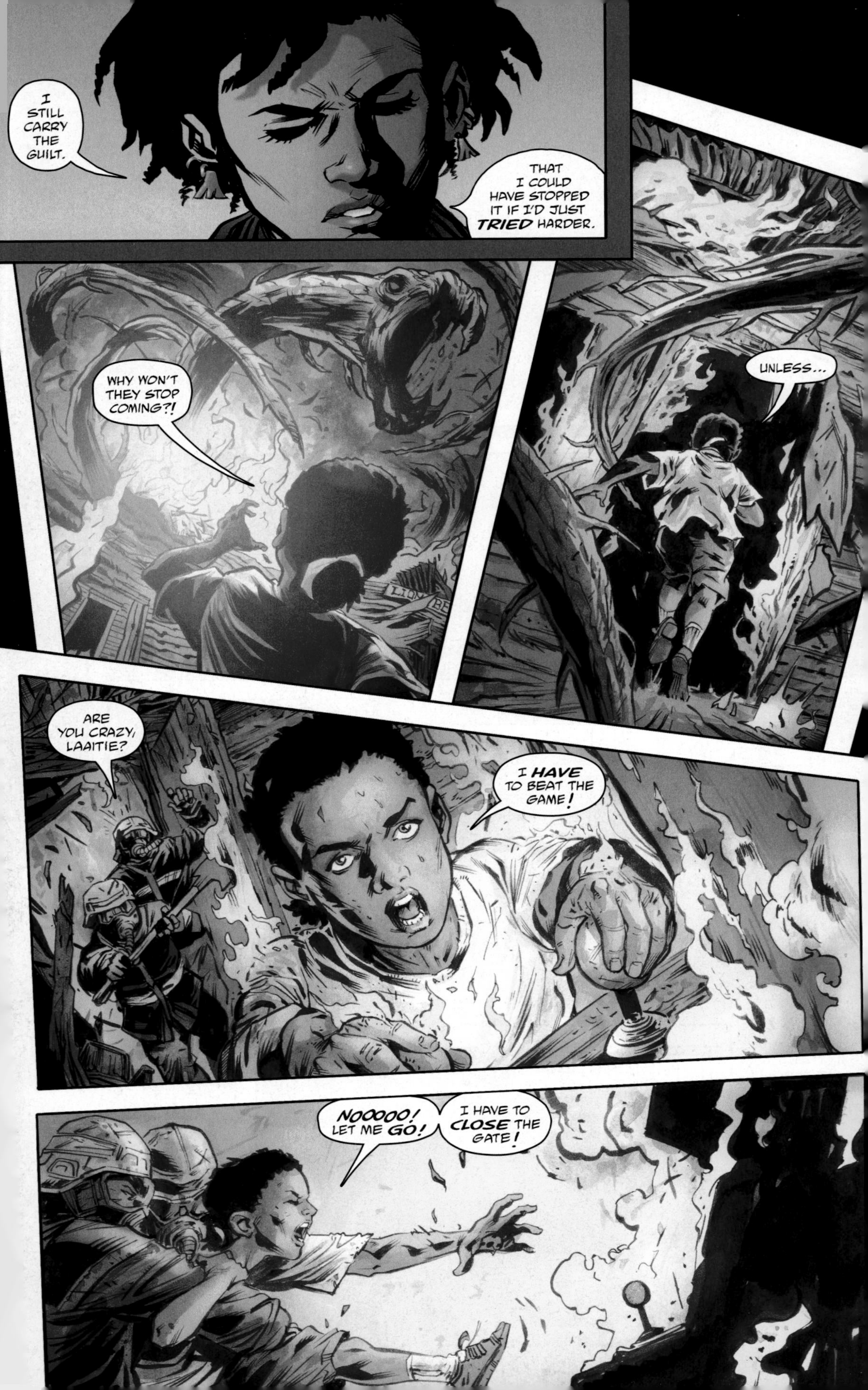
I STILL CARRY THE GUILT.
THAT I COULD HAVE STOPPED IT IF I'D JUST TRIED HARDER.
WHY WON'T THEY STOP COMING?!
UNLESS...
ARE YOU CRAZY, LAAITIE?
I HAVE TO BEAT THE GAME!
NOOOOO! LET ME GO!
I HAVE TO CLOSE THE GATE!

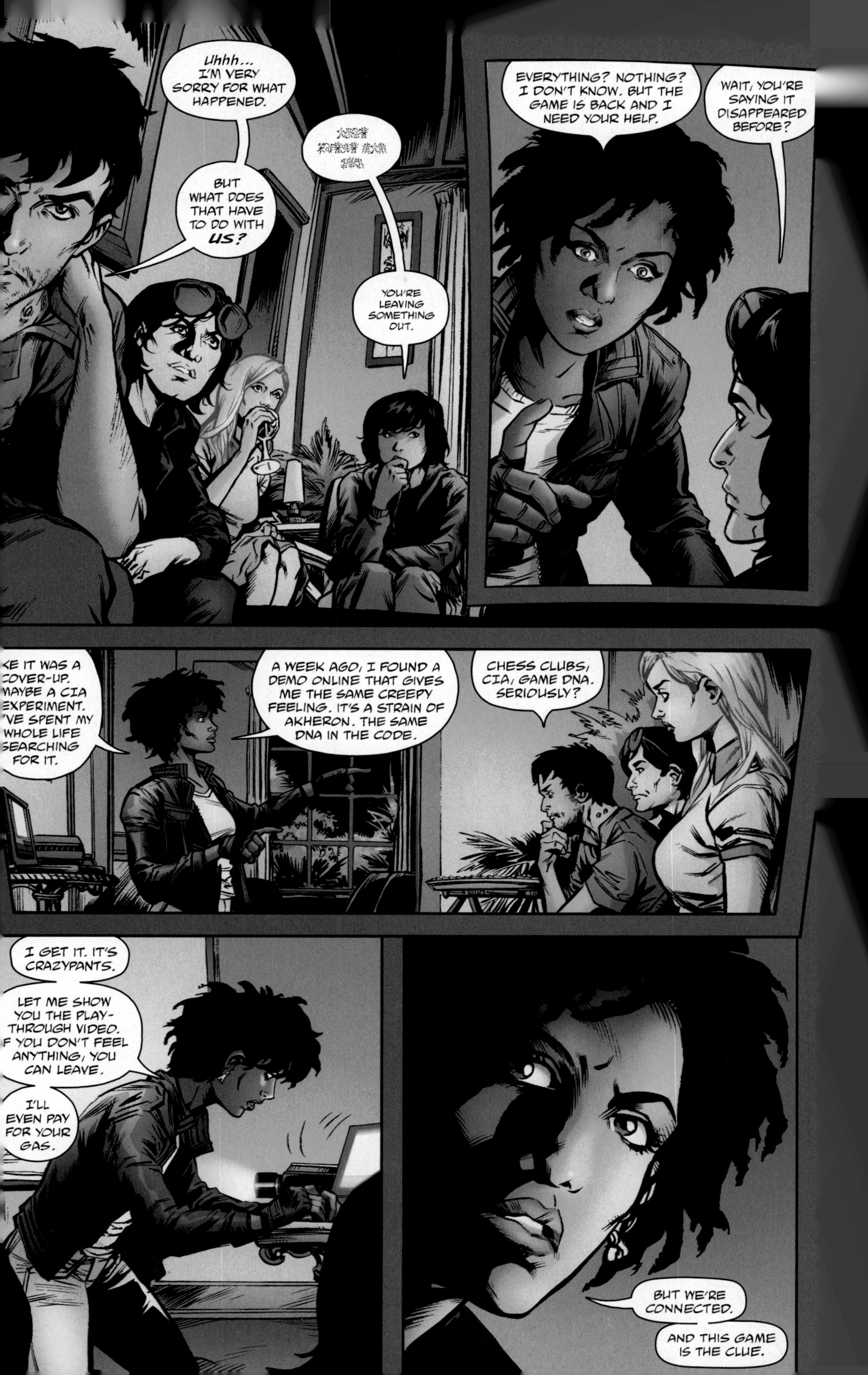
Uhhh... I'M VERY SORRY FOR WHAT HAPPENED.
BUT WHAT DOES THAT HAVE TO DO WITH US?
YOU'RE LEAVING SOMETHING OUT.
EVERYTHING? NOTHING? I DON'T KNOW. BUT THE GAME IS BACK AND I NEED YOUR HELP.
WAIT, YOU'RE SAYING IT DISAPPEARED BEFORE?
KE IT WAS A COVER-UP. MAYBE A CIA EXPERIMENT. 'VE SPENT MY WHOLE LIFE SEARCHING FOR IT.
A WEEK AGO, I FOUND A DEMO ONLINE THAT GIVES ME THE SAME CREEPY FEELING. IT'S A STRAIN OF AKHERON. THE SAME DNA IN THE CODE.
CHESS CLUBS, CIA, GAME DNA. SERIOUSLY?
I GET IT. IT'S CRAZYPANTS.
LET ME SHOW YOU THE PLAY-THROUGH VIDEO. F YOU DON'T FEEL ANYTHING, YOU CAN LEAVE.
I'LL EVEN PAY FOR YOUR GAS.
BUT WE'RE CONNECTED.
AND THIS GAME IS THE CLUE.

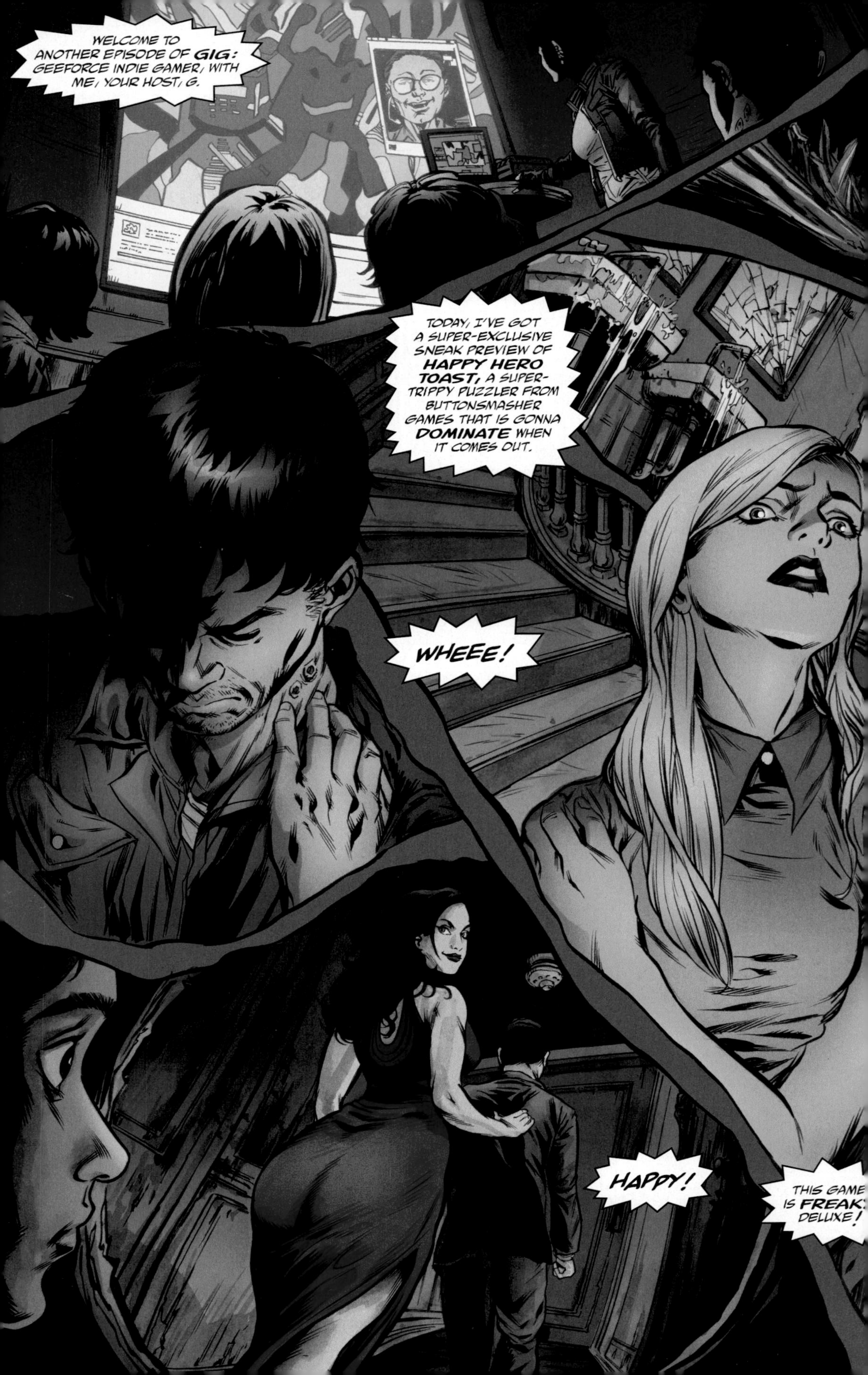
WELCOME TO ANOTHER EPISODE OF GIG: GEEFORCE INDIE GAMER, WITH ME, YOUR HOST, G.
TODAY, I'VE GOT A SUPER-EXCLUSIVE SNEAK PREVIEW OF HAPPY HERO TOAST, A SUPER-TRIPPY PUZZLER FROM BUTTONSMASHER GAMES THAT IS GONNA DOMINATE WHEN IT COMES OUT.
WHEEE!
HAPPY!
THIS GAME IS FREAK DELUXE!

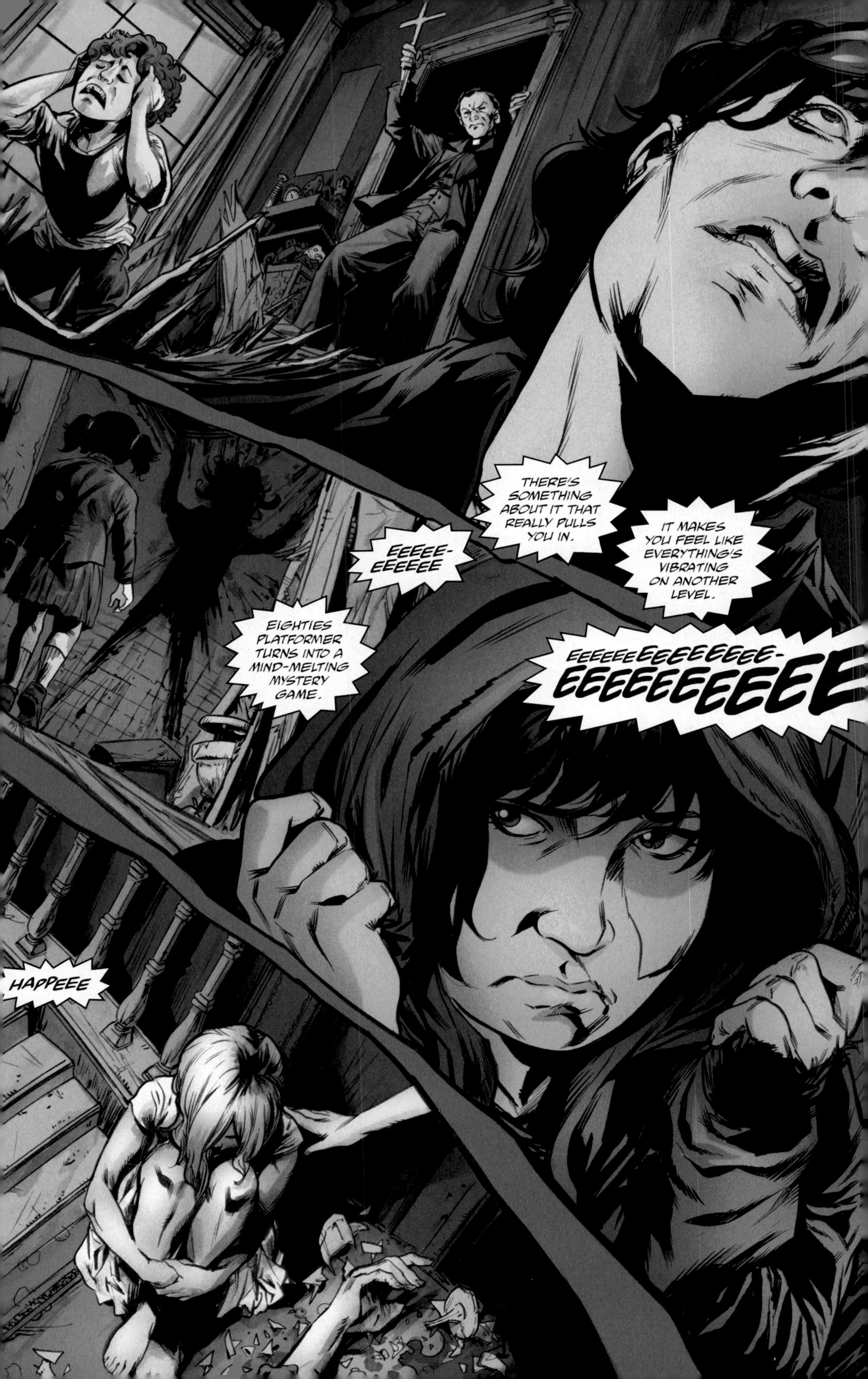
THERE'S SOMETHING ABOUT IT THAT REALLY PULLS YOU IN.
EEEEE-EEEEEE
IT MAKES YOU FEEL LIKE EVERYTHING'S VIBRATING ON ANOTHER LEVEL.
EIGHTIES PLATFORMER TURNS INTO A MIND-MELTING MYSTERY GAME.
EEEEEEEEEEEEEEE-EEEEEEEEEEE
HAPPEEE

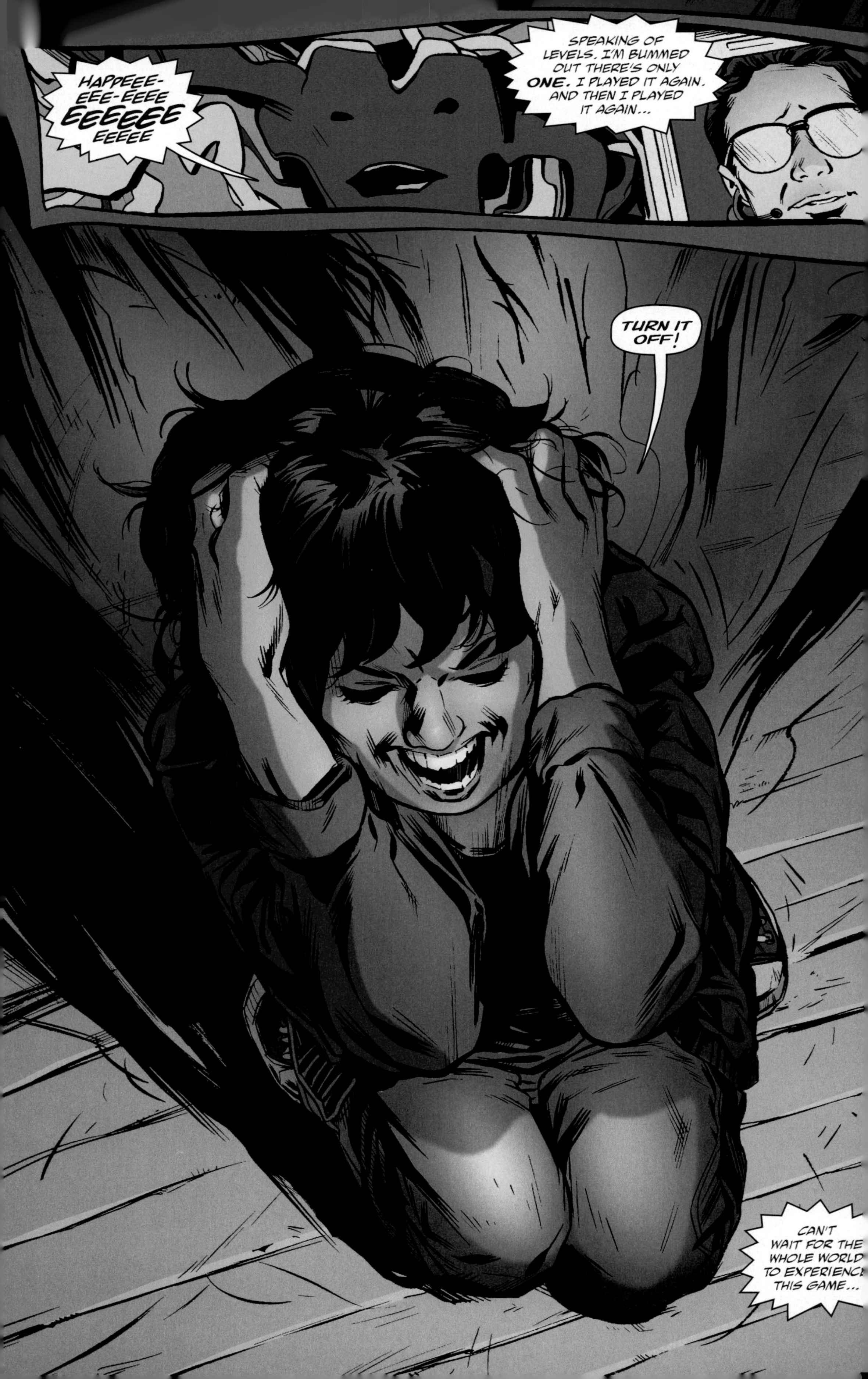
HAPPEEE-EEE-EEEE EEEEEE EEEEE
SPEAKING OF LEVELS. I'M BUMMED OUT THERE'S ONLY ONE. I PLAYED IT AGAIN. AND THEN I PLAYED IT AGAIN...
TURN IT OFF!
CAN'T WAIT FOR THE WHOLE WORLD TO EXPERIENCE THIS GAME...

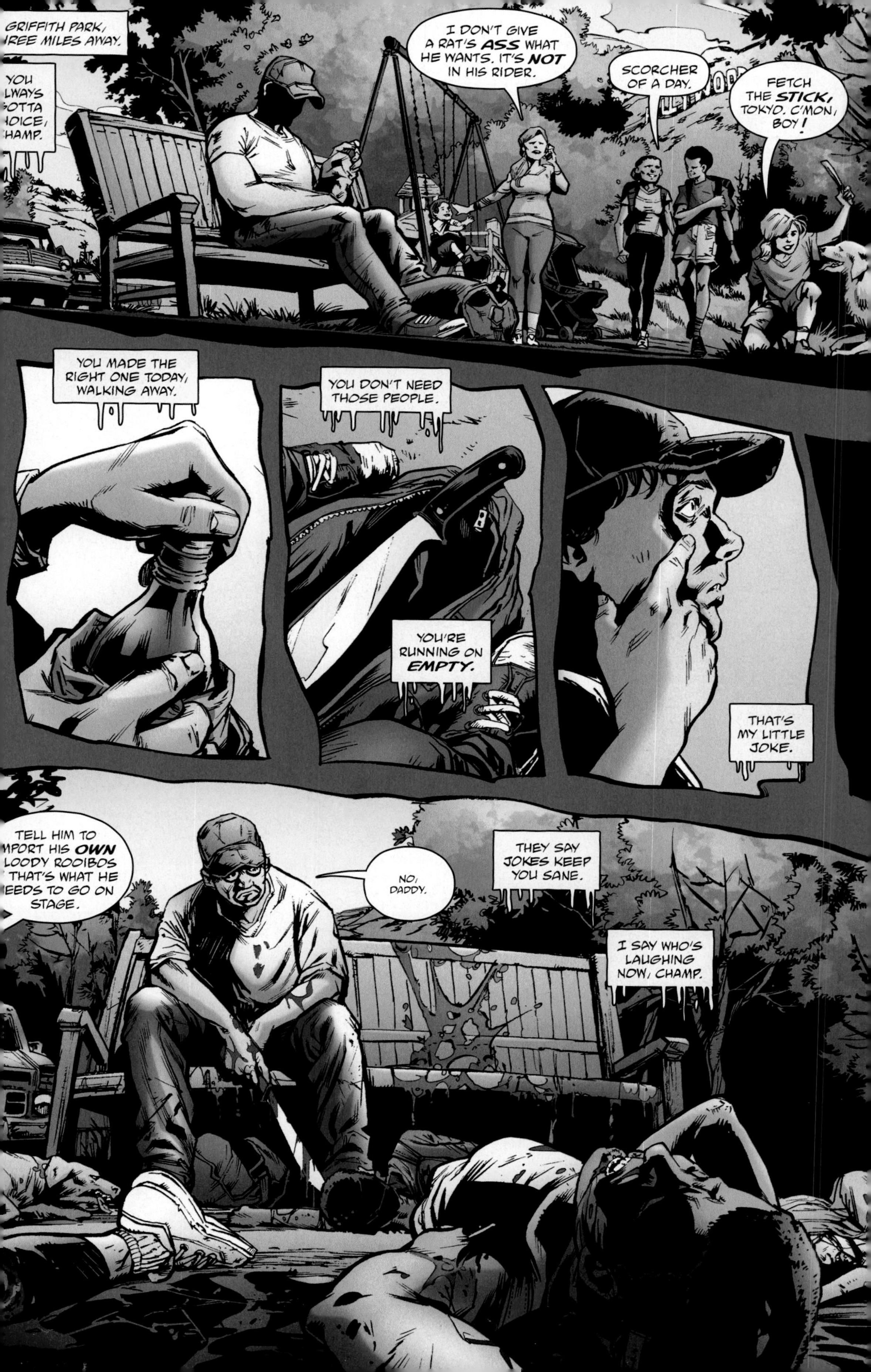
GRIFFITH PARK, THREE MILES AWAY.
YOU ALWAYS GOTTA CHOICE, CHAMP.
I DON'T GIVE A RAT'S ASS WHAT HE WANTS. IT'S NOT IN HIS RIDER.
SCORCHER OF A DAY.
FETCH THE STICK, TOKYO. C'MON, BOY!
YOU MADE THE RIGHT ONE TODAY, WALKING AWAY.
YOU DON'T NEED THOSE PEOPLE.
YOU'RE RUNNING ON EMPTY.
THAT'S MY LITTLE JOKE.
TELL HIM TO IMPORT HIS OWN BLOODY ROOIBOS IF THAT'S WHAT HE NEEDS TO GO ON STAGE.
NO, DADDY.
THEY SAY JOKES KEEP YOU SANE.
I SAY WHO'S LAUGHING NOW, CHAMP.

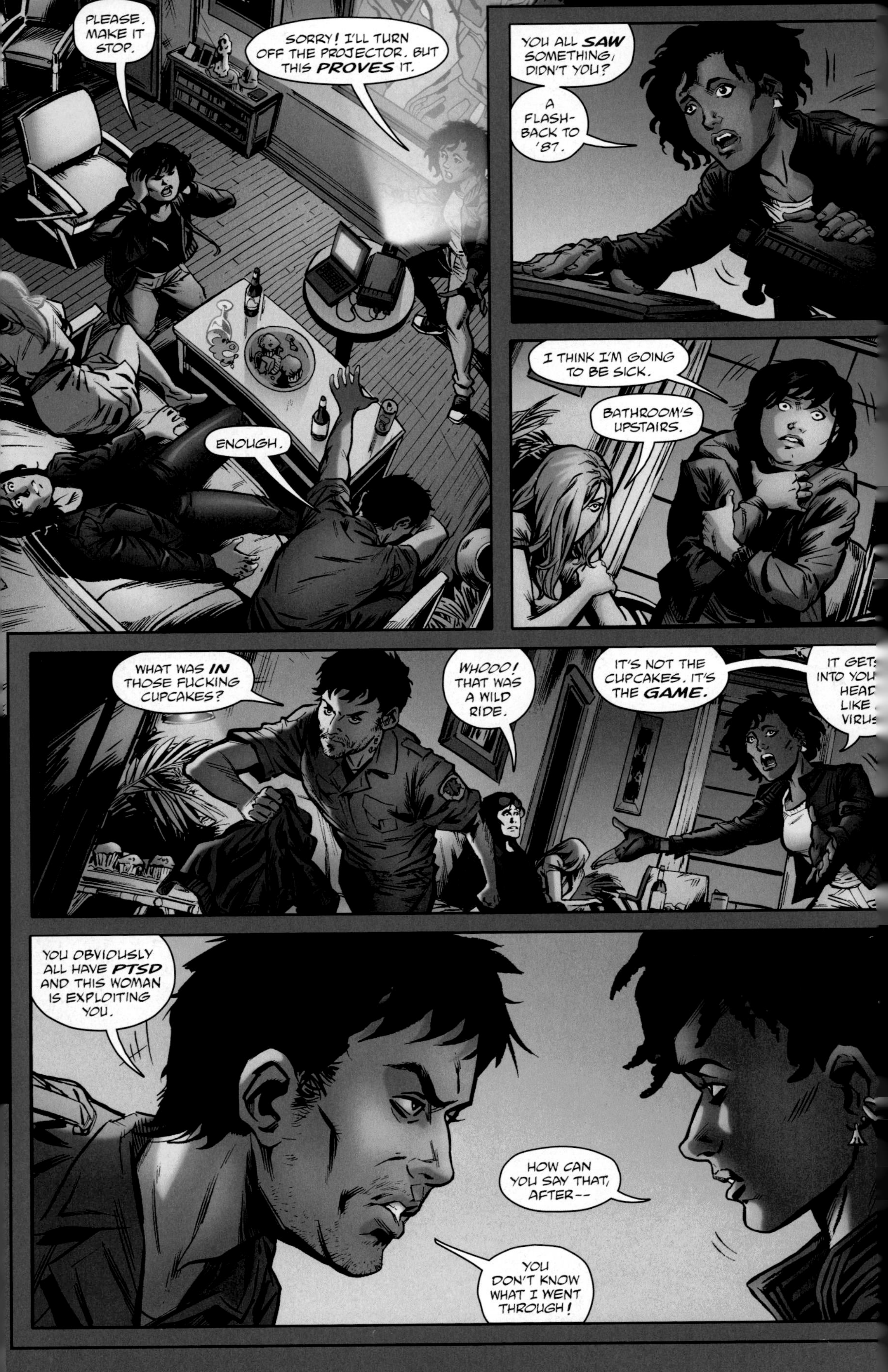
PLEASE. MAKE IT STOP.
SORRY! I'LL TURN OFF THE PROJECTOR. BUT THIS PROVES IT.
ENOUGH.
YOU ALL SAW SOMETHING, DIDN'T YOU?
A FLASH-BACK TO '87.
I THINK I'M GOING TO BE SICK.
BATHROOM'S UPSTAIRS.
WHAT WAS IN THOSE FUCKING CUPCAKES?
WHOOO! THAT WAS A WILD RIDE.
IT'S NOT THE CUPCAKES. IT'S THE GAME.
YOU OBVIOUSLY ALL HAVE PTSD AND THIS WOMAN IS EXPLOITING YOU.
HOW CAN YOU SAY THAT, AFTER--
YOU DON'T KNOW WHAT I WENT THROUGH!

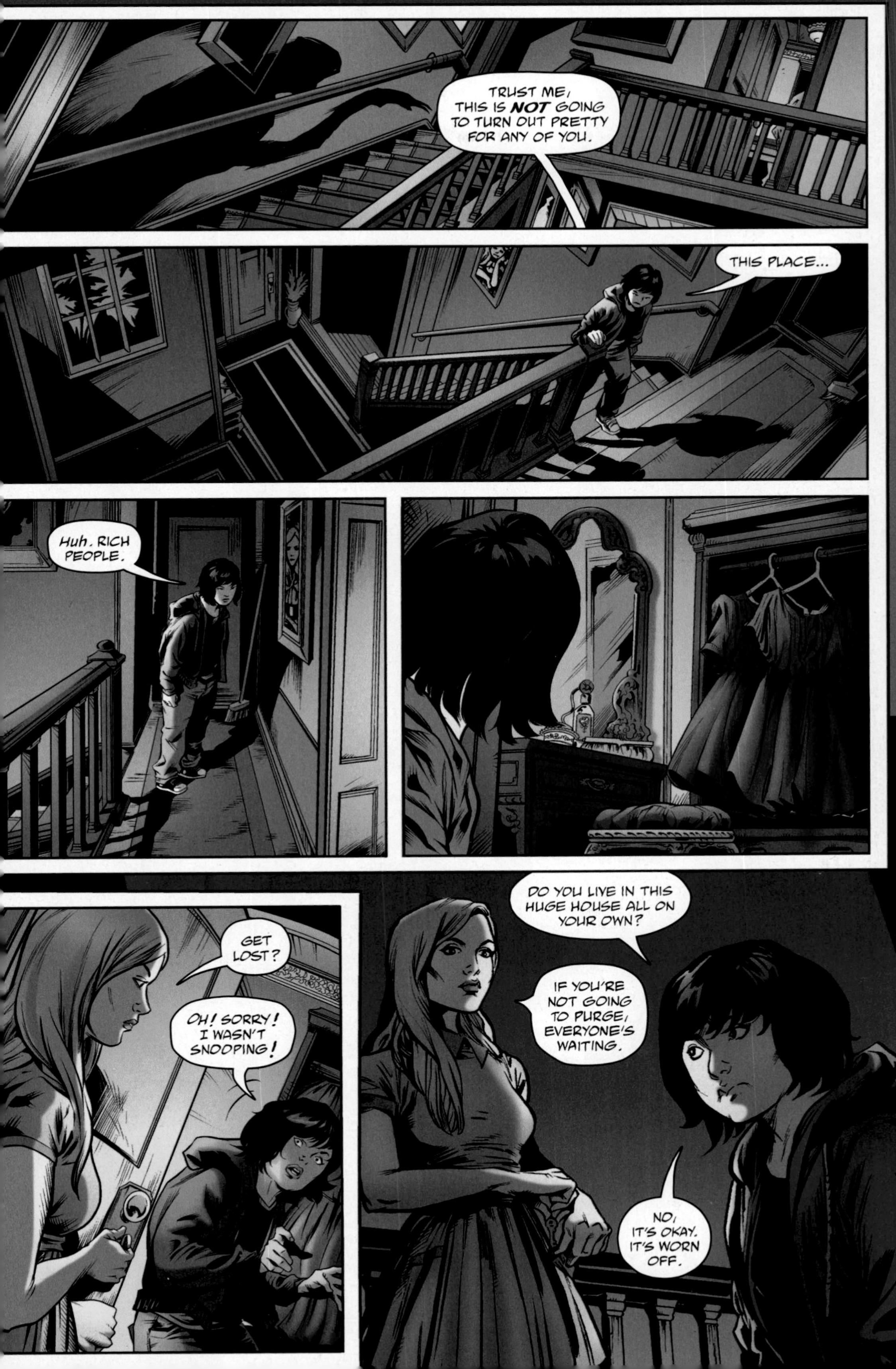
TRUST ME, THIS IS NOT GOING TO TURN OUT PRETTY FOR ANY OF YOU.
THIS PLACE...
Huh. RICH PEOPLE.
GET LOST?
OH! SORRY! I WASN'T SNOOPING!
DO YOU LIVE IN THIS HUGE HOUSE ALL ON YOUR OWN?
IF YOU'RE NOT GOING TO PURGE, EVERYONE'S WAITING.
NO, IT'S OKAY. IT'S WORN OFF.

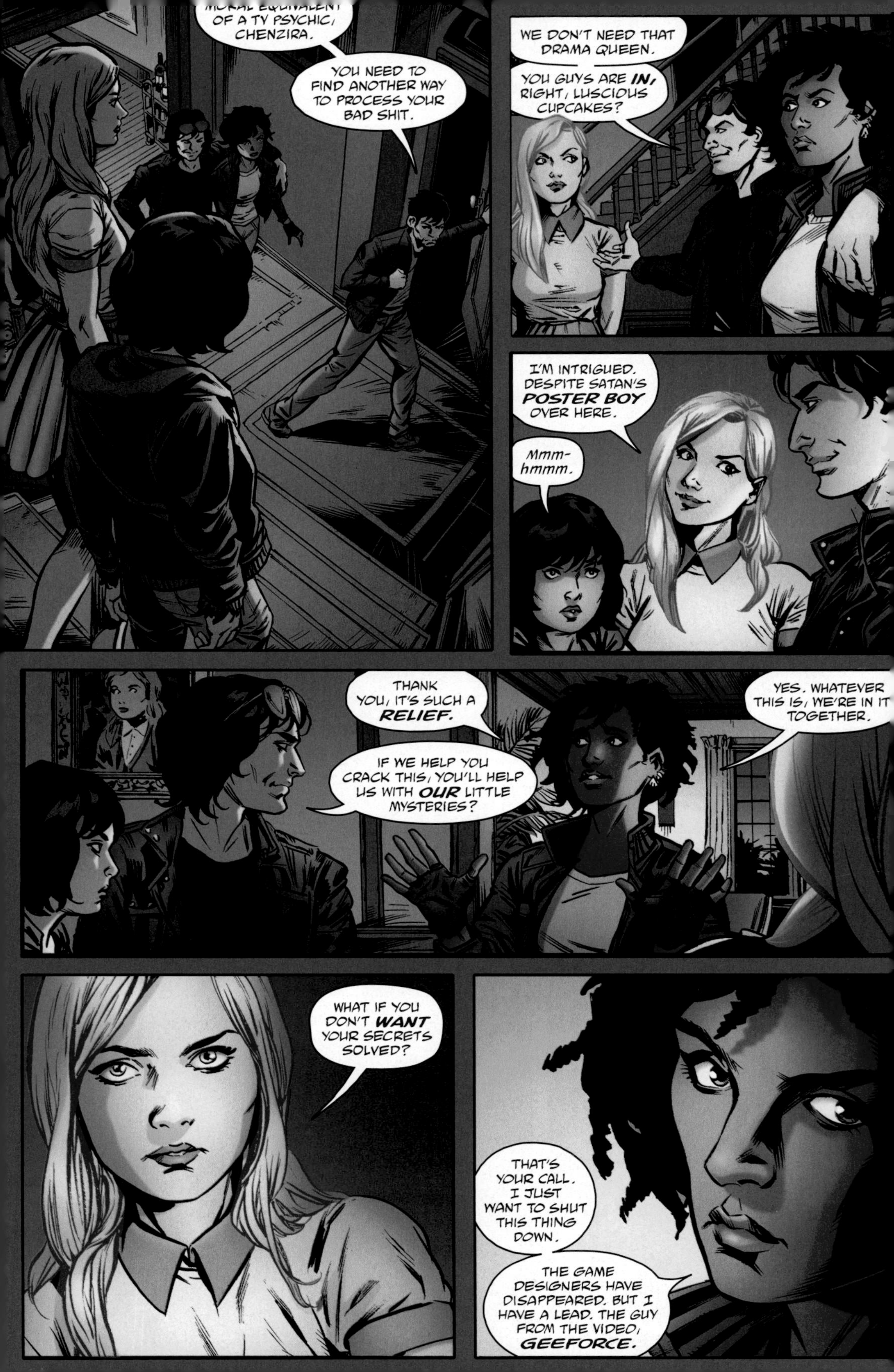
OF A TV PSYCHIC, CHENZIRA.
YOU NEED TO FIND ANOTHER WAY TO PROCESS YOUR BAD SHIT.
WE DON'T NEED THAT DRAMA QUEEN.
YOU GUYS ARE IN, RIGHT, LUSCIOUS CUPCAKES?
I'M INTRIGUED. DESPITE SATAN'S POSTER BOY OVER HERE.
Mmm-hmmm.
THANK YOU, IT'S SUCH A RELIEF.
IF WE HELP YOU CRACK THIS, YOU'LL HELP US WITH OUR LITTLE MYSTERIES?
YES. WHATEVER THIS IS, WE'RE IN IT TOGETHER.
WHAT IF YOU DON'T WANT YOUR SECRETS SOLVED?
THAT'S YOUR CALL. I JUST WANT TO SHUT THIS THING DOWN.
THE GAME DESIGNERS HAVE DISAPPEARED. BUT I HAVE A LEAD. THE GUY FROM THE VIDEO, GEEFORCE.

SAN LAZARO HOSPITAL, WEST HOLLYWOOD. NEXT SHIFT.

URGGGGGH!

SIR. I'M GOING TO NEED YOU TO REMAIN ON THE STRETCHER.

AAAAAGH!

HEY, TEO, YOU MISSED SOME CRAZY SHIT.

FOUR A.M. GUYS BROUGHT IN AN *EDP*. COLLEGE STUDENT, LAUGHING LIKE THE *JOKER*. TRIED TO RIP HIS OWN *THROAT* OUT.

I HAD *PLENTY* OF CRAZY LAST NIGHT. TRUST ME.

THIS WAS ALL KINDS OF SPECIAL. DUDE LOST HIS *SHIT* PLAYING SOME VIDEO GAME.

WHAT? WHERE IS HE?

PSYCH WARD. WHERE DO YOU THINK?

HEY MAN, WHERE YOU GOING?

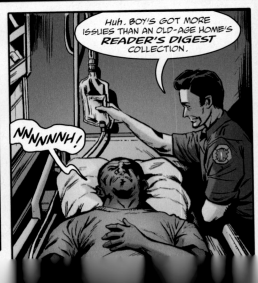

Huh. BOY'S GOT MORE ISSUES THAN AN OLD-AGE HOME'S *READER'S DIGEST* COLLECTION.

NNNNNNH!

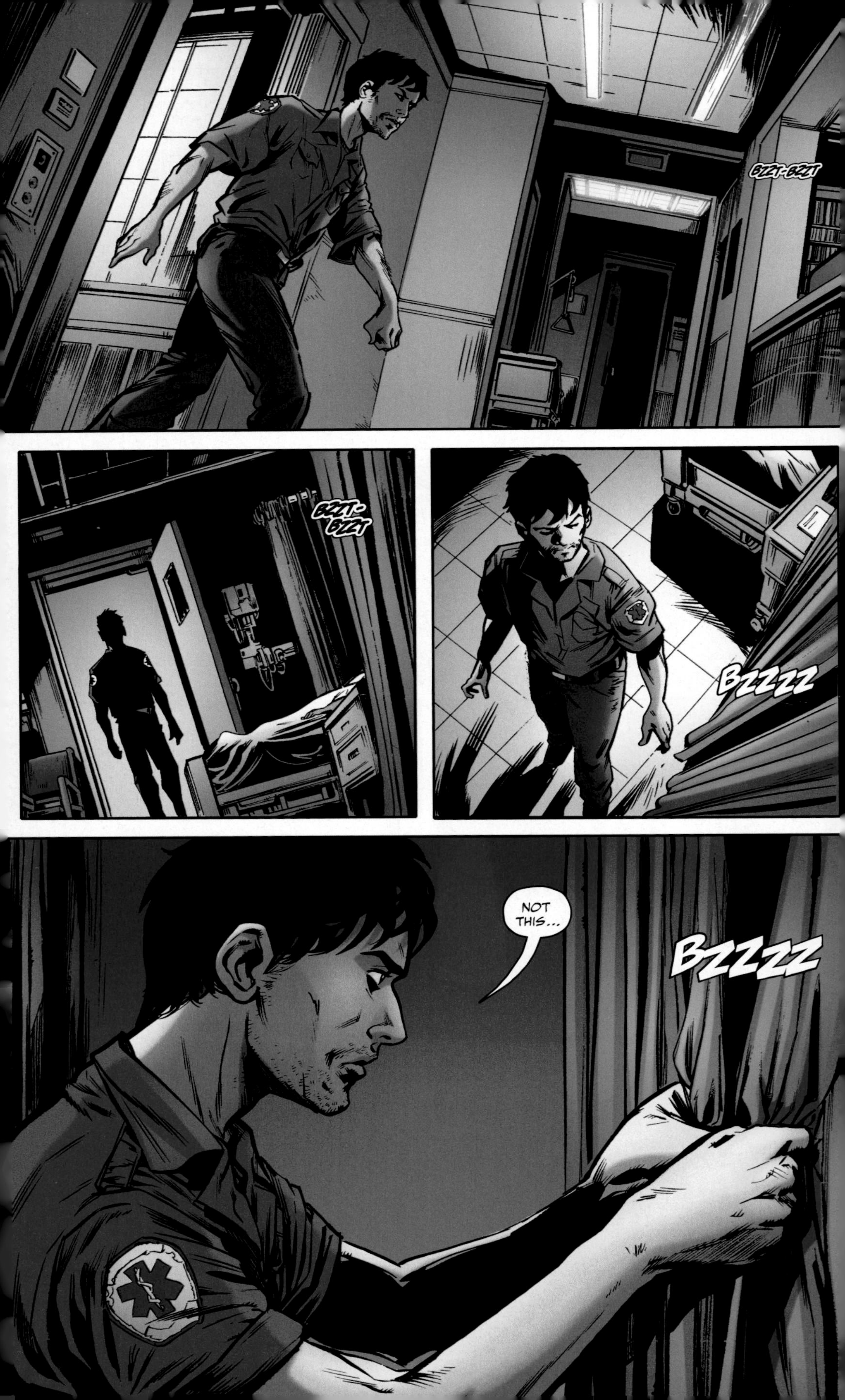
BZZT-BZZT
BZZT-BZZT
BZZZZ
NOT THIS...
BZZZZ

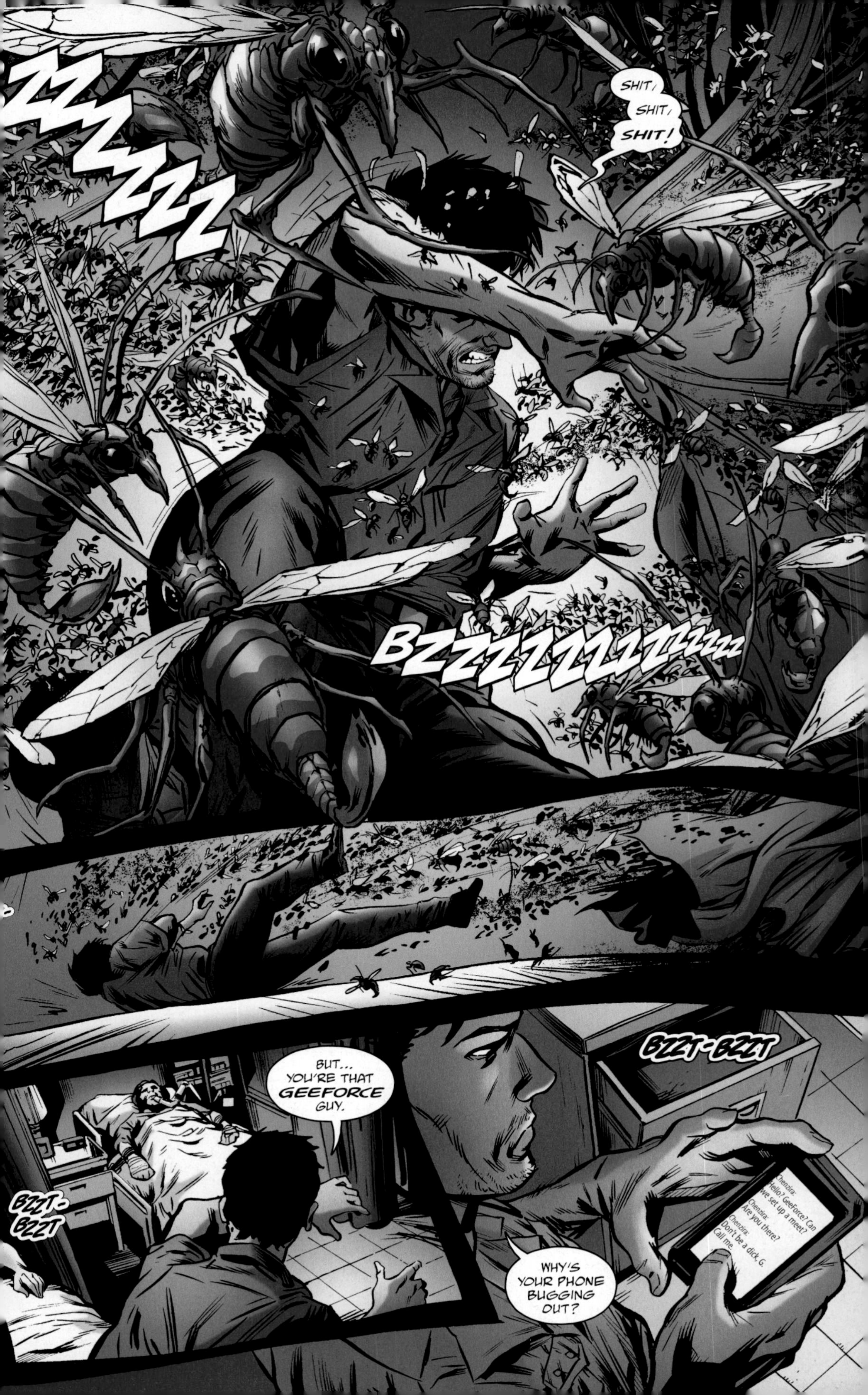
ZZZZZ
SHIT, SHIT, SHIT!
BZZZZZZZZZZzzz
BZZT-BZZT
BUT... YOU'RE THAT GEEFORCE GUY.
BZZT-BZZT
Chenzira: Hello? GeeForce? Can we set up a meet?
Chenzira: Are you there?
Chenzira: Don't be a dick, G. Call me.
WHY'S YOUR PHONE BUGGING OUT?

DON'T KNOW WHAT YOU WERE EXPECTING ME TO FIND, TEO, BUT YOUR **BRAIN** LOOKS NORMAL TO ME.

LIKE LAST TIME.

I CAN'T KEEP DOING THIS FOR YOU.

I'VE HAD EIGHTEEN YEARS TO PREPARE FOR THIS. I **RECOGNIZE** YOU, GAME.

I'M COMING TO **FIND** YOU. YOU'VE USED YOUR LAST LIFE.

PING

**PlayTube**
Happy Toast Behind

- This is where it all begin
- Stream-ing along (gettir'
- X-Mas Update!
- Boy genius: Pascal Fuentes in the house
- Pascal's Musings 402
- Pascal's Musings 407
- Going Away For A While BRB

New email from **Teo Reyes**
*I really need to talk to you. Sorry I was a pendejo before.*

**Plusbook**

Works at: Happy
(Buttonsmasher

**Likes**
Indie Games
Cult Gaming N
Sonic Secret L
Flower
Polybius
Creepypasta
Bon Iver
The Indoor Kids
Wolf In White Vai
AD&D Paladins, v
California Pagan:
LA Reiki Society
Tentra
Hermetic Order o
Timothy Leary
Trans-humanism
Alt. Religions

TELL ME GOOD THINGS, CAMPBELL, CAMPBELL & WULFSOHN.

SORRY, MISTER WICKMAN, THERE'S **NOTHING** WE CAN DO. THEY'VE GOT THE RIGHTS TO THE MUSKAGEE HOUSE SEWN UP.

YOU'RE LUCKY THEY LET YOU DO **HORROR** CONVENTIONS.

FUCK'S SAKE.

SO HO
THAT ORIG
**SCRIPT**
COMIN

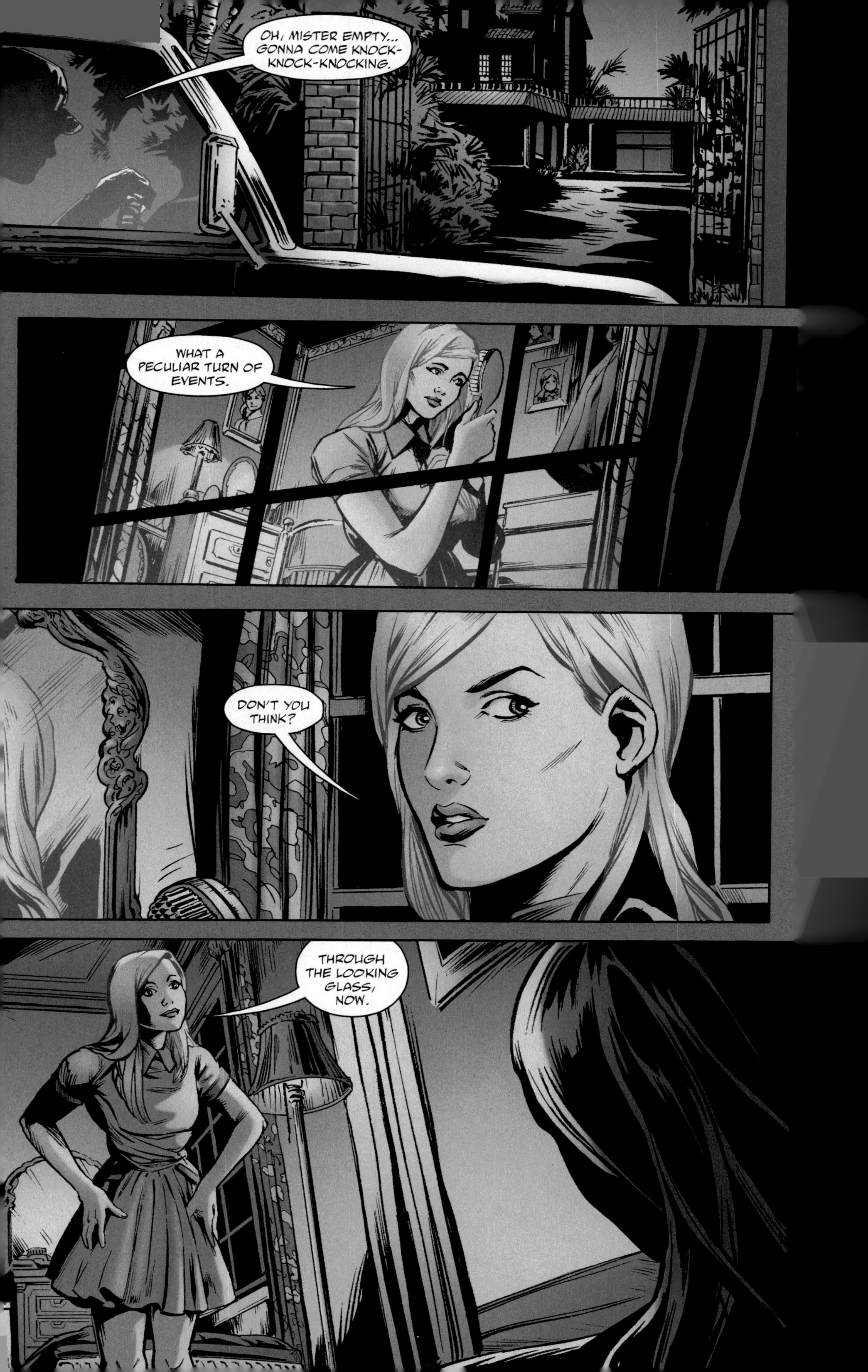
OH, MISTER EMPTY... GONNA COME KNOCK-KNOCK-KNOCKING.
WHAT A PECULIAR TURN OF EVENTS.
DON'T YOU THINK?
THROUGH THE LOOKING GLASS, NOW.

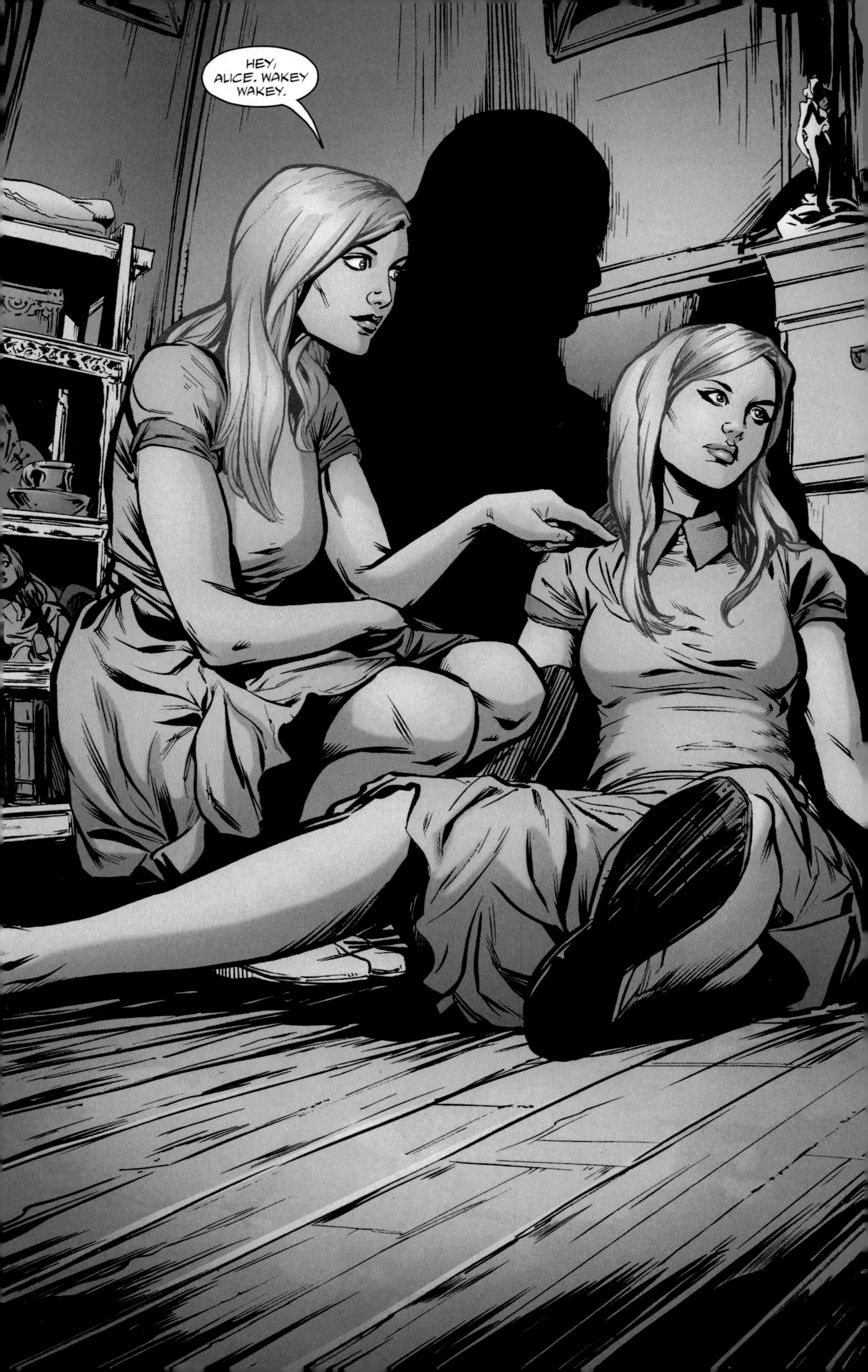
HEY, ALICE. WAKEY WAKEY.

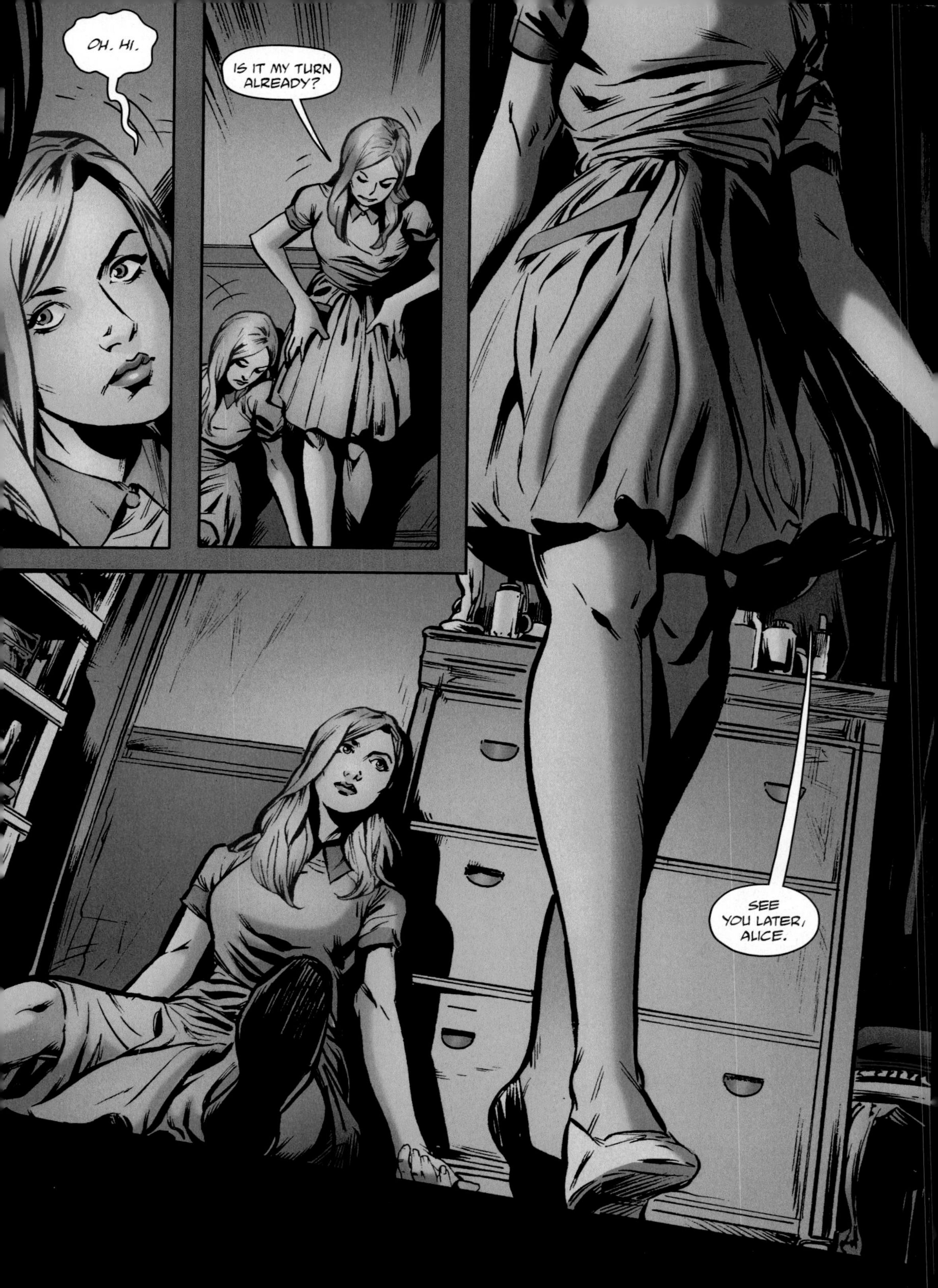
OH. HI.
IS IT MY TURN ALREADY?
SEE YOU LATER, ALICE.

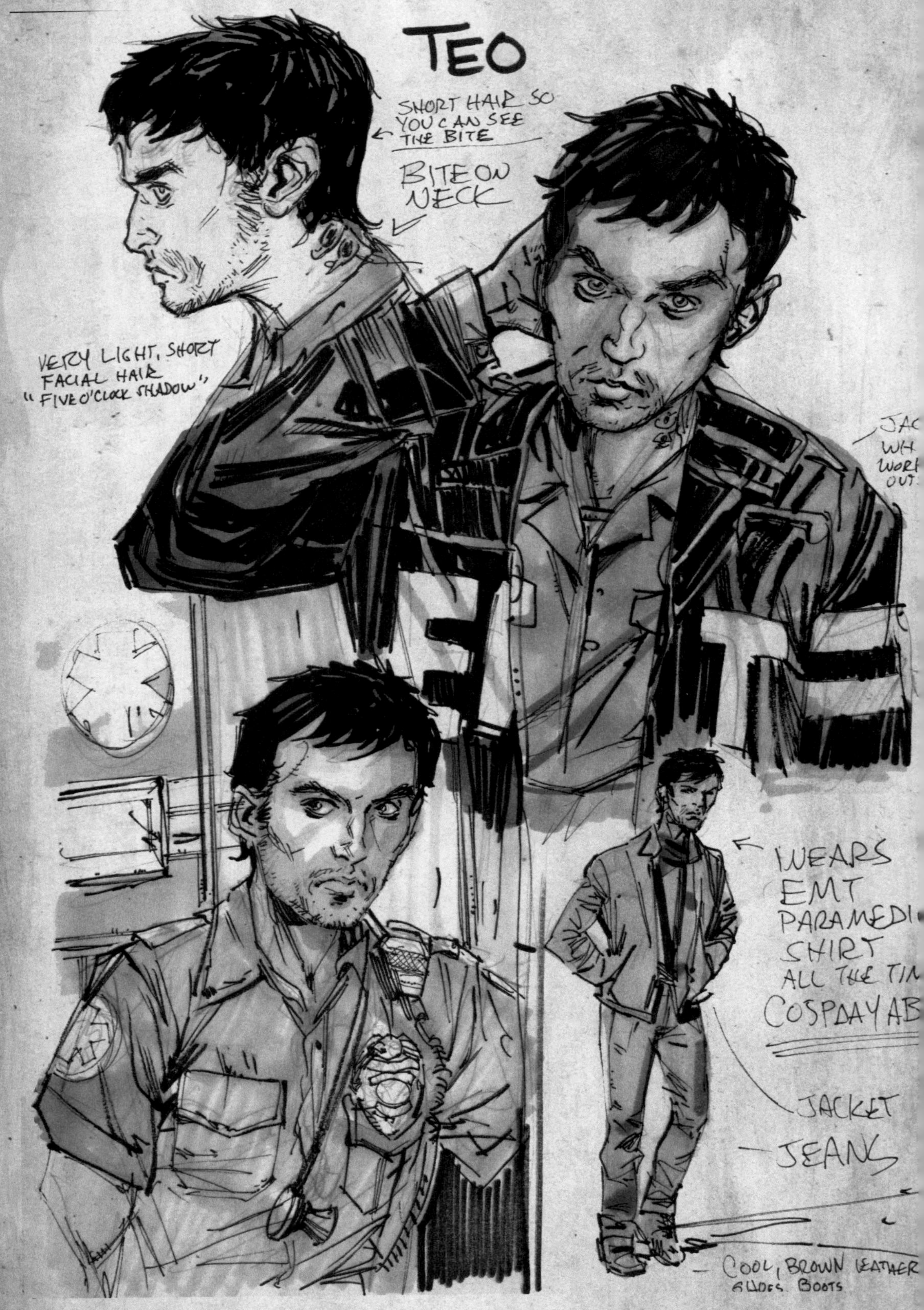

TEO
SHORT HAIR SO YOU CAN SEE THE BITE
BITE ON NECK
VERY LIGHT, SHORT FACIAL HAIR "FIVE O'CLOCK SHADOW"
WEARS EMT PARAMEDI SHIRT ALL THE TIM
JACKET
JEANS
COOL, BROWN LEATHER

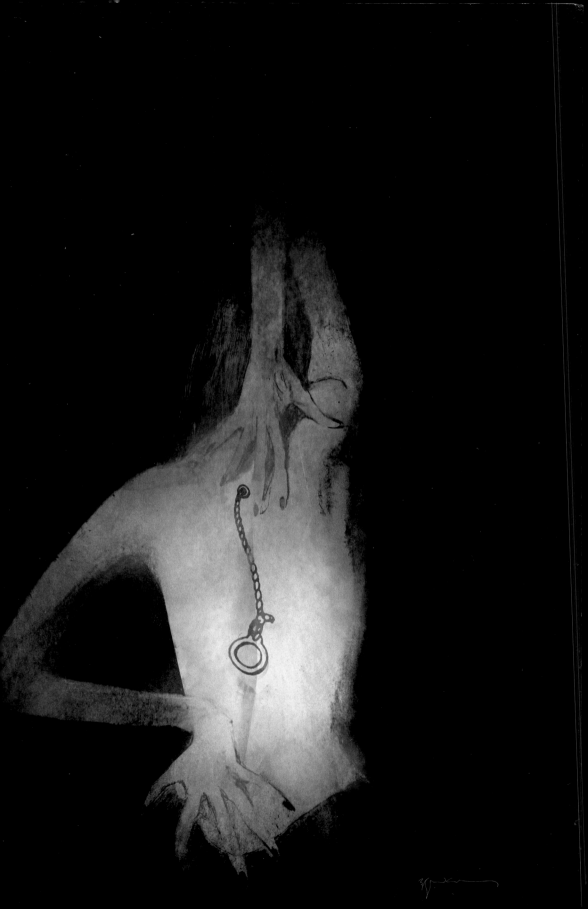

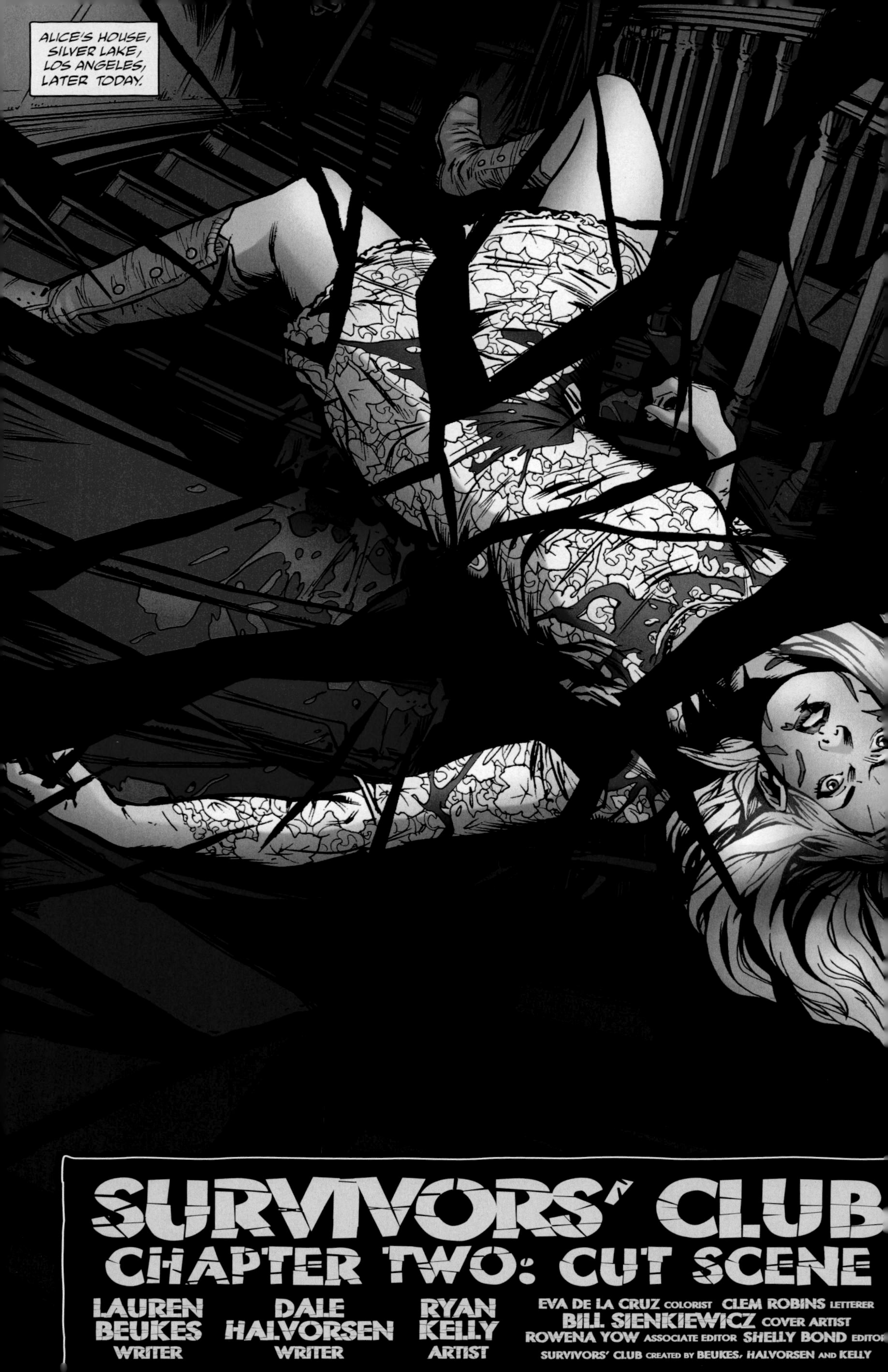
ALICE'S HOUSE, SILVER LAKE, LOS ANGELES, LATER TODAY.
SURVIVORS' CLUB
CHAPTER TWO: CUT SCENE
LAUREN BEUKES WRITER
DALE HALVORSEN WRITER
RYAN KELLY ARTIST
EVA DE LA CRUZ COLORIST CLEM ROBINS LETTERER
BILL SIENKIEWICZ COVER ARTIST
ROWENA YOW ASSOCIATE EDITOR SHELLY BOND EDITOR
SURVIVORS' CLUB CREATED BY BEUKES, HALVORSEN AND KELLY

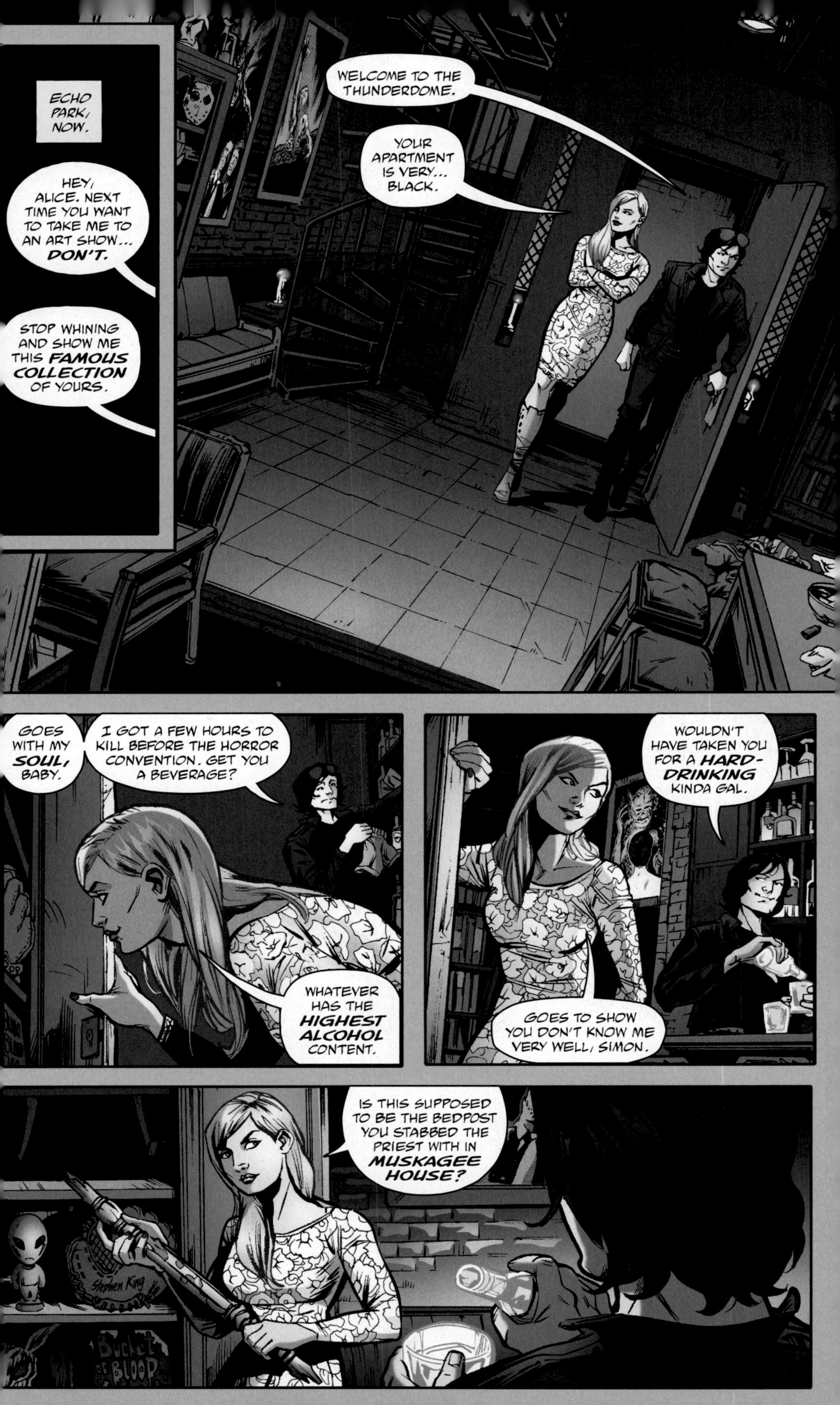

ECHO PARK, NOW.
HEY, ALICE. NEXT TIME YOU WANT TO TAKE ME TO AN ART SHOW... DON'T.
STOP WHINING AND SHOW ME THIS FAMOUS COLLECTION OF YOURS.
WELCOME TO THE THUNDERDOME.
YOUR APARTMENT IS VERY... BLACK.
GOES WITH MY SOUL, BABY.
I GOT A FEW HOURS TO KILL BEFORE THE HORROR CONVENTION. GET YOU A BEVERAGE?
WHATEVER HAS THE HIGHEST ALCOHOL CONTENT.
WOULDN'T HAVE TAKEN YOU FOR A HARD-DRINKING KINDA GAL.
GOES TO SHOW YOU DON'T KNOW ME VERY WELL, SIMON.
IS THIS SUPPOSED TO BE THE BEDPOST YOU STABBED THE PRIEST WITH IN MUSKAGEE HOUSE?
Stephen King
Bucket of Blood

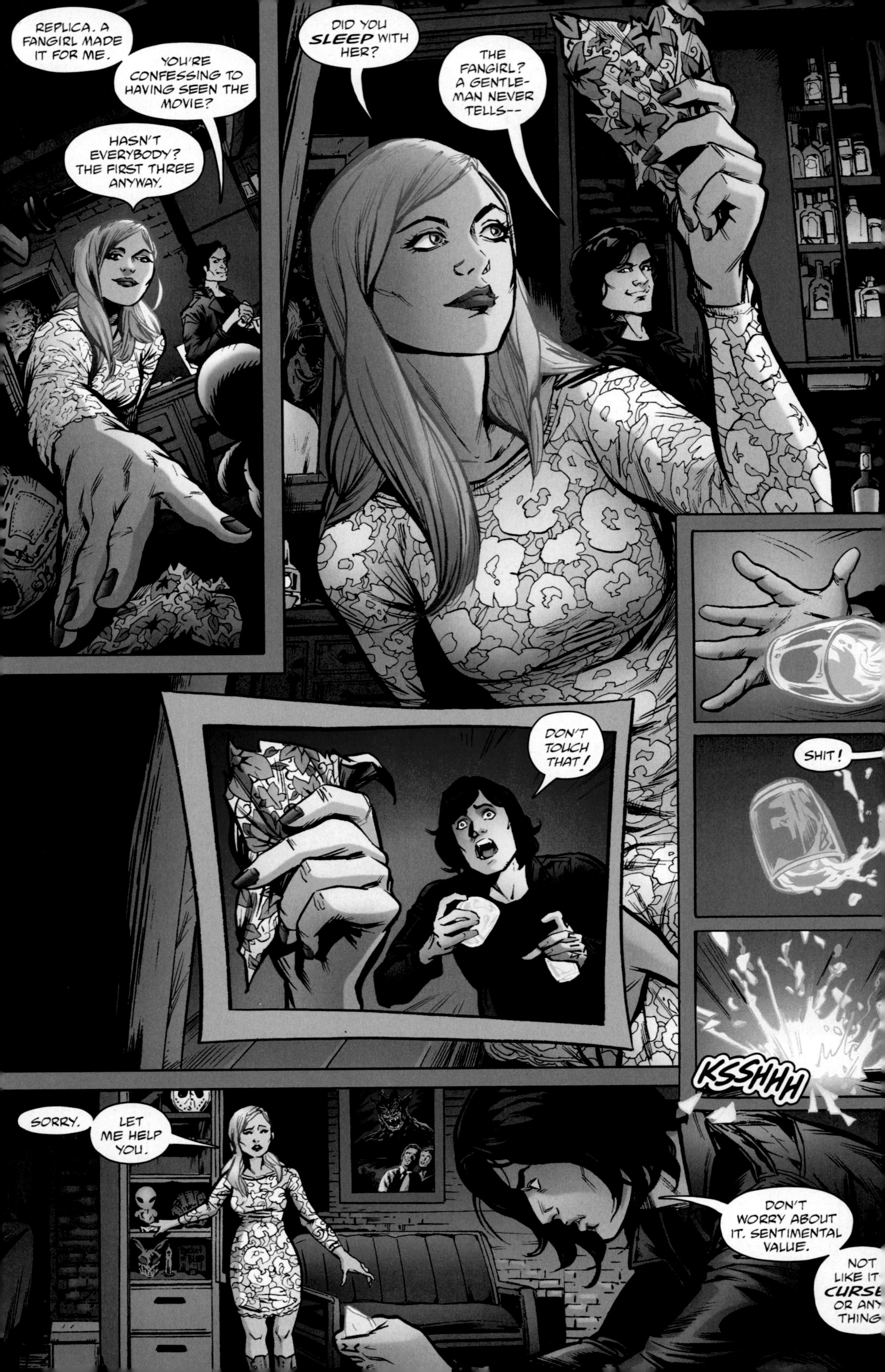
REPLICA. A FANGIRL MADE IT FOR ME.
YOU'RE CONFESSING TO HAVING SEEN THE MOVIE?
HASN'T EVERYBODY? THE FIRST THREE ANYWAY.
DID YOU SLEEP WITH HER?
THE FANGIRL? A GENTLE-MAN NEVER TELLS--
DON'T TOUCH THAT!
SHIT!
KSSHHH
SORRY.
LET ME HELP YOU.
DON'T WORRY ABOUT IT. SENTIMENTAL VALUE.

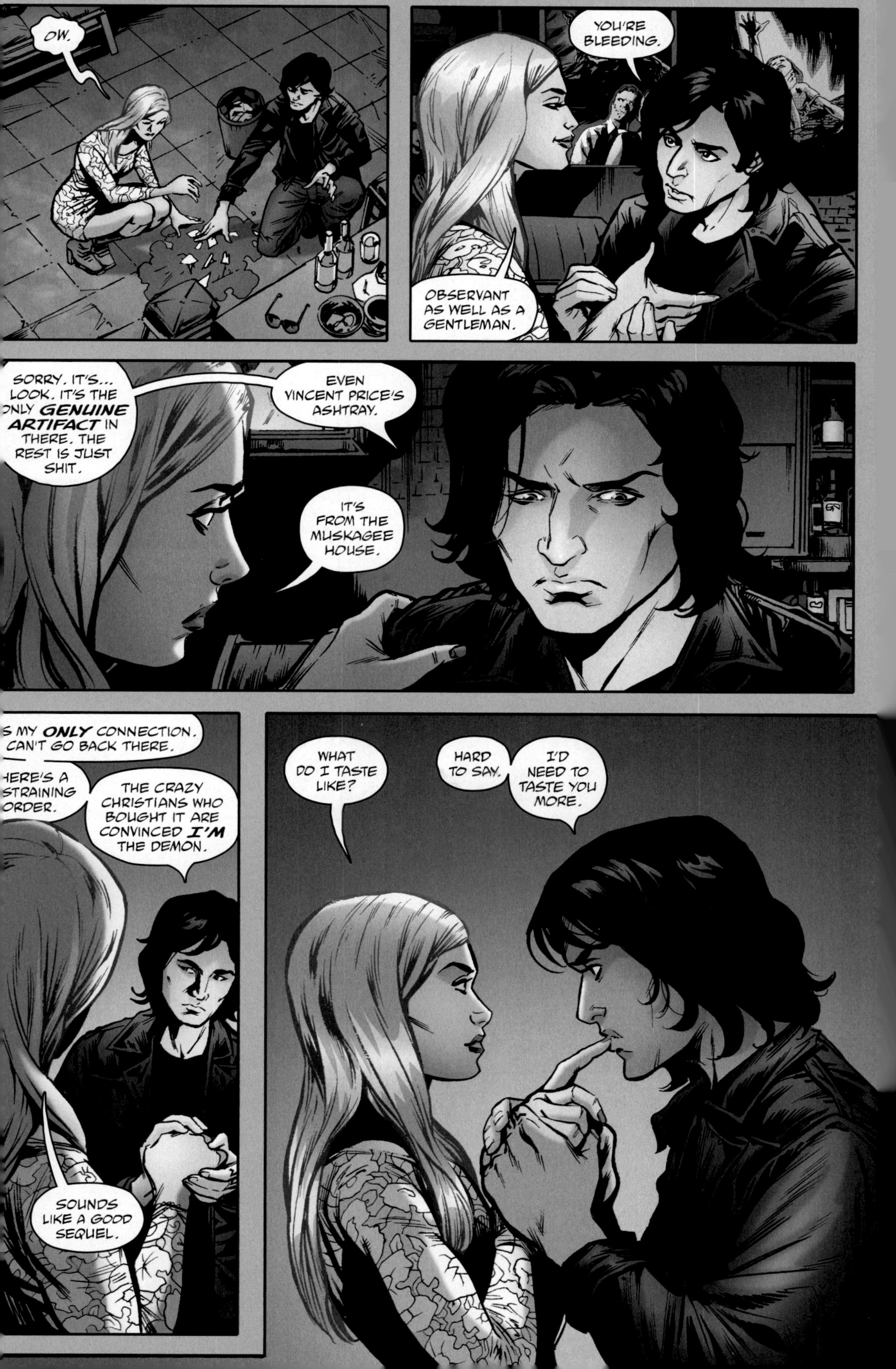
OW.
YOU'RE BLEEDING.
OBSERVANT AS WELL AS A GENTLEMAN.
SORRY. IT'S... LOOK. IT'S THE ONLY GENUINE ARTIFACT IN THERE. THE REST IS JUST SHIT.
EVEN VINCENT PRICE'S ASHTRAY.
IT'S FROM THE MUSKAGEE HOUSE.
S MY ONLY CONNECTION. CAN'T GO BACK THERE.
HERE'S A STRAINING ORDER.
THE CRAZY CHRISTIANS WHO BOUGHT IT ARE CONVINCED I'M THE DEMON.
SOUNDS LIKE A GOOD SEQUEL.
WHAT DO I TASTE LIKE?
HARD TO SAY.
I'D NEED TO TASTE YOU MORE.

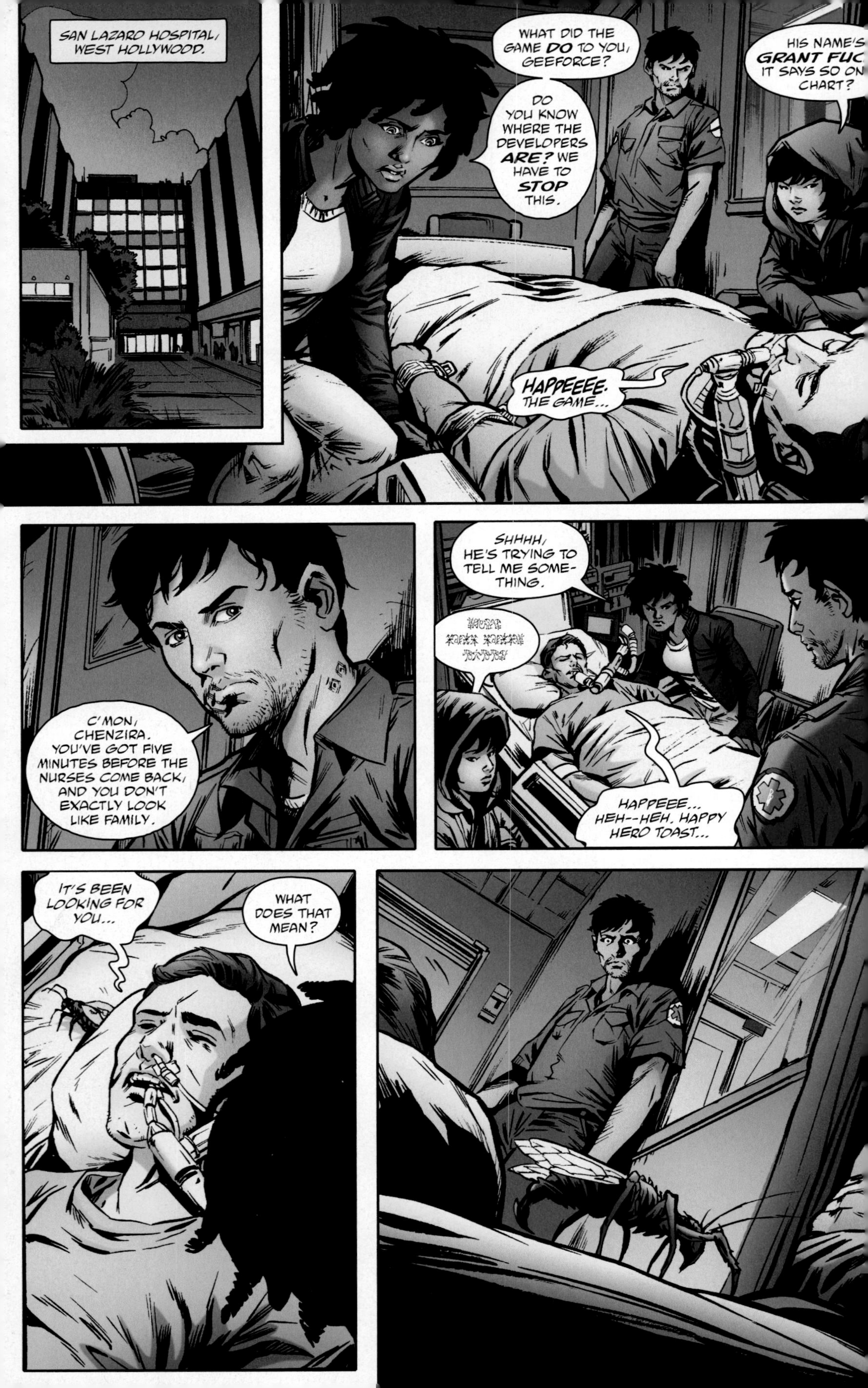
SAN LAZARO HOSPITAL, WEST HOLLYWOOD.
WHAT DID THE GAME DO TO YOU, GEEFORCE?
DO YOU KNOW WHERE THE DEVELOPERS ARE? WE HAVE TO STOP THIS.
HIS NAME'S GRANT FUC IT SAYS SO ON CHART?
HAPPEEEE. THE GAME...
C'MON, CHENZIRA. YOU'VE GOT FIVE MINUTES BEFORE THE NURSES COME BACK, AND YOU DON'T EXACTLY LOOK LIKE FAMILY.
SHHHH, HE'S TRYING TO TELL ME SOME-THING.
HAPPEEE... HEH--HEH. HAPPY HERO TOAST...
IT'S BEEN LOOKING FOR YOU...
WHAT DOES THAT MEAN?

HAHA HAHAHA HAHA

歡 甾吇吇喜
吜甾吇吇 吜大吇喜吇吇喜
喜吇吜大大吇吇 吇甾吇吇
吜甾吇吇吜 吇甾喜

THE GAME WANTS *YOU*, CHENZIRA.

LET ME GO. UN--FUCKING-- *TIE* ME....

I'LL TAKE YOU THERE. I'LL TAKE YOU TO *AKHERON!*

OKAY--

--THAT'S IT, EVERYBODY OUT.

OH, C'MON, TEO--

*HAHAHAHA!*

TAKE IT EASY, SIR. I NEED YOU TO CALM DOWN--

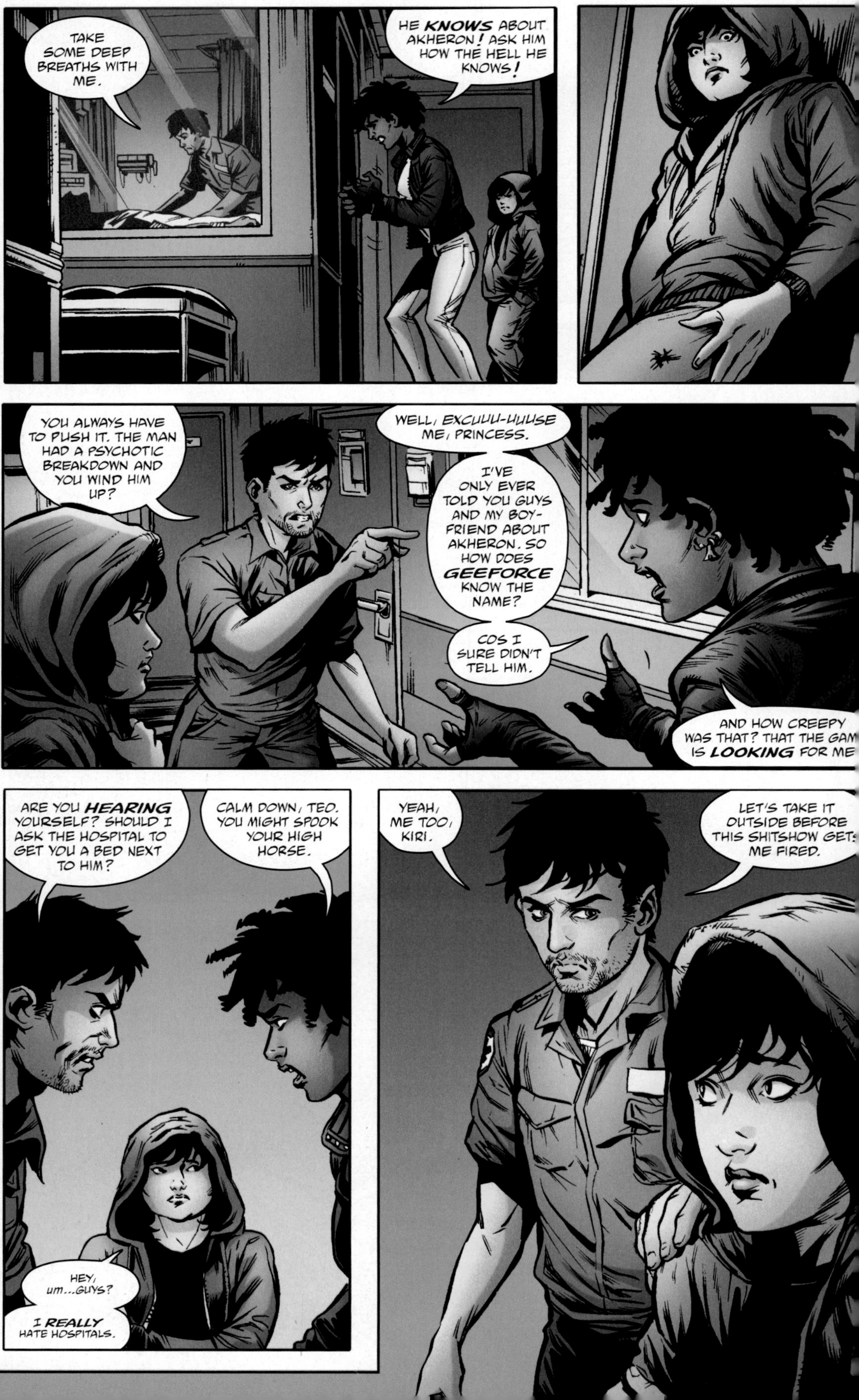
TAKE SOME DEEP BREATHS WITH ME.
HE **KNOWS** ABOUT AKHERON! ASK HIM HOW THE HELL HE KNOWS!
YOU ALWAYS HAVE TO PUSH IT. THE MAN HAD A PSYCHOTIC BREAKDOWN AND YOU WIND HIM UP?
WELL, EXCUUU-UUUSE ME, PRINCESS.
I'VE ONLY EVER TOLD YOU GUYS AND MY BOY-FRIEND ABOUT AKHERON. SO HOW DOES **GEEFORCE** KNOW THE NAME?
COS I SURE DIDN'T TELL HIM.
AND HOW CREEPY WAS THAT? THAT THE GAM IS **LOOKING** FOR ME
ARE YOU **HEARING** YOURSELF? SHOULD I ASK THE HOSPITAL TO GET YOU A BED NEXT TO HIM?
CALM DOWN, TEO. YOU MIGHT SPOOK YOUR HIGH HORSE.
HEY, um...GUYS?
I **REALLY** HATE HOSPITALS.
YEAH, ME TOO, KIRI.
LET'S TAKE IT OUTSIDE BEFORE THIS SHITSHOW GETS ME FIRED.

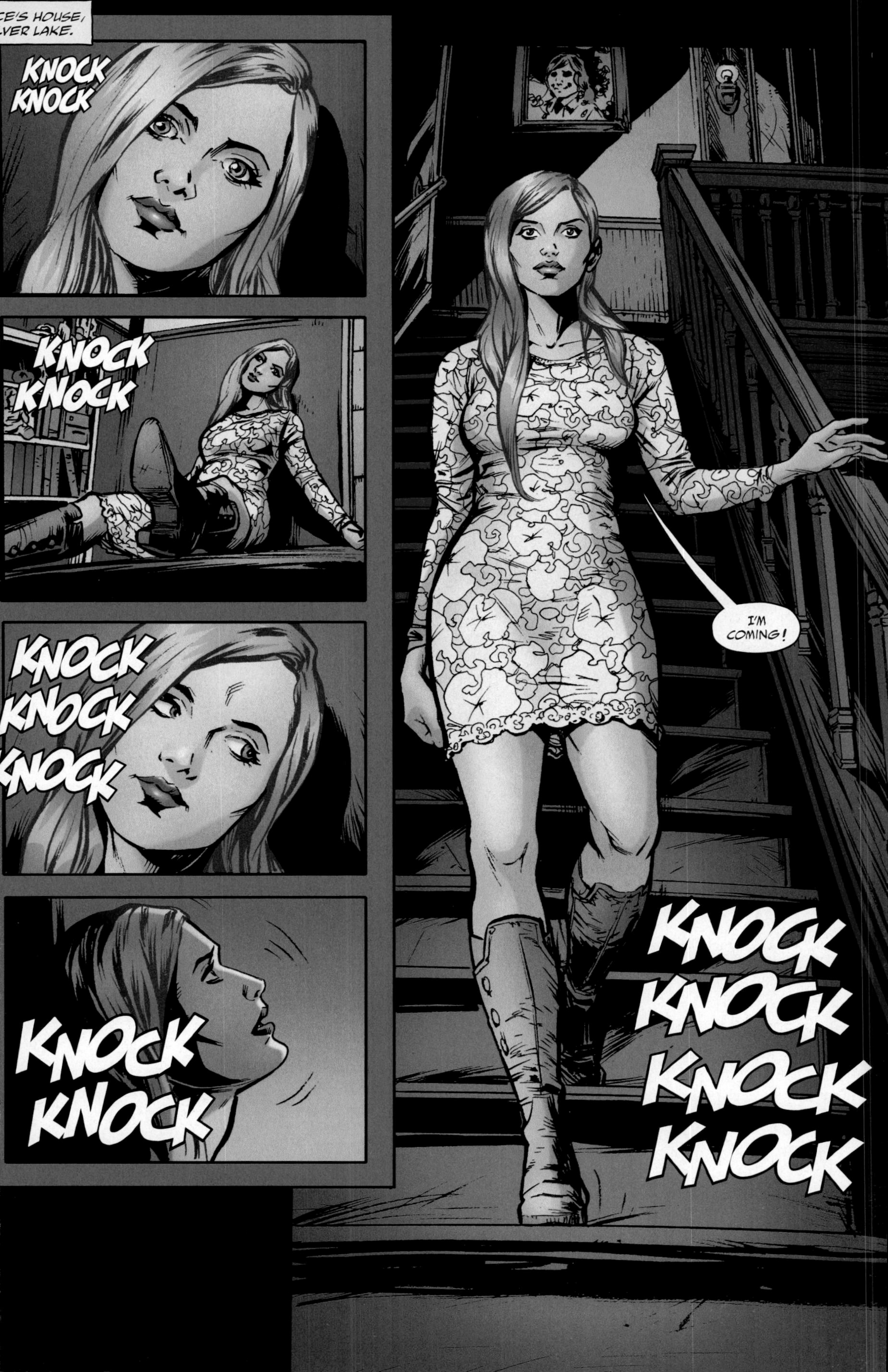
CE'S HOUSE,
LVER LAKE.
KNOCK KNOCK
KNOCK KNOCK
KNOCK KNOCK KNOCK
KNOCK KNOCK
I'M COMING!
KNOCK KNOCK KNOCK KNOCK

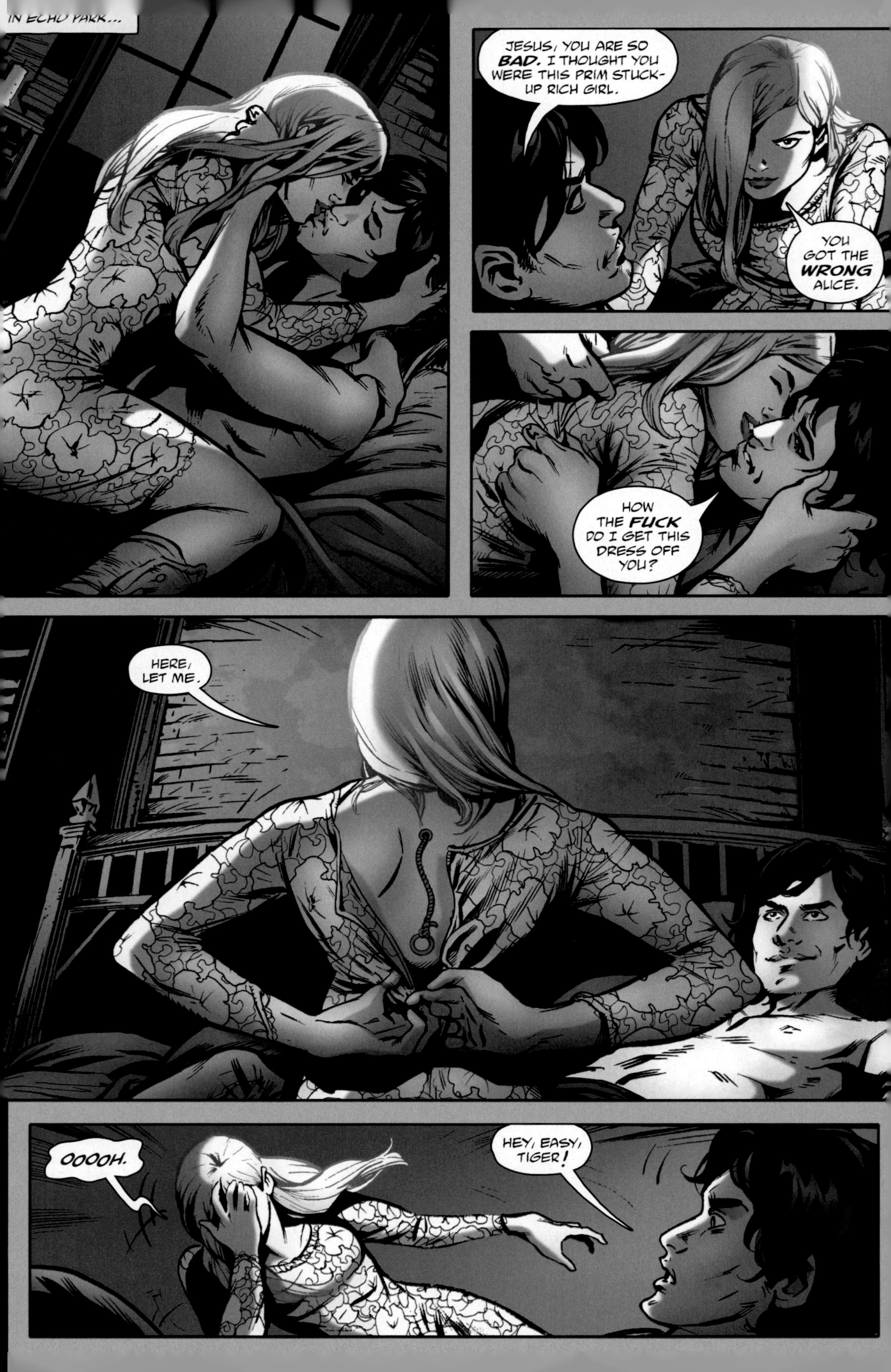
IN ECHO PARK...
JESUS, YOU ARE SO BAD. I THOUGHT YOU WERE THIS PRIM STUCK-UP RICH GIRL.
YOU GOT THE WRONG ALICE.
HOW THE FUCK DO I GET THIS DRESS OFF YOU?
HERE, LET ME.
OOOOH.
HEY, EASY, TIGER!

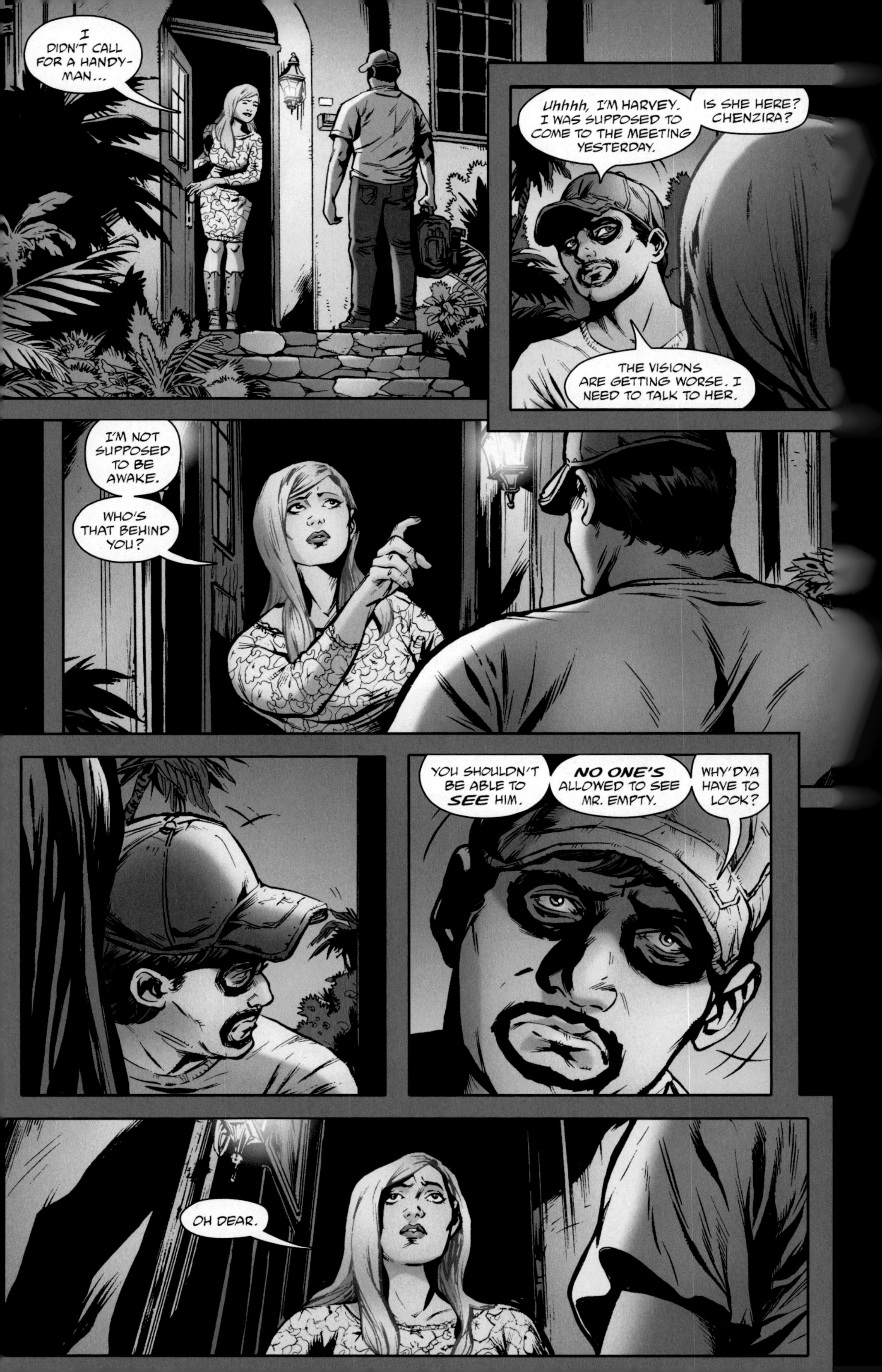
I DIDN'T CALL FOR A HANDY-MAN...
Uhhhh, I'M HARVEY. I WAS SUPPOSED TO COME TO THE MEETING YESTERDAY.
IS SHE HERE? CHENZIRA?
THE VISIONS ARE GETTING WORSE. I NEED TO TALK TO HER.
I'M NOT SUPPOSED TO BE AWAKE.
WHO'S THAT BEHIND YOU?
YOU SHOULDN'T BE ABLE TO SEE HIM.
NO ONE'S ALLOWED TO SEE MR. EMPTY.
WHY'DYA HAVE TO LOOK?
OH DEAR.

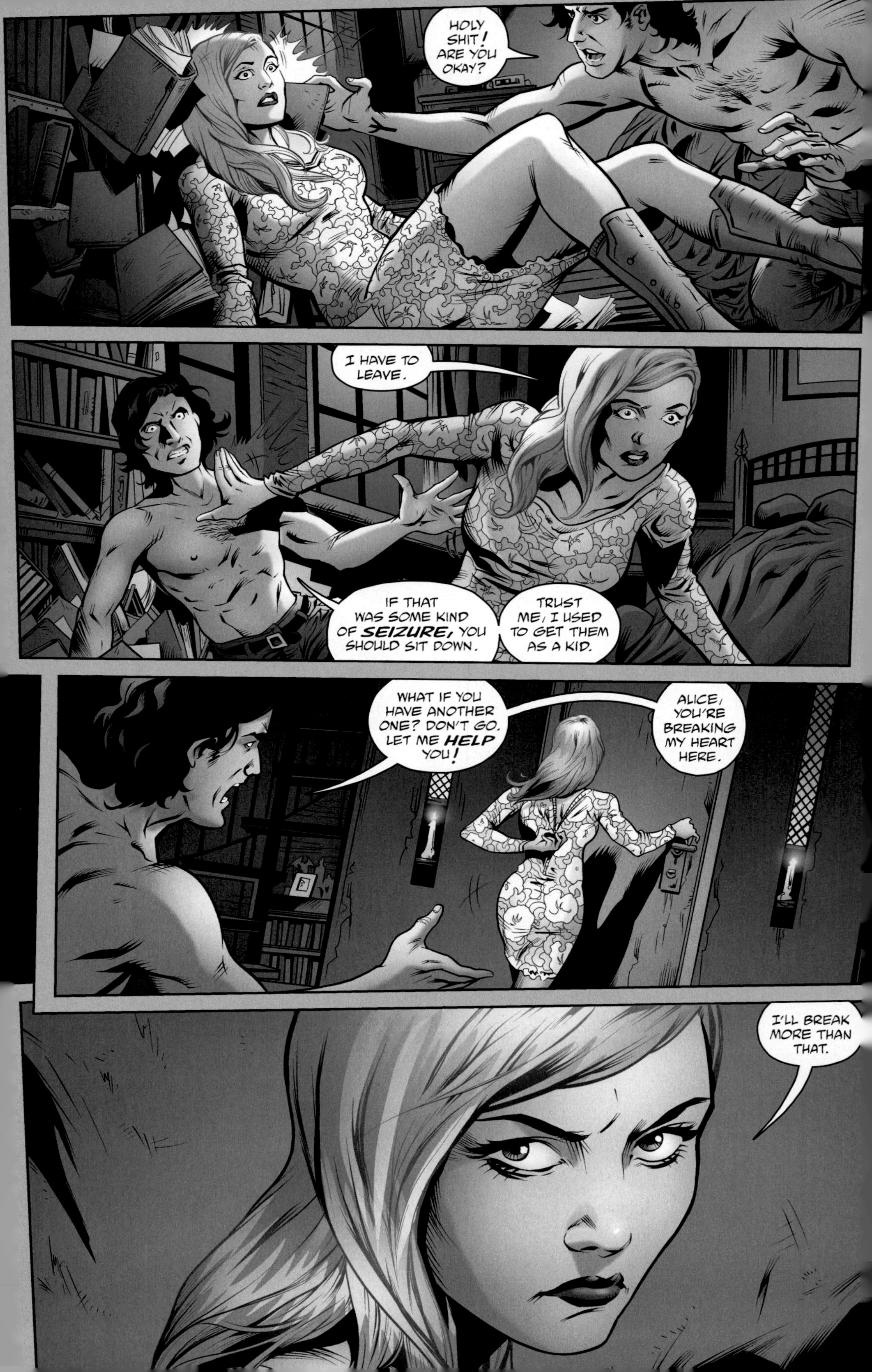
HOLY SHIT! ARE YOU OKAY?
I HAVE TO LEAVE.
IF THAT WAS SOME KIND OF SEIZURE, YOU SHOULD SIT DOWN.
TRUST ME, I USED TO GET THEM AS A KID.
WHAT IF YOU HAVE ANOTHER ONE? DON'T GO. LET ME HELP YOU!
ALICE, YOU'RE BREAKING MY HEART HERE.
I'LL BREAK MORE THAN THAT.

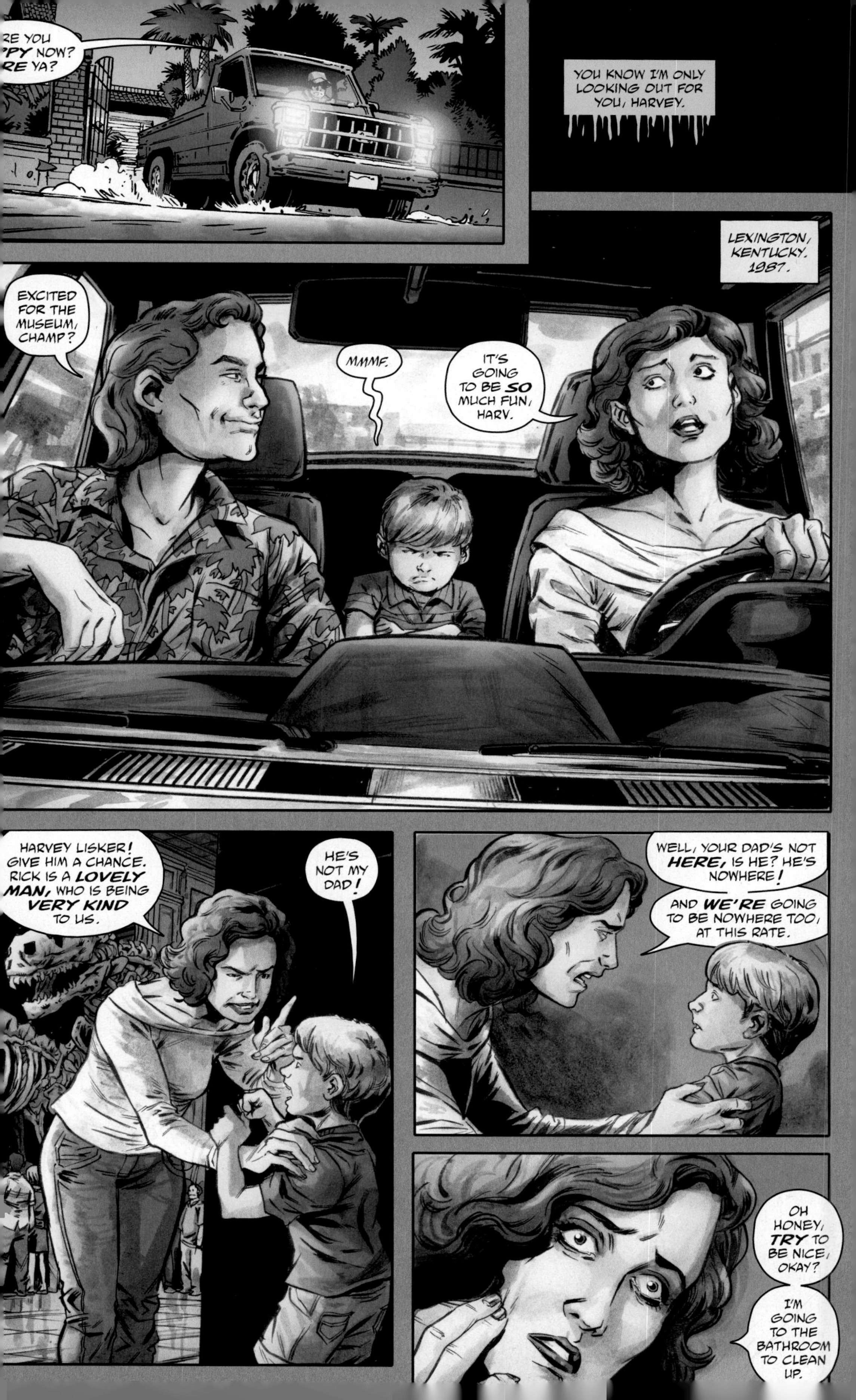

RE YOU PPY NOW? RE YA?
YOU KNOW I'M ONLY LOOKING OUT FOR YOU, HARVEY.
LEXINGTON, KENTUCKY. 1987.
EXCITED FOR THE MUSEUM, CHAMP?
MMMF.
IT'S GOING TO BE SO MUCH FUN, HARV.
HARVEY LISKER! GIVE HIM A CHANCE. RICK IS A LOVELY MAN, WHO IS BEING VERY KIND TO US.
HE'S NOT MY DAD!
WELL, YOUR DAD'S NOT HERE, IS HE? HE'S NOWHERE!
AND WE'RE GOING TO BE NOWHERE TOO, AT THIS RATE.
OH HONEY, TRY TO BE NICE, OKAY?
I'M GOING TO THE BATHROOM TO CLEAN UP.

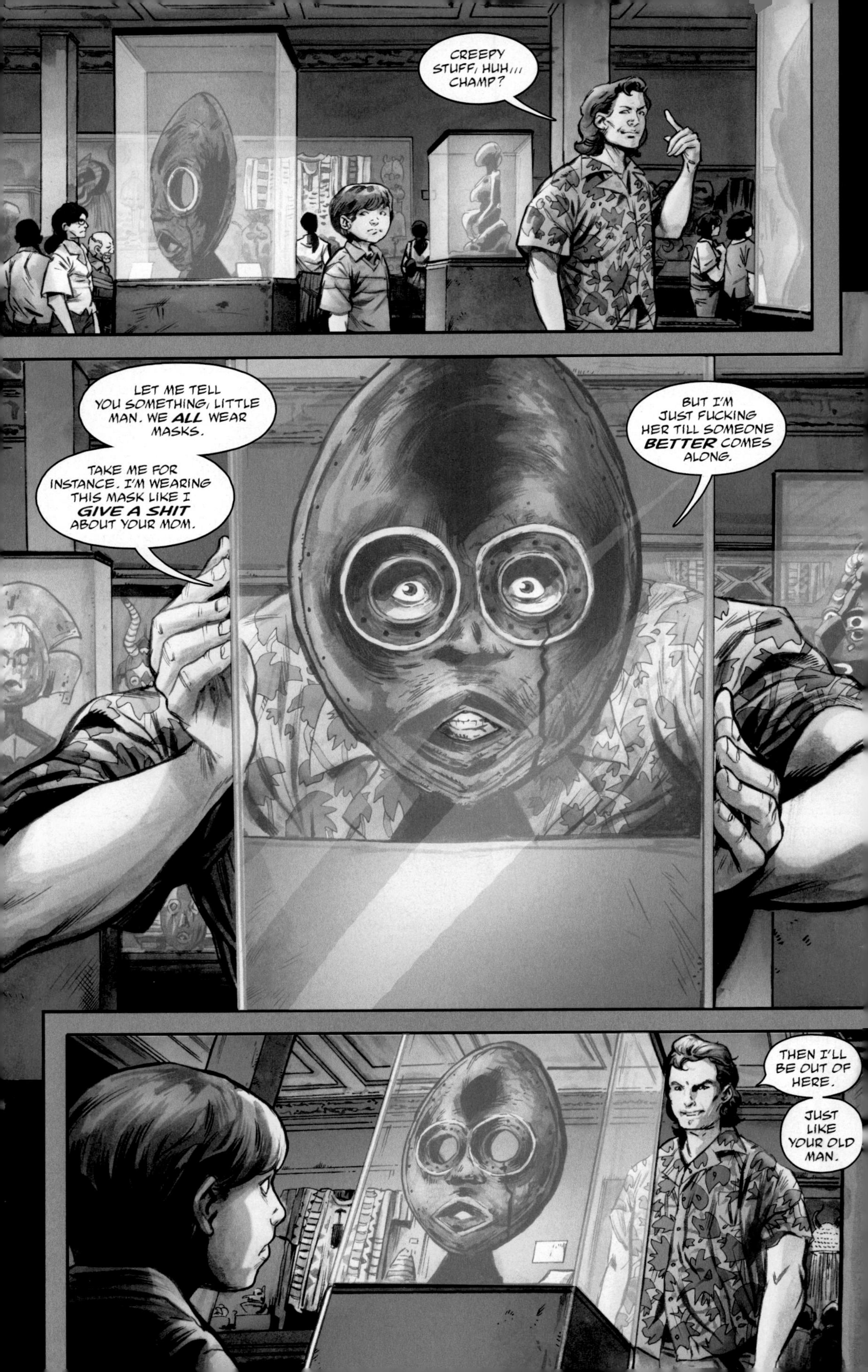
CREEPY STUFF, HUH... CHAMP?
LET ME TELL YOU SOMETHING, LITTLE MAN. WE ALL WEAR MASKS.
TAKE ME FOR INSTANCE. I'M WEARING THIS MASK LIKE I GIVE A SHIT ABOUT YOUR MOM.
BUT I'M JUST FUCKING HER TILL SOMEONE BETTER COMES ALONG.
THEN I'LL BE OUT OF HERE.
JUST LIKE YOUR OLD MAN.

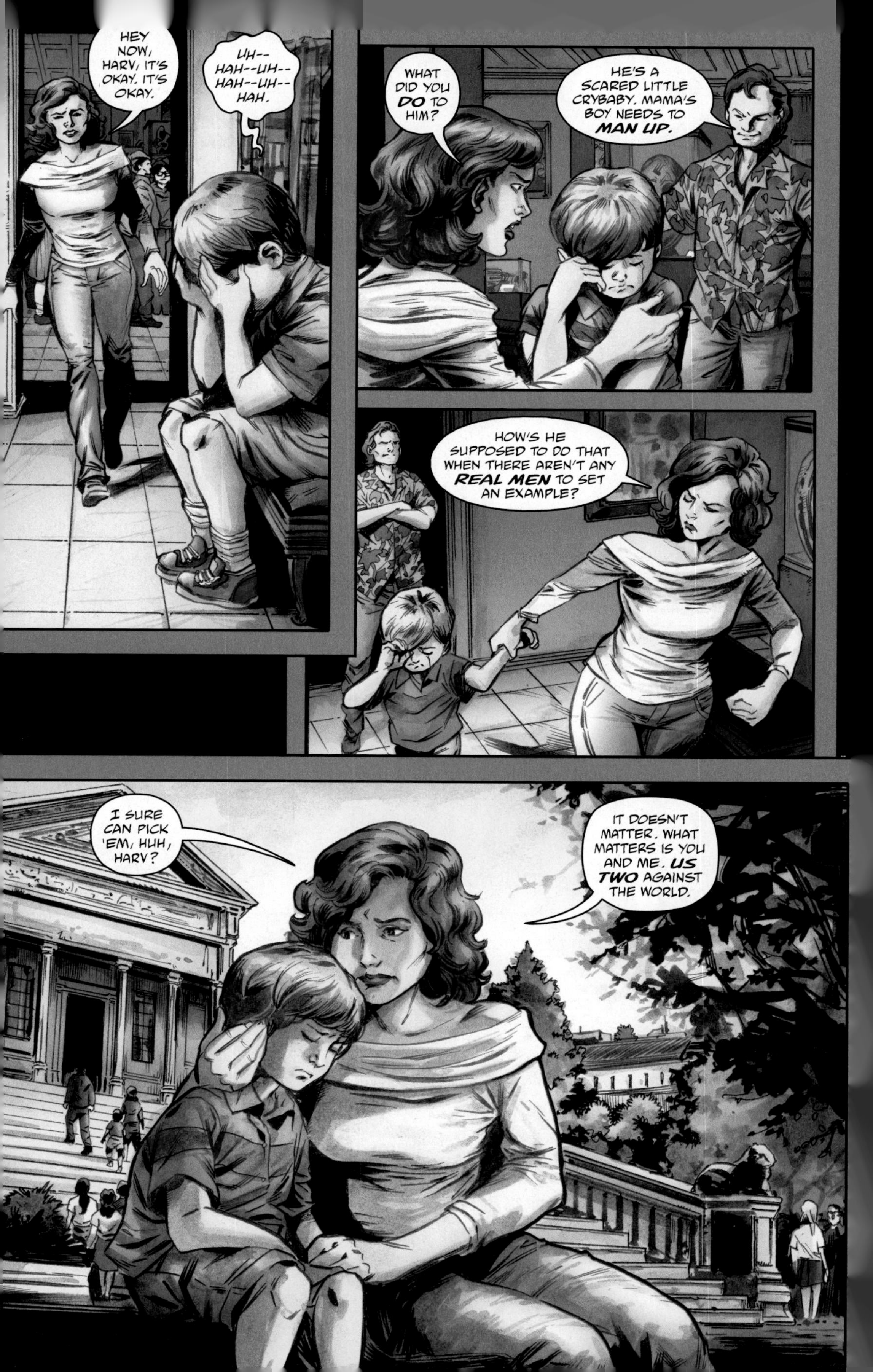
HEY NOW, HARV, IT'S OKAY. IT'S OKAY.
UH-- HAH--UH-- HAH--UH-- HAH.
WHAT DID YOU DO TO HIM?
HE'S A SCARED LITTLE CRYBABY. MAMA'S BOY NEEDS TO MAN UP.
HOW'S HE SUPPOSED TO DO THAT WHEN THERE AREN'T ANY REAL MEN TO SET AN EXAMPLE?
I SURE CAN PICK 'EM, HUH, HARV?
IT DOESN'T MATTER. WHAT MATTERS IS YOU AND ME. US TWO AGAINST THE WORLD.

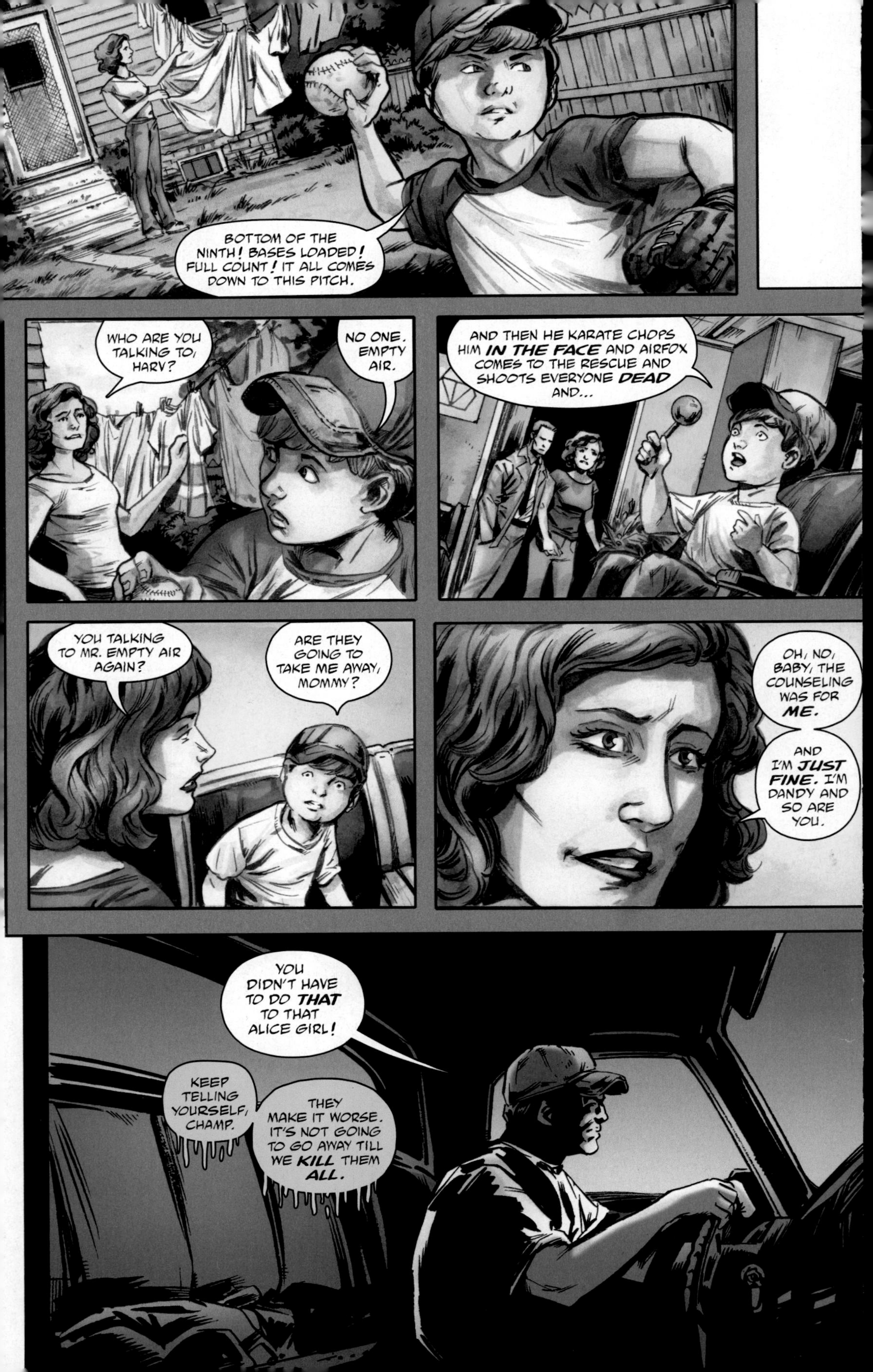

BOTTOM OF THE NINTH! BASES LOADED! FULL COUNT! IT ALL COMES DOWN TO THIS PITCH.
WHO ARE YOU TALKING TO, HARV?
NO ONE. EMPTY AIR.
AND THEN HE KARATE CHOPS HIM IN THE FACE AND AIRFOX COMES TO THE RESCUE AND SHOOTS EVERYONE DEAD AND...
YOU TALKING TO MR. EMPTY AIR AGAIN?
ARE THEY GOING TO TAKE ME AWAY, MOMMY?
OH, NO, BABY, THE COUNSELING WAS FOR ME.
AND I'M JUST FINE. I'M DANDY AND SO ARE YOU.
YOU DIDN'T HAVE TO DO THAT TO THAT ALICE GIRL!
KEEP TELLING YOURSELF, CHAMP.
THEY MAKE IT WORSE. IT'S NOT GOING TO GO AWAY TILL WE KILL THEM ALL.

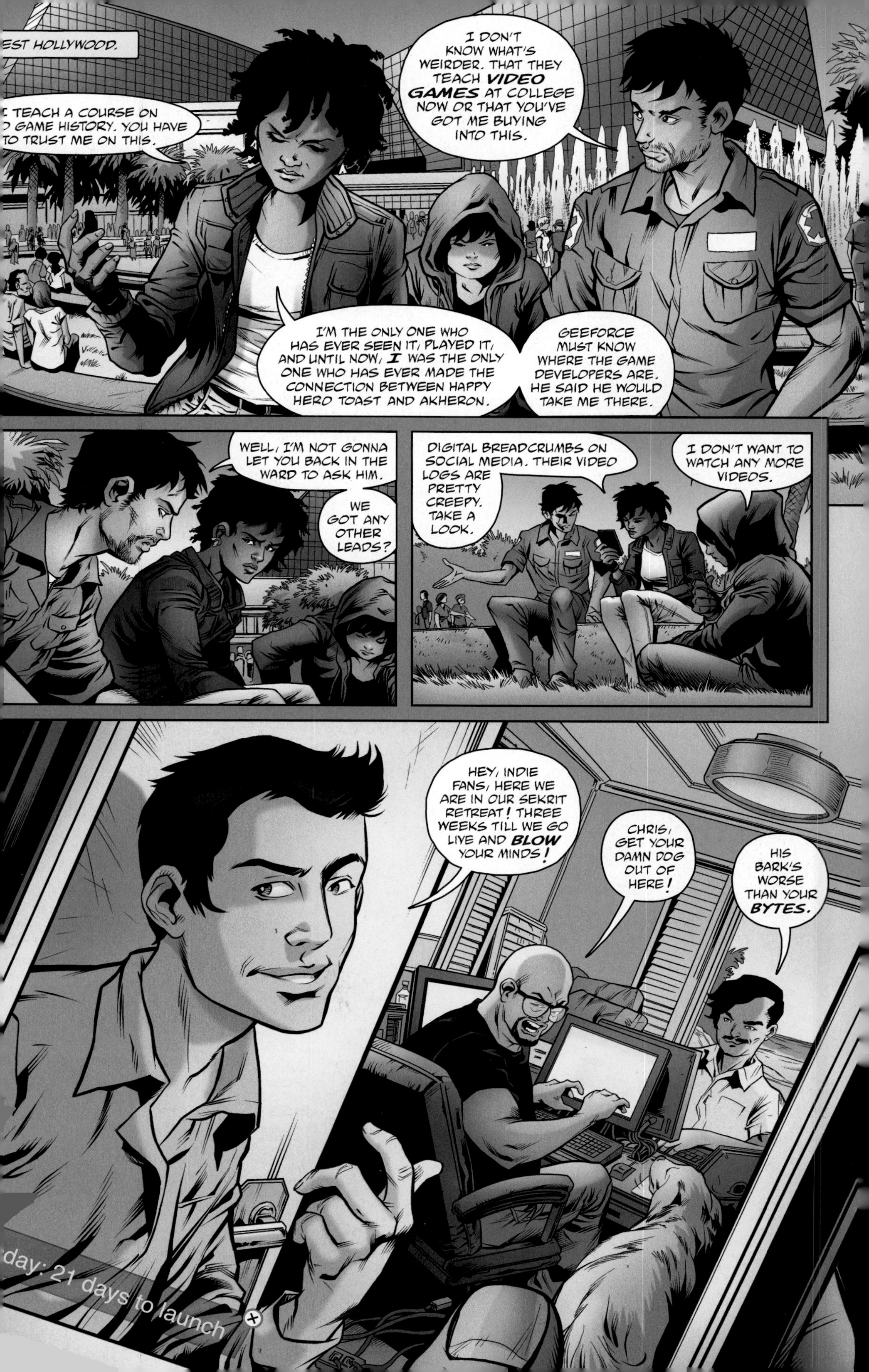
EST HOLLYWOOD.
I TEACH A COURSE ON
D GAME HISTORY. YOU HAVE
O TRUST ME ON THIS.
I DON'T KNOW WHAT'S WEIRDER. THAT THEY TEACH VIDEO GAMES AT COLLEGE NOW OR THAT YOU'VE GOT ME BUYING INTO THIS.
I'M THE ONLY ONE WHO HAS EVER SEEN IT, PLAYED IT, AND UNTIL NOW, I WAS THE ONLY ONE WHO HAS EVER MADE THE CONNECTION BETWEEN HAPPY HERO TOAST AND AKHERON.
GEEFORCE MUST KNOW WHERE THE GAME DEVELOPERS ARE. HE SAID HE WOULD TAKE ME THERE.
WELL, I'M NOT GONNA LET YOU BACK IN THE WARD TO ASK HIM.
WE GOT ANY OTHER LEADS?
DIGITAL BREADCRUMBS ON SOCIAL MEDIA. THEIR VIDEO LOGS ARE PRETTY CREEPY. TAKE A LOOK.
I DON'T WANT TO WATCH ANY MORE VIDEOS.
HEY, INDIE FANS, HERE WE ARE IN OUR SEKRIT RETREAT! THREE WEEKS TILL WE GO LIVE AND BLOW YOUR MINDS!
CHRIS, GET YOUR DAMN DOG OUT OF HERE!
HIS BARK'S WORSE THAN YOUR BYTES.
day: 21 days to launch

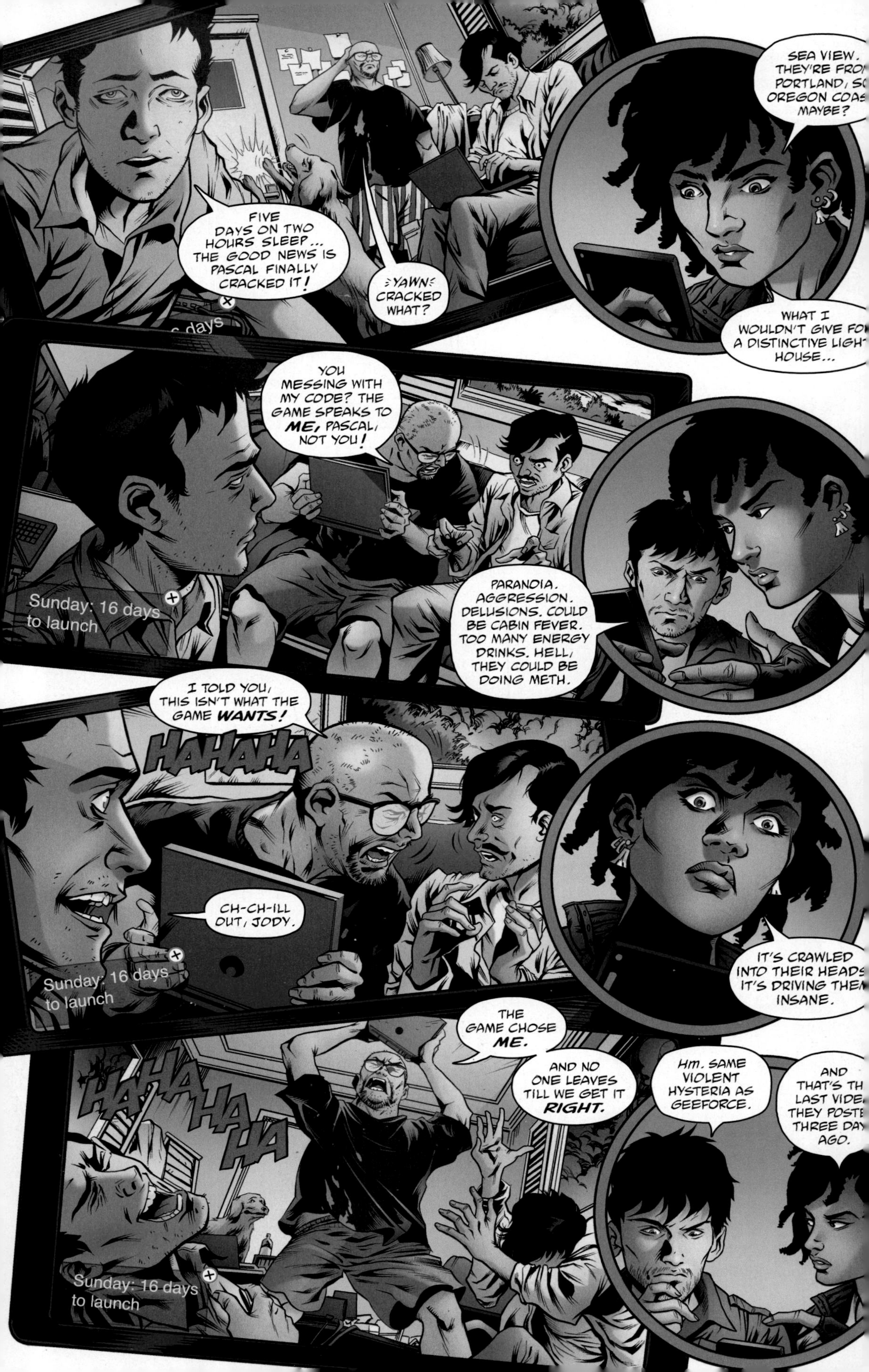
FIVE DAYS ON TWO HOURS SLEEP... THE GOOD NEWS IS PASCAL FINALLY CRACKED IT!
YAWN CRACKED WHAT?
SEA VIEW. THEY'RE FROM PORTLAND, SO OREGON COAST MAYBE?
WHAT I WOULDN'T GIVE FOR A DISTINCTIVE LIGHTHOUSE...
YOU MESSING WITH MY CODE? THE GAME SPEAKS TO ME, PASCAL, NOT YOU!
Sunday: 16 days to launch
PARANOIA. AGGRESSION. DELUSIONS. COULD BE CABIN FEVER. TOO MANY ENERGY DRINKS. HELL, THEY COULD BE DOING METH.
I TOLD YOU, THIS ISN'T WHAT THE GAME WANTS!
HAHAHA
CH-CH-ILL OUT, JODY.
Sunday: 16 days to launch
IT'S CRAWLED INTO THEIR HEADS. IT'S DRIVING THEM INSANE.
THE GAME CHOSE ME.
AND NO ONE LEAVES TILL WE GET IT RIGHT.
HAHAHAHA
Hm. SAME VIOLENT HYSTERIA AS GEEFORCE.
AND THAT'S THE LAST VIDEO THEY POSTED THREE DAYS AGO.
Sunday: 16 days to launch

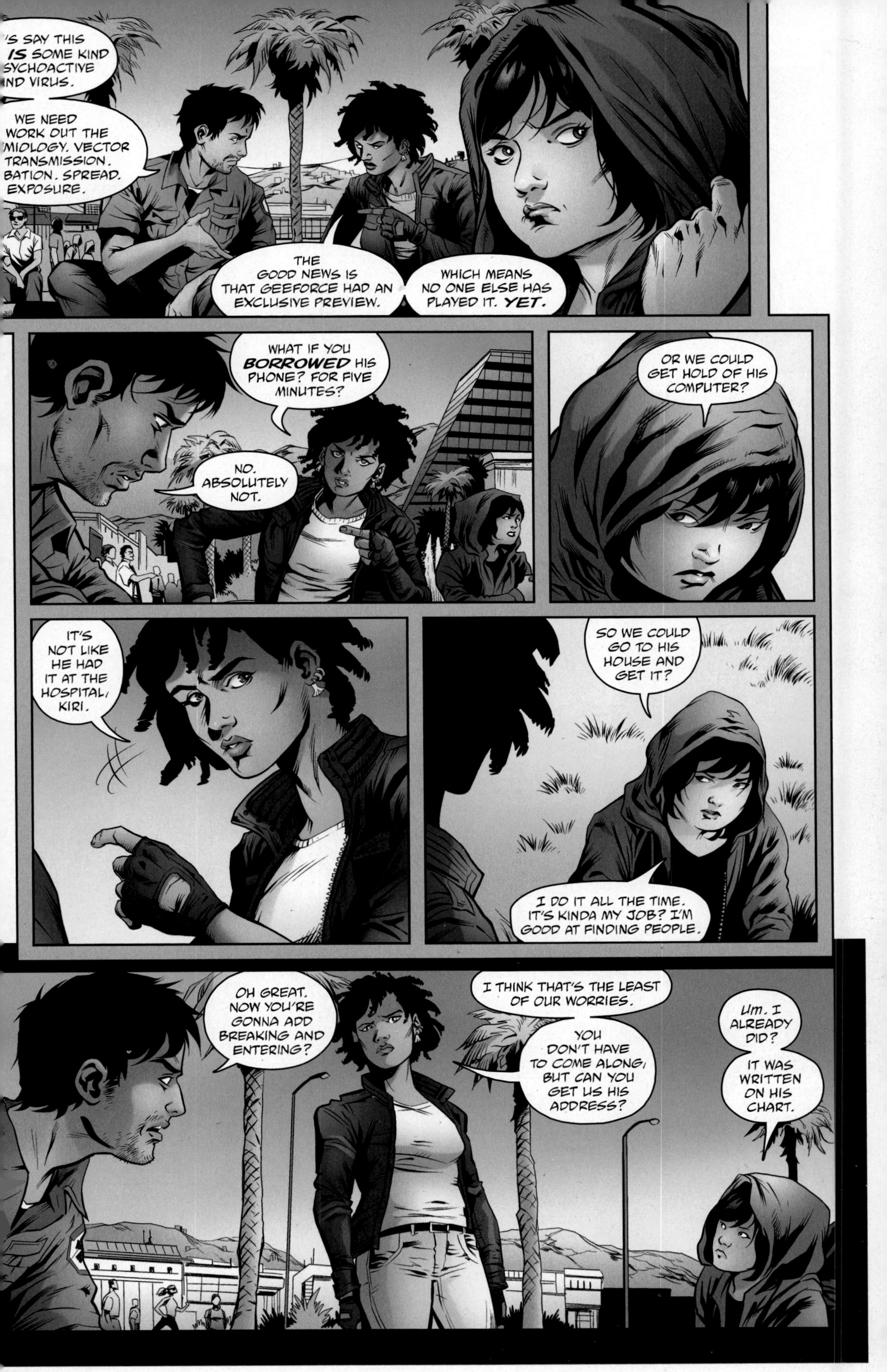
'S SAY THIS IS SOME KIND SYCHOACTIVE IND VIRUS.
WE NEED WORK OUT THE MIOLOGY. VECTOR TRANSMISSION. BATION. SPREAD. EXPOSURE.
THE GOOD NEWS IS THAT GEEFORCE HAD AN EXCLUSIVE PREVIEW.
WHICH MEANS NO ONE ELSE HAS PLAYED IT. YET.
WHAT IF YOU BORROWED HIS PHONE? FOR FIVE MINUTES?
NO. ABSOLUTELY NOT.
OR WE COULD GET HOLD OF HIS COMPUTER?
IT'S NOT LIKE HE HAD IT AT THE HOSPITAL, KIRI.
SO WE COULD GO TO HIS HOUSE AND GET IT?
I DO IT ALL THE TIME. IT'S KINDA MY JOB? I'M GOOD AT FINDING PEOPLE.
OH GREAT. NOW YOU'RE GONNA ADD BREAKING AND ENTERING?
I THINK THAT'S THE LEAST OF OUR WORRIES.
YOU DON'T HAVE TO COME ALONG, BUT CAN YOU GET US HIS ADDRESS?
UM. I ALREADY DID?
IT WAS WRITTEN ON HIS CHART.

THE LARGO THEATER.

"FRITEFEST 5."

MOVIE SCREENINGS! MERCH! MEET YOUR FAVE HORROR STARS!

FRITE FEST 5

OMG! I CAN'T BELIEVE IT'S REALLY *YOU!* MUSKAGEE'S LIKE MY ALL-TIME FAVORITE MOVIE.

EXCEPT NUMBER FOUR. THAT WAS SHIT.

Um. THAT'S NOT MY PHOTO.

AUTOGRAPHS $5
SIGNED POSTERS $25
PHOTOGRAPHS $10

I'M THE *REAL GUY.* YOU'RE LOOKING FOR THE ACTOR WHO PLAYED ME IN THE MOVIE.

OMIGOSH! SOZ! ≶Giggle≶ I'M *SO* EMBARRASSED.

NEXT TABLE.

TELL CODY HIS HAIRPLUGS LOOK GREAT.

CAN YOU BELIEVE THIS SHIT? MY SISTER SAYS I SHOULD GET A *REAL* JOB.

Meet the Star of Muskagee House! Cody Whitman-Tekker

WOW, VHS. HAVEN'T SEEN ONE OF THOSE IN A WHILE. RETRO.

IN THE ORIGINAL MOVIE THE PRIEST GOT SUCKED INTO THE WALLPAPER, BUT I READ THIS INTERVIEW WITH YOU IN 1992 THAT YOU SAID THE HOUSE ATE HIM? IS THAT WHAT HAPPENED TO YOUR PARENTS? I SAW A GHOST ONCE. OR MAYBE IT WAS A DEMON. I THINK IT WAS LONELY? HOW DO YOU TELL IF SOMETHING IS MALEVOLENT?

T BELIEVE

HEY, HEY, EASY. I GOTTA SAVE *SOMETHING* FOR THE TELL-ALL MEMOIR.

THER WE G THIS ON ON "T HOUSE

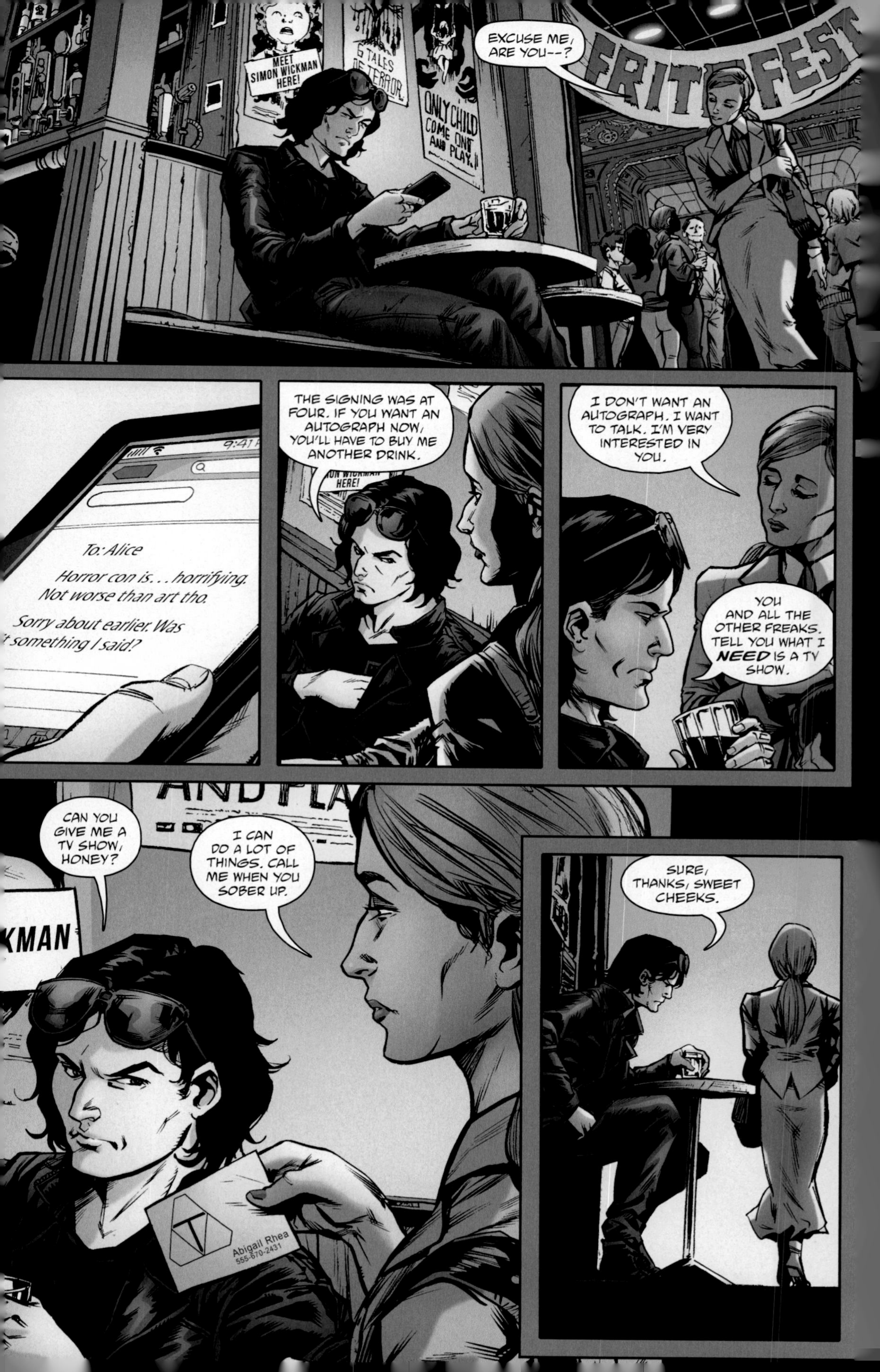
MEET SIMON WICKMAN HERE!
6 TALES OF TERROR
ONLY CHILD COME ON AND PLAY.
FRIGHTFEST
EXCUSE ME, ARE YOU--?
To: Alice
Horror con is... horrifying. Not worse than art tho.
Sorry about earlier. Was it something I said?
THE SIGNING WAS AT FOUR. IF YOU WANT AN AUTOGRAPH NOW, YOU'LL HAVE TO BUY ME ANOTHER DRINK.
I DON'T WANT AN AUTOGRAPH. I WANT TO TALK. I'M VERY INTERESTED IN YOU.
YOU AND ALL THE OTHER FREAKS. TELL YOU WHAT I NEED IS A TV SHOW.
CAN YOU GIVE ME A TV SHOW, HONEY?
I CAN DO A LOT OF THINGS. CALL ME WHEN YOU SOBER UP.
Abigail Rhea
555-670-2431
SURE, THANKS, SWEET CHEEKS.

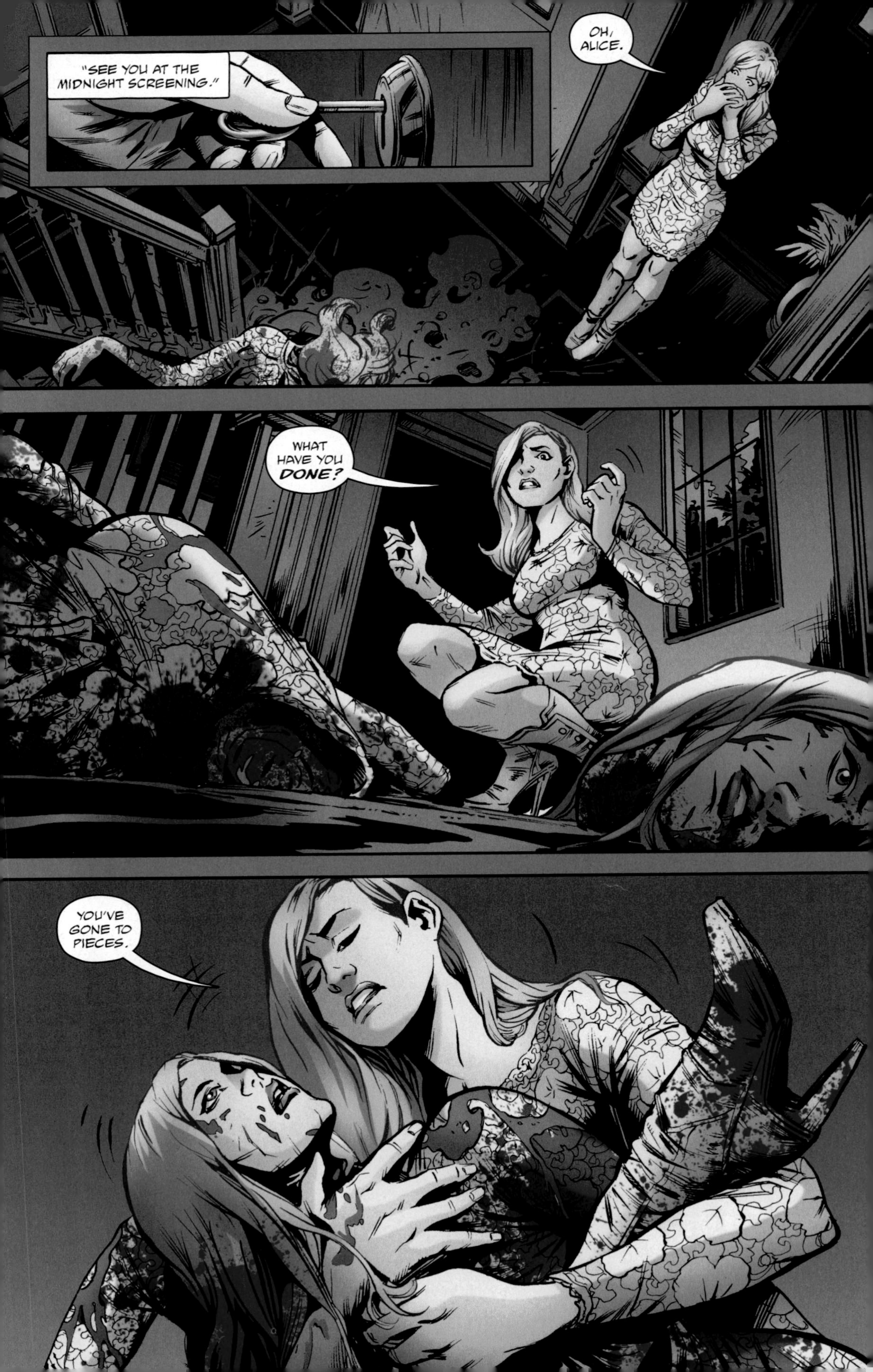
"SEE YOU AT THE MIDNIGHT SCREENING."
OH, ALICE.
WHAT HAVE YOU DONE?
YOU'VE GONE TO PIECES.

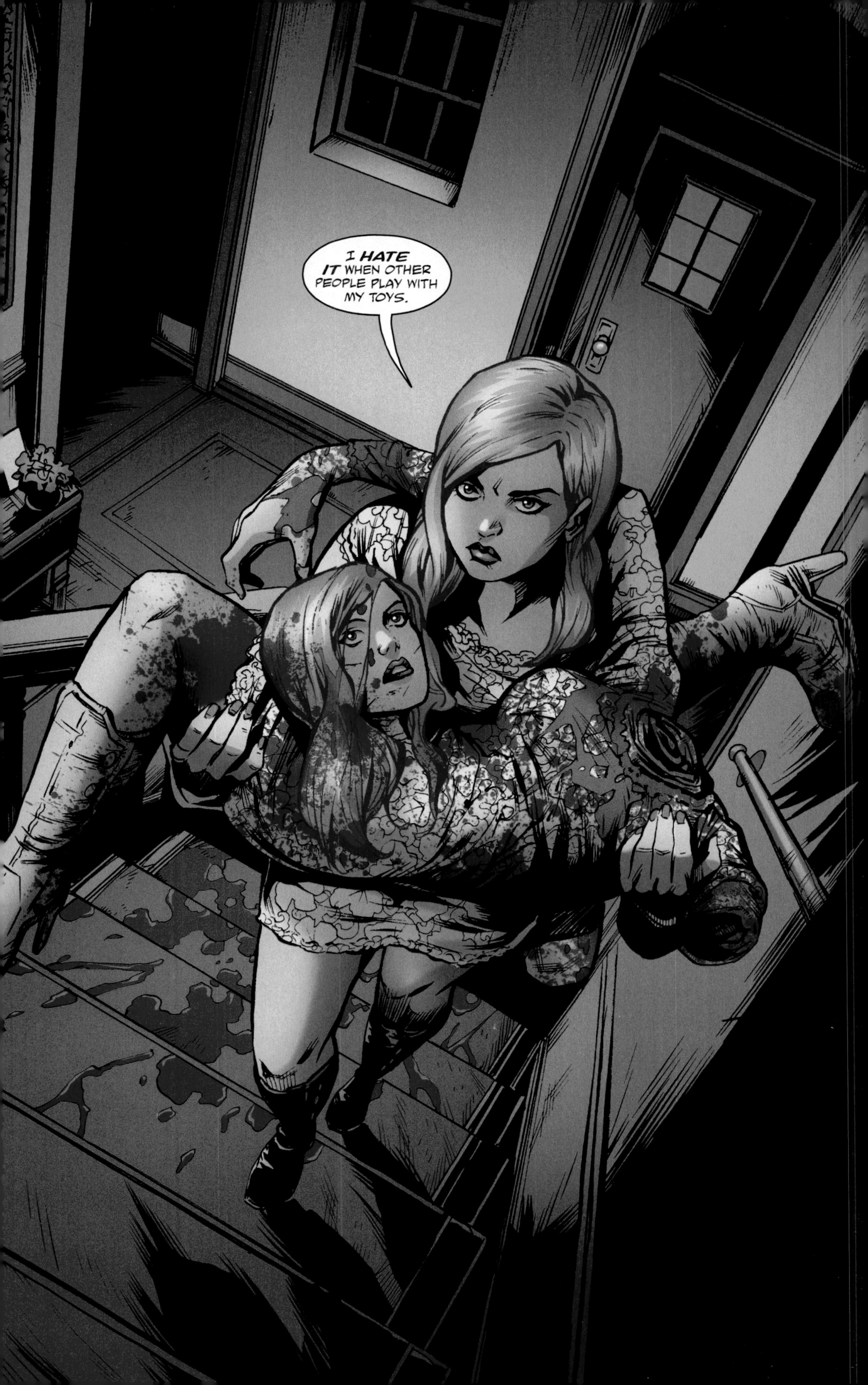
I HATE IT WHEN OTHER PEOPLE PLAY WITH MY TOYS.

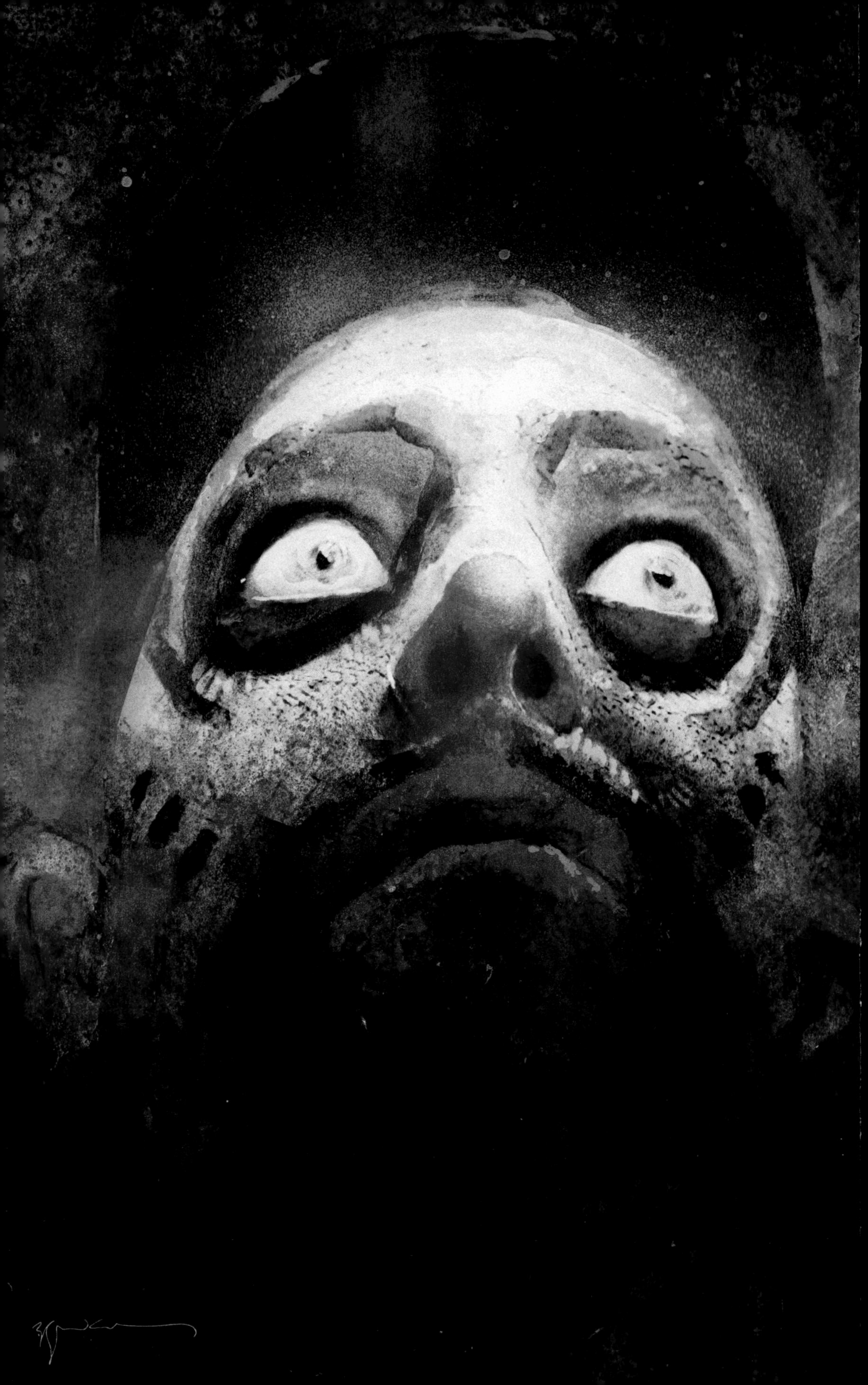

OFFREY
ET POOL,
PEDRO.

RONALD BRANNAN?

苯 腐苯苯啡
苯大苯腐功欠欠
腐欠功欠 苯腐啡
欠苯 苯腐

THE FUCK, *YOU* AGAIN, LITTLE CHINK?

YOU'RE NOT GONNA FOOL ME WITH THE PIZZA DELIVERY STORY THIS TIME.

YOU GOT ME, RONNY. HERE TO SERVE YOU *ANOTHER* PIPING-HOT RESTRAINING ORDER.

LIKE I TOLD THE COPS, BITCH FELL DOWN THE STAIRS.

YOU SEEM TO ATTRACT A *LOT* OF CLUMSY BITCHES. THIS IS THE FOURTH ONE IN SIX MONTHS.

YOU KNOW, RONNY, YOU ARE MY *NUMBER ONE* REPEAT CUSTOMER. THAT QUALIFIES YOU FOR A SPECIAL PRIZE.

YEAH? YOU GONNA BLOW ME?

OH, BETTER THAN THAT.

苯腐欠
测腐大苯 腐腻
苯腐苯腐腻珠 欠欠
功 腐大苯

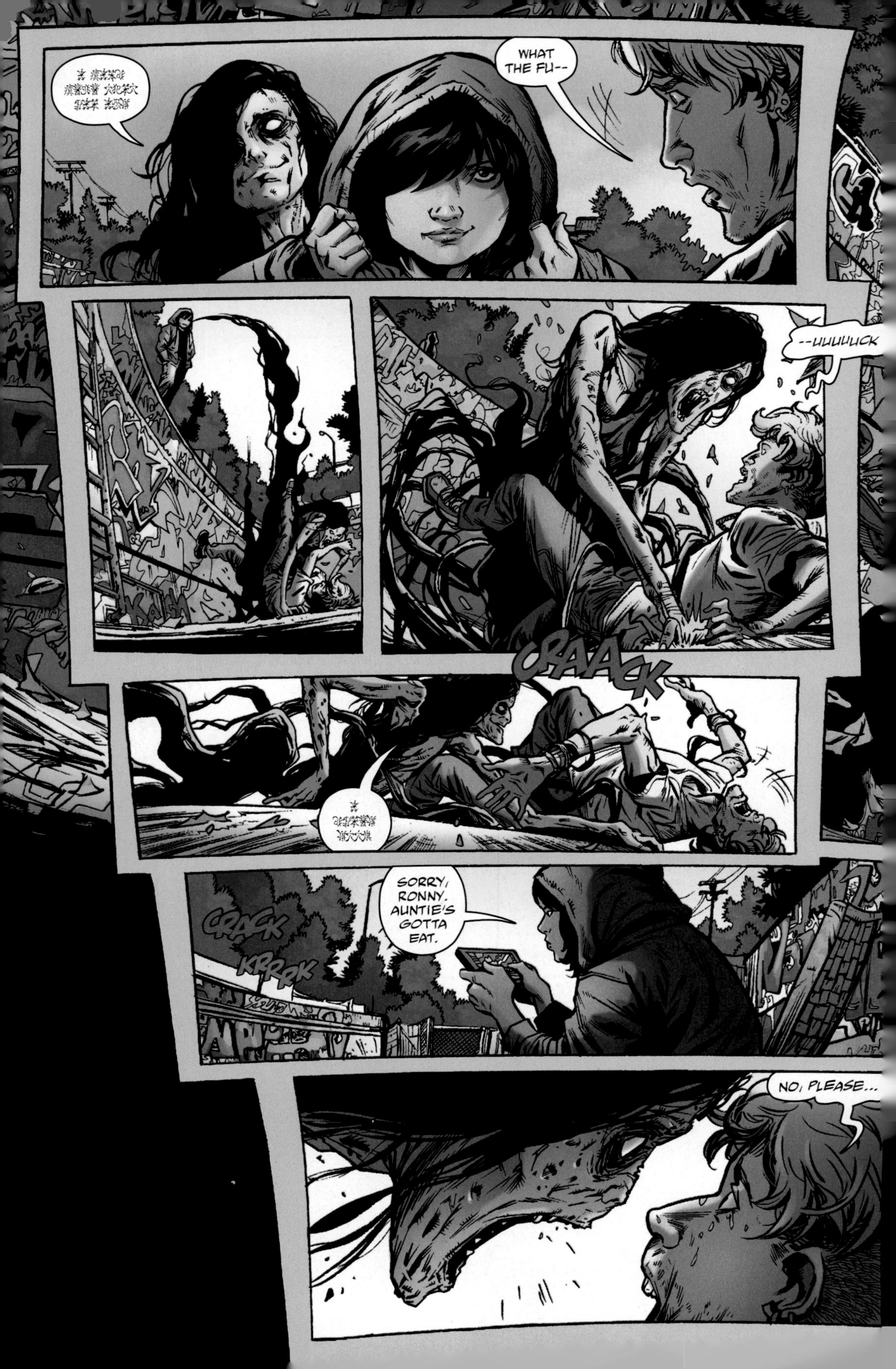
WHAT THE FU--
--UUUUUCK
CRAAACK
SORRY, RONNY. AUNTIE'S GOTTA EAT.
CRACK
KRRRK
NO, PLEASE...

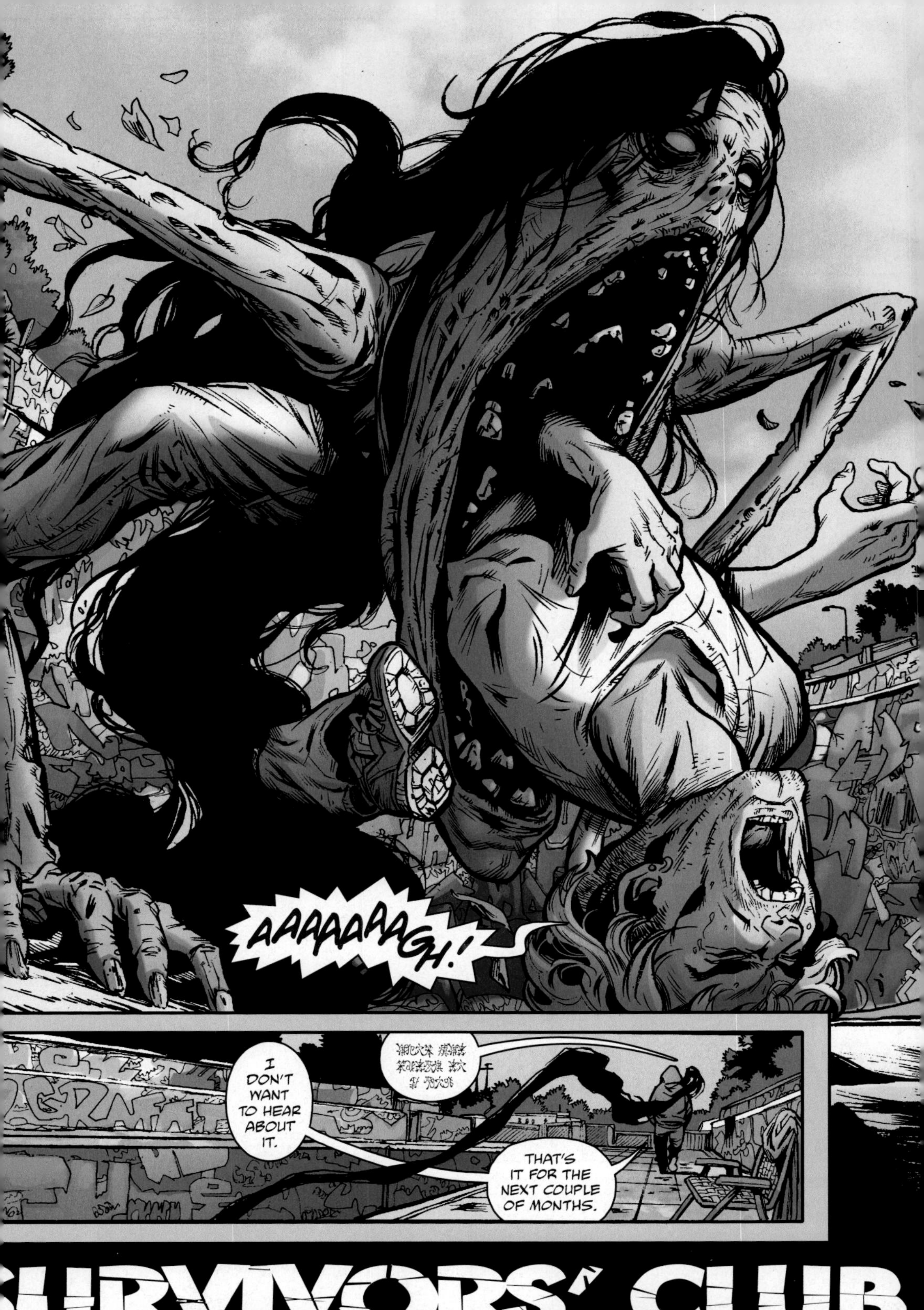
AAAAAAAAGH!
I DON'T WANT TO HEAR ABOUT IT.
THAT'S IT FOR THE NEXT COUPLE OF MONTHS.

# SURVIVORS' CLUB
## CHAPTER THREE: RESPAWN

REN KES · DALE HALVORSEN · RYAN KELLY

EVA DE LA CRUZ COLORIST CLEM ROBINS LETTERER
BILL SIENKIEWICZ COVER ARTIST
ROWENA YOW ASSOCIATE EDITOR SHELLY BOND EDITOR

AKWASI AMO-ADDAE GHANAIAN TRANSLATIONS

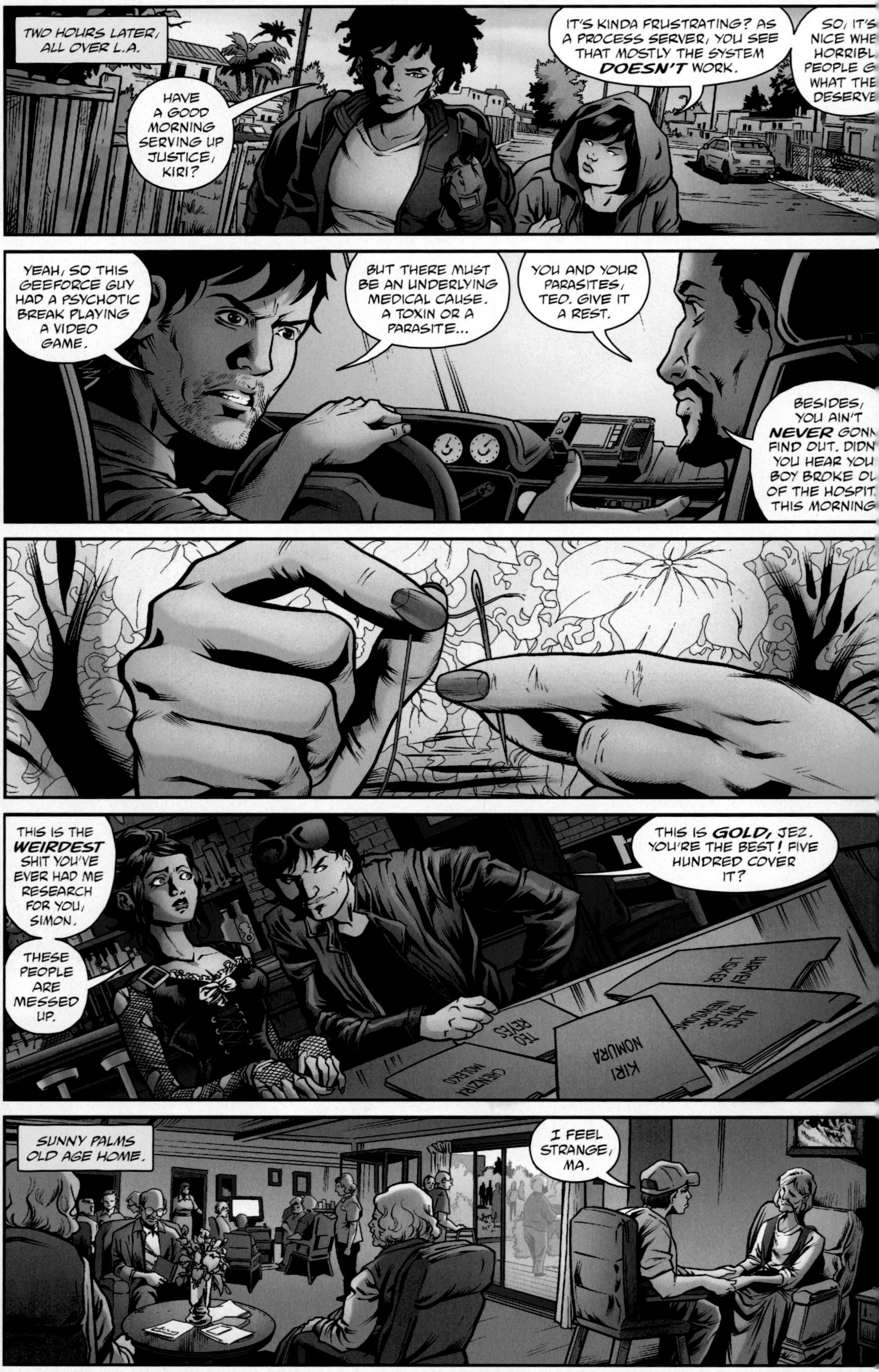
TWO HOURS LATER, ALL OVER L.A.
HAVE A GOOD MORNING SERVING UP JUSTICE, KIRI?
IT'S KINDA FRUSTRATING? AS A PROCESS SERVER, YOU SEE THAT MOSTLY THE SYSTEM DOESN'T WORK.
SO, IT'S NICE WHE HORRIBL PEOPLE G WHAT THE DESERVE
YEAH, SO THIS GEEFORCE GUY HAD A PSYCHOTIC BREAK PLAYING A VIDEO GAME.
BUT THERE MUST BE AN UNDERLYING MEDICAL CAUSE. A TOXIN OR A PARASITE...
YOU AND YOUR PARASITES, TEO. GIVE IT A REST.
BESIDES, YOU AIN'T NEVER GONN FIND OUT. DIDN YOU HEAR YOU BOY BROKE OU OF THE HOSPIT THIS MORNING
THIS IS THE WEIRDEST SHIT YOU'VE EVER HAD ME RESEARCH FOR YOU, SIMON.
THESE PEOPLE ARE MESSED UP.
THIS IS GOLD, JEZ. YOU'RE THE BEST! FIVE HUNDRED COVER IT?
HARVEY LISKER
TEO REYES
KIRI NOMURA
SUNNY PALMS OLD AGE HOME.
I FEEL STRANGE, MA.

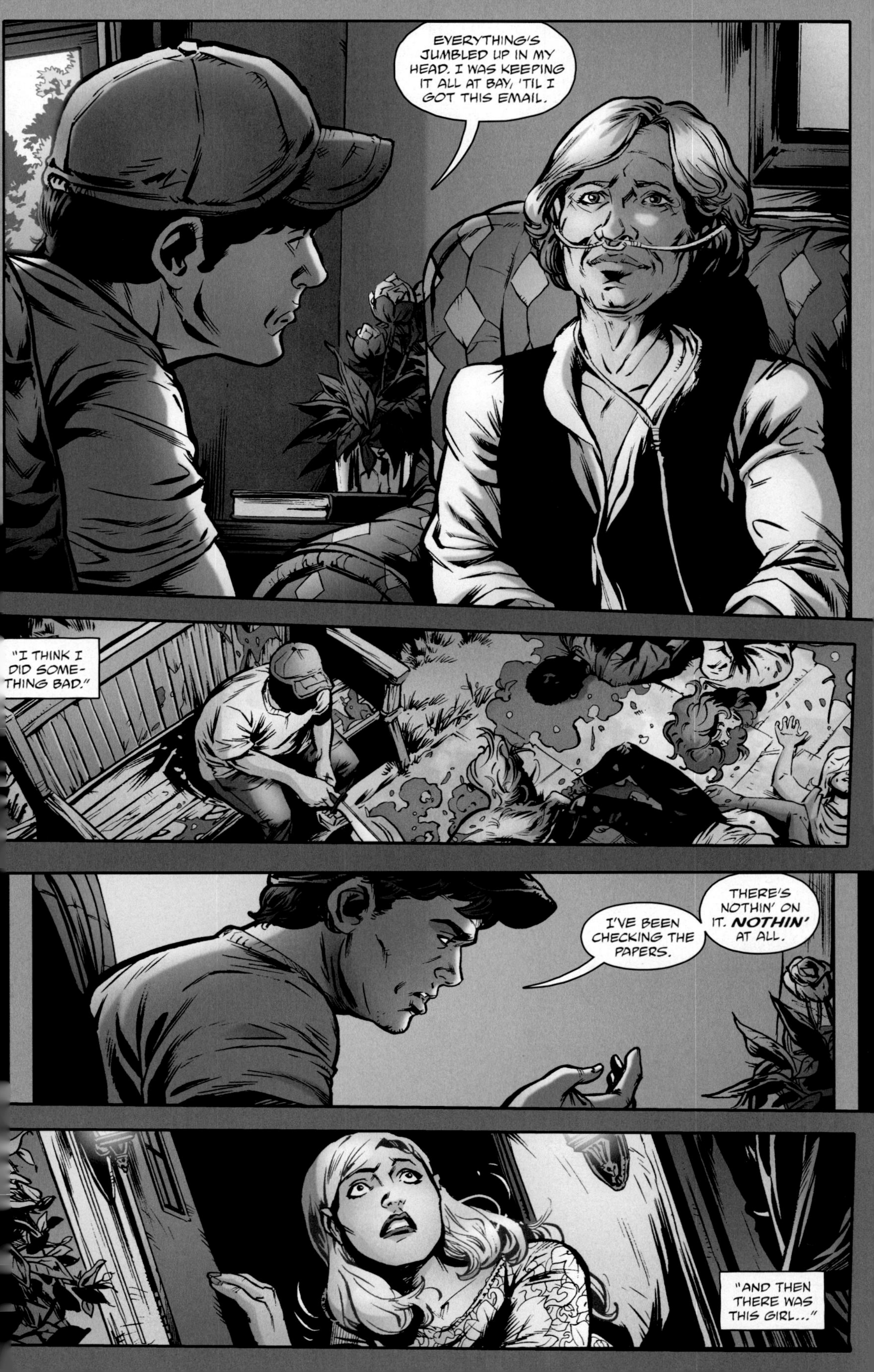
EVERYTHING'S JUMBLED UP IN MY HEAD. I WAS KEEPING IT ALL AT BAY, 'TIL I GOT THIS EMAIL.
"I THINK I DID SOMETHING BAD."
I'VE BEEN CHECKING THE PAPERS.
THERE'S NOTHIN' ON IT. NOTHIN' AT ALL.
"AND THEN THERE WAS THIS GIRL..."

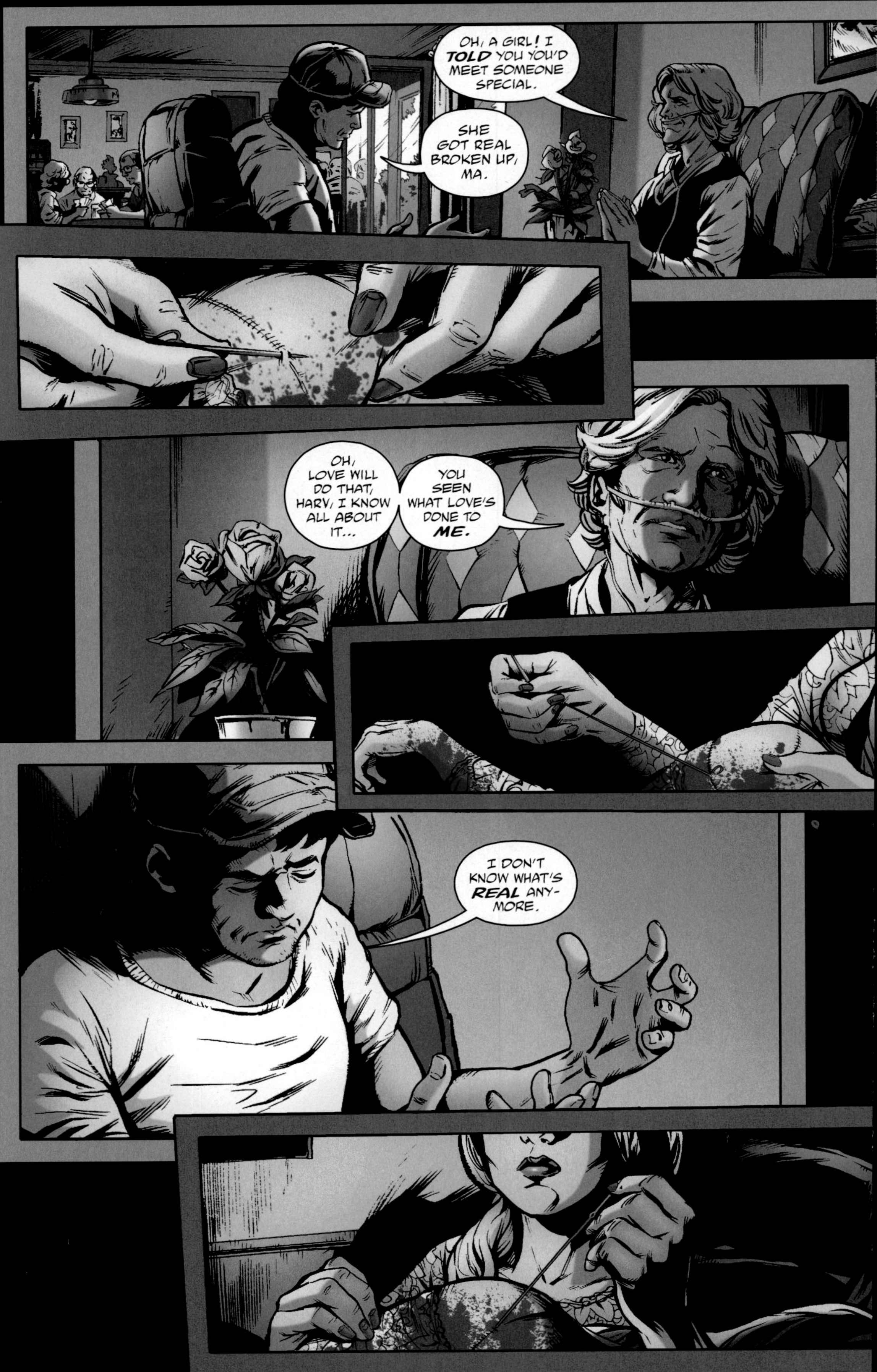
OH, A GIRL! I TOLD YOU YOU'D MEET SOMEONE SPECIAL.
SHE GOT REAL BROKEN UP, MA.
OH, LOVE WILL DO THAT, HARV, I KNOW ALL ABOUT IT...
YOU SEEN WHAT LOVE'S DONE TO ME.
I DON'T KNOW WHAT'S REAL ANY-MORE.

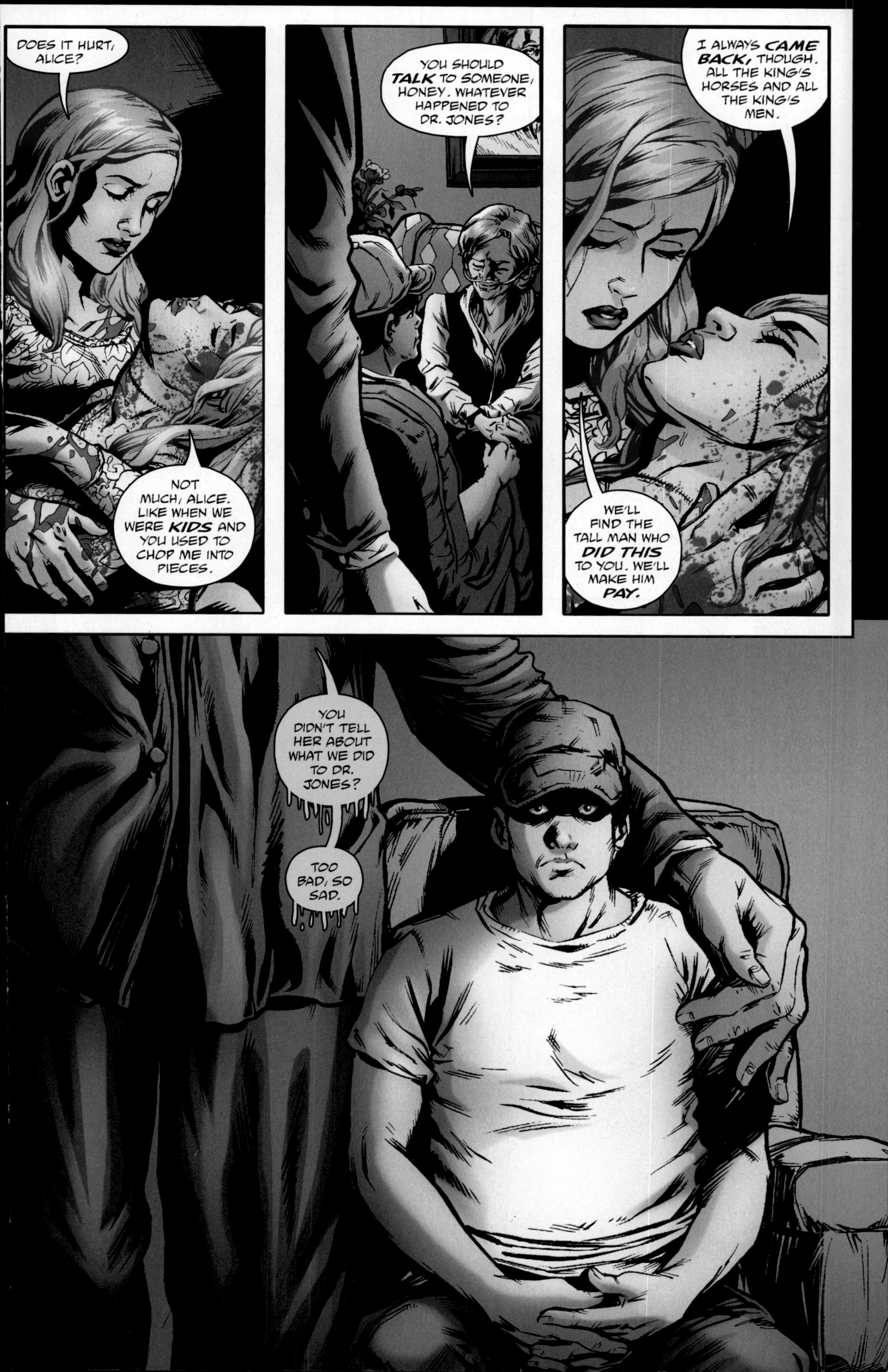
DOES IT HURT, ALICE?
NOT MUCH, ALICE. LIKE WHEN WE WERE KIDS AND YOU USED TO CHOP ME INTO PIECES.
YOU SHOULD TALK TO SOMEONE, HONEY. WHATEVER HAPPENED TO DR. JONES?
I ALWAYS CAME BACK, THOUGH. ALL THE KING'S HORSES AND ALL THE KING'S MEN.
WE'LL FIND THE TALL MAN WHO DID THIS TO YOU. WE'LL MAKE HIM PAY.
YOU DIDN'T TELL HER ABOUT WHAT WE DID TO DR. JONES?
TOO BAD, SO SAD.

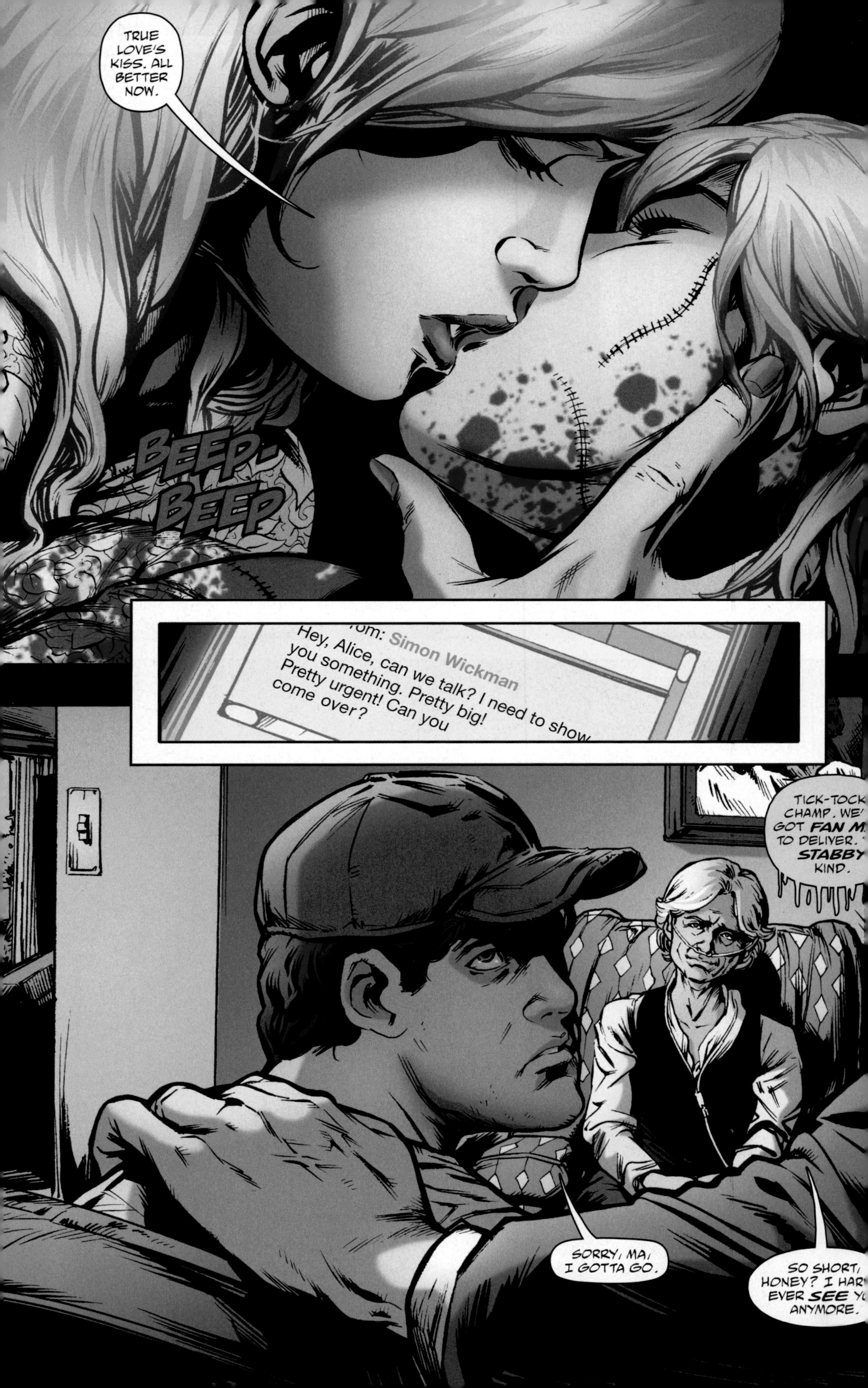
TRUE LOVE'S KISS. ALL BETTER NOW.
BEEP-BEEP
...rom: Simon Wickman
Hey, Alice, can we talk? I need to show you something. Pretty big! Pretty urgent! Can you come over?
TICK-TOCK CHAMP. WE' GOT FAN M TO DELIVER. STABBY KIND.
SORRY, MA, I GOTTA GO.
SO SHORT, HONEY? I HAR EVER SEE Y ANYMORE.

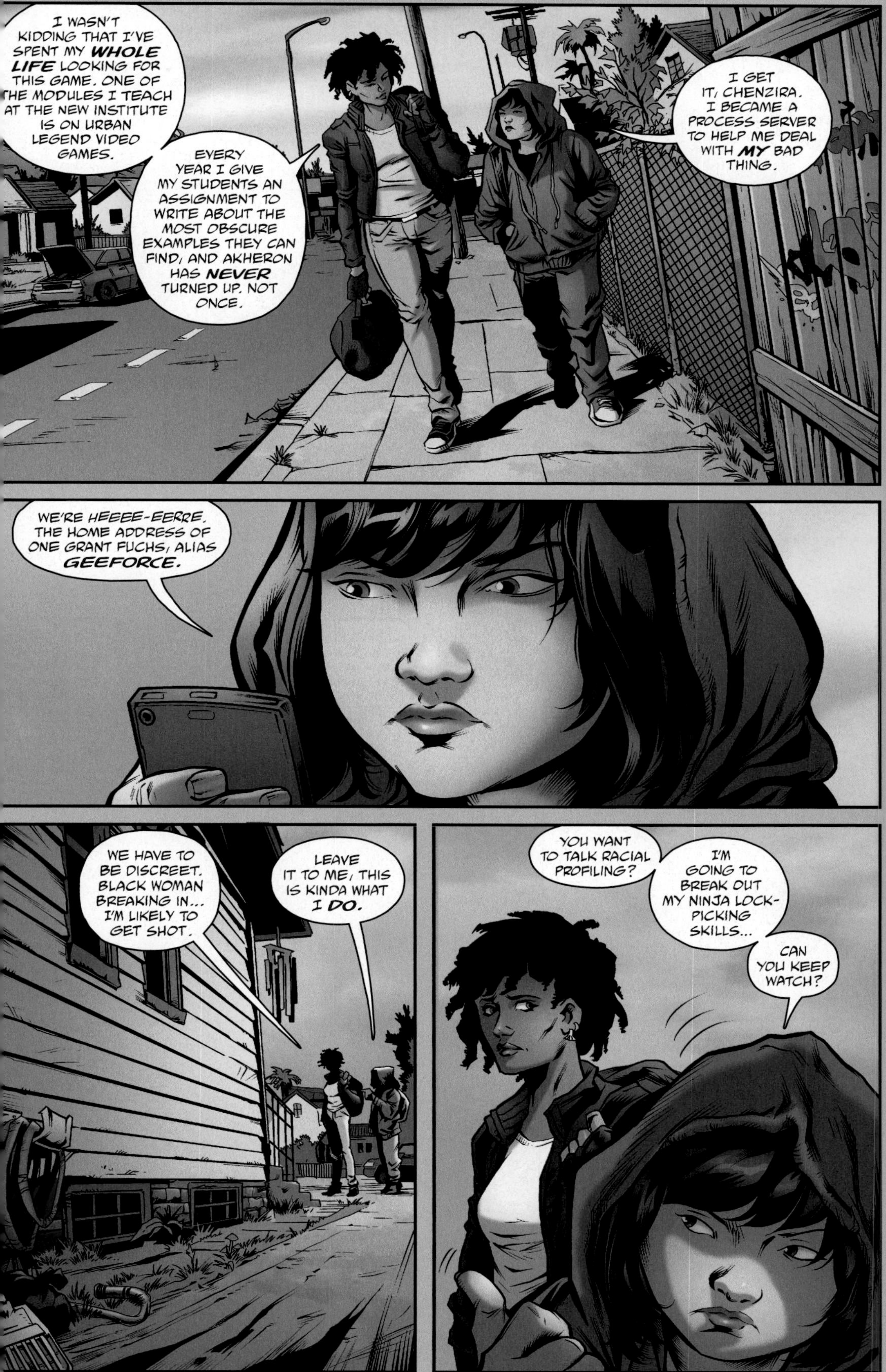
I WASN'T KIDDING THAT I'VE SPENT MY WHOLE LIFE LOOKING FOR THIS GAME. ONE OF THE MODULES I TEACH AT THE NEW INSTITUTE IS ON URBAN LEGEND VIDEO GAMES.
EVERY YEAR I GIVE MY STUDENTS AN ASSIGNMENT TO WRITE ABOUT THE MOST OBSCURE EXAMPLES THEY CAN FIND, AND AKHERON HAS NEVER TURNED UP. NOT ONCE.
I GET IT, CHENZIRA. I BECAME A PROCESS SERVER TO HELP ME DEAL WITH MY BAD THING.
WE'RE HEEEE-EERRE. THE HOME ADDRESS OF ONE GRANT FUCHS, ALIAS GEEFORCE.
WE HAVE TO BE DISCREET. BLACK WOMAN BREAKING IN... I'M LIKELY TO GET SHOT.
LEAVE IT TO ME, THIS IS KINDA WHAT I DO.
YOU WANT TO TALK RACIAL PROFILING?
I'M GOING TO BREAK OUT MY NINJA LOCK-PICKING SKILLS...
CAN YOU KEEP WATCH?

GOT IT! YOU CAN LOOK NOW.

KLIK

NICE WORK, JILL, MASTER OF UNLOCKING.

HUH?

GAMER HUMOR. WOW, *LOOK* AT THIS PLACE. DECOR BY GUY-WHO-WENT-MENTAL-PLAYING-A-VIDEO-GAME-AND-TRIED-TO-RIP-HIS-THROAT-OUT.

WHAT'S WITH THE MASK AND GLOVES?

TEO SAID WE SHOULD WEAR THESE IN CASE OF TOXINS.

OH PLEASE. LET'S JUST GET THIS DONE. IF YOU SEE GEEFORCE'S LAPTOP, THAT'S FIRST PRIZE.

BUT WE'RE LOOKING FOR ANYTHING THAT MIGHT BE CONNECTED TO *HAPPY HERO TOAST.*

OR, I DUNNO, ENVELOPES MARKED "DANGER: CRAZYPANTS ANTHRAX," IF YOU WANT TO BUY INTO TEO'S THEORY.

HOW DID THE GAME EVEN *GET* TO L.A.? I THOUGHT YOU SAID IT WAS DESTROYED IN THE FIRE IN 1987?

IT SHOULD HAVE BEEN DEAD AND BURIED.

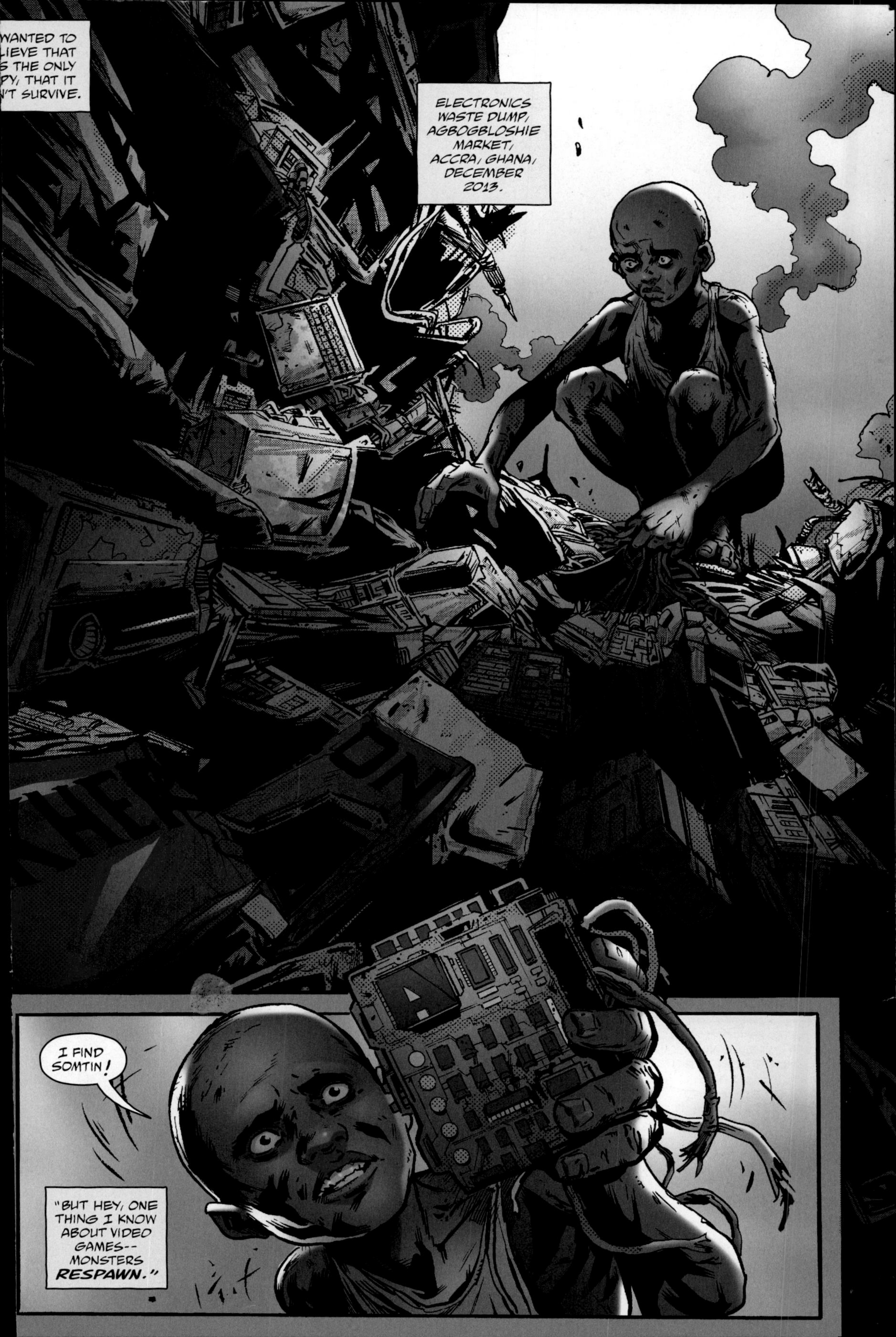
WANTED TO
LIEVE THAT
S THE ONLY
PY, THAT IT
N'T SURVIVE.
ELECTRONICS WASTE DUMP, AGBOGBLOSHIE MARKET, ACCRA, GHANA, DECEMBER 2013.
I FIND SOMTIN!
"BUT HEY, ONE THING I KNOW ABOUT VIDEO GAMES-- MONSTERS **RESPAWN.**"

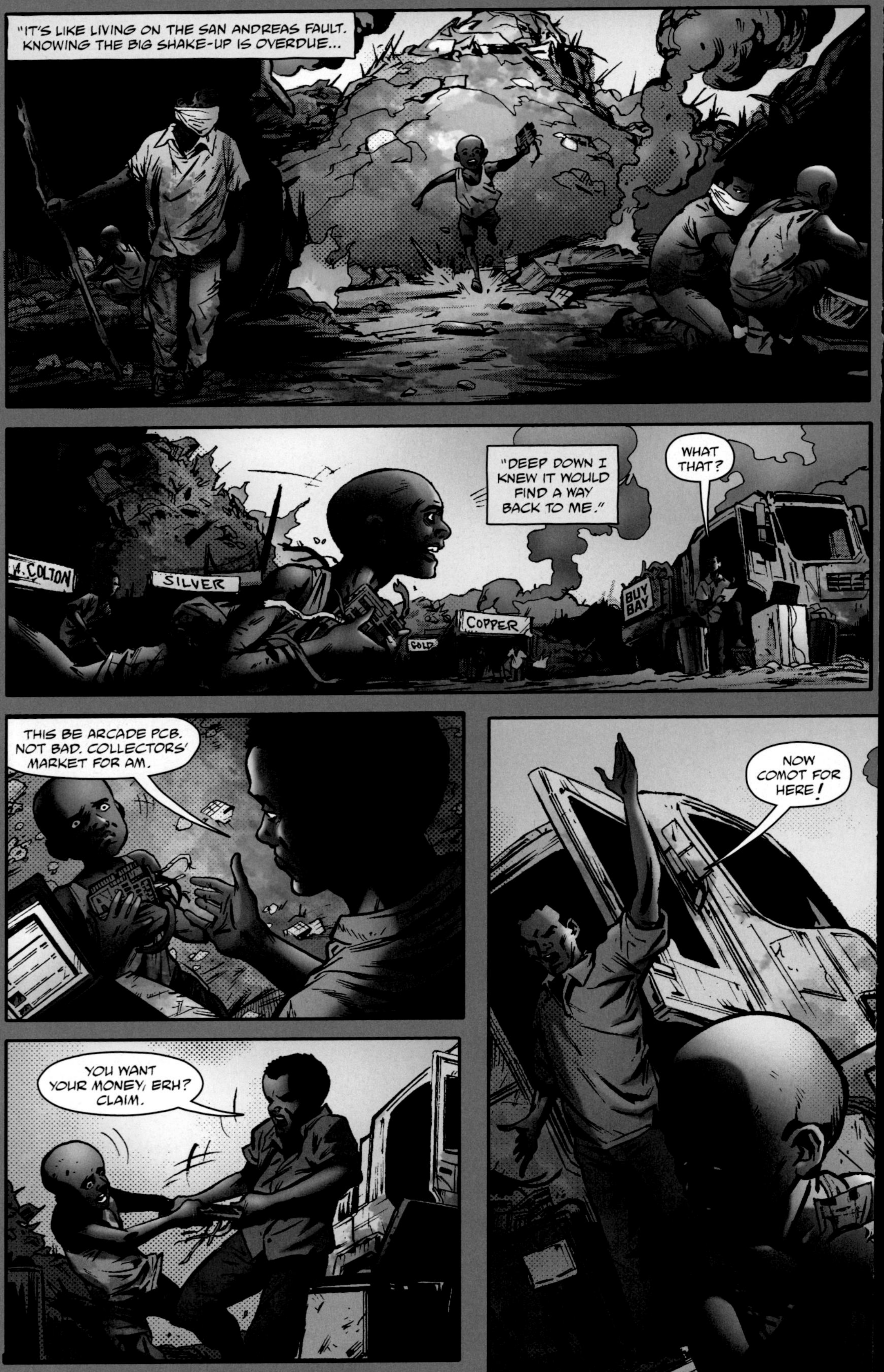
"IT'S LIKE LIVING ON THE SAN ANDREAS FAULT. KNOWING THE BIG SHAKE-UP IS OVERDUE...
"DEEP DOWN I KNEW IT WOULD FIND A WAY BACK TO ME."
WHAT THAT?
A.COLTON
SILVER
GOLD
COPPER
BUY BAY
THIS BE ARCADE PCB. NOT BAD. COLLECTORS' MARKET FOR AM.
YOU WANT YOUR MONEY, ERH? CLAIM.
NOW COMOT FOR HERE!

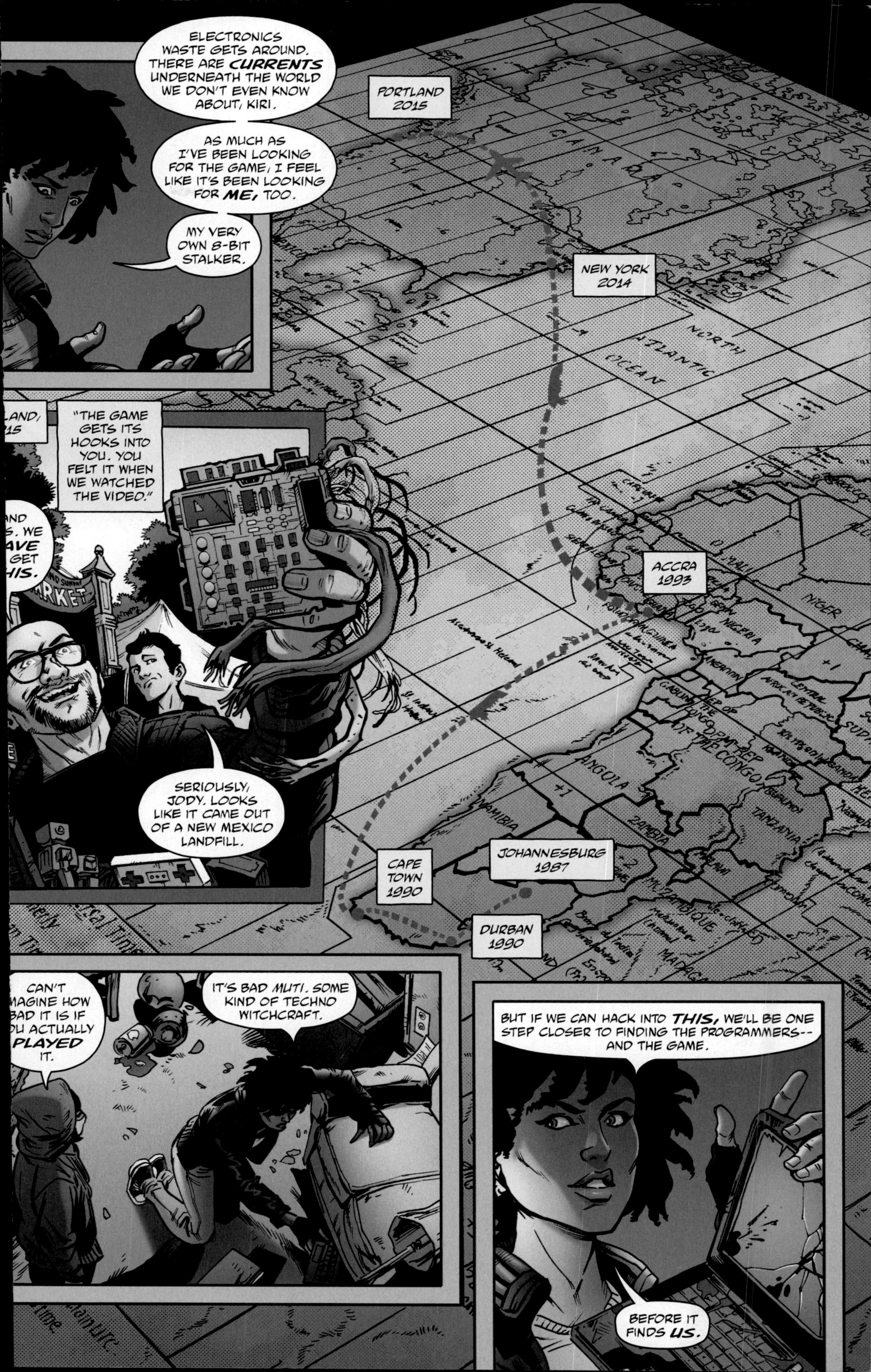
ELECTRONICS WASTE GETS AROUND. THERE ARE CURRENTS UNDERNEATH THE WORLD WE DON'T EVEN KNOW ABOUT, KIRI.
AS MUCH AS I'VE BEEN LOOKING FOR THE GAME, I FEEL LIKE IT'S BEEN LOOKING FOR ME, TOO.
MY VERY OWN 8-BIT STALKER.
PORTLAND 2015
NEW YORK 2014
NORTH ATLANTIC OCEAN
ACCRA 1993
NIGERIA
NIGER
ANGOLA
NAMIBIA
ZAMBIA
TANZANIA
JOHANNESBURG 1987
CAPE TOWN 1990
DURBAN 1990
"THE GAME GETS ITS HOOKS INTO YOU. YOU FELT IT WHEN WE WATCHED THE VIDEO."
MARKET
SERIOUSLY, JODY. LOOKS LIKE IT CAME OUT OF A NEW MEXICO LANDFILL.
CAN'T IMAGINE HOW BAD IT IS IF YOU ACTUALLY PLAYED IT.
IT'S BAD MUTI. SOME KIND OF TECHNO WITCHCRAFT.
BUT IF WE CAN HACK INTO THIS, WE'LL BE ONE STEP CLOSER TO FINDING THE PROGRAMMERS-- AND THE GAME.
BEFORE IT FINDS US.

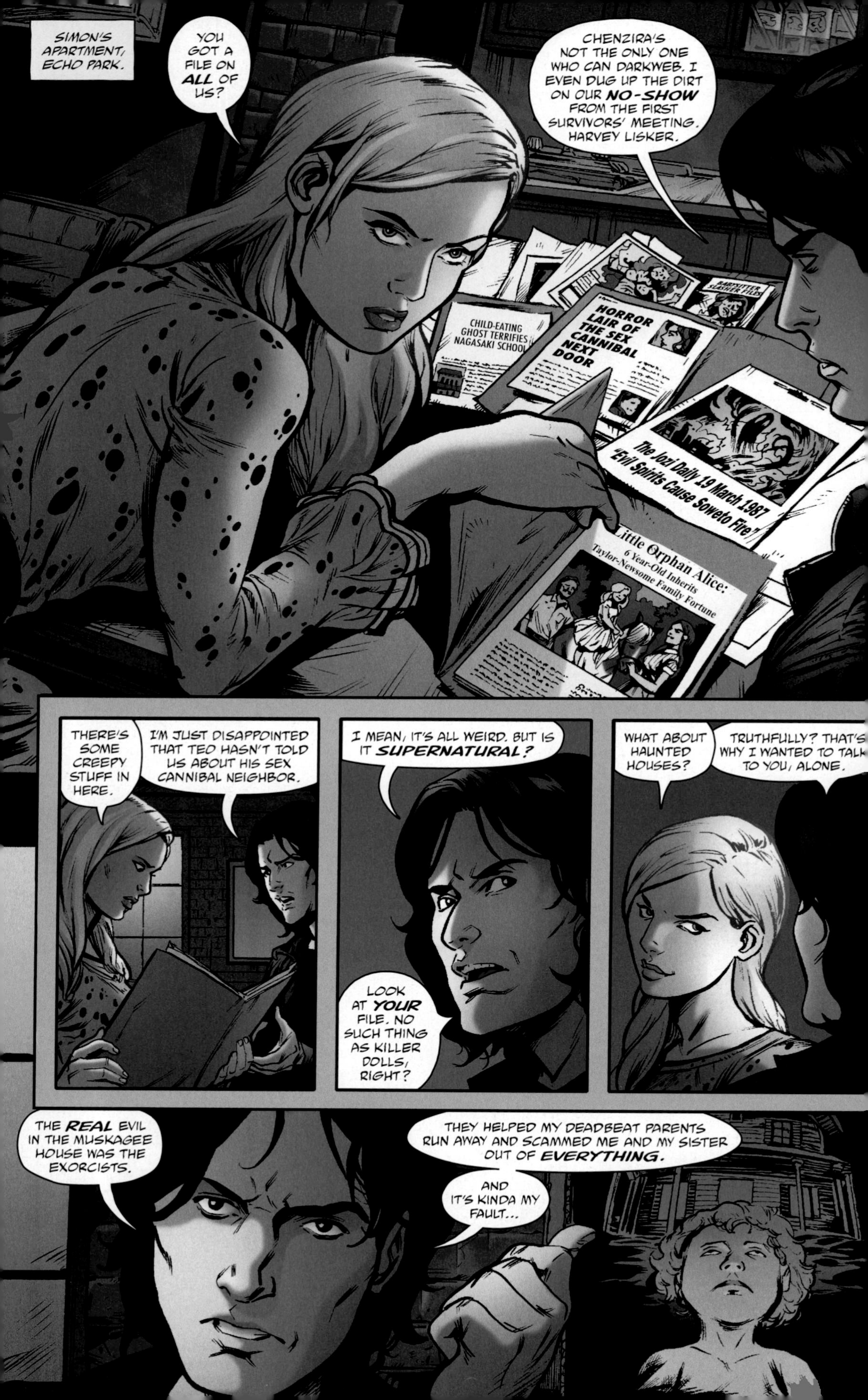
SIMON'S APARTMENT, ECHO PARK.
YOU GOT A FILE ON ALL OF US?
CHENZIRA'S NOT THE ONLY ONE WHO CAN DARKWEB. I EVEN DUG UP THE DIRT ON OUR NO-SHOW FROM THE FIRST SURVIVORS' MEETING. HARVEY LISKER.
CHILD-EATING GHOST TERRIFIES NAGASAKI SCHOOL
HORROR LAIR OF THE SEX CANNIBAL NEXT DOOR
The Jozi Daily 19 March 1987
"Evil Spirits Cause Soweto Fire"
Little Orphan Alice:
6 Year-Old Inherits Taylor-Newsome Family Fortune
THERE'S SOME CREEPY STUFF IN HERE.
I'M JUST DISAPPOINTED THAT TEO HASN'T TOLD US ABOUT HIS SEX CANNIBAL NEIGHBOR.
I MEAN, IT'S ALL WEIRD. BUT IS IT SUPERNATURAL?
LOOK AT YOUR FILE. NO SUCH THING AS KILLER DOLLS, RIGHT?
WHAT ABOUT HAUNTED HOUSES?
TRUTHFULLY? THAT'S WHY I WANTED TO TALK TO YOU, ALONE.
THE REAL EVIL IN THE MUSKAGEE HOUSE WAS THE EXORCISTS.
THEY HELPED MY DEADBEAT PARENTS RUN AWAY AND SCAMMED ME AND MY SISTER OUT OF EVERYTHING.
AND IT'S KINDA MY FAULT...

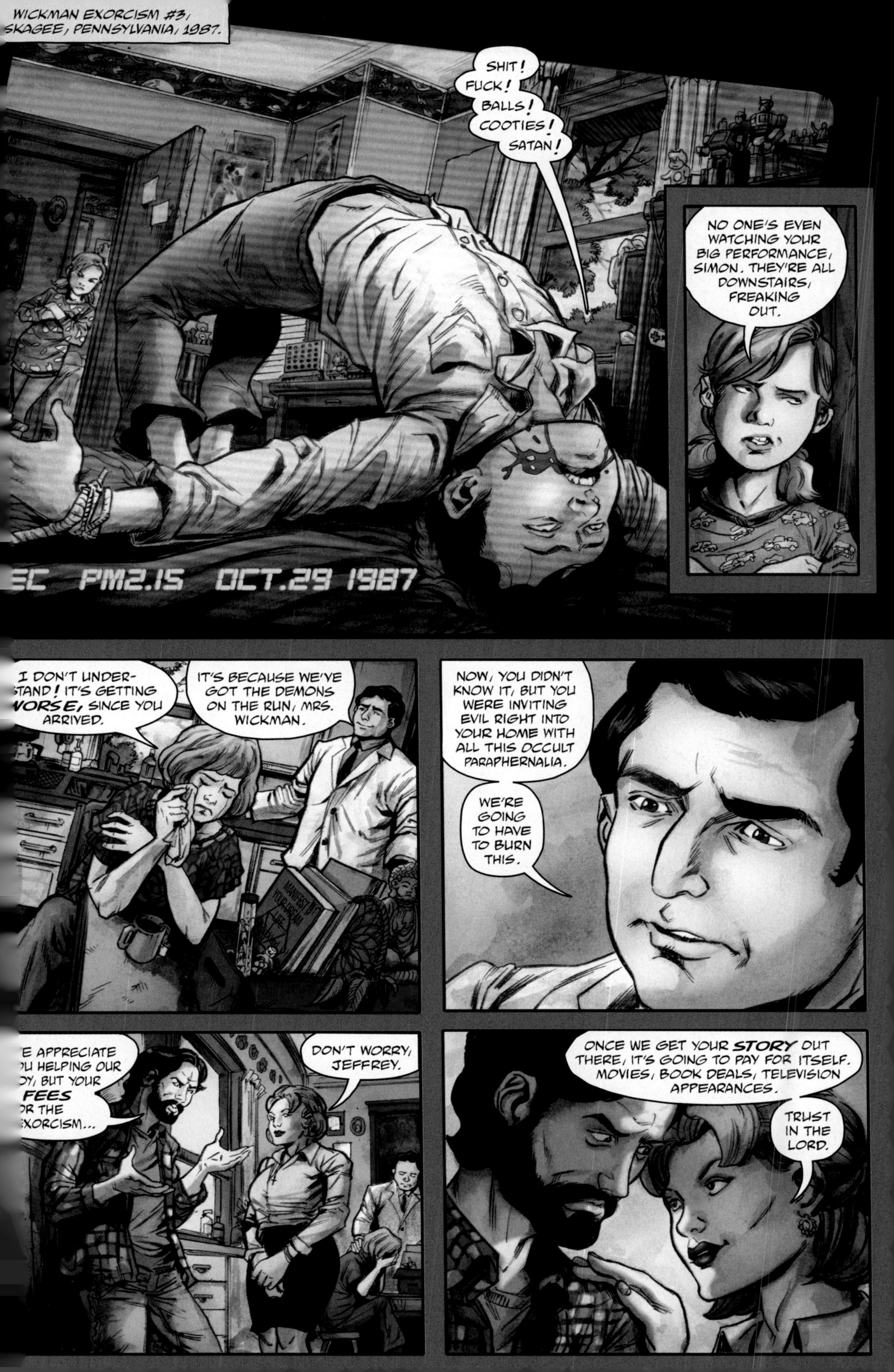

WICKMAN EXORCISM #3, SKAGEE, PENNSYLVANIA, 1987.
SHIT! FUCK! BALLS! COOTIES! SATAN!
EC PM2.15 OCT.29 1987
NO ONE'S EVEN WATCHING YOUR BIG PERFORMANCE, SIMON. THEY'RE ALL DOWNSTAIRS, FREAKING OUT.
I DON'T UNDERSTAND! IT'S GETTING WORSE, SINCE YOU ARRIVED.
IT'S BECAUSE WE'VE GOT THE DEMONS ON THE RUN, MRS. WICKMAN.
MANIFEST YOUR DREAM LIFE
NOW, YOU DIDN'T KNOW IT, BUT YOU WERE INVITING EVIL RIGHT INTO YOUR HOME WITH ALL THIS OCCULT PARAPHERNALIA.
WE'RE GOING TO HAVE TO BURN THIS.
E APPRECIATE OU HELPING OUR OY, BUT YOUR FEES OR THE EXORCISM...
DON'T WORRY, JEFFREY.
ONCE WE GET YOUR STORY OUT THERE, IT'S GOING TO PAY FOR ITSELF. MOVIES, BOOK DEALS, TELEVISION APPEARANCES.
TRUST IN THE LORD.

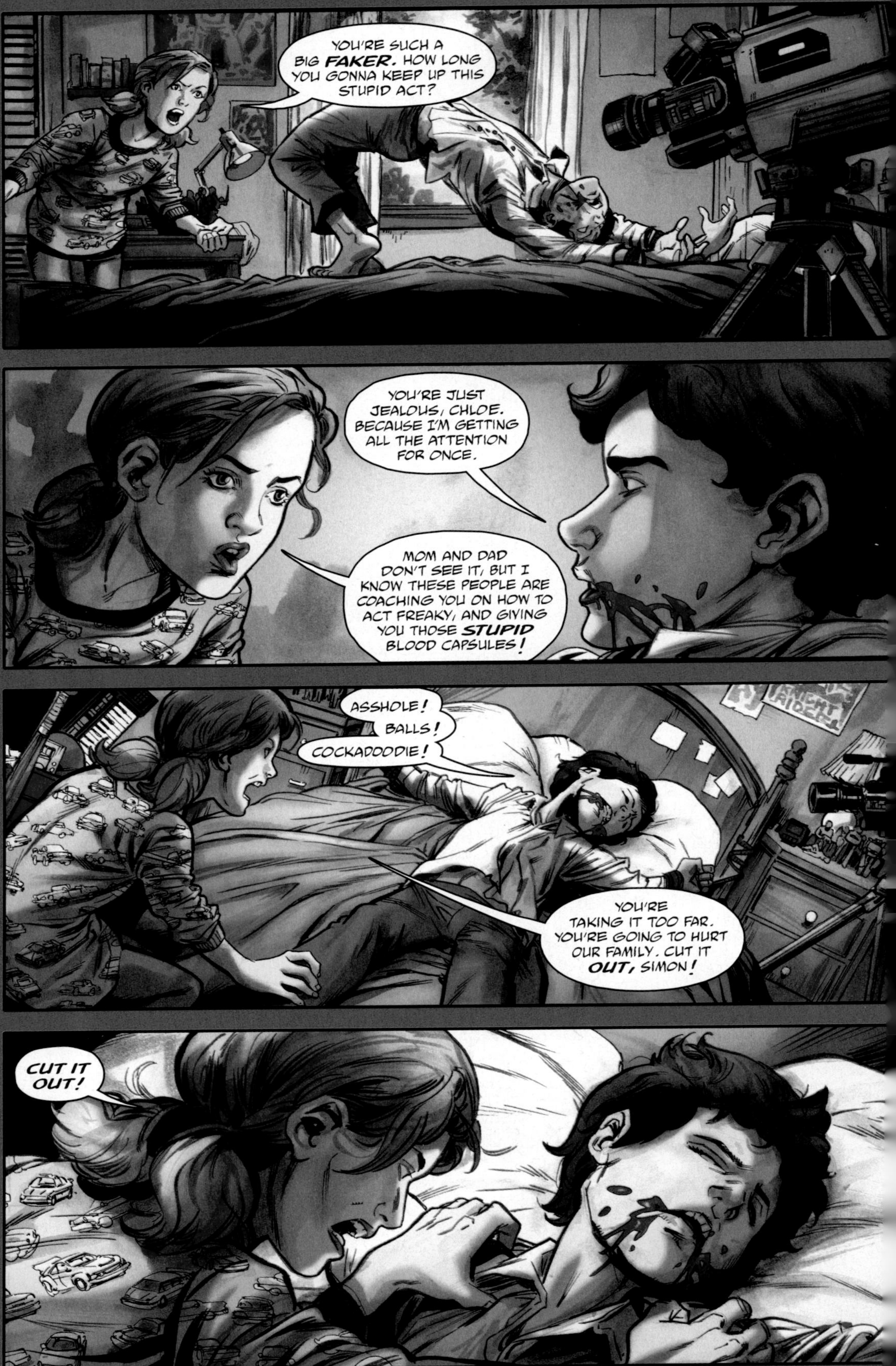
YOU'RE SUCH A BIG FAKER. HOW LONG YOU GONNA KEEP UP THIS STUPID ACT?
YOU'RE JUST JEALOUS, CHLOE. BECAUSE I'M GETTING ALL THE ATTENTION FOR ONCE.
MOM AND DAD DON'T SEE IT, BUT I KNOW THESE PEOPLE ARE COACHING YOU ON HOW TO ACT FREAKY, AND GIVING YOU THOSE STUPID BLOOD CAPSULES!
ASSHOLE!
BALLS!
COCKADOODIE!
YOU'RE TAKING IT TOO FAR. YOU'RE GOING TO HURT OUR FAMILY. CUT IT OUT, SIMON!
CUT IT OUT!

EVERY-THING IN THE **MUSKAGEE MOVIES**--

--THE WALLPAPER COMING ALIVE, THE DEAD PRIEST, THE FLOORBOARDS OPENING UP AND SWALLOWING MY PARENTS?

SATANIC PANIC FAKE-MEMORY **BULLSHIT.**

JUST LIKE WE PRACTICED, CHAMP.

I'VE HAD TO KEEP UP THIS DAMN ACT SINCE I WAS SEVEN YEARS OLD. AND I AM **DONE.**

YEAH?

CAN I HELP YOU?

UH. HI. YES. UM. GOTTA PACKAGE. FAN MAIL DELIVERY FOR MR. SIMON WICKMAN.

SURE. COME ON UP.

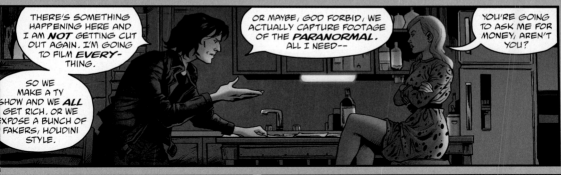

THERE'S SOMETHING HAPPENING HERE AND I AM **NOT** GETTING CUT OUT AGAIN. I'M GOING TO FILM **EVERY-**THING.

SO WE MAKE A TV SHOW AND WE **ALL** GET RICH. OR WE EXPOSE A BUNCH OF FAKERS, HOUDINI STYLE.

OR MAYBE, GOD FORBID, WE ACTUALLY CAPTURE FOOTAGE OF THE **PARANORMAL.** ALL I NEED--

YOU'RE GOING TO ASK ME FOR MONEY, AREN'T YOU?

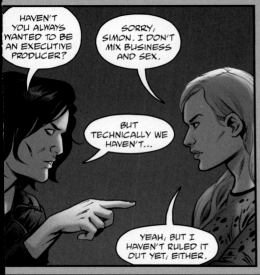

HAVEN'T YOU ALWAYS WANTED TO BE AN EXECUTIVE PRODUCER?

SORRY, SIMON. I DON'T MIX BUSINESS AND SEX.

BUT TECHNICALLY WE HAVEN'T...

YEAH, BUT I HAVEN'T RULED IT OUT YET, EITHER.

ARE YOU OKAY?

UGH. SORRY, ALICE. I SUDDENLY FEEL REALLY STRANGE...

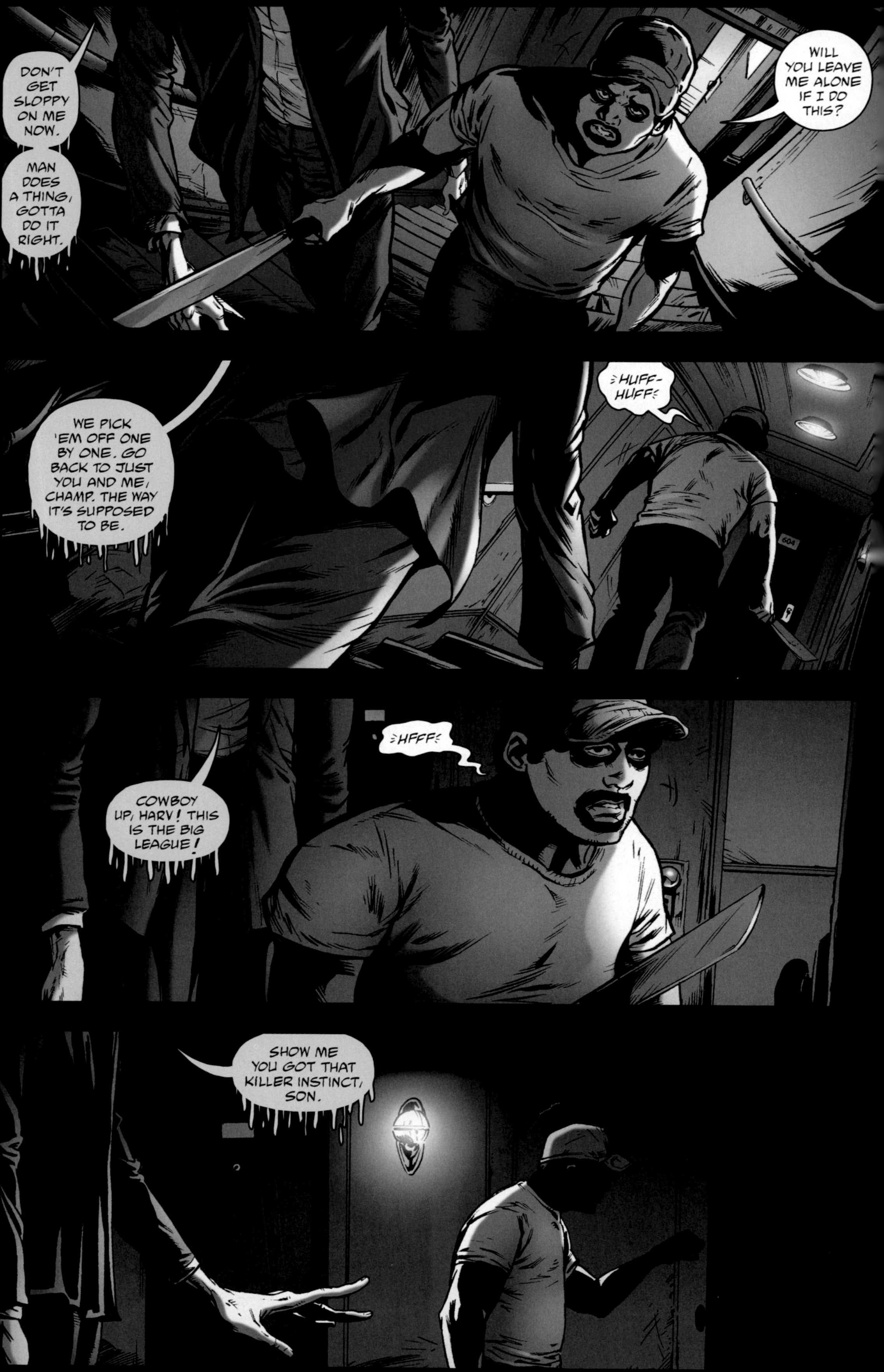
DON'T GET SLOPPY ON ME NOW.
MAN DOES A THING, GOTTA DO IT RIGHT.
WILL YOU LEAVE ME ALONE IF I DO THIS?
WE PICK 'EM OFF ONE BY ONE. GO BACK TO JUST YOU AND ME, CHAMP. THE WAY IT'S SUPPOSED TO BE.
HUFF-HUFF
604
COWBOY UP, HARV! THIS IS THE BIG LEAGUE!
HFFF
SHOW ME YOU GOT THAT KILLER INSTINCT, SON.

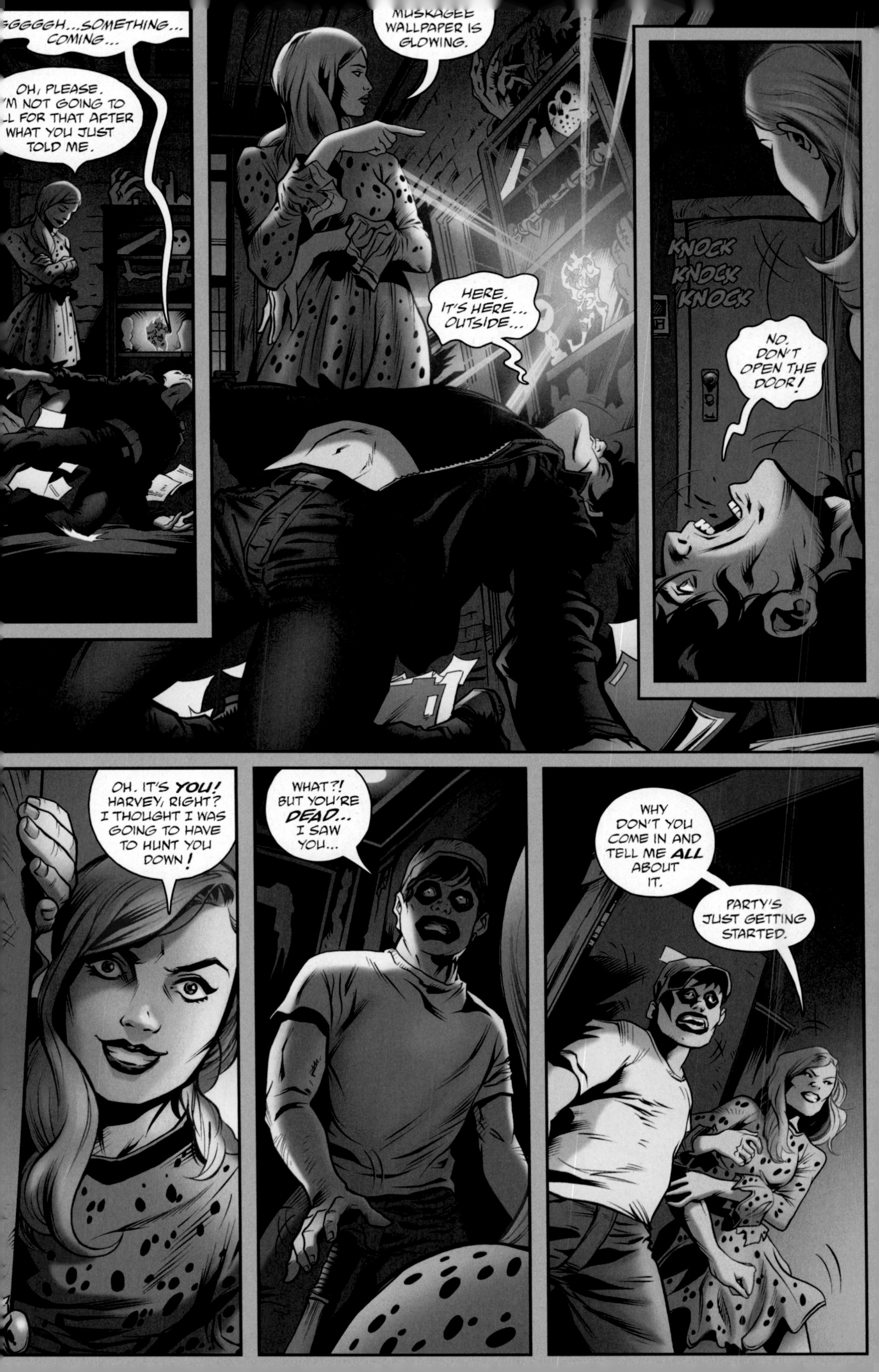
GGGGGH...SOMETHING... COMING...
OH, PLEASE. I'M NOT GOING TO FALL FOR THAT AFTER WHAT YOU JUST TOLD ME.
MUSKAGEE WALLPAPER IS GLOWING.
HERE. IT'S HERE... OUTSIDE...
KNOCK KNOCK KNOCK
NO. DON'T OPEN THE DOOR!
OH. IT'S YOU! HARVEY, RIGHT? I THOUGHT I WAS GOING TO HAVE TO HUNT YOU DOWN!
WHAT?! BUT YOU'RE DEAD... I SAW YOU...
WHY DON'T YOU COME IN AND TELL ME ALL ABOUT IT.
PARTY'S JUST GETTING STARTED.

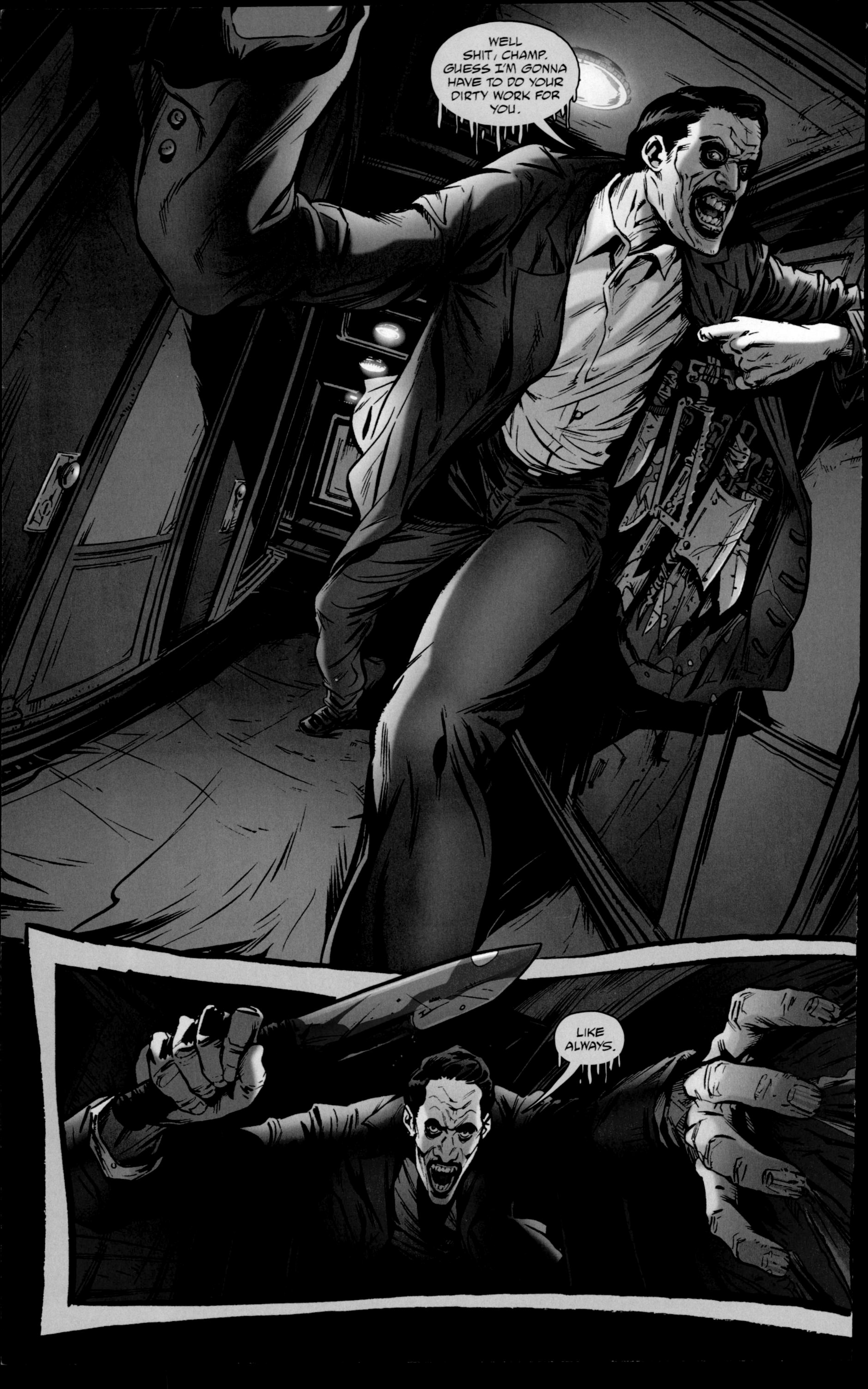
WELL SHIT, CHAMP. GUESS I'M GONNA HAVE TO DO YOUR DIRTY WORK FOR YOU.
LIKE ALWAYS.

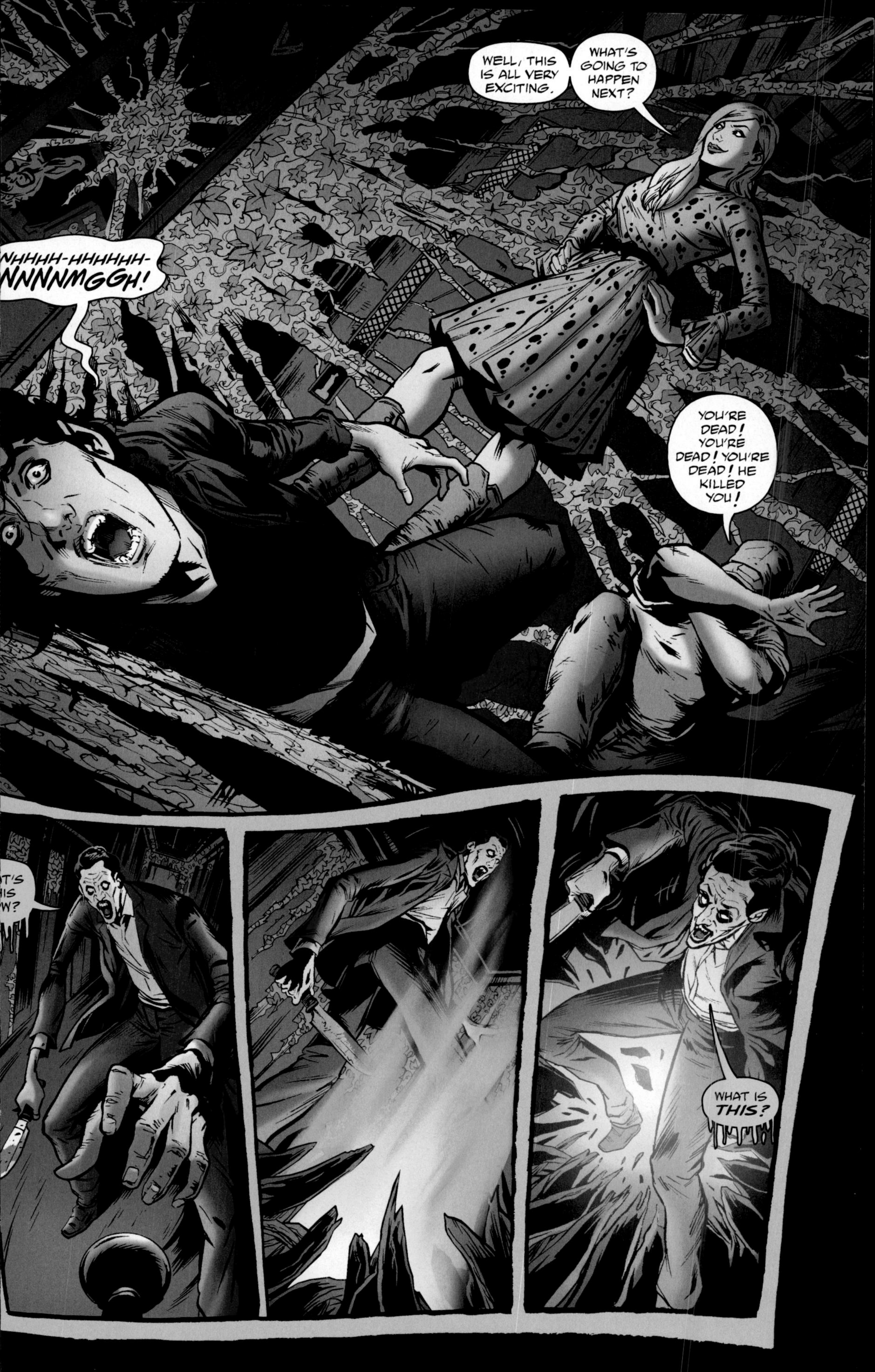
WELL, THIS IS ALL VERY EXCITING.
WHAT'S GOING TO HAPPEN NEXT?
NHHHH-HHHHHH-NNNNMGGH!
YOU'RE DEAD! YOU'RE DEAD! YOU'RE DEAD! HE KILLED YOU!
WHAT IS THIS?

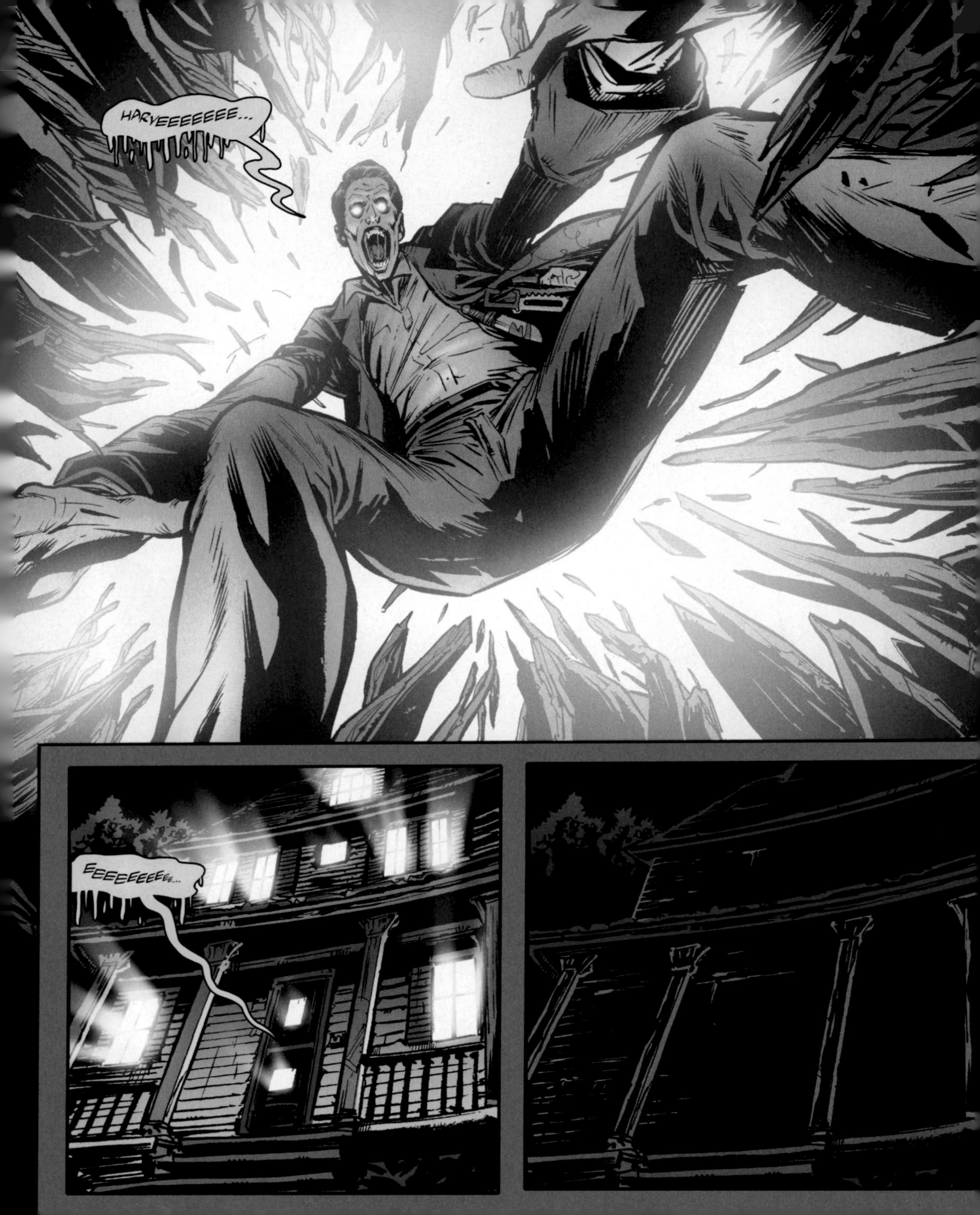
HARVEEEEEEE...
EEEEEEEEEe...

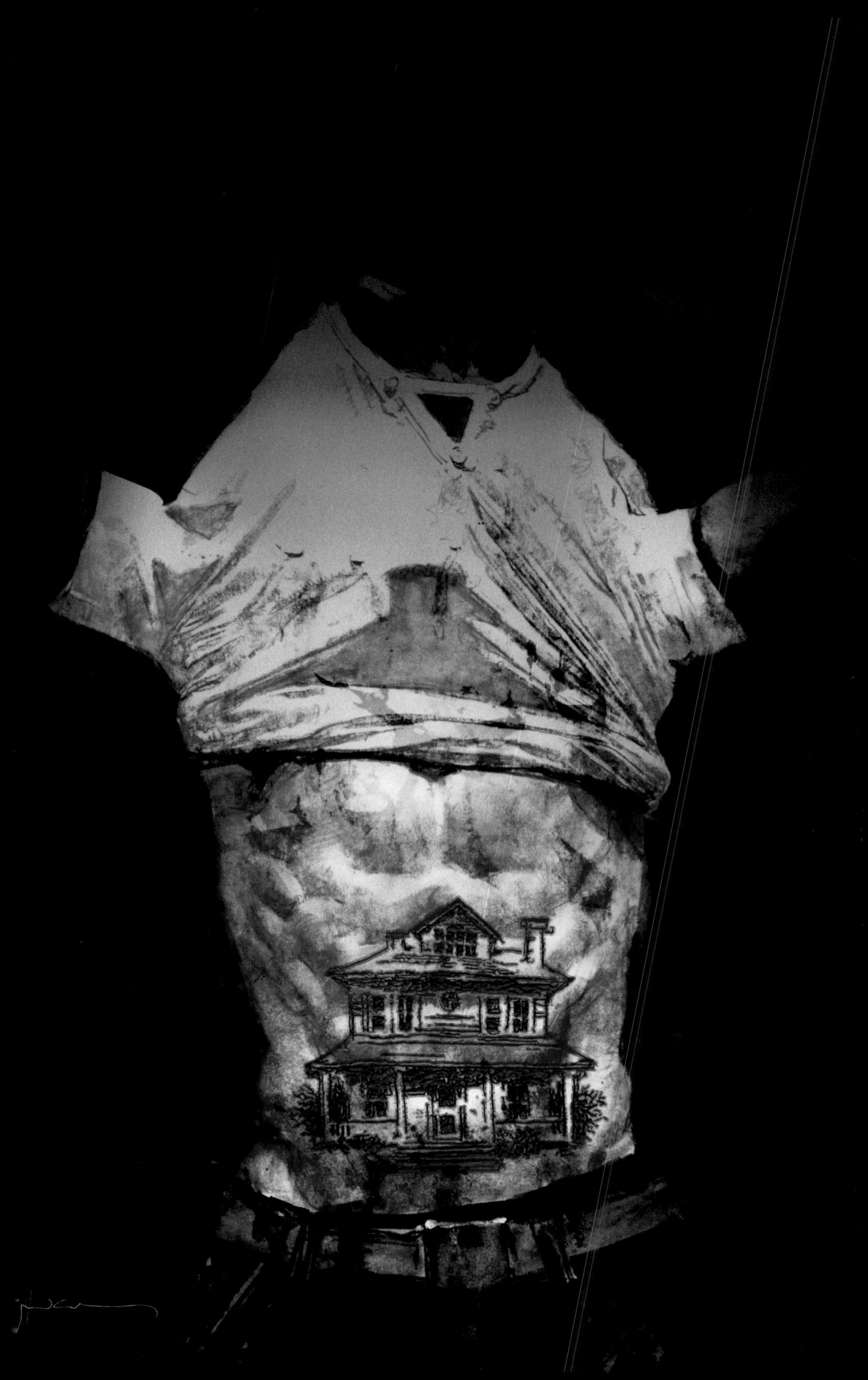

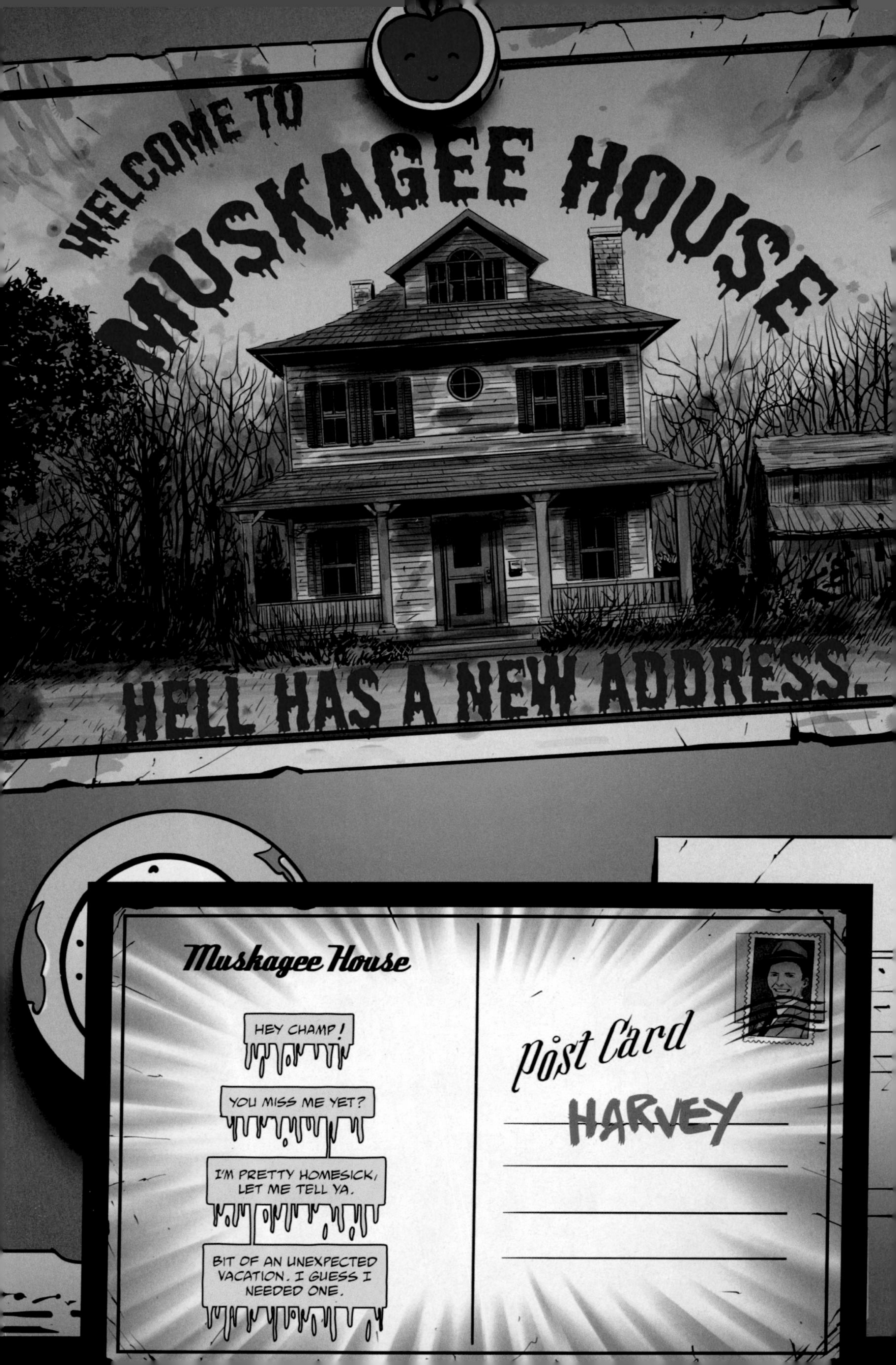
WELCOME TO
MUSKAGEE HOUSE
HELL HAS A NEW ADDRESS.
Muskagee House
HEY CHAMP!
YOU MISS ME YET?
I'M PRETTY HOMESICK, LET ME TELL YA.
BIT OF AN UNEXPECTED VACATION. I GUESS I NEEDED ONE.
Post Card
HARVEY

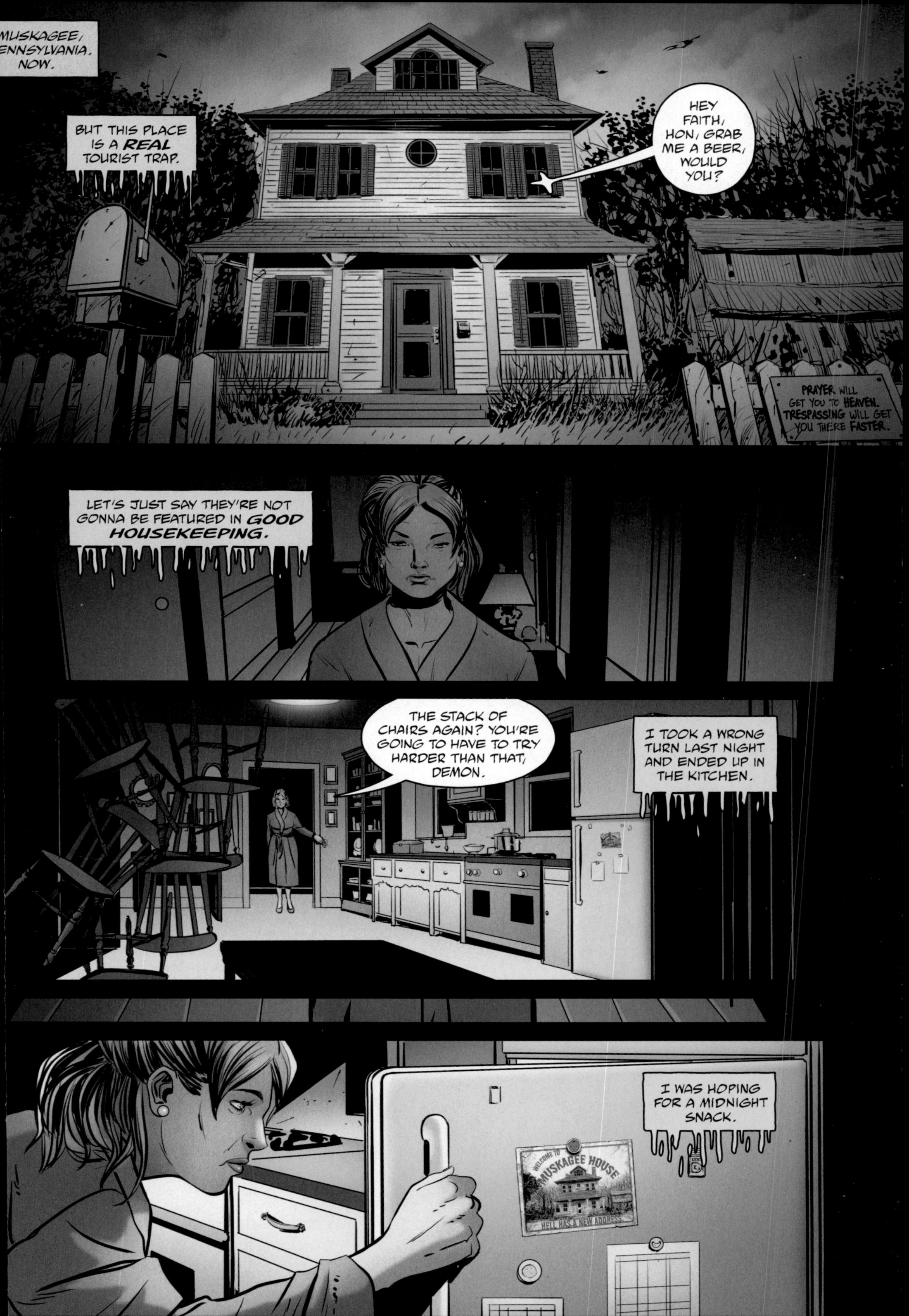
MUSKAGEE,
ENNSYLVANIA.
NOW.
BUT THIS PLACE IS A REAL TOURIST TRAP.
HEY FAITH, HON, GRAB ME A BEER, WOULD YOU?
PRAYER WILL GET YOU TO HEAVEN. TRESPASSING WILL GET YOU THERE FASTER.
LET'S JUST SAY THEY'RE NOT GONNA BE FEATURED IN GOOD HOUSEKEEPING.
THE STACK OF CHAIRS AGAIN? YOU'RE GOING TO HAVE TO TRY HARDER THAN THAT, DEMON.
I TOOK A WRONG TURN LAST NIGHT AND ENDED UP IN THE KITCHEN.
I WAS HOPING FOR A MIDNIGHT SNACK.
WELCOME TO MUSKAGEE HOUSE
HELL HAS A NEW ADDRESS

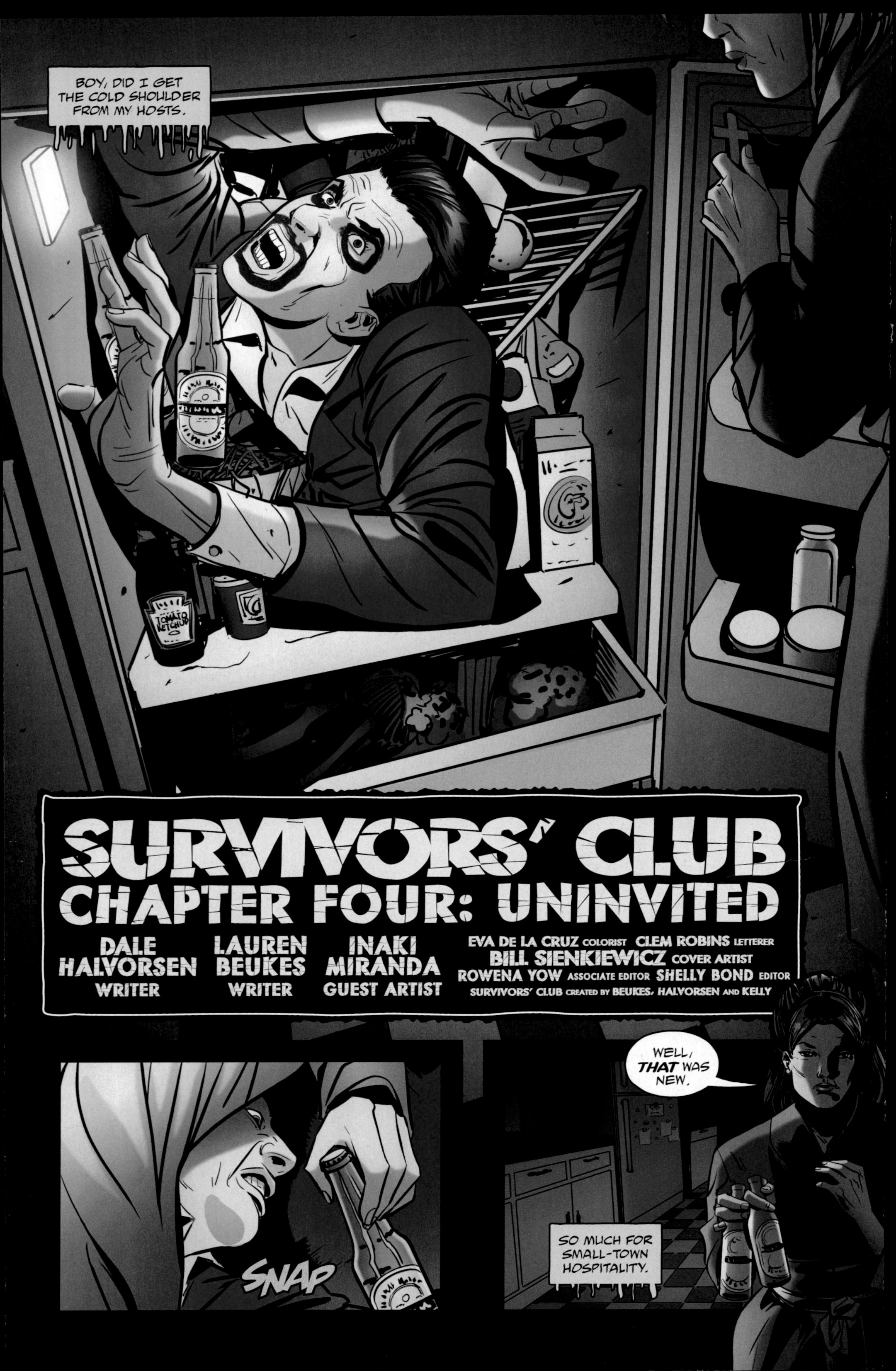
BOY, DID I GET THE COLD SHOULDER FROM MY HOSTS.
TOMATO KETCHUP
SURVIVORS' CLUB
CHAPTER FOUR: UNINVITED
DALE HALVORSEN WRITER
LAUREN BEUKES WRITER
INAKI MIRANDA GUEST ARTIST
EVA DE LA CRUZ COLORIST CLEM ROBINS LETTERER
BILL SIENKIEWICZ COVER ARTIST
ROWENA YOW ASSOCIATE EDITOR SHELLY BOND EDITOR
SURVIVORS' CLUB CREATED BY BEUKES, HALVORSEN AND KELLY
SNAP
WELL, THAT WAS NEW.
SO MUCH FOR SMALL-TOWN HOSPITALITY.

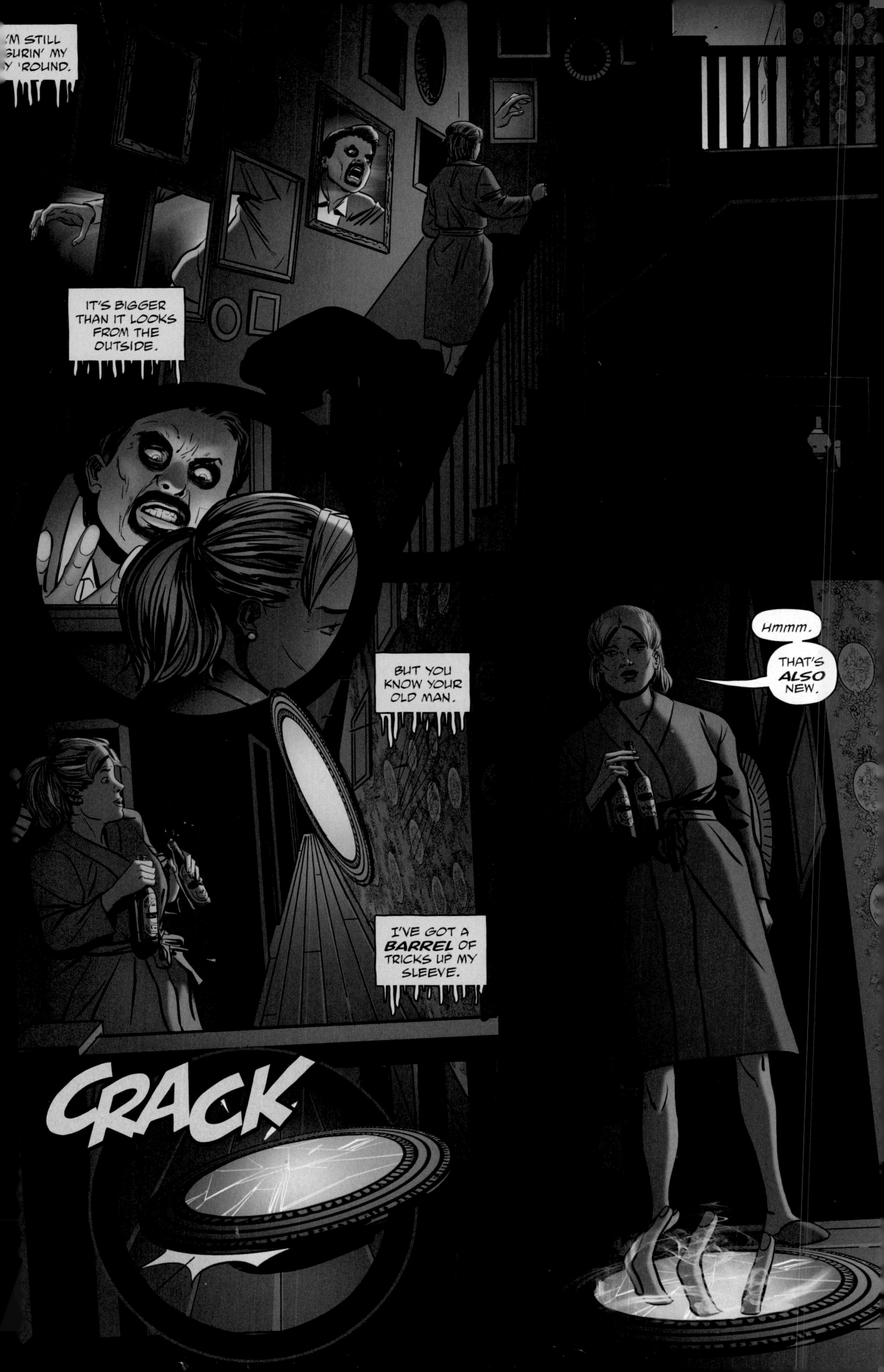

'M STILL
GURIN' MY
Y 'ROUND.
IT'S BIGGER THAN IT LOOKS FROM THE OUTSIDE.
BUT YOU KNOW YOUR OLD MAN.
I'VE GOT A BARREL OF TRICKS UP MY SLEEVE.
Hmmm.
THAT'S ALSO NEW.
CRACK

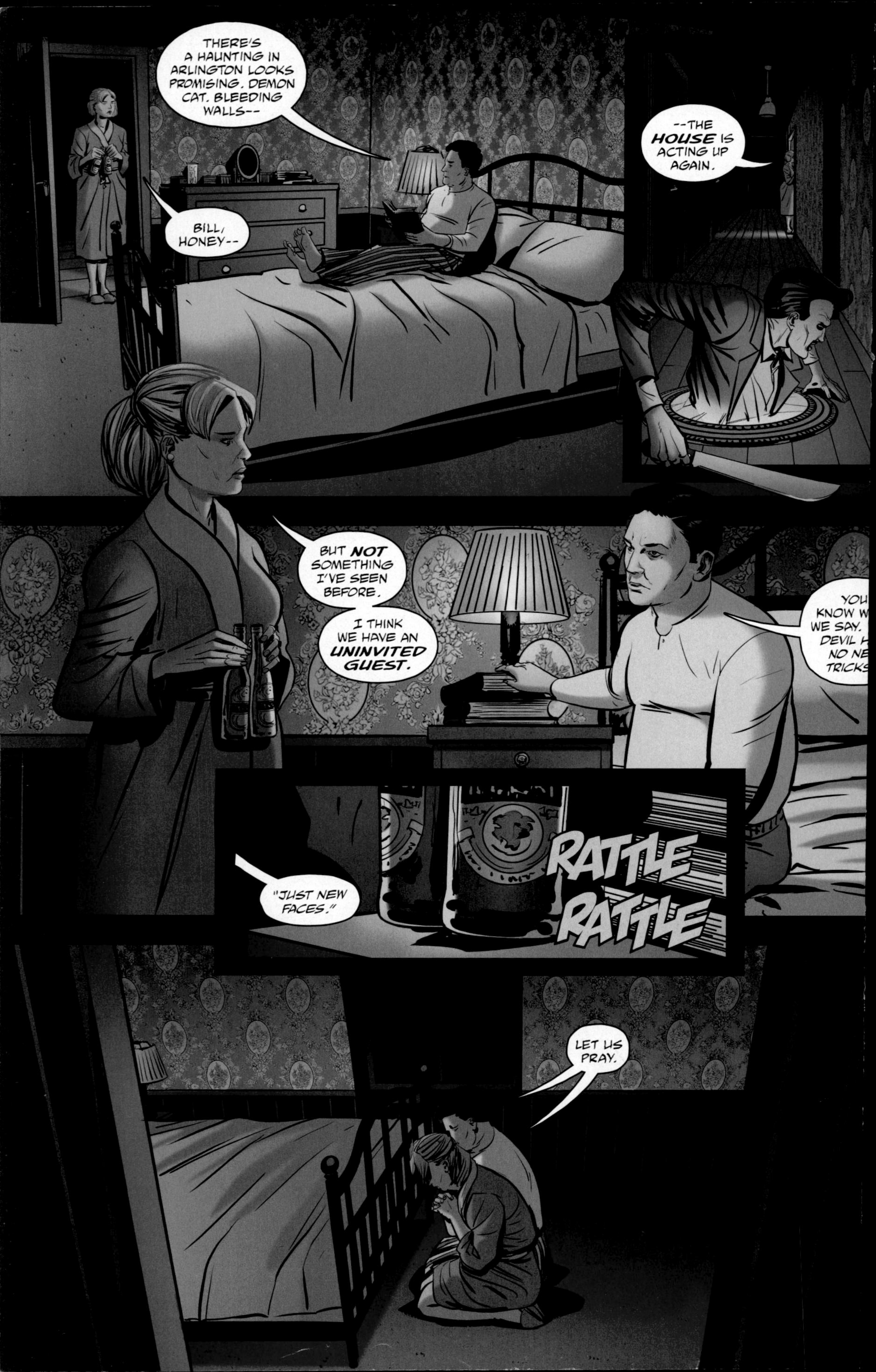
BILL, HONEY--
THERE'S A HAUNTING IN ARLINGTON LOOKS PROMISING. DEMON CAT. BLEEDING WALLS--
--THE HOUSE IS ACTING UP AGAIN.
BUT NOT SOMETHING I'VE SEEN BEFORE.
I THINK WE HAVE AN UNINVITED GUEST.
YOU KNOW W WE SAY. DEVIL H NO NE TRICKS
"JUST NEW FACES."
RATTLE RATTLE
LET US PRAY.

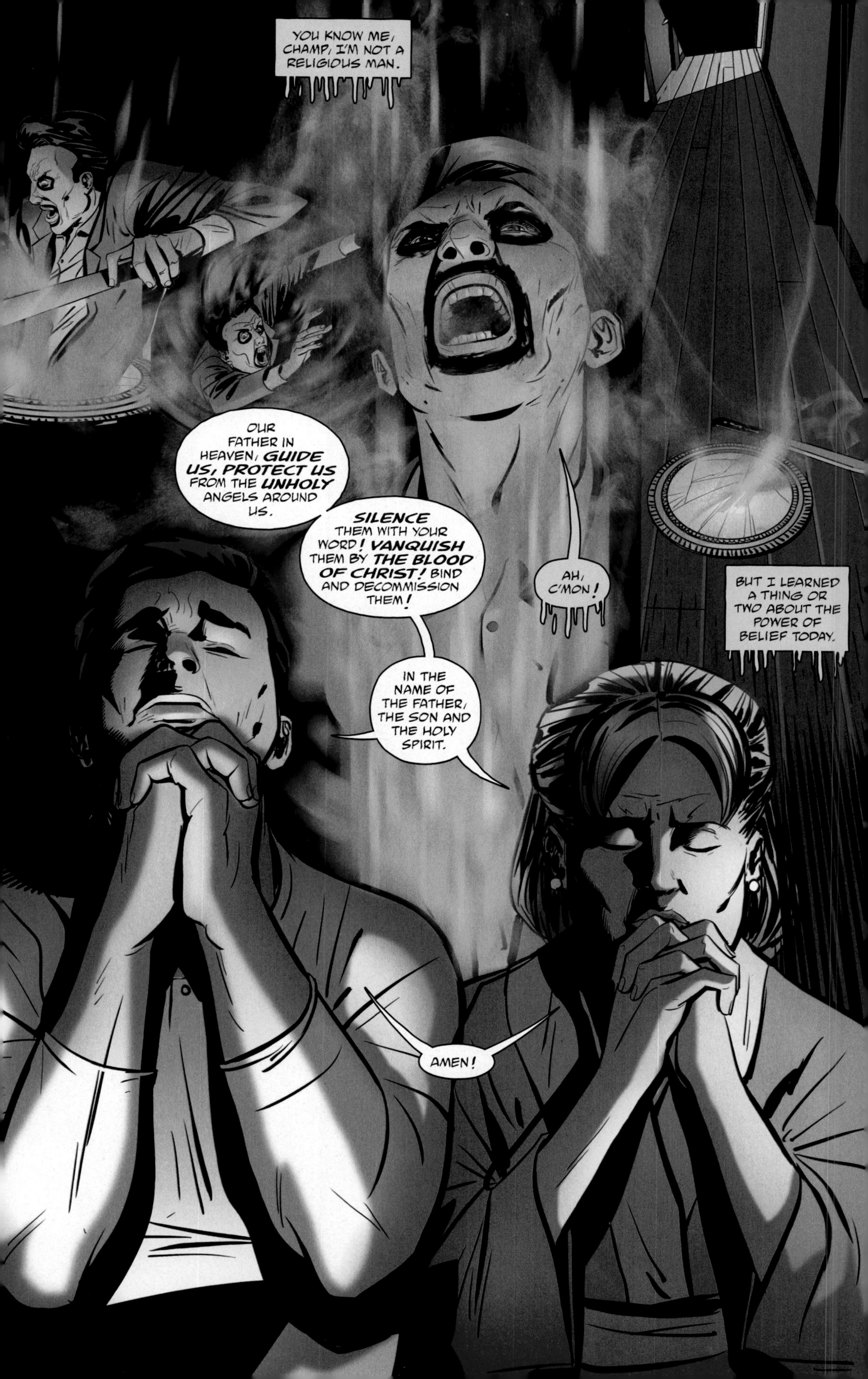
YOU KNOW ME, CHAMP, I'M NOT A RELIGIOUS MAN.
OUR FATHER IN HEAVEN, GUIDE US, PROTECT US FROM THE UNHOLY ANGELS AROUND US.
SILENCE THEM WITH YOUR WORD! VANQUISH THEM BY THE BLOOD OF CHRIST! BIND AND DECOMMISSION THEM!
AH, C'MON!
BUT I LEARNED A THING OR TWO ABOUT THE POWER OF BELIEF TODAY.
IN THE NAME OF THE FATHER, THE SON AND THE HOLY SPIRIT.
AMEN!

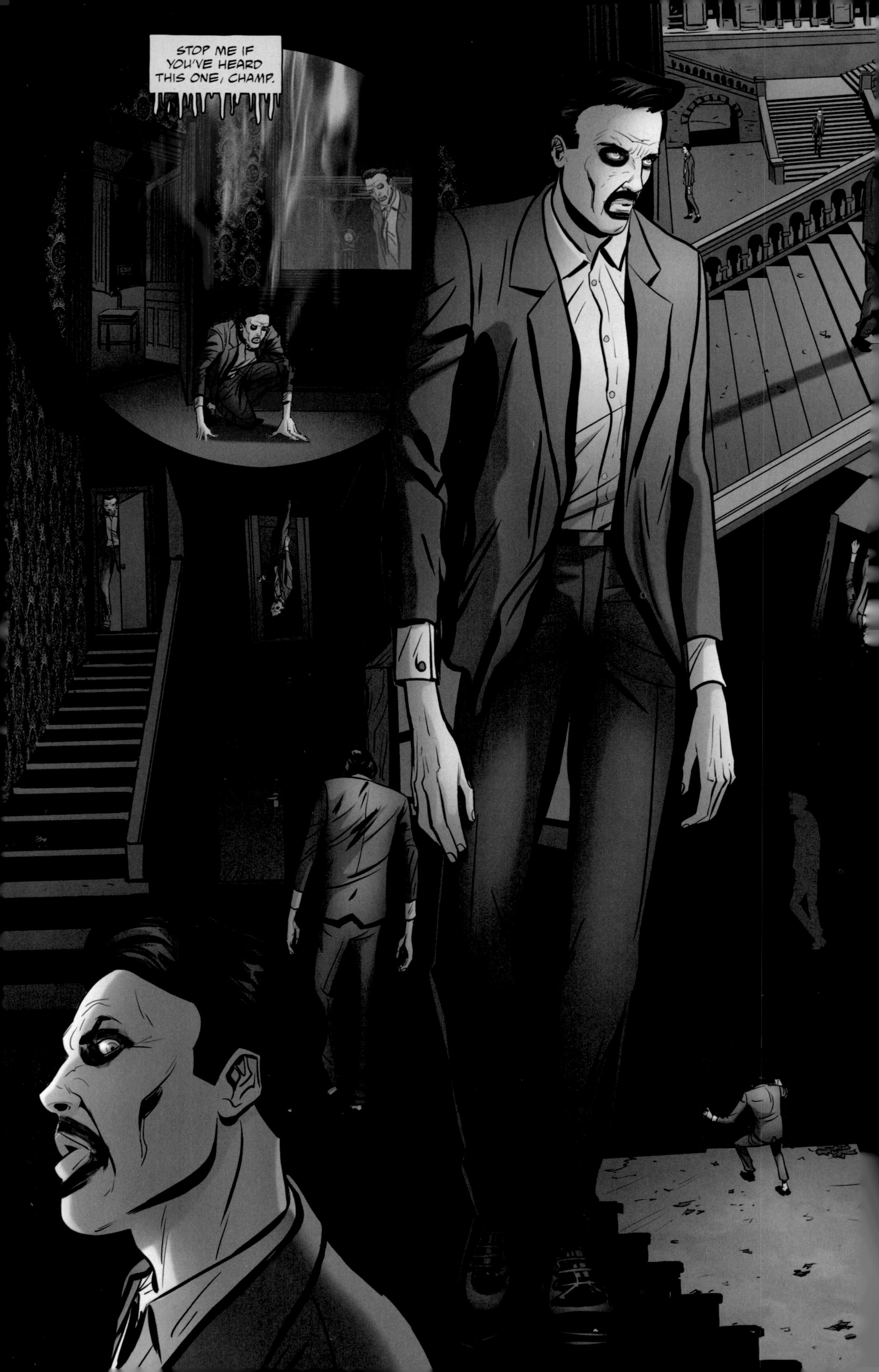
STOP ME IF YOU'VE HEARD THIS ONE, CHAMP.

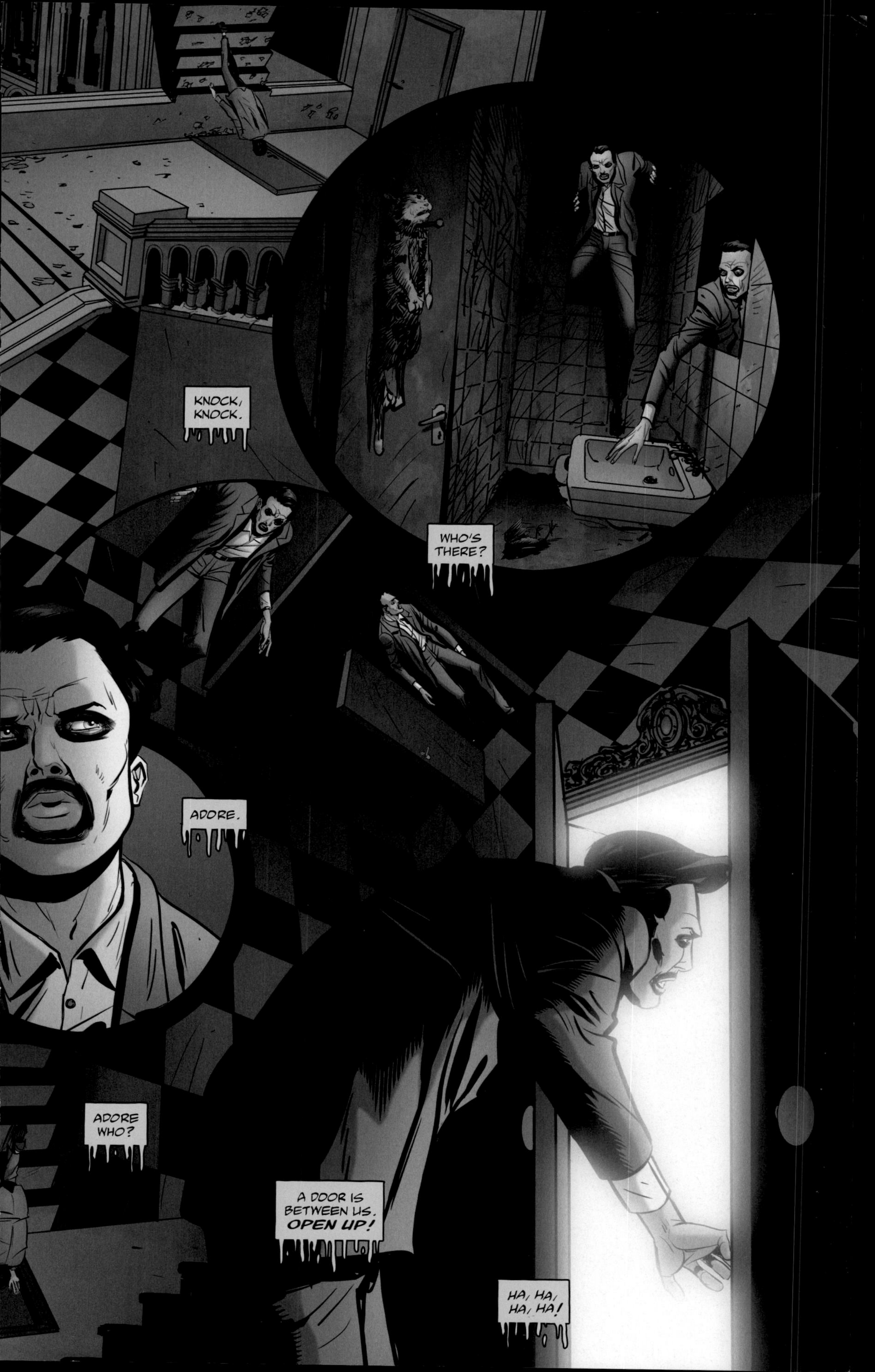
KNOCK, KNOCK.
WHO'S THERE?
ADORE.
ADORE WHO?
A DOOR IS BETWEEN US. OPEN UP!
HA, HA, HA, HA!

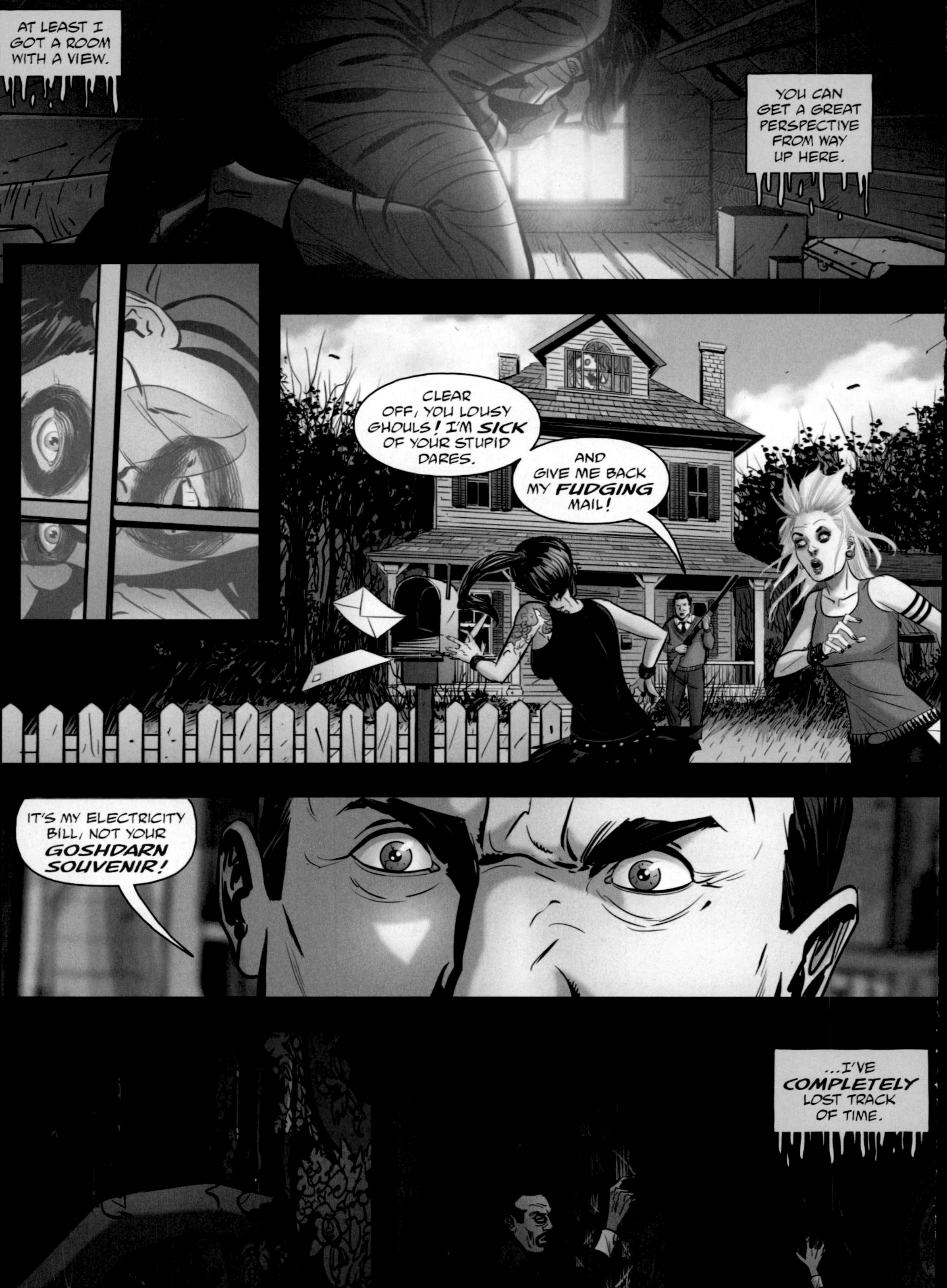
AT LEAST I GOT A ROOM WITH A VIEW.
YOU CAN GET A GREAT PERSPECTIVE FROM WAY UP HERE.
CLEAR OFF, YOU LOUSY GHOULS! I'M SICK OF YOUR STUPID DARES.
AND GIVE ME BACK MY FUDGING MAIL!
IT'S MY ELECTRICITY BILL, NOT YOUR GOSHDARN SOUVENIR!
...I'VE COMPLETELY LOST TRACK OF TIME.

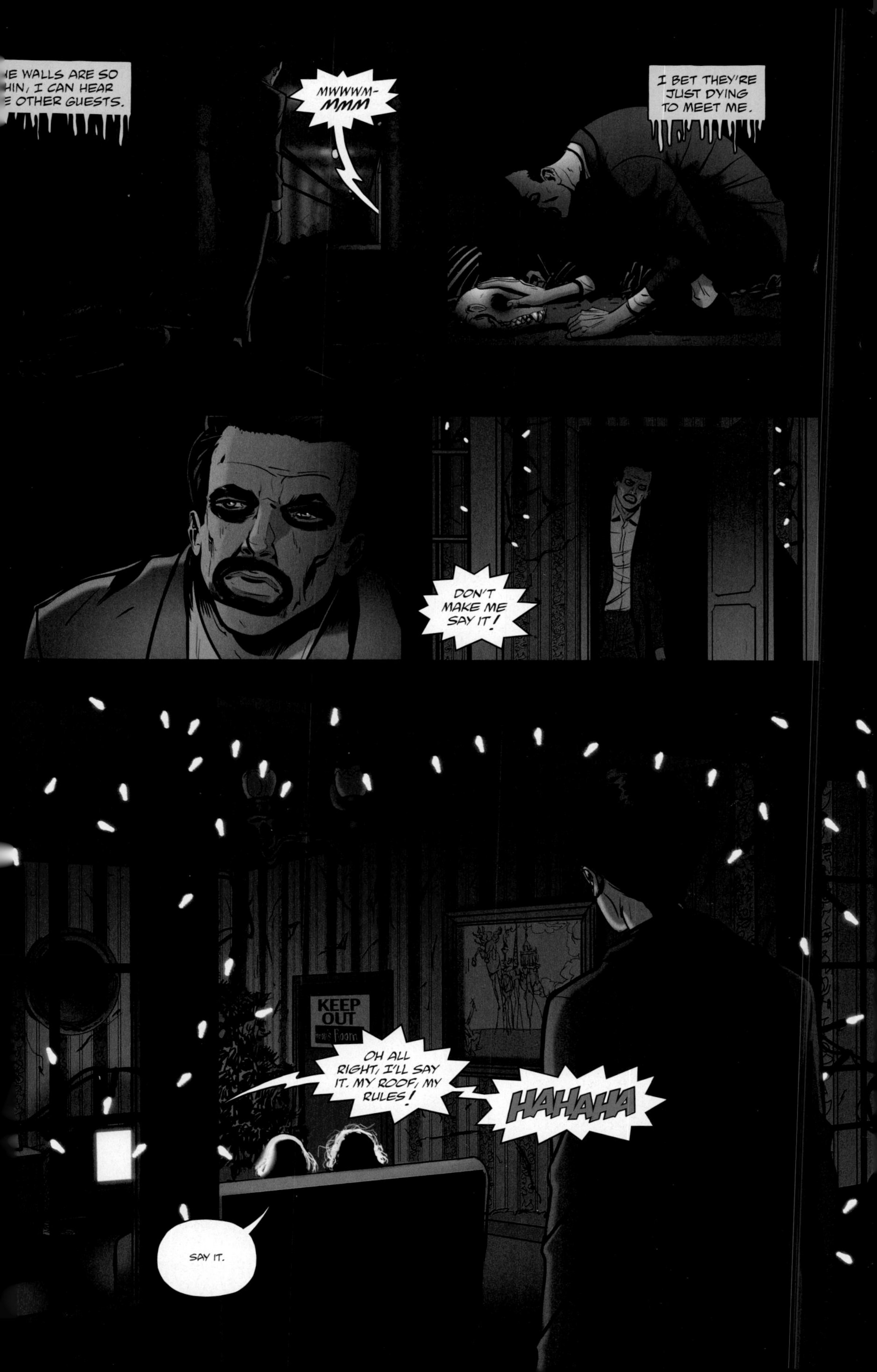

HE WALLS ARE SO
HIN, I CAN HEAR
E OTHER GUESTS.
MWWWM-MMM
I BET THEY'RE JUST DYING TO MEET ME.
DON'T MAKE ME SAY IT!
KEEP OUT
SAY IT.
OH ALL RIGHT, I'LL SAY IT. MY ROOF, MY RULES!
HAHAHA

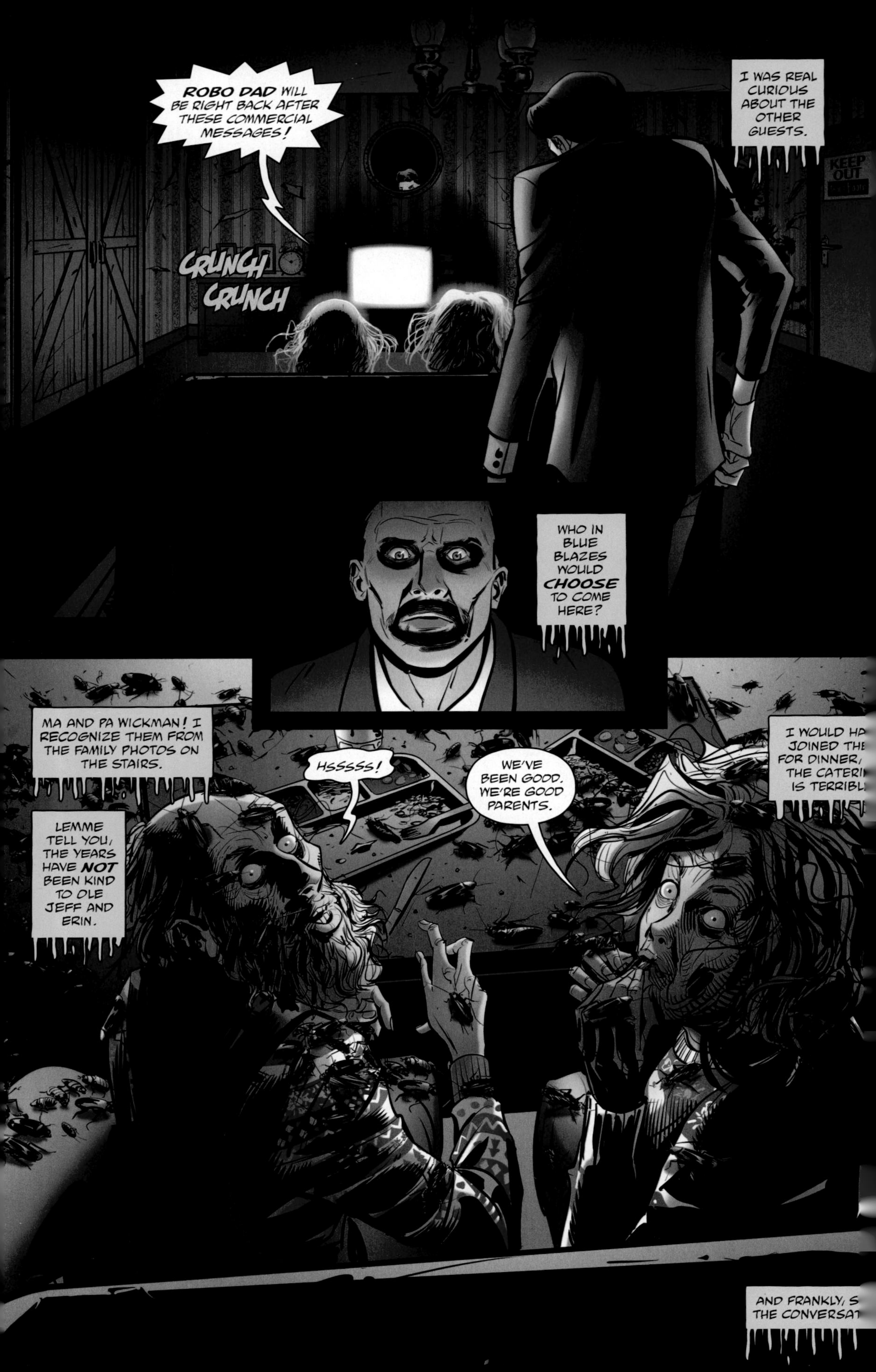
ROBO DAD WILL BE RIGHT BACK AFTER THESE COMMERCIAL MESSAGES!
I WAS REAL CURIOUS ABOUT THE OTHER GUESTS.
KEEP OUT
CRUNCH
CRUNCH
WHO IN BLUE BLAZES WOULD CHOOSE TO COME HERE?
MA AND PA WICKMAN! I RECOGNIZE THEM FROM THE FAMILY PHOTOS ON THE STAIRS.
HSSSSS!
WE'VE BEEN GOOD. WE'RE GOOD PARENTS.
I WOULD HA
JOINED THE
FOR DINNER,
THE CATERI
IS TERRIBL
LEMME TELL YOU, THE YEARS HAVE NOT BEEN KIND TO OLE JEFF AND ERIN.
AND FRANKLY, S
THE CONVERSAT

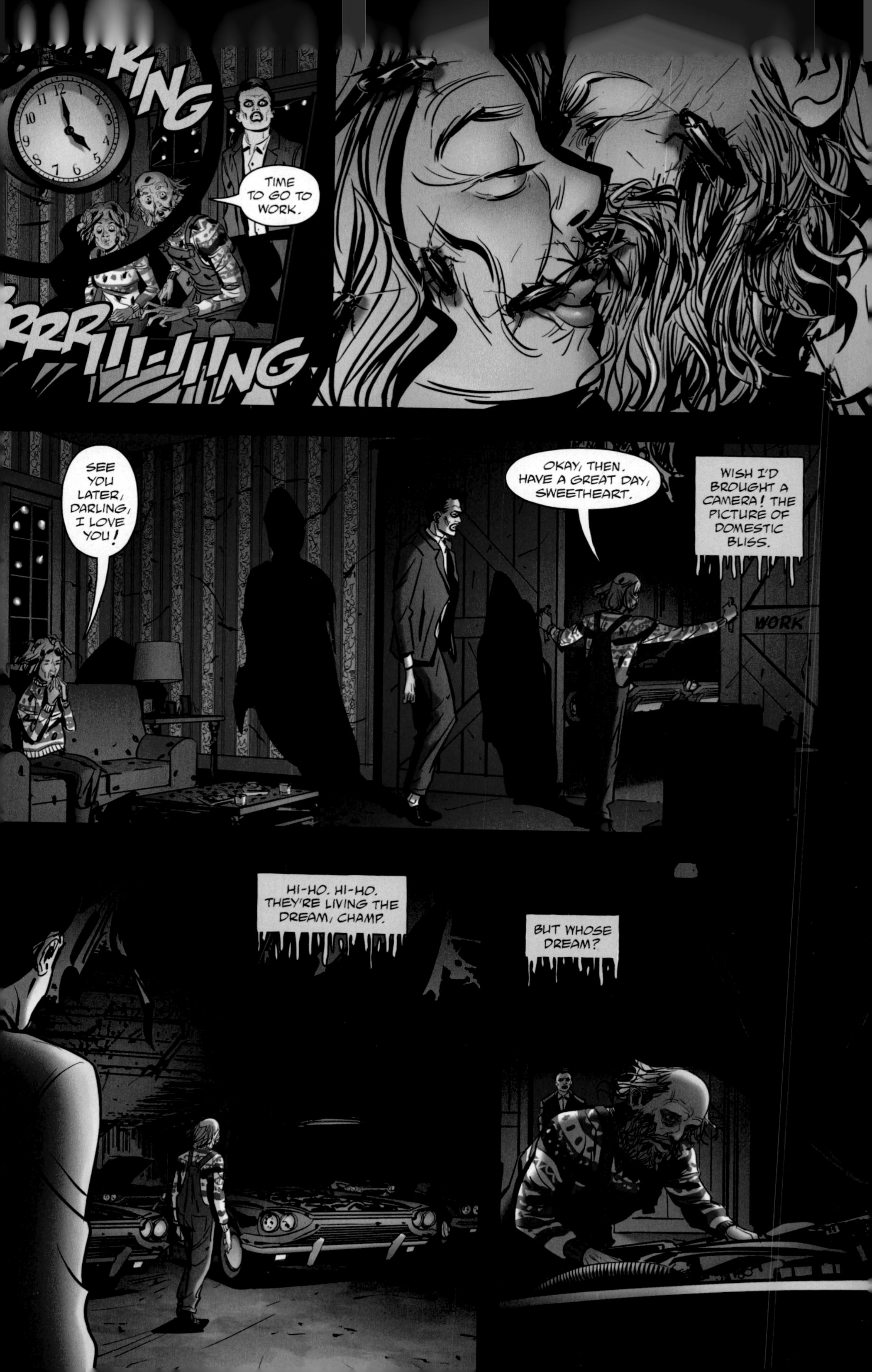
KING
TIME TO GO TO WORK.
RRRRIII-IIING
SEE YOU LATER, DARLING, I LOVE YOU!
OKAY, THEN. HAVE A GREAT DAY, SWEETHEART.
WISH I'D BROUGHT A CAMERA! THE PICTURE OF DOMESTIC BLISS.
WORK
HI-HO. HI-HO. THEY'RE LIVING THE DREAM, CHAMP.
BUT WHOSE DREAM?

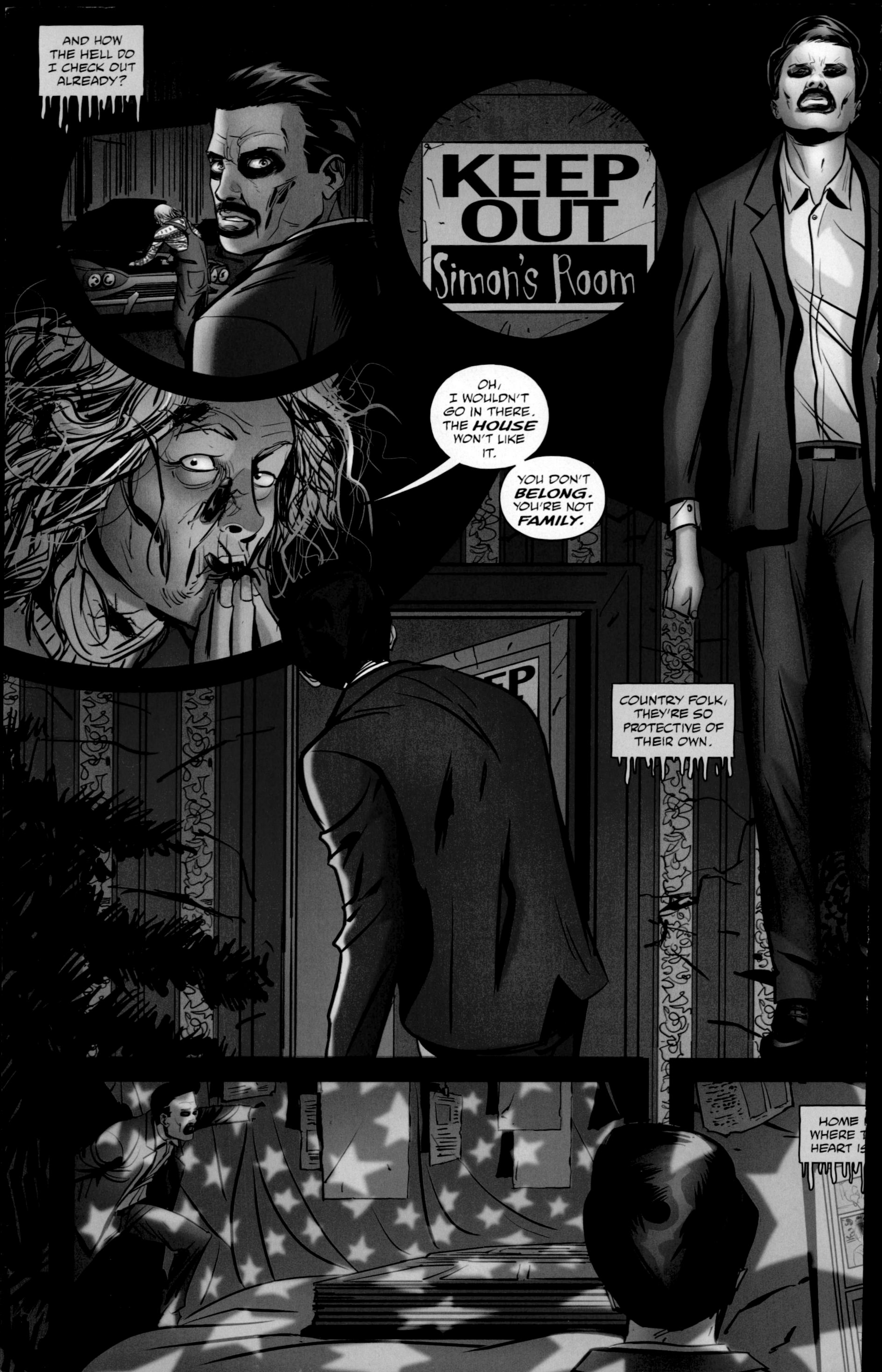
AND HOW THE HELL DO I CHECK OUT ALREADY?
KEEP OUT
Simon's Room
OH, I WOULDN'T GO IN THERE. THE HOUSE WON'T LIKE IT.
YOU DON'T BELONG. YOU'RE NOT FAMILY.
COUNTRY FOLK, THEY'RE SO PROTECTIVE OF THEIR OWN.

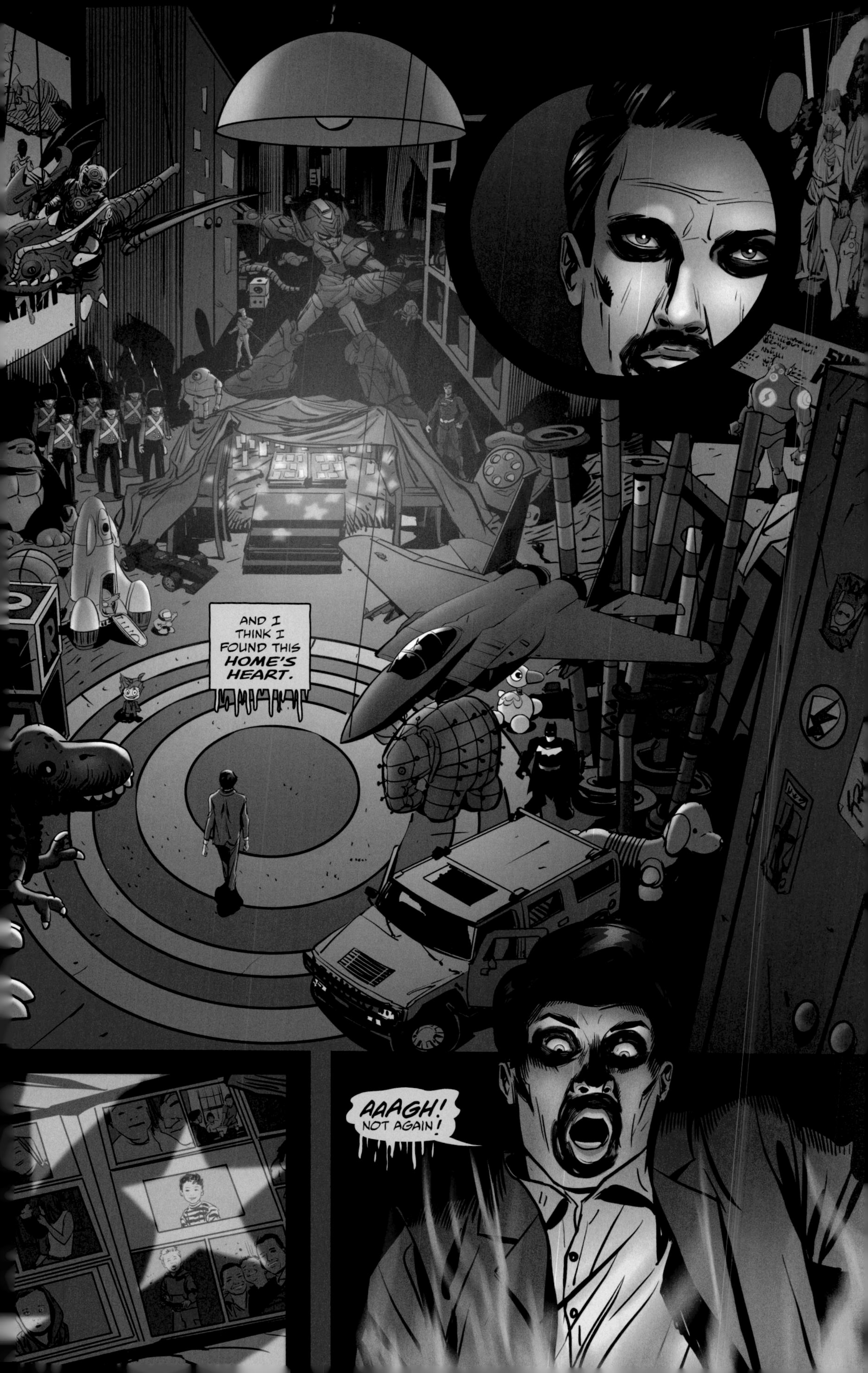
AND I THINK I FOUND THIS HOME'S HEART.
AAAGH! NOT AGAIN!

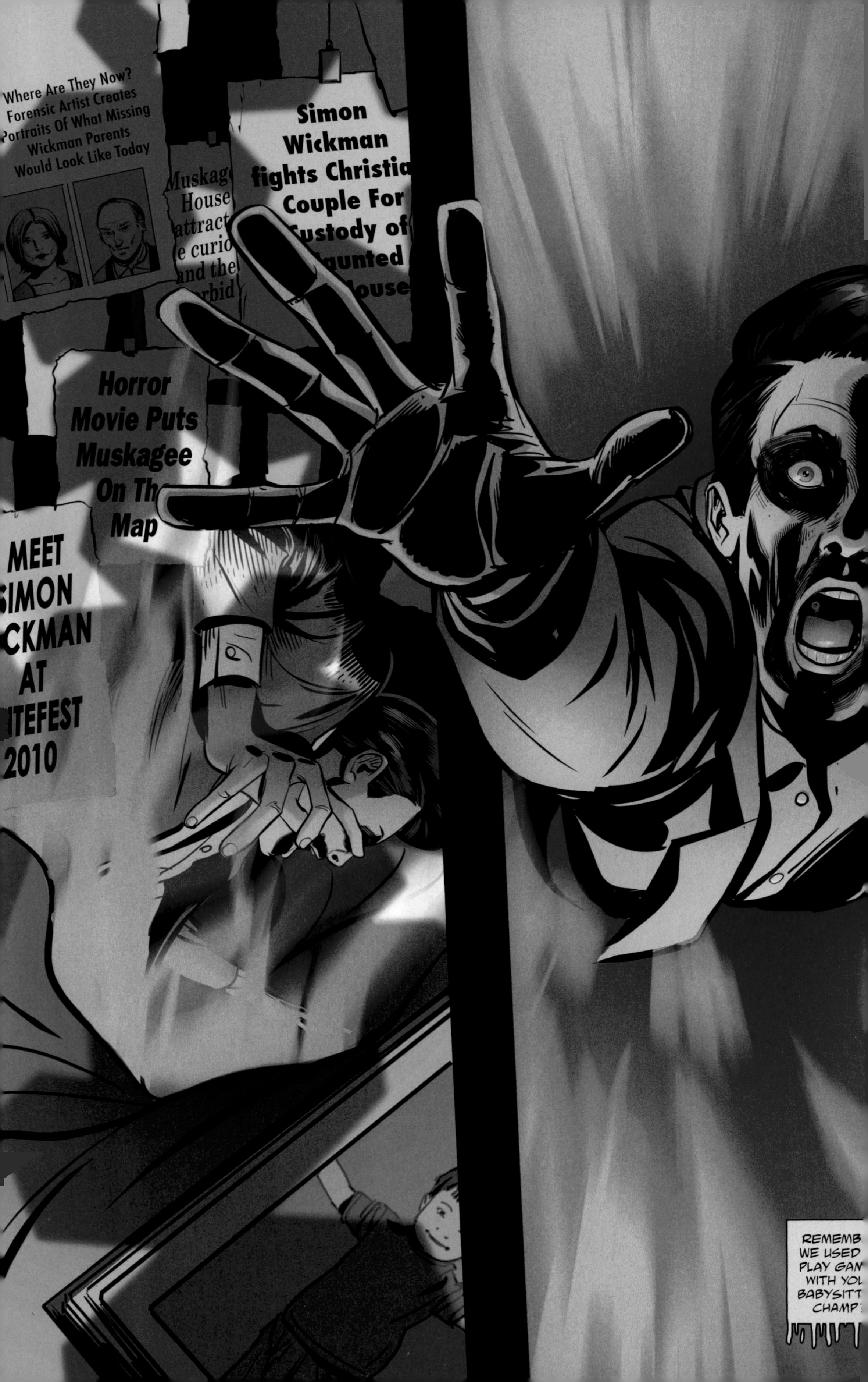

Where Are They Now? Forensic Artist Creates Portraits Of What Missing Wickman Parents Would Look Like Today
Muskage House attract e curio and the rbid
Simon Wickman fights Christia Couple For Custody of aunted House
Horror Movie Puts Muskagee On Th Map
MEET SIMON CKMAN AT ITEFEST 2010
REMEMB WE USED PLAY GAM WITH YOU BABYSITT CHAMP?

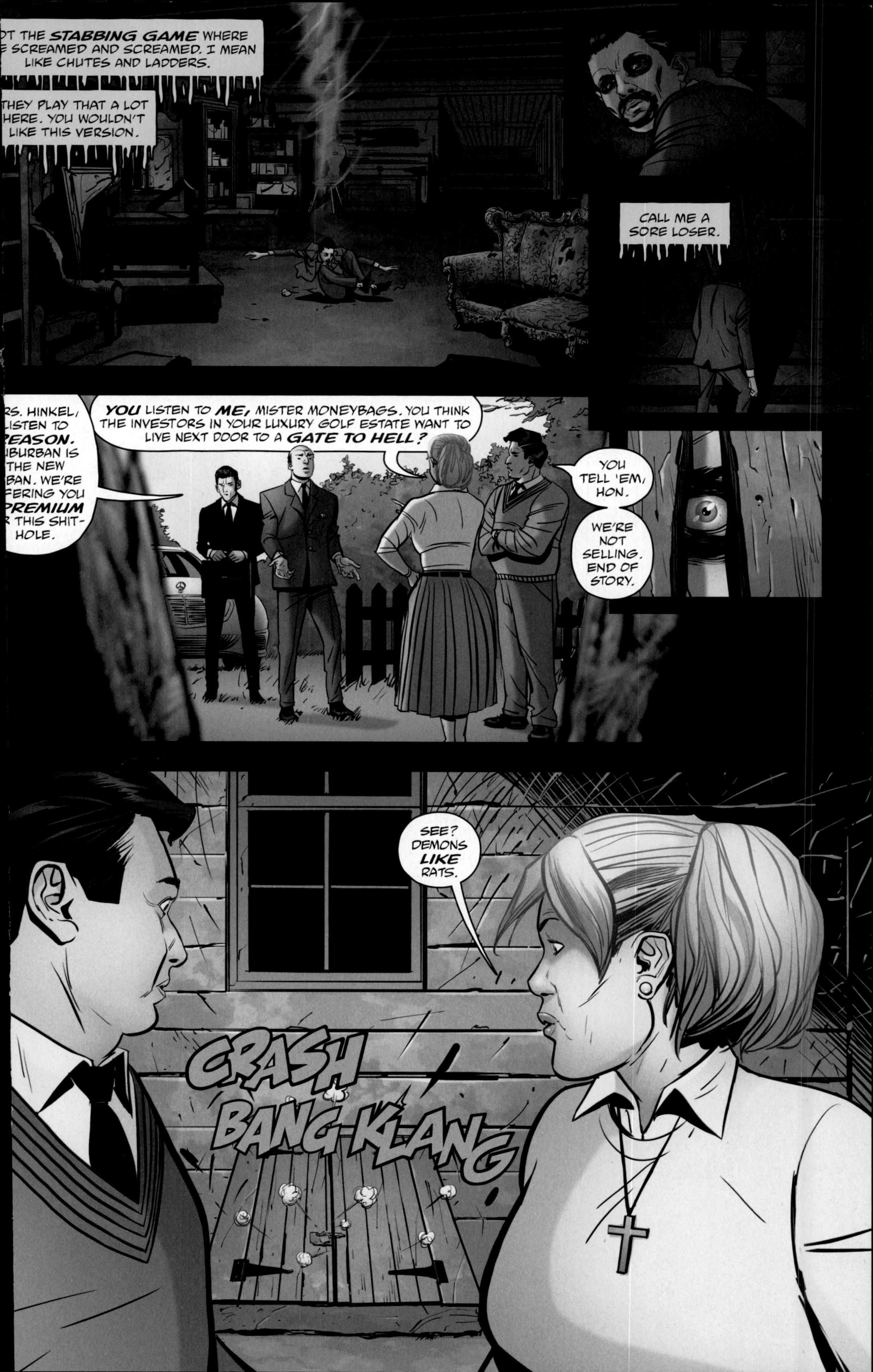
OT THE STABBING GAME WHERE
E SCREAMED AND SCREAMED. I MEAN LIKE CHUTES AND LADDERS.
THEY PLAY THAT A LOT HERE. YOU WOULDN'T LIKE THIS VERSION.
CALL ME A SORE LOSER.
RS. HINKEL, LISTEN TO REASON. UBURBAN IS THE NEW BAN. WE'RE FERING YOU PREMIUM R THIS SHIT-HOLE.
YOU LISTEN TO ME, MISTER MONEYBAGS. YOU THINK THE INVESTORS IN YOUR LUXURY GOLF ESTATE WANT TO LIVE NEXT DOOR TO A GATE TO HELL?
YOU TELL 'EM, HON.
WE'RE NOT SELLING. END OF STORY.
SEE? DEMONS LIKE RATS.
CRASH
BANG-KLANG

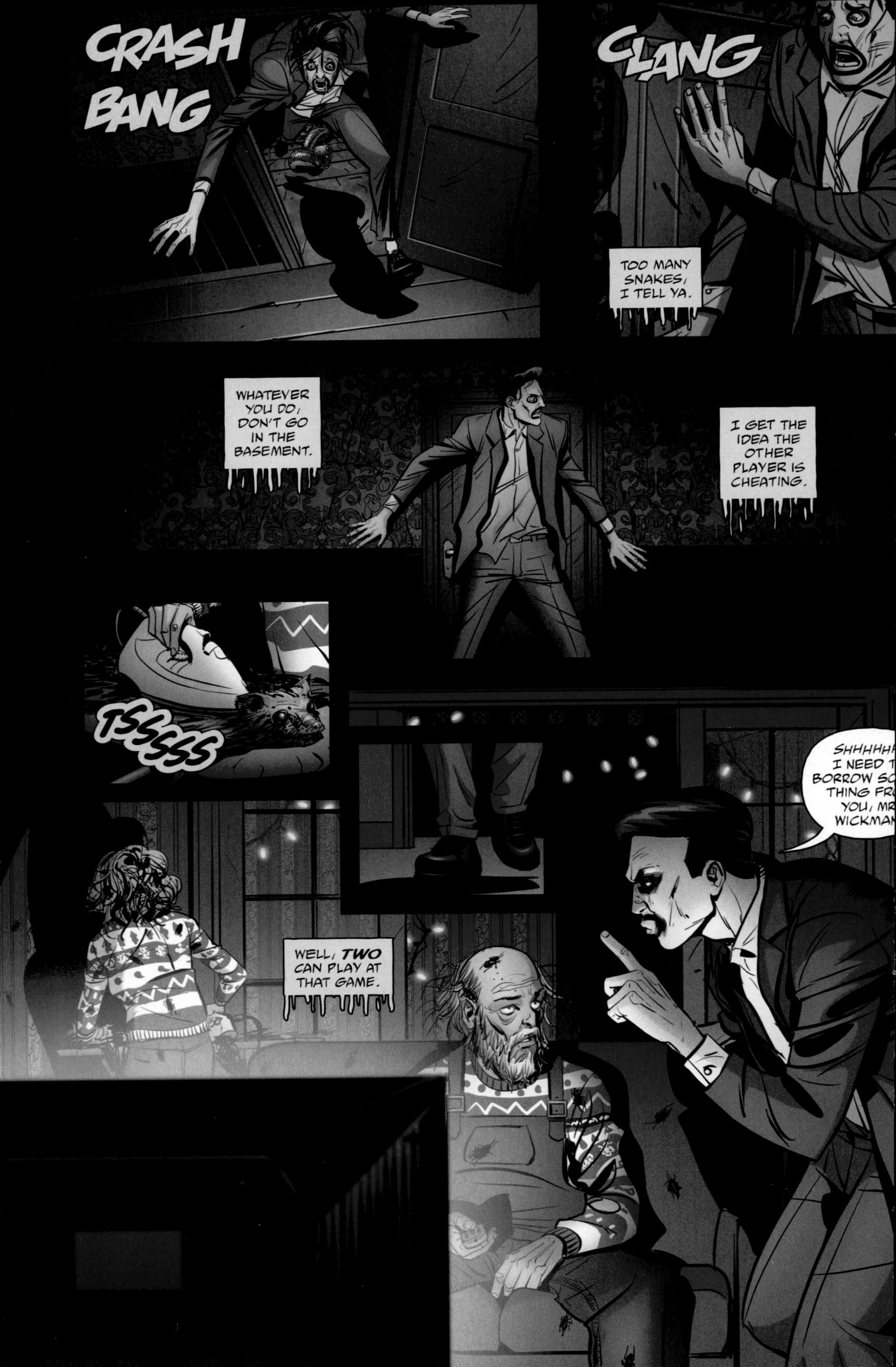
CRASH
BANG
CLANG
TOO MANY SNAKES, I TELL YA.
WHATEVER YOU DO, DON'T GO IN THE BASEMENT.
I GET THE IDEA THE OTHER PLAYER IS CHEATING.
TSSSSSS
SHHHHH I NEED BORROW THING YOU, MR WICKMAN
WELL, **TWO** CAN PLAY AT THAT GAME.

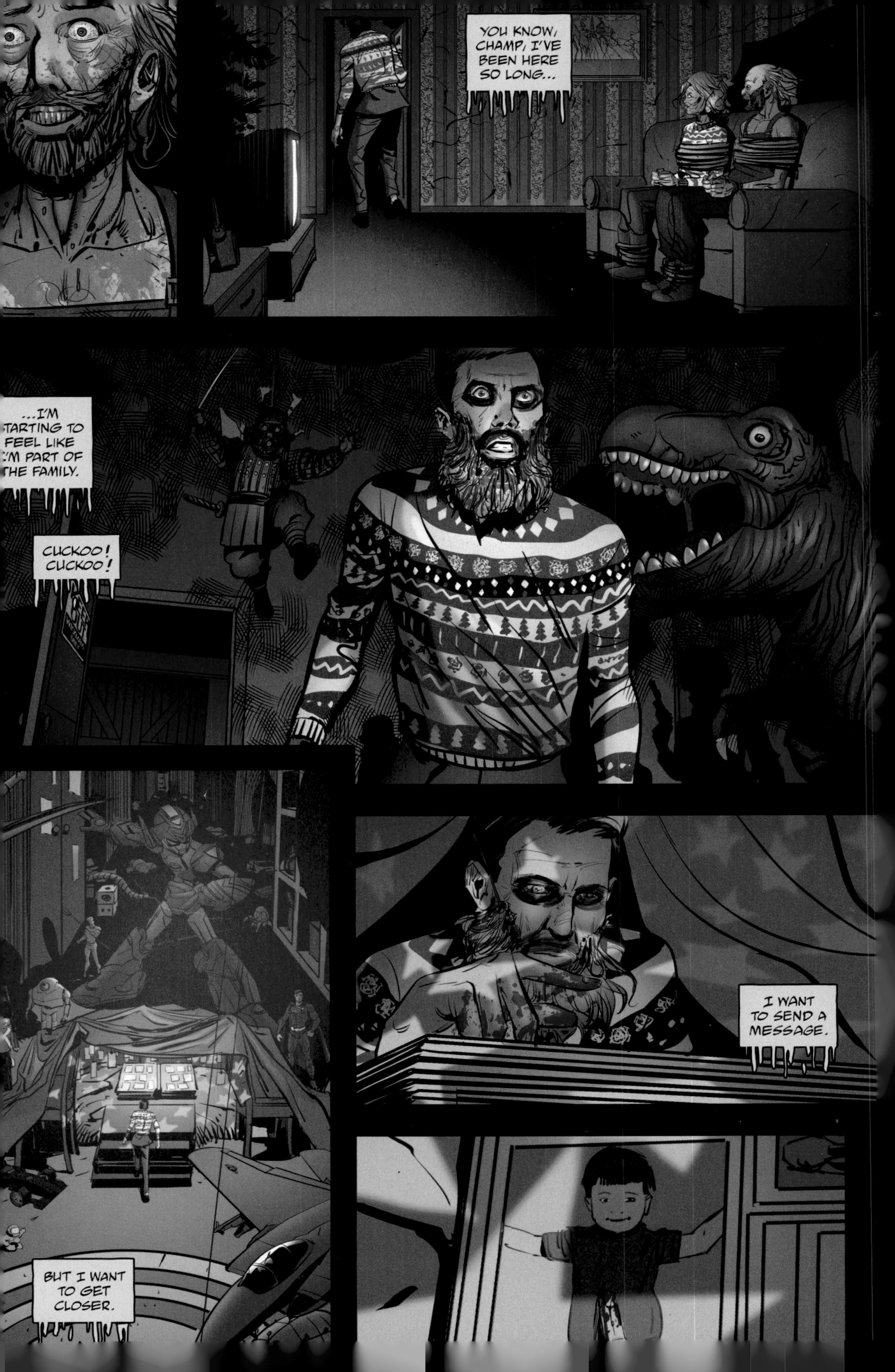
YOU KNOW, CHAMP, I'VE BEEN HERE SO LONG...
...I'M STARTING TO FEEL LIKE I'M PART OF THE FAMILY.
CUCKOO! CUCKOO!
BUT I WANT TO GET CLOSER.
I WANT TO SEND A MESSAGE.

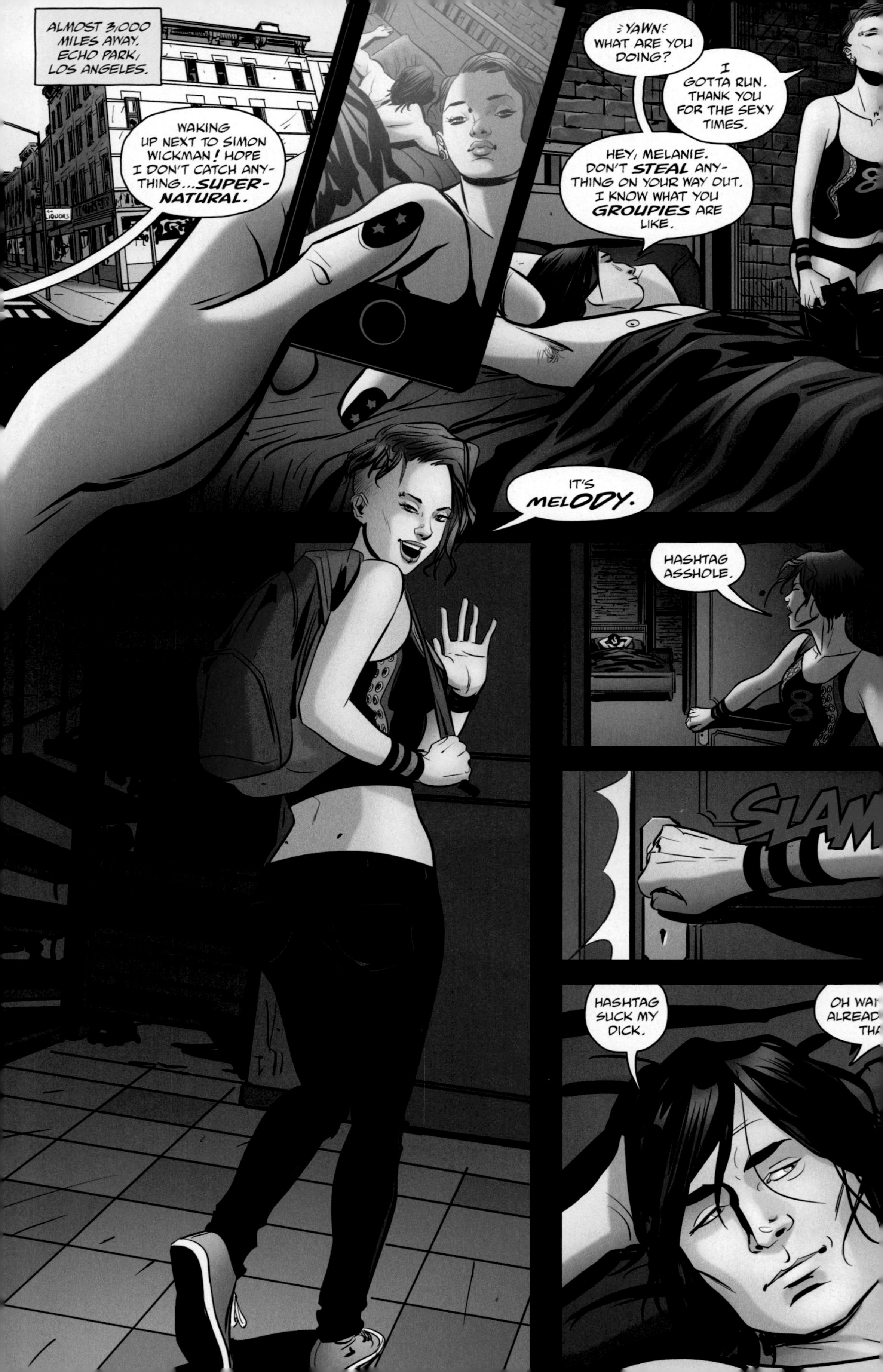
ALMOST 3,000 MILES AWAY. ECHO PARK, LOS ANGELES.
LIQUORS
WAKING UP NEXT TO SIMON WICKMAN! HOPE I DON'T CATCH ANY-THING...SUPER-NATURAL.
YAWN WHAT ARE YOU DOING?
I GOTTA RUN. THANK YOU FOR THE SEXY TIMES.
HEY, MELANIE. DON'T STEAL ANY-THING ON YOUR WAY OUT. I KNOW WHAT YOU GROUPIES ARE LIKE.
IT'S MELODY.
HASHTAG ASSHOLE.
SLAM
HASHTAG SUCK MY DICK.

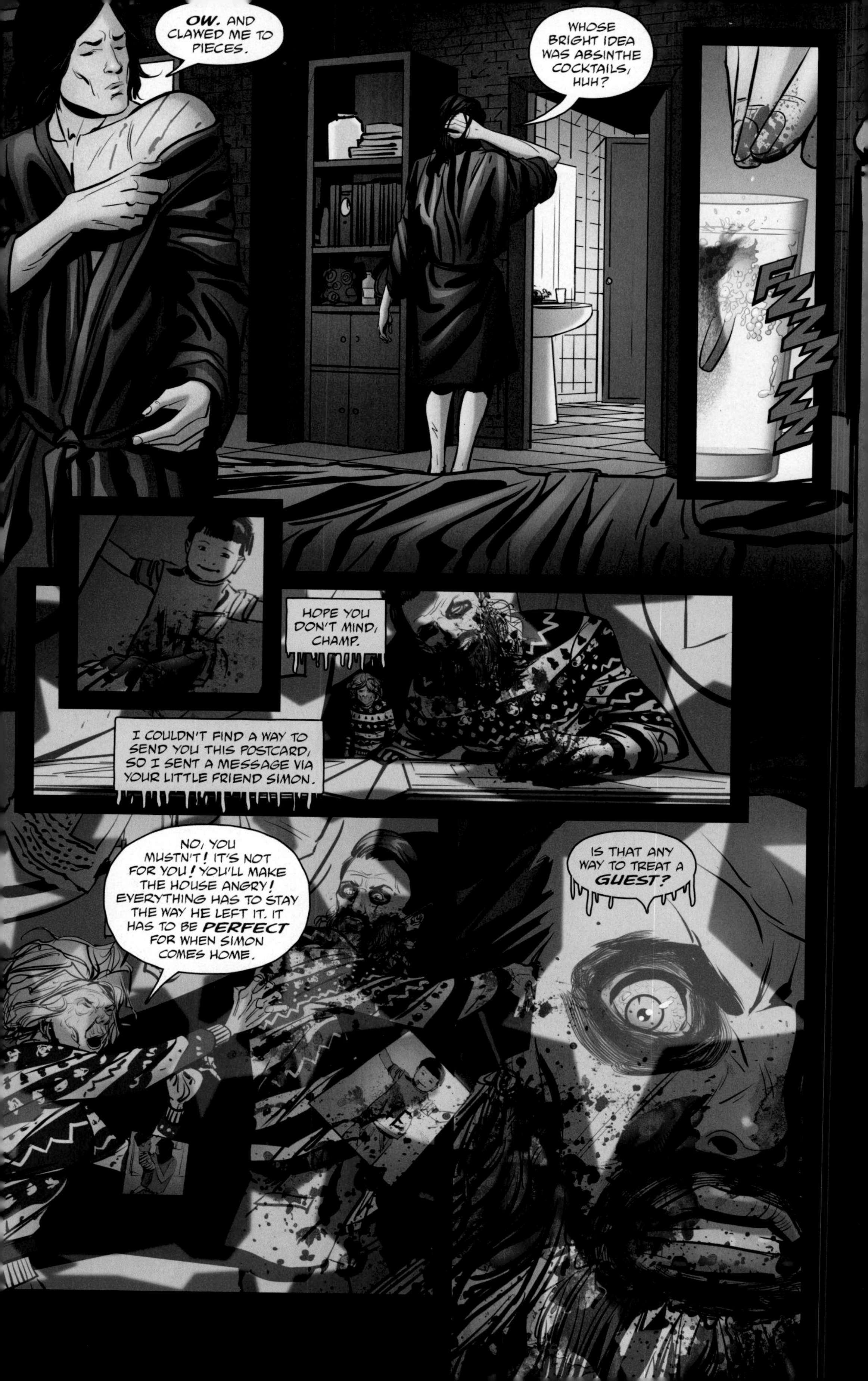
OW. AND CLAWED ME TO PIECES.
WHOSE BRIGHT IDEA WAS ABSINTHE COCKTAILS, HUH?
FZZZZZZ
HOPE YOU DON'T MIND, CHAMP.
I COULDN'T FIND A WAY TO SEND YOU THIS POSTCARD, SO I SENT A MESSAGE VIA YOUR LITTLE FRIEND SIMON.
NO, YOU MUSTN'T! IT'S NOT FOR YOU! YOU'LL MAKE THE HOUSE ANGRY! EVERYTHING HAS TO STAY THE WAY HE LEFT IT. IT HAS TO BE PERFECT FOR WHEN SIMON COMES HOME.
IS THAT ANY WAY TO TREAT A GUEST?

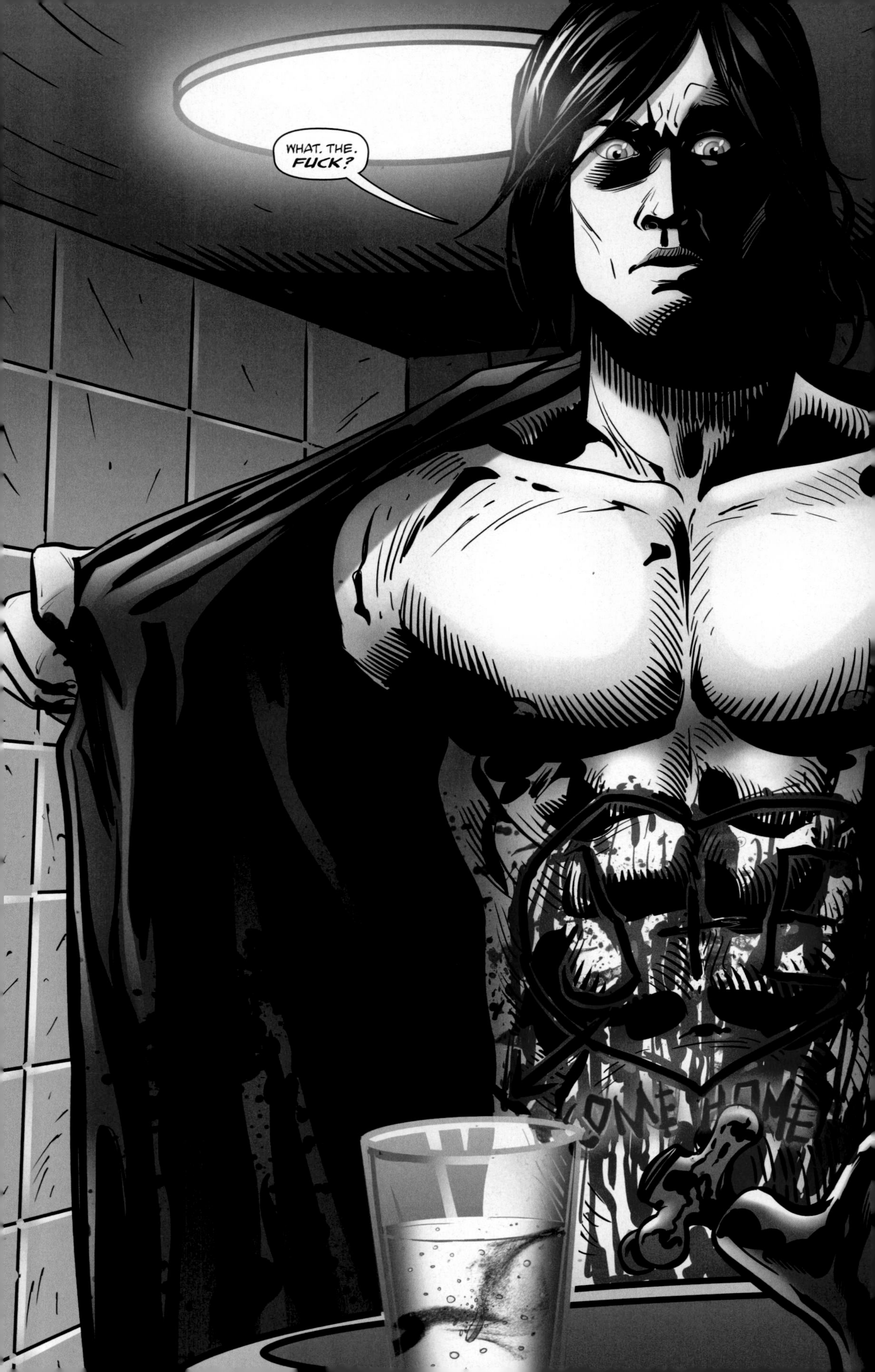
WHAT. THE. FUCK?

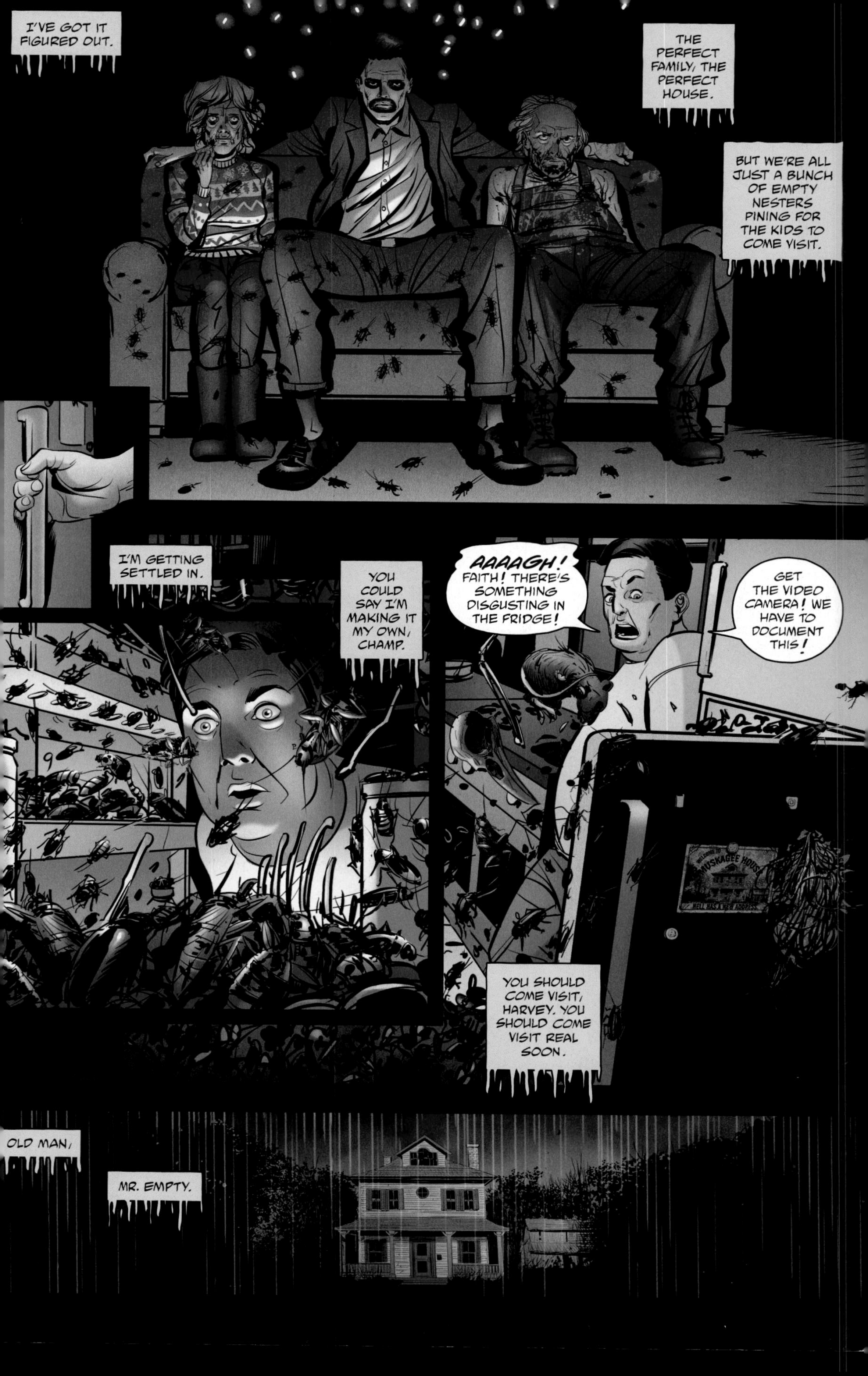
I'VE GOT IT FIGURED OUT.
THE PERFECT FAMILY, THE PERFECT HOUSE.
BUT WE'RE ALL JUST A BUNCH OF EMPTY NESTERS PINING FOR THE KIDS TO COME VISIT.
I'M GETTING SETTLED IN.
YOU COULD SAY I'M MAKING IT MY OWN, CHAMP.
AAAAGH! FAITH! THERE'S SOMETHING DISGUSTING IN THE FRIDGE!
GET THE VIDEO CAMERA! WE HAVE TO DOCUMENT THIS!
MUSKAGEE HOUSE
HELL HAS A NEW ADDRESS
YOU SHOULD COME VISIT, HARVEY. YOU SHOULD COME VISIT REAL SOON.
OLD MAN,
MR. EMPTY.

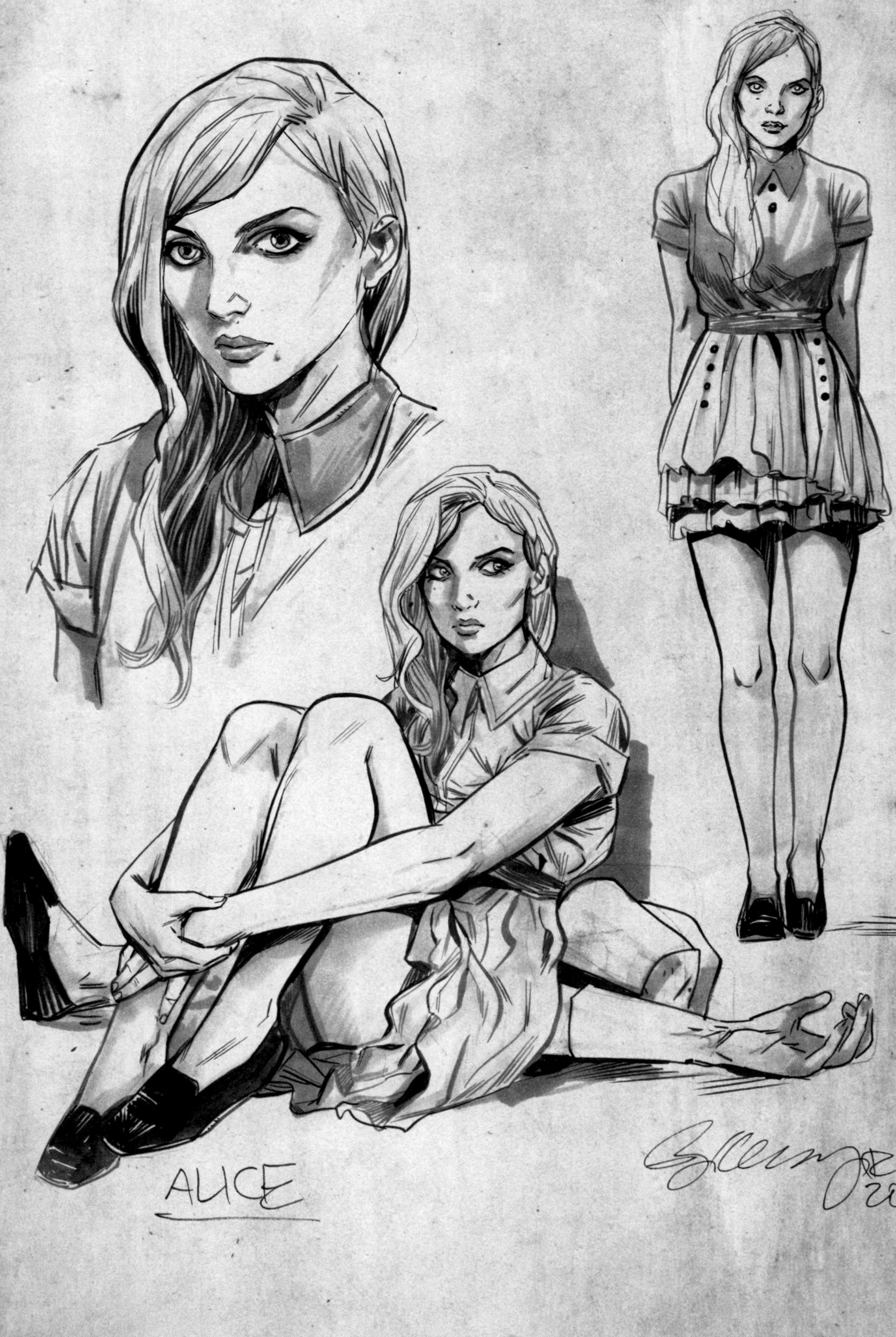
ALICE

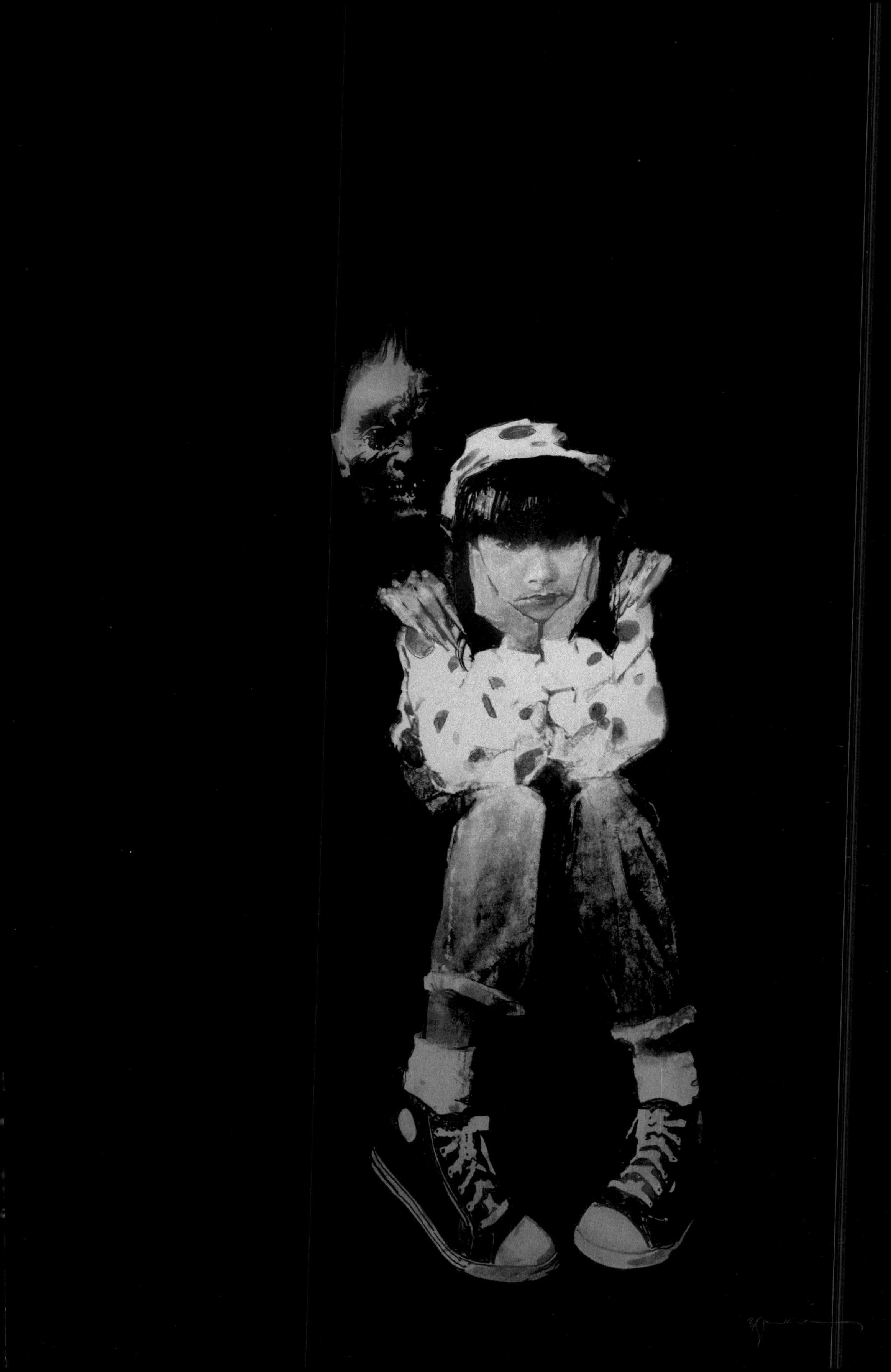

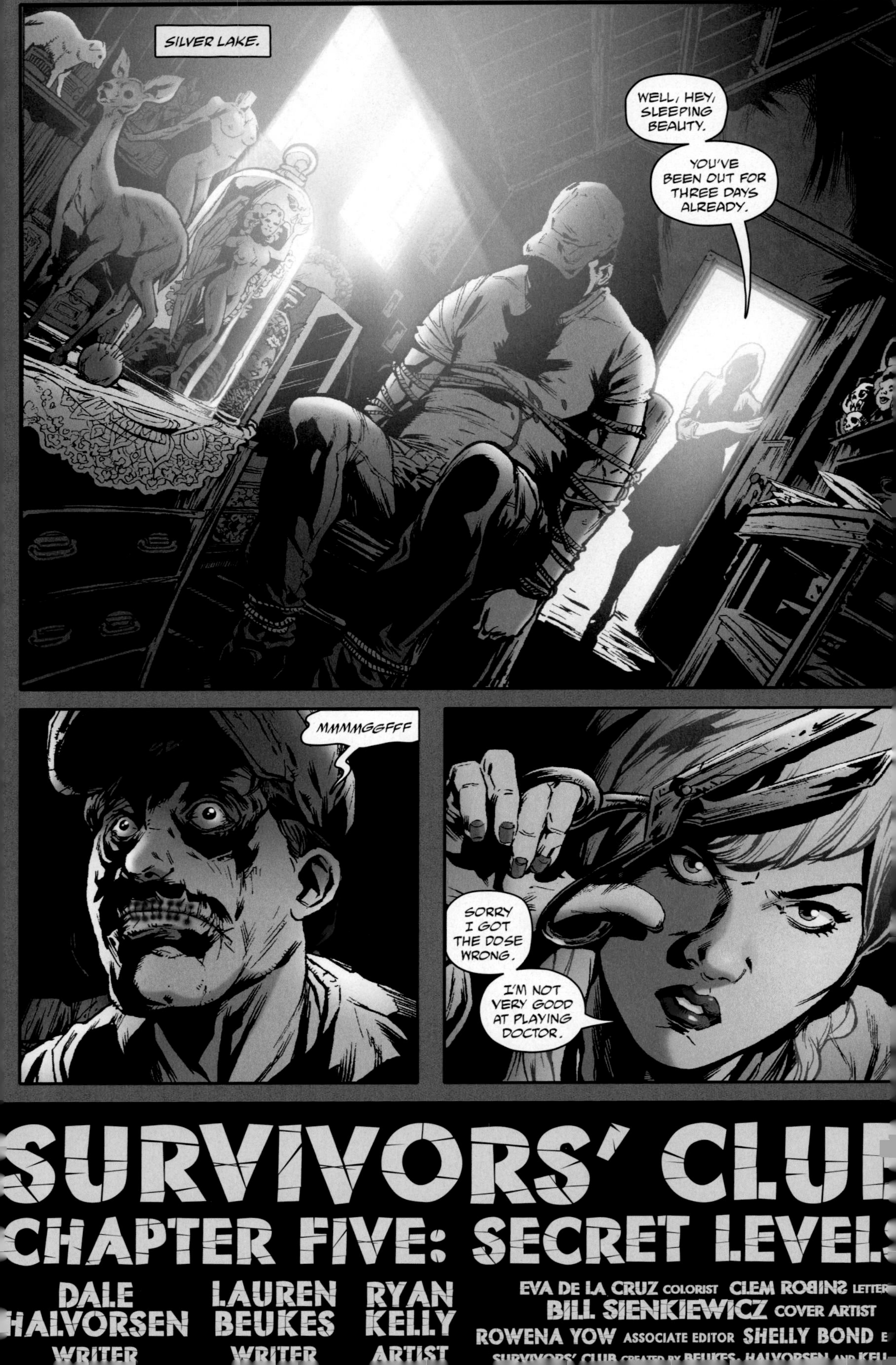
SILVER LAKE.
WELL, HEY, SLEEPING BEAUTY.
YOU'VE BEEN OUT FOR THREE DAYS ALREADY.
MMMMGGFFF
SORRY I GOT THE DOSE WRONG.
I'M NOT VERY GOOD AT PLAYING DOCTOR.

# SURVIVORS' CLUB

## CHAPTER FIVE: SECRET LEVELS

DALE HALVORSEN WRITER
LAUREN BEUKES WRITER
RYAN KELLY ARTIST
EVA DE LA CRUZ COLORIST CLEM ROBINS LETTER
BILL SIENKIEWICZ COVER ARTIST
ROWENA YOW ASSOCIATE EDITOR SHELLY BOND E
SURVIVORS' CLUB CREATED BY BEUKES, HALVORSEN AND KEL

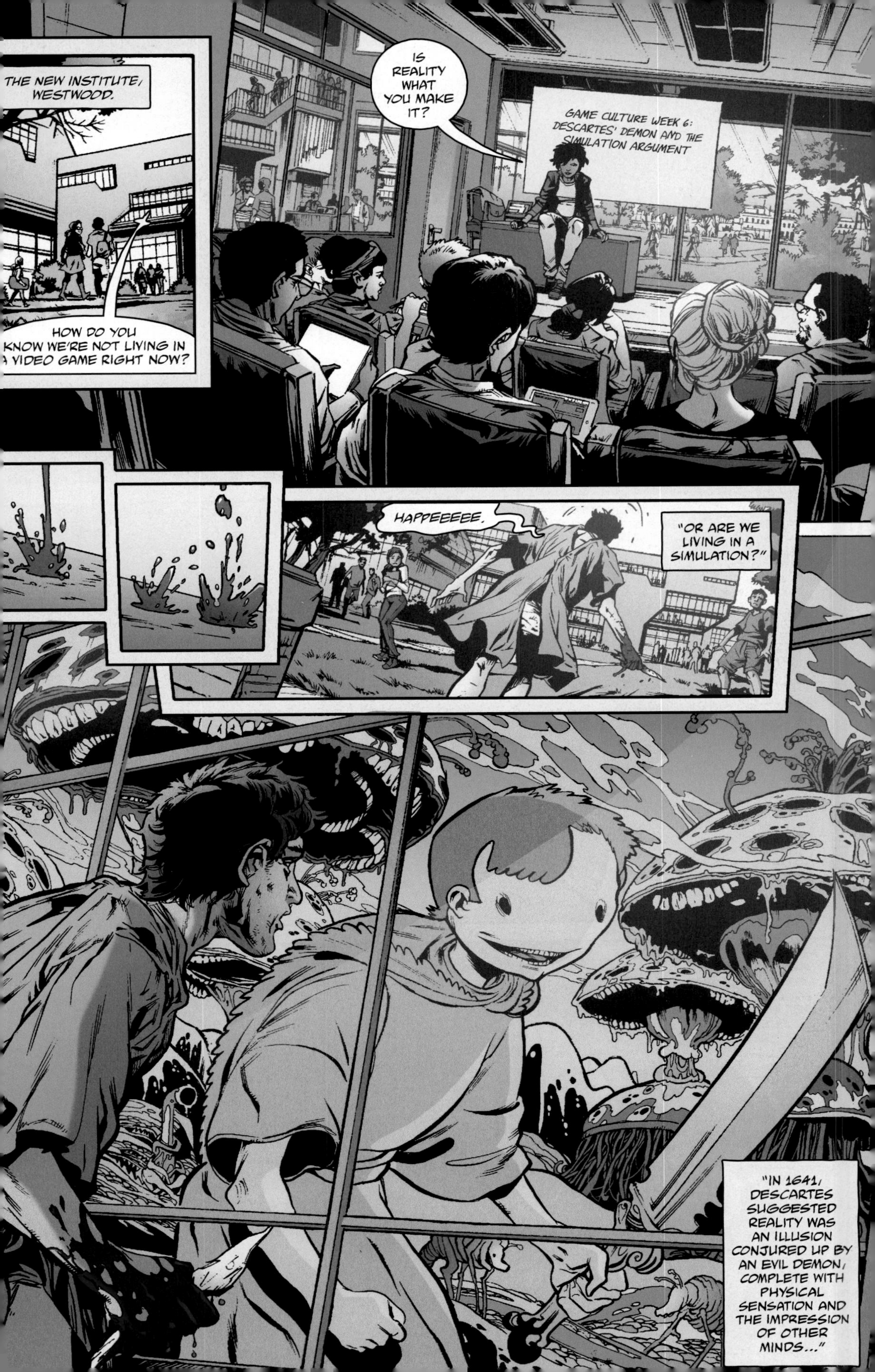
THE NEW INSTITUTE, WESTWOOD.
HOW DO YOU KNOW WE'RE NOT LIVING IN A VIDEO GAME RIGHT NOW?
IS REALITY WHAT YOU MAKE IT?
GAME CULTURE WEEK 6: DESCARTES' DEMON AND THE SIMULATION ARGUMENT
HAPPEEEEEE.
"OR ARE WE LIVING IN A SIMULATION?"
"IN 1641, DESCARTES SUGGESTED REALITY WAS AN ILLUSION CONJURED UP BY AN EVIL DEMON, COMPLETE WITH PHYSICAL SENSATION AND THE IMPRESSION OF OTHER MINDS..."

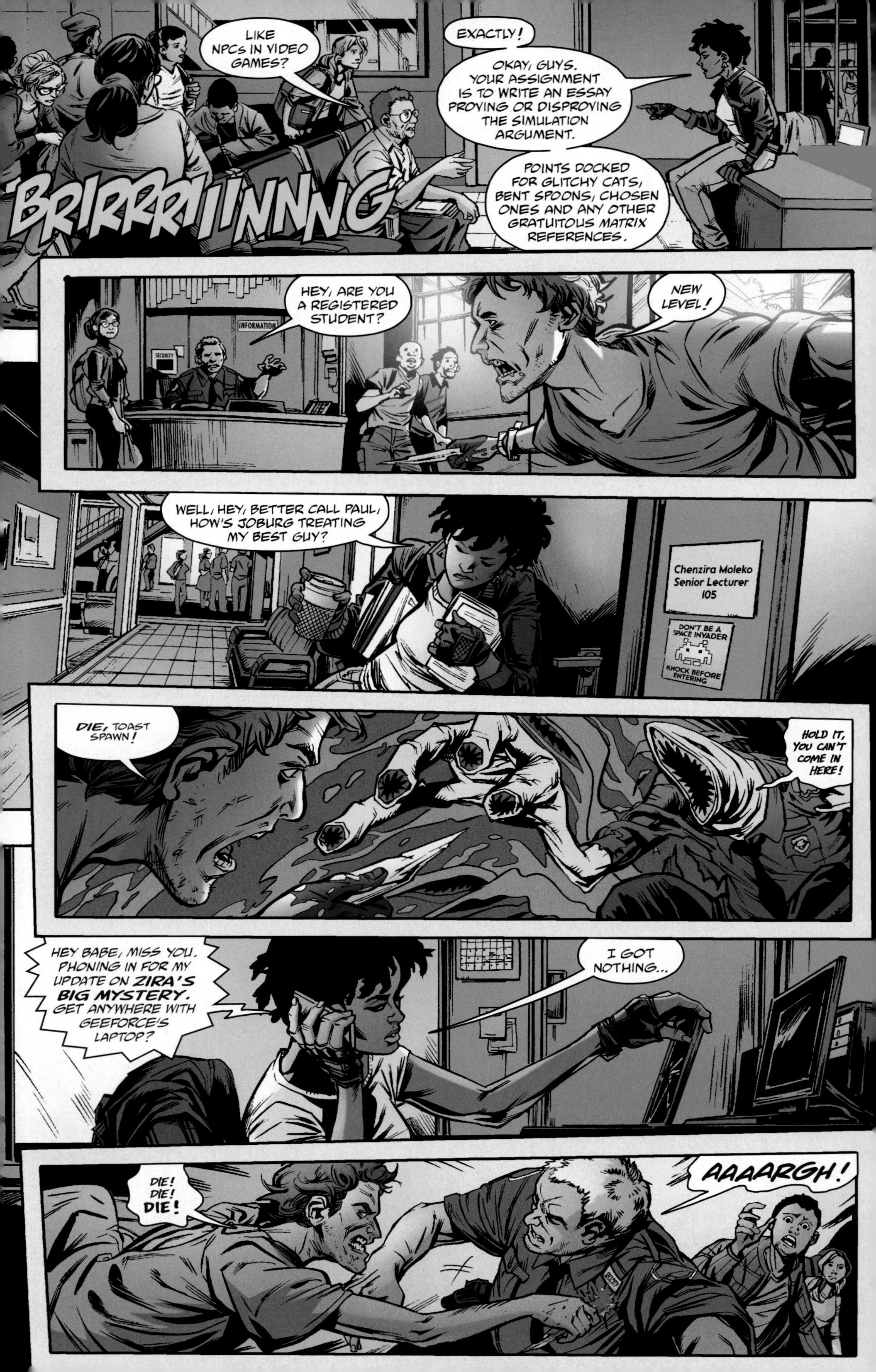

LIKE NPCs IN VIDEO GAMES?
EXACTLY!
OKAY, GUYS. YOUR ASSIGNMENT IS TO WRITE AN ESSAY PROVING OR DISPROVING THE SIMULATION ARGUMENT.
POINTS DOCKED FOR GLITCHY CATS, BENT SPOONS, CHOSEN ONES AND ANY OTHER GRATUITOUS MATRIX REFERENCES.
BRIRRRIIINNNG
INFORMATION
SECURITY
HEY, ARE YOU A REGISTERED STUDENT?
NEW LEVEL!
WELL, HEY, BETTER CALL PAUL, HOW'S JOBURG TREATING MY BEST GUY?
Chenzira Moleko
Senior Lecturer
105
DON'T BE A SPACE INVADER
KNOCK BEFORE ENTERING
DIE, TOAST SPAWN!
HOLD IT, YOU CAN'T COME IN HERE!
HEY BABE, MISS YOU. PHONING IN FOR MY UPDATE ON ZIRA'S BIG MYSTERY. GET ANYWHERE WITH GEEFORCE'S LAPTOP?
I GOT NOTHING...
DIE! DIE! DIE!
AAAARGH!

WELL... THERE'S **ONE** THING. PLAYING THE DEMO ON GEEFORCE'S 'APTOP. BUT I'M NOT SURE I'M READY TO GO THERE YET.

I'D LOVE TO ASK GEEFORCE MORE ABOUT IT, BUT HE BUSTED OUT OF THE HOSPITAL.

"WHO KNOWS WHERE HE IS NOW?"

I'M COMING TO **FIND** YOU, PRINCESS! I'M GONNA SAVE THE DAY!

AND YOUR SCOOBY DOO GANG?

IT'S A BIT LIKE HORROR SUDOKU. WISH EVERYONE WOULD OPEN UP ABOUT WHAT HAPPENED TO THEM.

I SHOULD TALK, RIGHT? I GOT MORE SECRETS THAN THE **NSA.** IT'S BRINGING OUT THAT BURNING RASH.

ALICE

KENT

SIMON

TEO

MUSKAGEE

NEW YORK

KIRI

NAGASAKI

GBENZIRA

JOBURG

ON YOUR HANDS? YOU HAVEN'T HAD THAT SINCE YOU WATCHED THE VIDEO OF THAT CRAZY GAME...

MAYBE IT'S ALL CONNECTED.

AAAAGGGHHH!! WHAT ARE YOU DOING?!

THERE'S SOME- THING GOING ON. I'LL CALL YOU BACK.

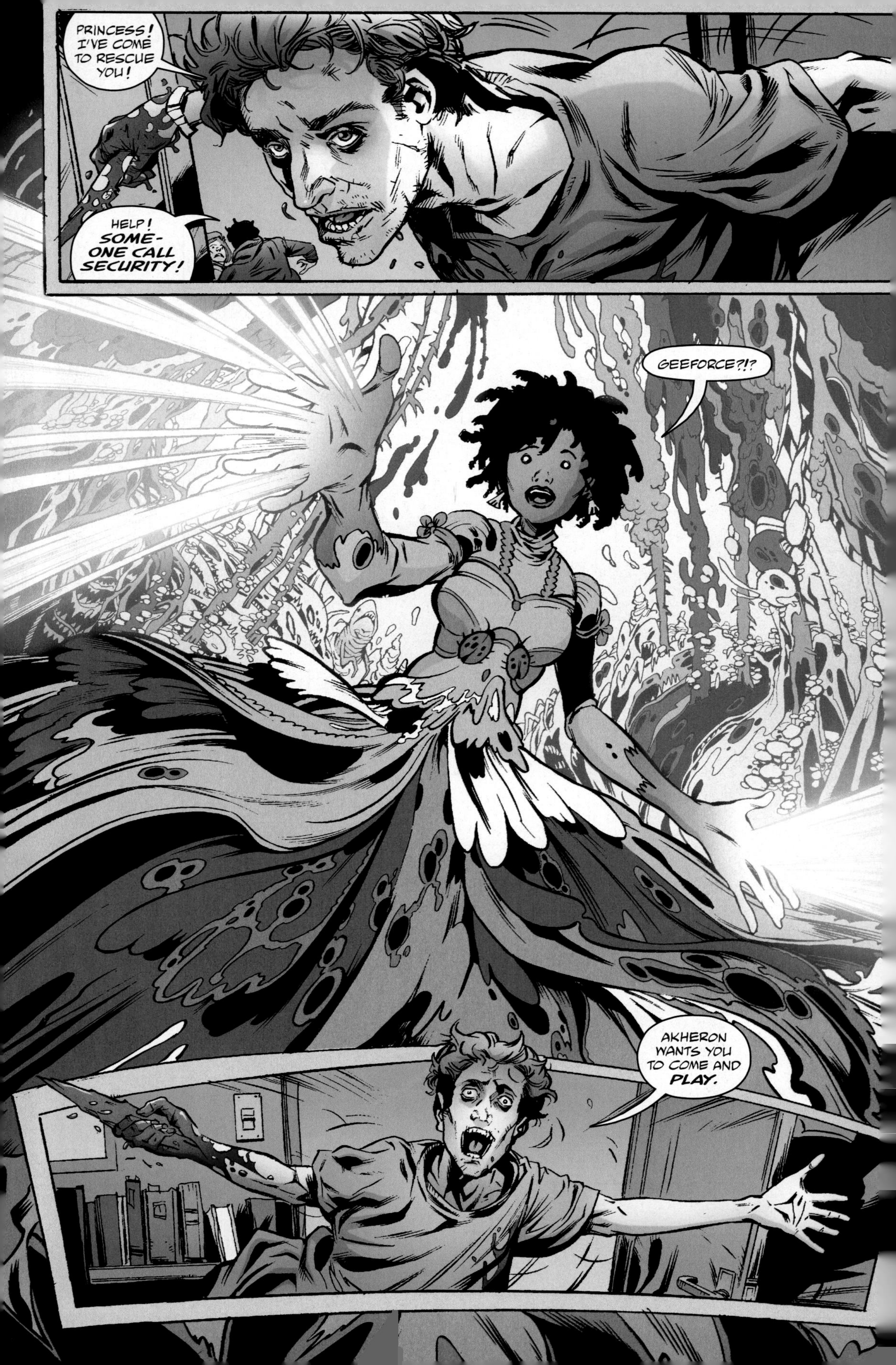
PRINCESS! I'VE COME TO RESCUE YOU!
HELP! SOME-ONE CALL SECURITY!
GEEFORCE?!?
AKHERON WANTS YOU TO COME AND PLAY.

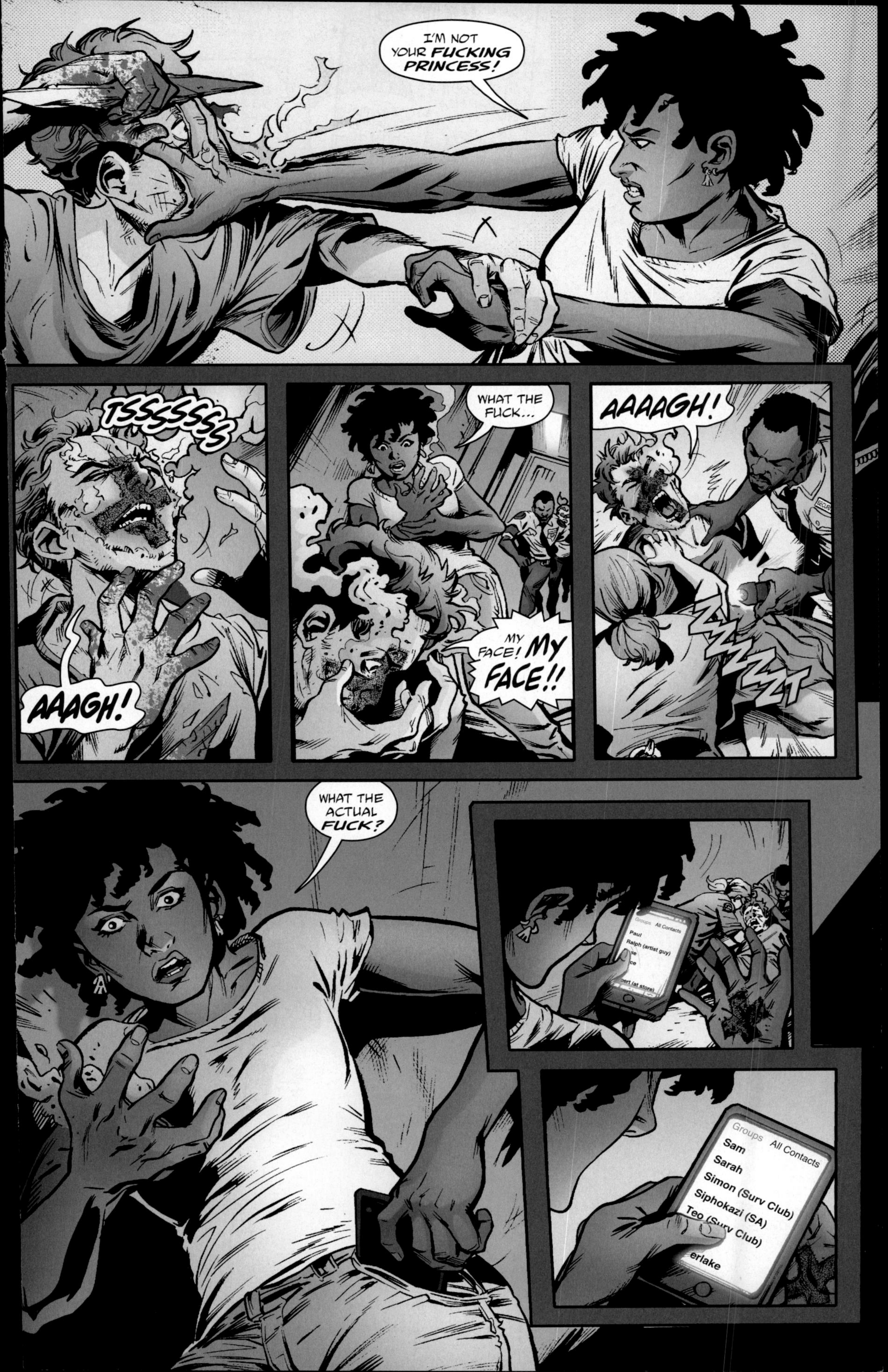
I'M NOT YOUR FUCKING PRINCESS!
TSSSSSSS
AAAGH!
WHAT THE FUCK...
MY FACE! MY FACE!!
AAAAGH!
ZZZZZT
WHAT THE ACTUAL FUCK?
Groups
All Contacts
Paul
Ralph (artist guy)
Groups
All Contacts
Sam
Sarah
Simon (Surv Club)
Siphokazi (SA)
Teo (Surv Club)

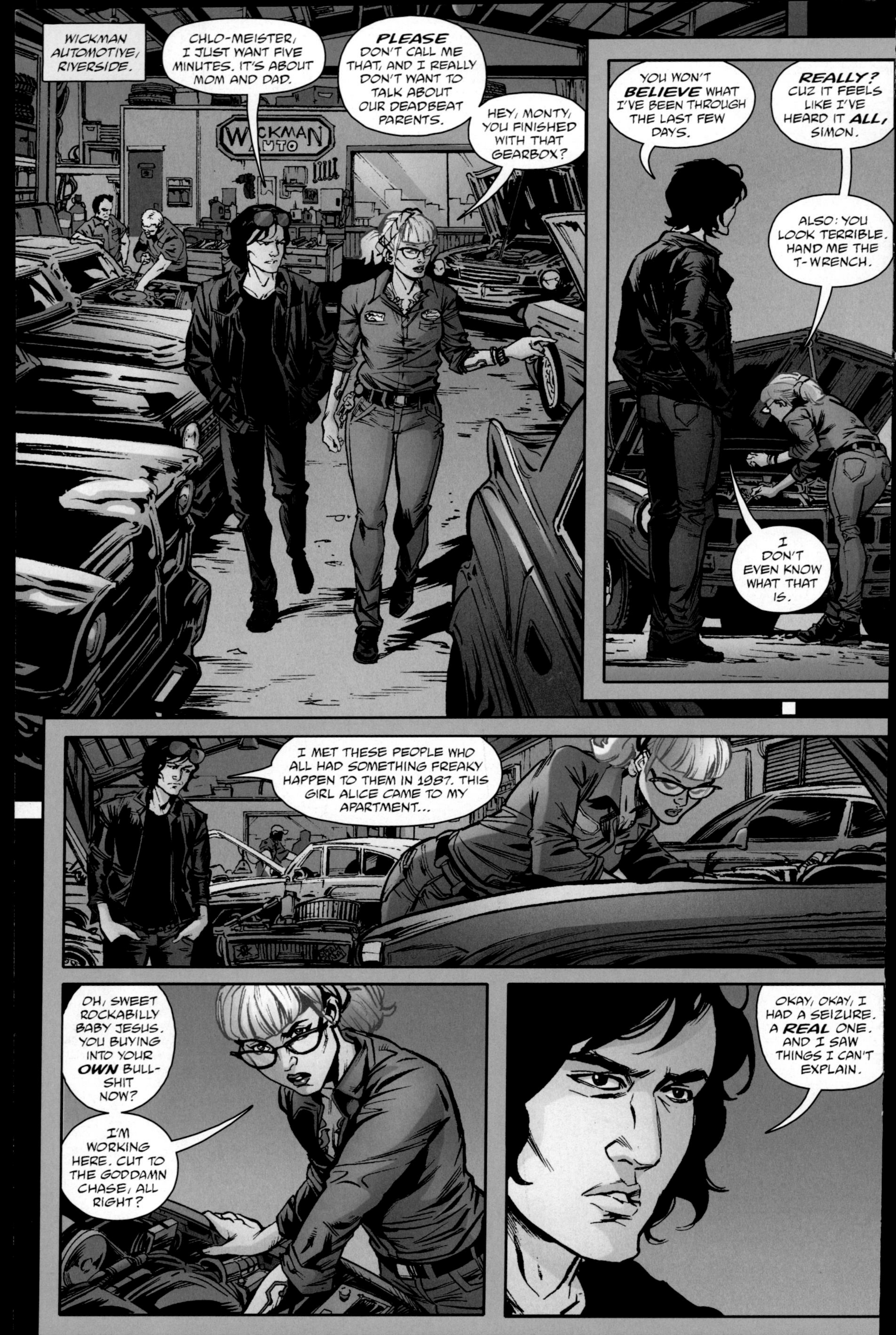
WICKMAN AUTOMOTIVE, RIVERSIDE.
CHLO-MEISTER, I JUST WANT FIVE MINUTES. IT'S ABOUT MOM AND DAD.
PLEASE DON'T CALL ME THAT, AND I REALLY DON'T WANT TO TALK ABOUT OUR DEADBEAT PARENTS.
HEY, MONTY, YOU FINISHED WITH THAT GEARBOX?
WICKMAN AUTO
YOU WON'T BELIEVE WHAT I'VE BEEN THROUGH THE LAST FEW DAYS.
REALLY? CUZ IT FEELS LIKE I'VE HEARD IT ALL, SIMON.
ALSO: YOU LOOK TERRIBLE. HAND ME THE T-WRENCH.
I DON'T EVEN KNOW WHAT THAT IS.
I MET THESE PEOPLE WHO ALL HAD SOMETHING FREAKY HAPPEN TO THEM IN 1987. THIS GIRL ALICE CAME TO MY APARTMENT...
OH, SWEET ROCKABILLY BABY JESUS. YOU BUYING INTO YOUR OWN BULL-SHIT NOW?
I'M WORKING HERE. CUT TO THE GODDAMN CHASE, ALL RIGHT?
OKAY, OKAY, I HAD A SEIZURE. A REAL ONE. AND I SAW THINGS I CAN'T EXPLAIN.

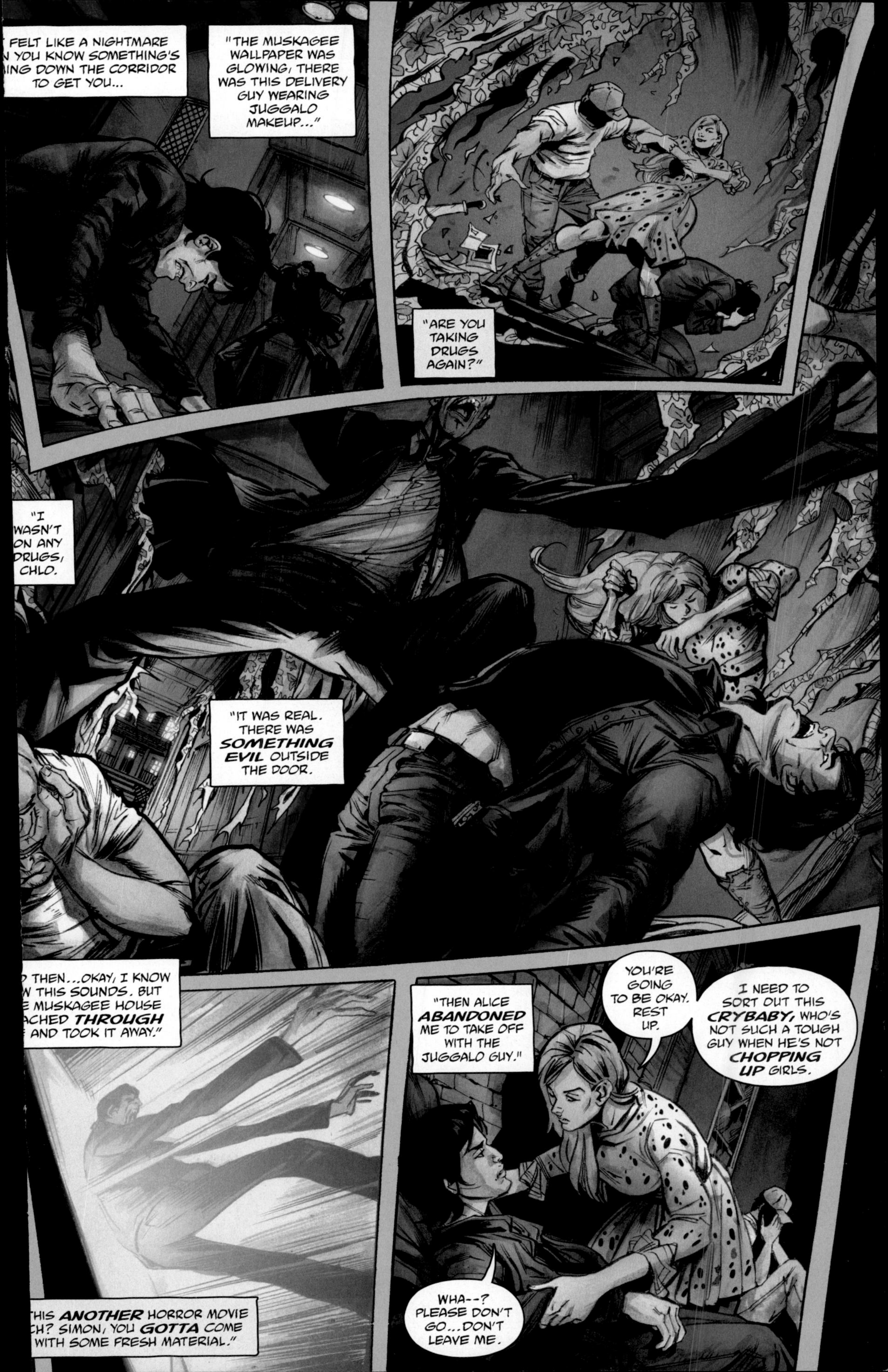
T FELT LIKE A NIGHTMARE
N YOU KNOW SOMETHING'S
AING DOWN THE CORRIDOR
TO GET YOU...
"THE MUSKAGEE WALLPAPER WAS GLOWING; THERE WAS THIS DELIVERY GUY WEARING JUGGALO MAKEUP..."
"ARE YOU TAKING DRUGS AGAIN?"
"I WASN'T ON ANY DRUGS, CHLO.
"IT WAS REAL. THERE WAS SOMETHING EVIL OUTSIDE THE DOOR.
D THEN...OKAY, I KNOW W THIS SOUNDS. BUT E MUSKAGEE HOUSE ACHED THROUGH E AND TOOK IT AWAY."
"THEN ALICE ABANDONED ME TO TAKE OFF WITH THE JUGGALO GUY."
YOU'RE GOING TO BE OKAY. REST UP.
I NEED TO SORT OUT THIS CRYBABY, WHO'S NOT SUCH A TOUGH GUY WHEN HE'S NOT CHOPPING UP GIRLS.
THIS ANOTHER HORROR MOVIE CH? SIMON, YOU GOTTA COME WITH SOME FRESH MATERIAL."
WHA--? PLEASE DON'T GO...DON'T LEAVE ME.

NOW ALICE WON'T TAKE MY CALLS. SHE SAYS SHE'S BUSY, WITH SOME PROJECT. I STILL DON'T KNOW WHAT HAPPENED.

YOU KNOW W YOU SOUN LIKE? THO SCAM ART EXORCIS

OH YEAH? IT GETS WEIRDER. YESTERDAY, I WOKE UP WITH *THIS*...

J+E COME HOME

WHAT IS *WRONG* WITH YOU? YOU CARVED MOM AND DAD'S INITIALS INTO YOUR *STOMACH?!*

YOU'VE TAKEN THIS TOO FAR. JUST LIKE WHEN YOU WERE SIX.

IT WASN'T ME! IT WASN'T ANYBODY. IT'S SOMEHOW... CONNECTED TO THE HOUSE. I THINK OUR PARENTS ARE ALIVE IN THERE, CHLO.

WE NEED TO GO BACK.

I'LL TELL YOU EXACTLY WHERE OUR PARENTS ARE: STILL ON THE *RUN* FROM THE DEBT COLLECTORS.

YOU REALLY WANT TO FIND *THOSE PEOPLE,* WHO ABANDONED THEIR KIDS TO BE RAISED BY NUTSO UNCLE PHIL WHO WAS MORE INTERESTED IN HIS GUN COLLECTION THAN US?

KNOCK YOURSELF OUT.

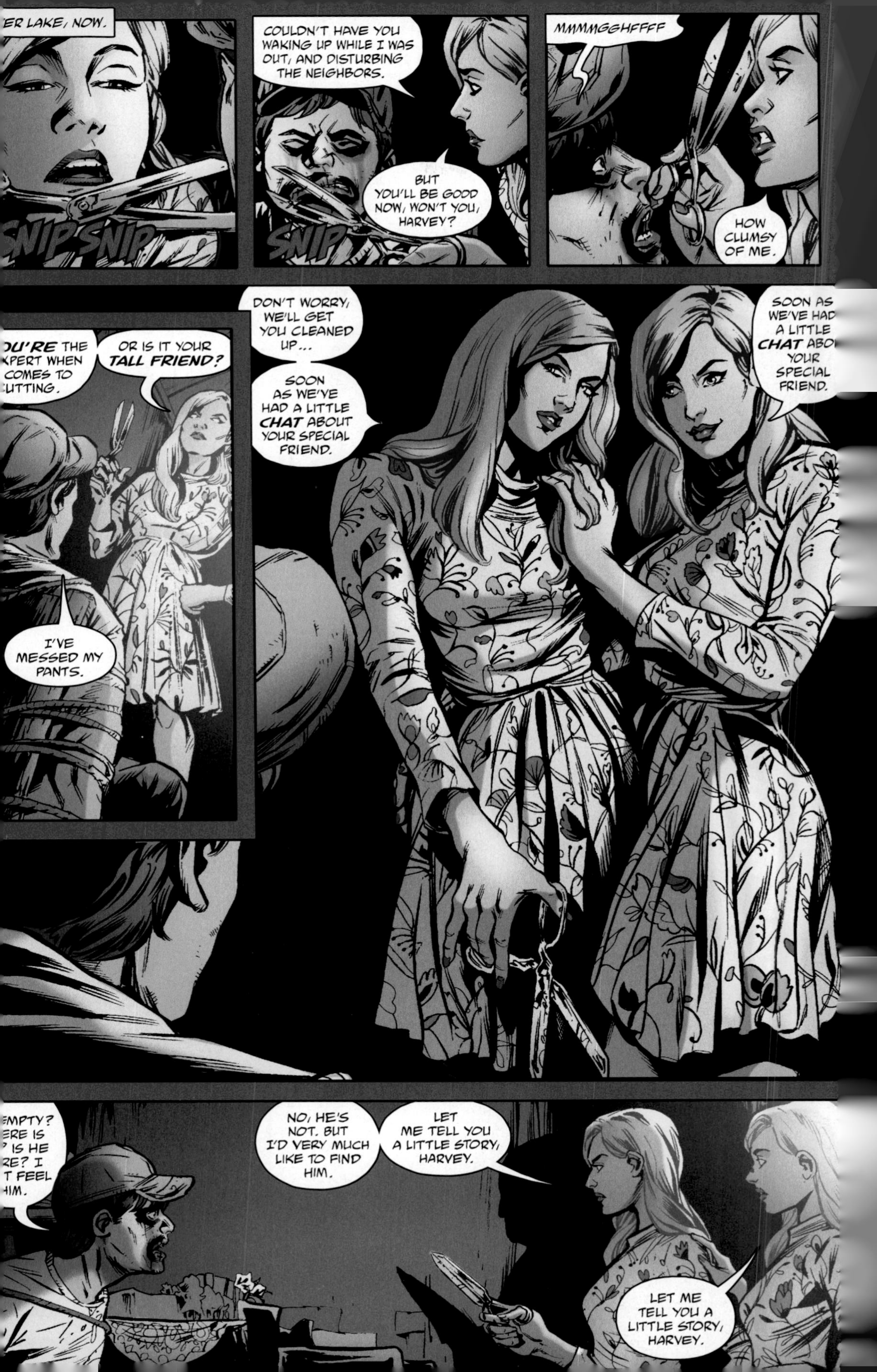
ER LAKE, NOW.
SNIP SNIP
COULDN'T HAVE YOU WAKING UP WHILE I WAS OUT, AND DISTURBING THE NEIGHBORS.
BUT YOU'LL BE GOOD NOW, WON'T YOU, HARVEY?
SNIP
MMMMGGHFFFF
HOW CLUMSY OF ME.
OU'RE THE XPERT WHEN COMES TO UTTING.
OR IS IT YOUR TALL FRIEND?
I'VE MESSED MY PANTS.
DON'T WORRY, WE'LL GET YOU CLEANED UP...
SOON AS WE'VE HAD A LITTLE CHAT ABOUT YOUR SPECIAL FRIEND.
SOON AS WE'VE HAD A LITTLE CHAT ABO YOUR SPECIAL FRIEND.
EMPTY? ERE IS IS HE RE? I T FEEL HIM.
NO, HE'S NOT. BUT I'D VERY MUCH LIKE TO FIND HIM.
LET ME TELL YOU A LITTLE STORY, HARVEY.
LET ME TELL YOU A LITTLE STORY, HARVEY.

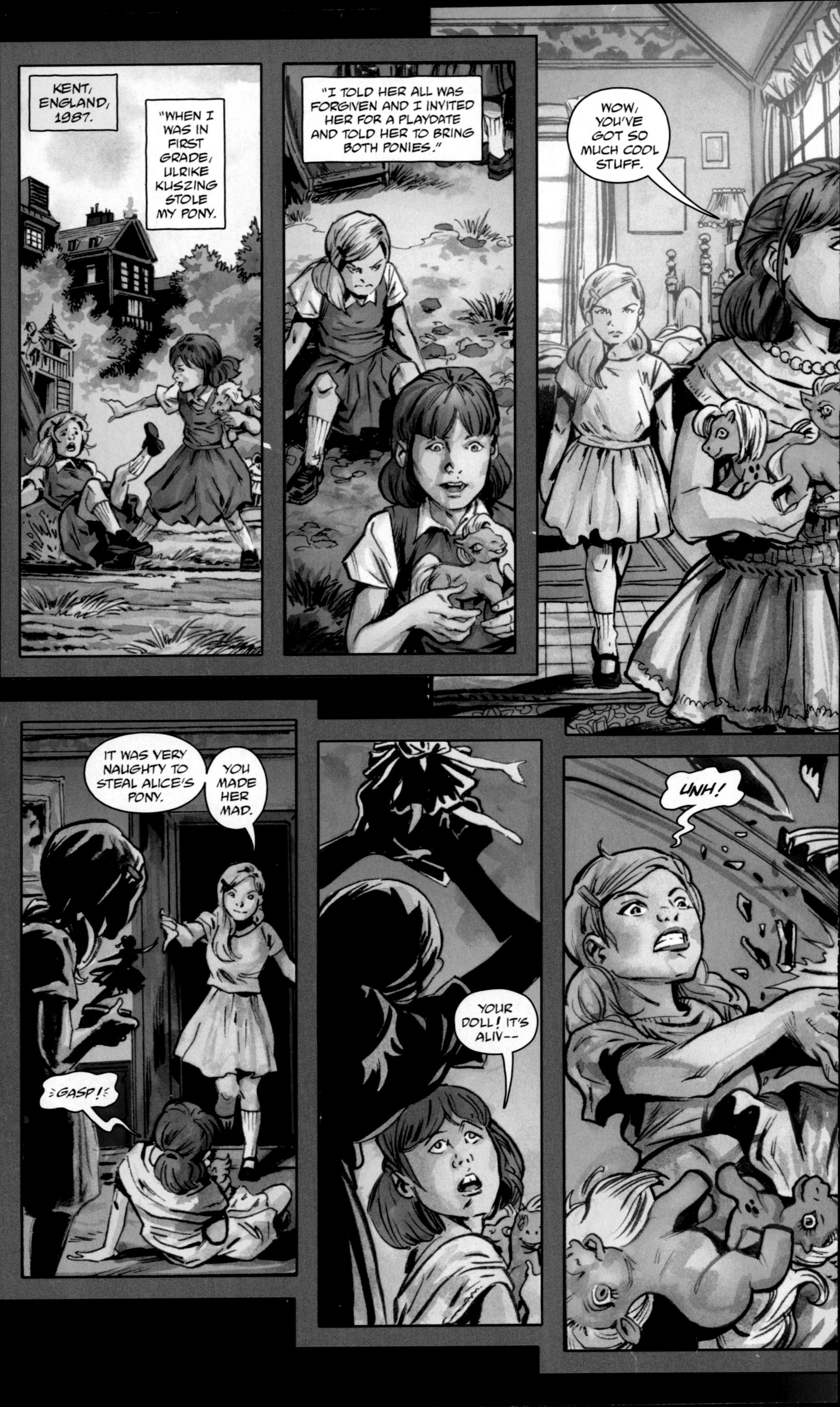

KENT, ENGLAND, 1987.
"WHEN I WAS IN FIRST GRADE, ULRIKE KUSZING STOLE MY PONY.
"I TOLD HER ALL WAS FORGIVEN AND I INVITED HER FOR A PLAYDATE AND TOLD HER TO BRING BOTH PONIES."
WOW, YOU'VE GOT SO MUCH COOL STUFF.
IT WAS VERY NAUGHTY TO STEAL ALICE'S PONY.
YOU MADE HER MAD.
GASP!
YOUR DOLL! IT'S ALIV--
UNH!

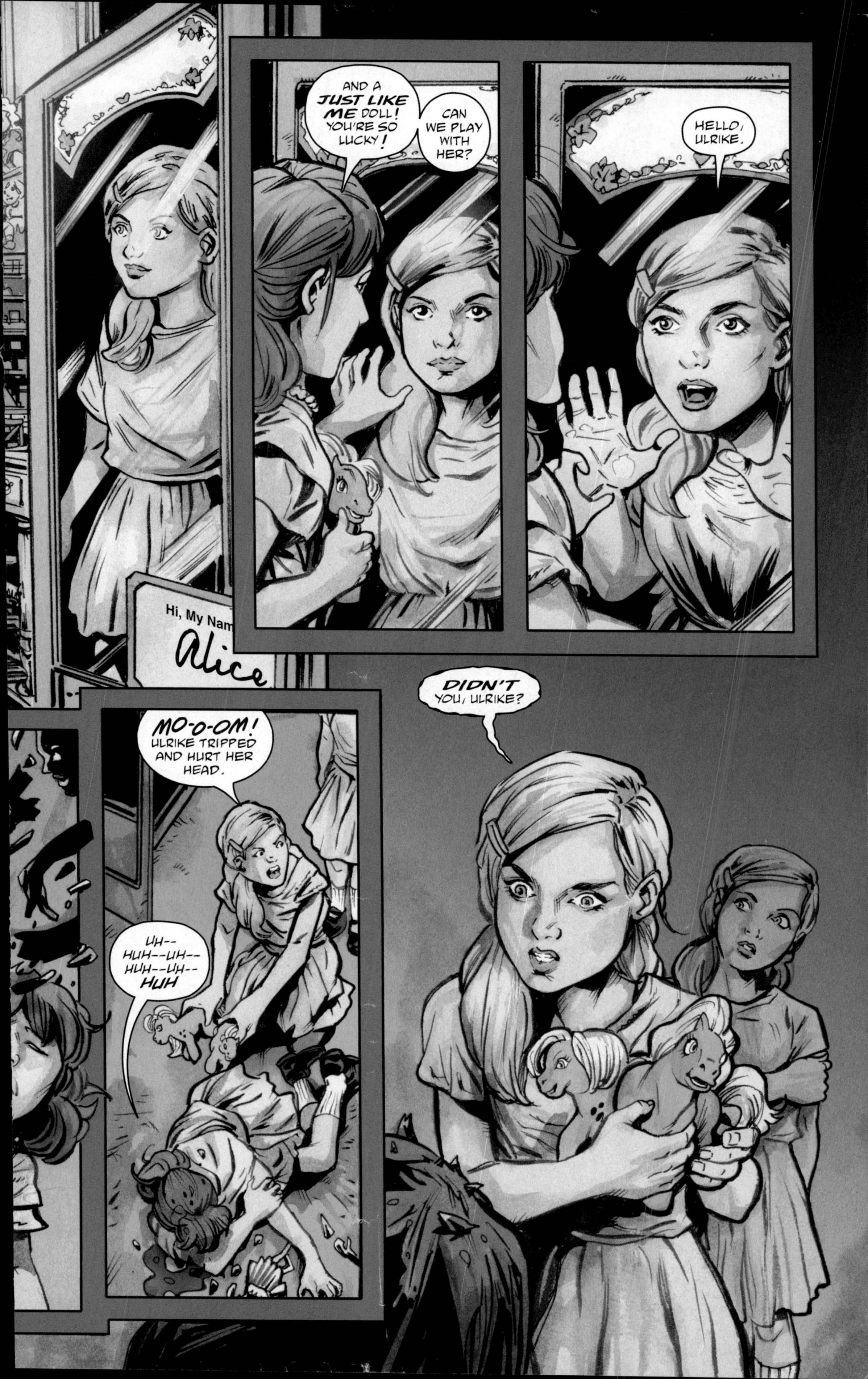
Hi, My Nam
Alice
AND A JUST LIKE ME DOLL! YOU'RE SO LUCKY!
CAN WE PLAY WITH HER?
HELLO, ULRIKE.
MO-O-OM! ULRIKE TRIPPED AND HURT HER HEAD.
UH-- HUH--UH-- HUH--UH-- HUH
DIDN'T YOU, ULRIKE?

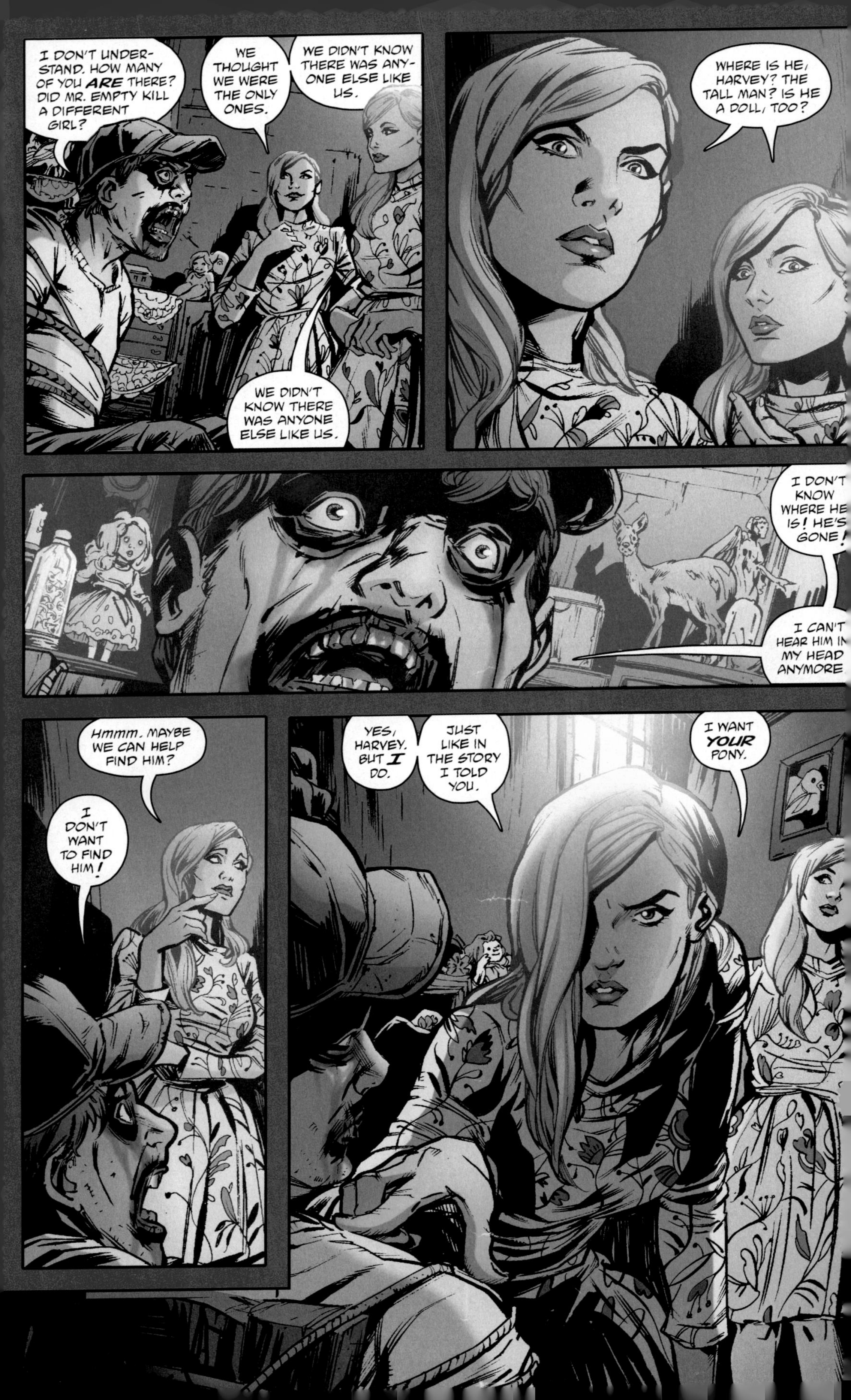
I DON'T UNDER-STAND. HOW MANY OF YOU **ARE** THERE? DID MR. EMPTY KILL A DIFFERENT GIRL?
WE THOUGHT WE WERE THE ONLY ONES.
WE DIDN'T KNOW THERE WAS ANY-ONE ELSE LIKE US.
WE DIDN'T KNOW THERE WAS ANYONE ELSE LIKE US.
WHERE IS HE, HARVEY? THE TALL MAN? IS HE A DOLL, TOO?
I DON'T KNOW WHERE HE IS! HE'S GONE!
I CAN'T HEAR HIM IN MY HEAD ANYMORE
Hmmm. MAYBE WE CAN HELP FIND HIM?
I DON'T WANT TO FIND HIM!
YES, HARVEY. BUT **I** DO.
JUST LIKE IN THE STORY I TOLD YOU.
I WANT **YOUR** PONY.

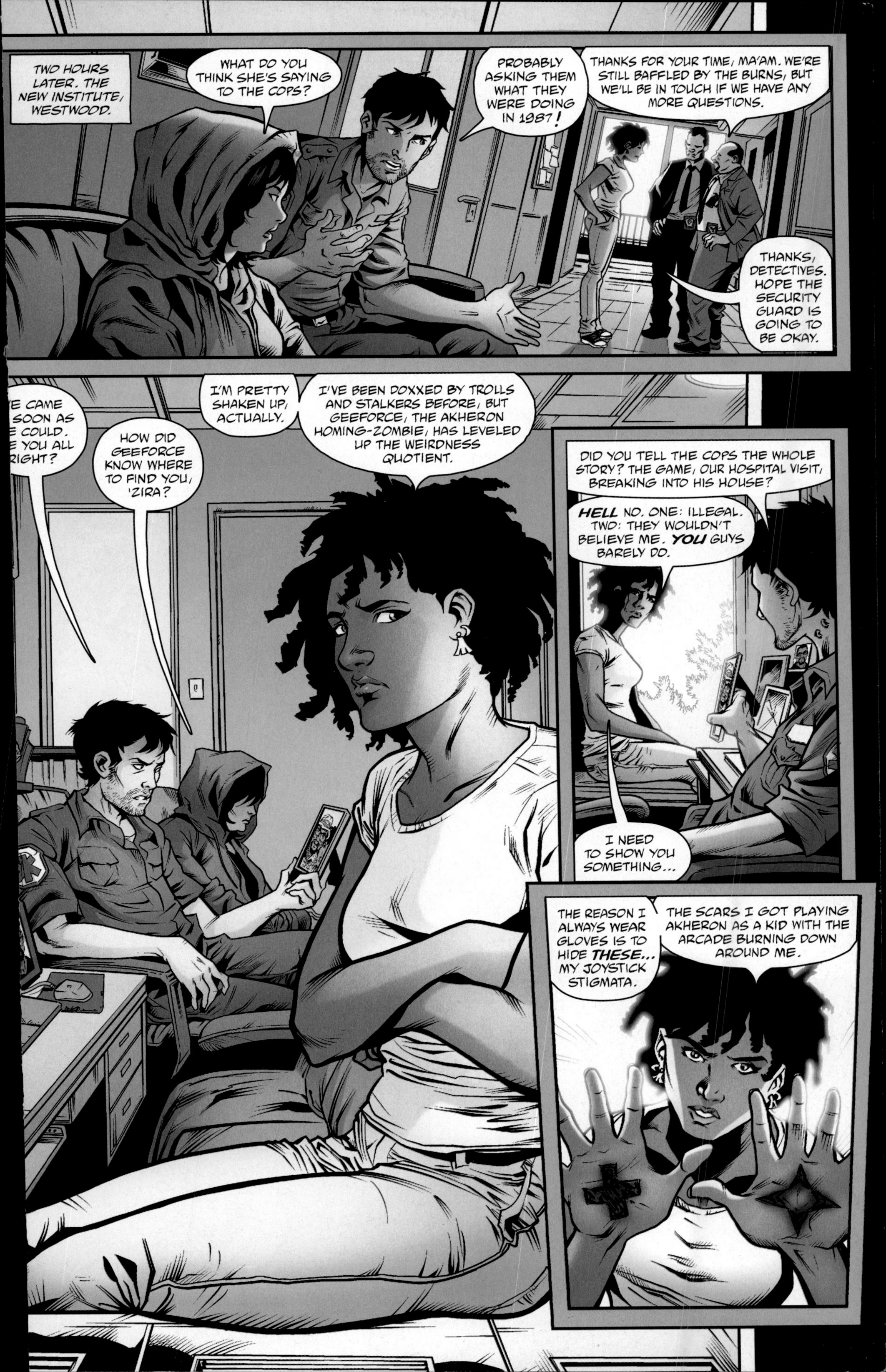
TWO HOURS LATER. THE NEW INSTITUTE, WESTWOOD.
WHAT DO YOU THINK SHE'S SAYING TO THE COPS?
PROBABLY ASKING THEM WHAT THEY WERE DOING IN 1987!
THANKS FOR YOUR TIME, MA'AM. WE'RE STILL BAFFLED BY THE BURNS, BUT WE'LL BE IN TOUCH IF WE HAVE ANY MORE QUESTIONS.
THANKS, DETECTIVES. HOPE THE SECURITY GUARD IS GOING TO BE OKAY.
SOON AS
COULD.
YOU ALL
RIGHT?
HOW DID GEEFORCE KNOW WHERE TO FIND YOU, 'ZIRA?
I'M PRETTY SHAKEN UP, ACTUALLY.
I'VE BEEN DOXXED BY TROLLS AND STALKERS BEFORE, BUT GEEFORCE, THE AKHERON HOMING-ZOMBIE, HAS LEVELED UP THE WEIRDNESS QUOTIENT.
DID YOU TELL THE COPS THE WHOLE STORY? THE GAME, OUR HOSPITAL VISIT, BREAKING INTO HIS HOUSE?
HELL NO. ONE: ILLEGAL. TWO: THEY WOULDN'T BELIEVE ME. YOU GUYS BARELY DO.
I NEED TO SHOW YOU SOMETHING...
THE REASON I ALWAYS WEAR GLOVES IS TO HIDE THESE... MY JOYSTICK STIGMATA.
THE SCARS I GOT PLAYING AKHERON AS A KID WITH THE ARCADE BURNING DOWN AROUND ME.

YIKES. LOOKS LIKE THIRD-DEGREE BURNS. HORRIBLE THING TO HAPPEN TO A KID.

AND THEY'RE-- HOT? DO YOU HAVE A FEVER?

UHH...IT'S MORE COMPLICATED THAN THAT.

I TOOK A VIDEO TO SHOW YOU. CUZ IT'S TOO INSANE OTHERWISE.

WHERE DID YOU GET THAT MARK ON YOUR FACE, GEEFORCE? DID YOU HAVE IT BEFORE?

YOU DID THIS! YOU BURNED ME, PRINCESS! WHY DID YOU BURN ME?

MA'AM, I KNOW YOU'RE UPSET. YOU NEED TO BACK AWAY. STOP FILMING.

GOT A RATIONAL MEDICAL EXPLANATION FOR THAT, TEO?

ALL RIGHT.

SHIT.

NO.

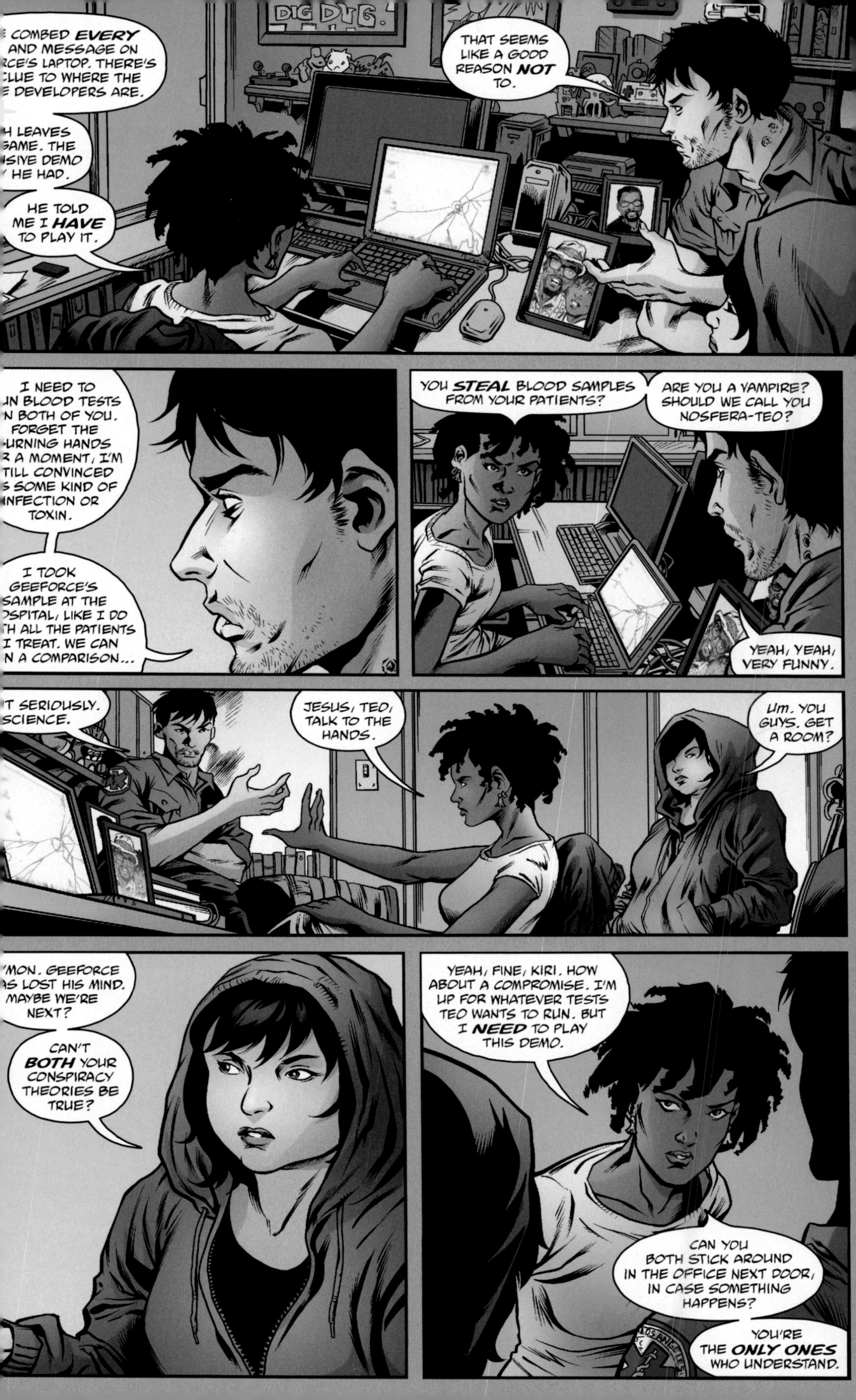
DIG DUG.
E COMBED EVERY AND MESSAGE ON RCE'S LAPTOP. THERE'S CLUE TO WHERE THE E DEVELOPERS ARE.
H LEAVES GAME. THE NSIVE DEMO HE HAD.
HE TOLD ME I HAVE TO PLAY IT.
THAT SEEMS LIKE A GOOD REASON NOT TO.
I NEED TO UN BLOOD TESTS N BOTH OF YOU. FORGET THE URNING HANDS R A MOMENT, I'M TILL CONVINCED S SOME KIND OF INFECTION OR TOXIN.
I TOOK GEEFORCE'S SAMPLE AT THE OSPITAL, LIKE I DO TH ALL THE PATIENTS I TREAT. WE CAN N A COMPARISON...
YOU STEAL BLOOD SAMPLES FROM YOUR PATIENTS?
ARE YOU A VAMPIRE? SHOULD WE CALL YOU NOSFERA-TEO?
YEAH, YEAH, VERY FUNNY.
T SERIOUSLY. SCIENCE.
JESUS, TEO, TALK TO THE HANDS.
UM. YOU GUYS. GET A ROOM?
'MON. GEEFORCE AS LOST HIS MIND. MAYBE WE'RE NEXT?
CAN'T BOTH YOUR CONSPIRACY THEORIES BE TRUE?
YEAH, FINE, KIRI. HOW ABOUT A COMPROMISE. I'M UP FOR WHATEVER TESTS TEO WANTS TO RUN. BUT I NEED TO PLAY THIS DEMO.
CAN YOU BOTH STICK AROUND IN THE OFFICE NEXT DOOR, IN CASE SOMETHING HAPPENS?
YOU'RE THE ONLY ONES WHO UNDERSTAND.

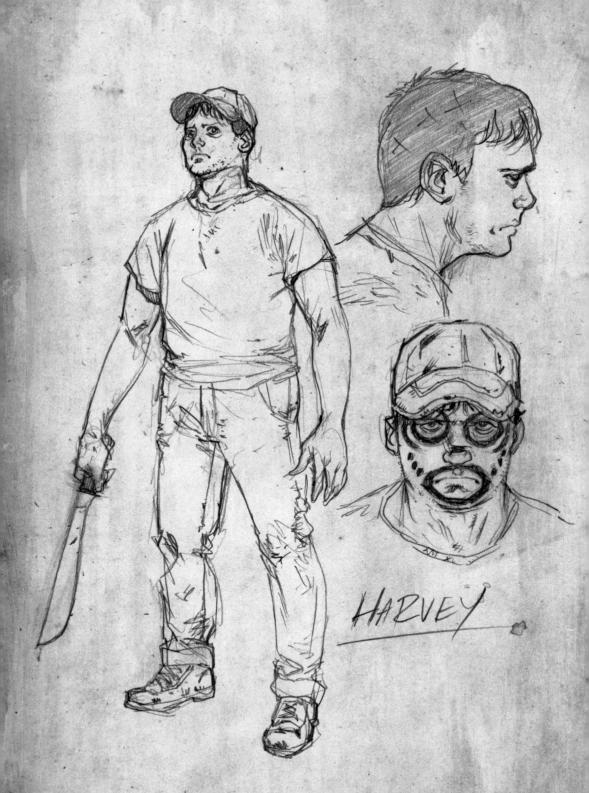

HARVEY

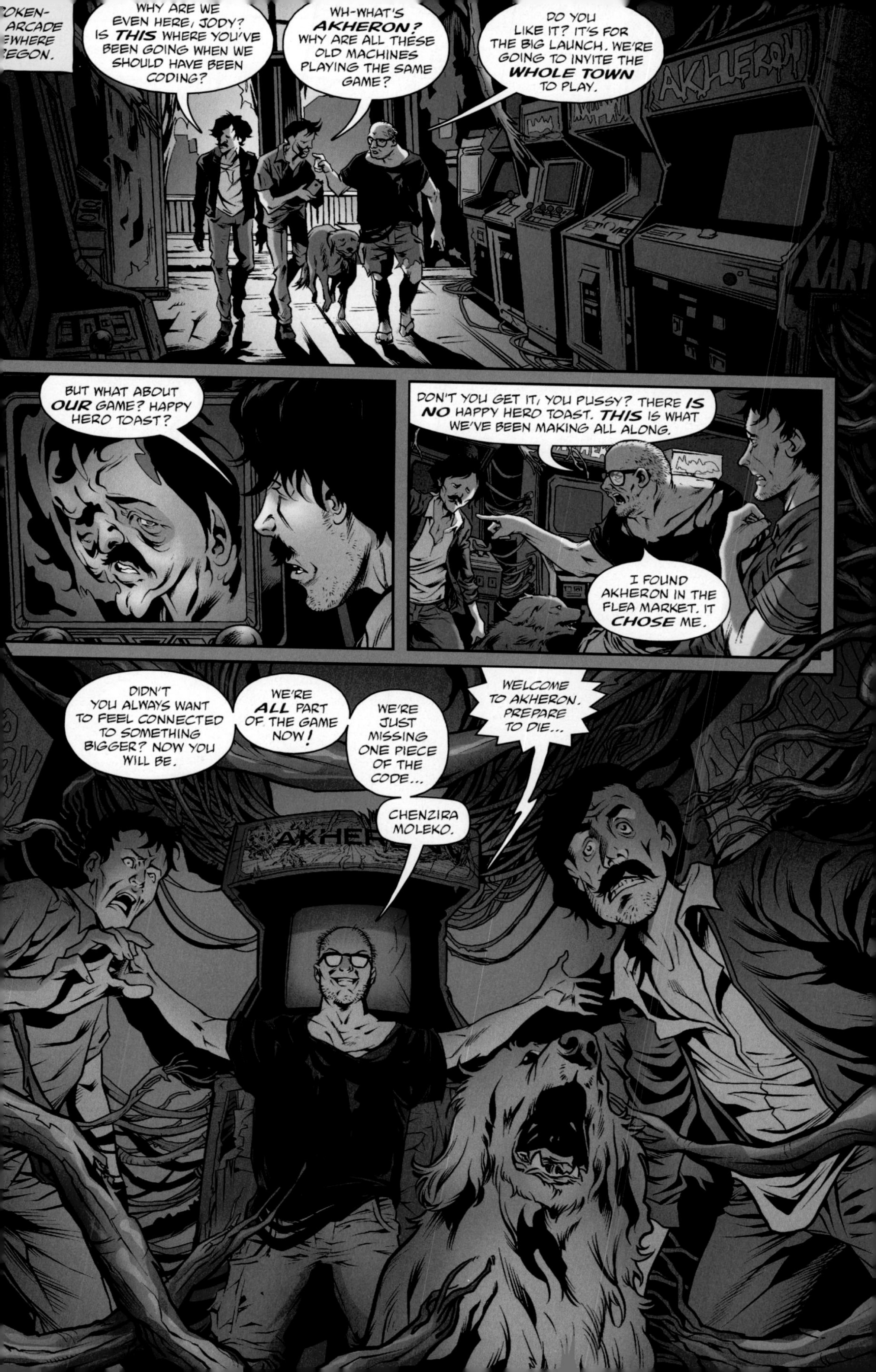
OKEN-
ARCADE
EWHERE
EGON.
WHY ARE WE EVEN HERE, JODY? IS **THIS** WHERE YOU'VE BEEN GOING WHEN WE SHOULD HAVE BEEN CODING?
WH-WHAT'S **AKHERON?** WHY ARE ALL THESE OLD MACHINES PLAYING THE SAME GAME?
DO YOU LIKE IT? IT'S FOR THE BIG LAUNCH. WE'RE GOING TO INVITE THE **WHOLE TOWN** TO PLAY.
BUT WHAT ABOUT **OUR** GAME? HAPPY HERO TOAST?
DON'T YOU GET IT, YOU PUSSY? THERE **IS NO** HAPPY HERO TOAST. **THIS** IS WHAT WE'VE BEEN MAKING ALL ALONG.
I FOUND AKHERON IN THE FLEA MARKET. IT **CHOSE** ME.
DIDN'T YOU ALWAYS WANT TO FEEL CONNECTED TO SOMETHING BIGGER? NOW YOU WILL BE.
WE'RE **ALL** PART OF THE GAME NOW!
WE'RE JUST MISSING ONE PIECE OF THE CODE...
CHENZIRA MOLEKO.
WELCOME TO AKHERON. PREPARE TO DIE...

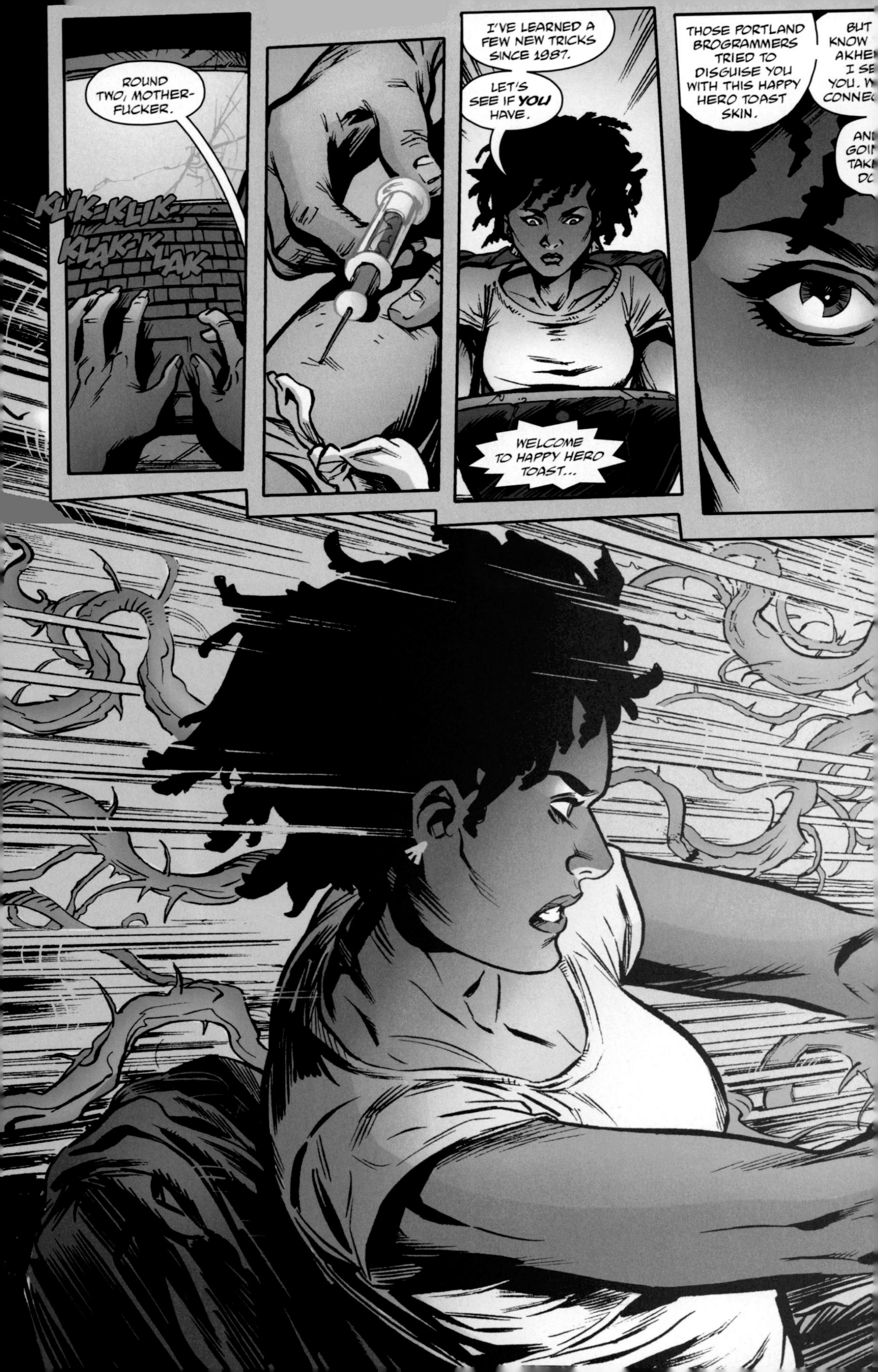
ROUND TWO, MOTHER-FUCKER.
KLIK-KLIK-KLAK-KLAK
I'VE LEARNED A FEW NEW TRICKS SINCE 1987.
LET'S SEE IF YOU HAVE.
WELCOME TO HAPPY HERO TOAST...
THOSE PORTLAND BROGRAMMERS TRIED TO DISGUISE YOU WITH THIS HAPPY HERO TOAST SKIN.

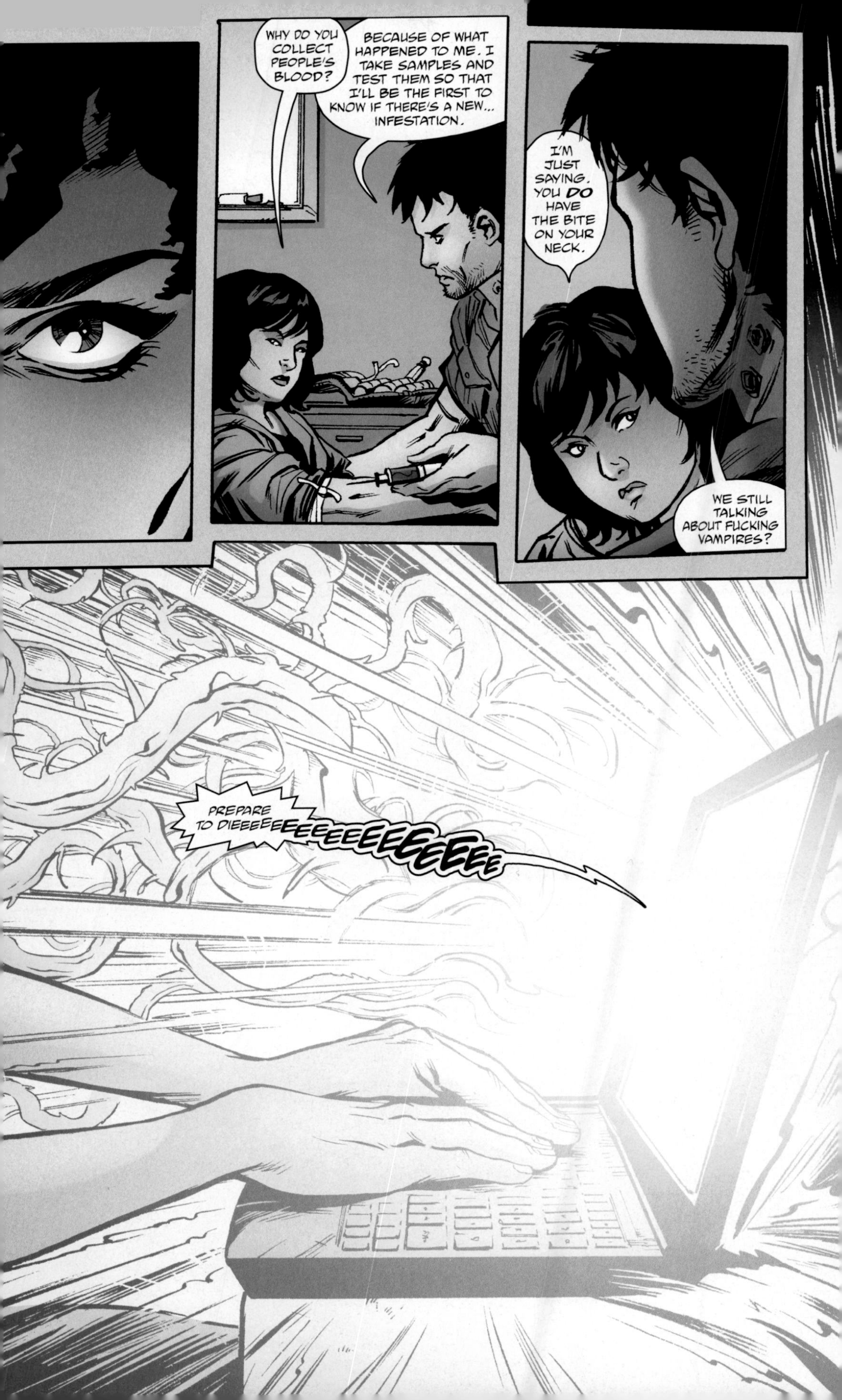

WHY DO YOU COLLECT PEOPLE'S BLOOD?
BECAUSE OF WHAT HAPPENED TO ME. I TAKE SAMPLES AND TEST THEM SO THAT I'LL BE THE FIRST TO KNOW IF THERE'S A NEW... INFESTATION.
I'M JUST SAYING. YOU **DO** HAVE THE BITE ON YOUR NECK.
WE STILL TALKING ABOUT FUCKING VAMPIRES?
PREPARE TO DIEEEEEEEEEEEEEEEEEEE

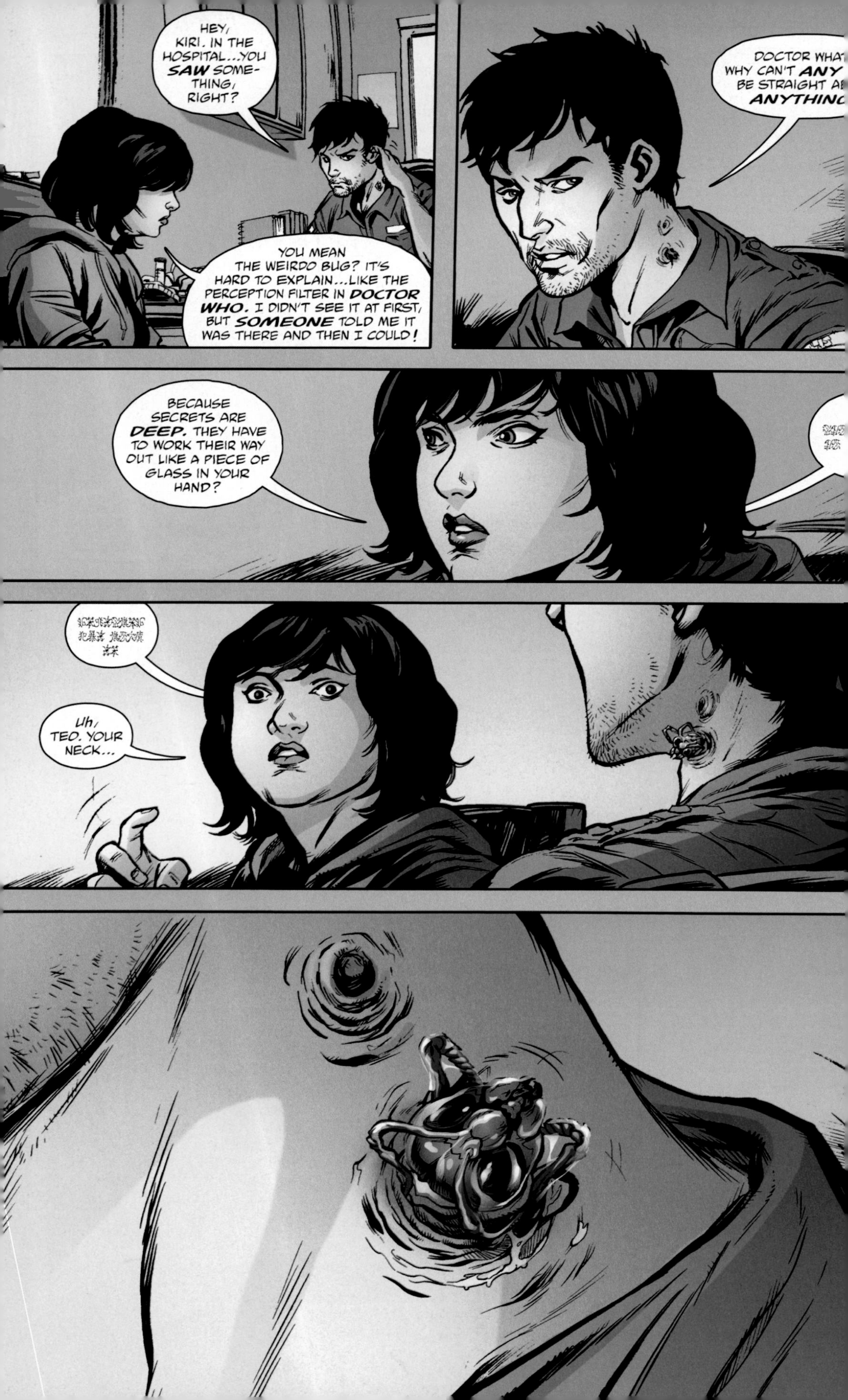
HEY, KIRI. IN THE HOSPITAL...YOU SAW SOMETHING, RIGHT?
YOU MEAN THE WEIRDO BUG? IT'S HARD TO EXPLAIN...LIKE THE PERCEPTION FILTER IN DOCTOR WHO. I DIDN'T SEE IT AT FIRST, BUT SOMEONE TOLD ME IT WAS THERE AND THEN I COULD!
DOCTOR WHAT WHY CAN'T ANY BE STRAIGHT A ANYTHING
BECAUSE SECRETS ARE DEEP. THEY HAVE TO WORK THEIR WAY OUT LIKE A PIECE OF GLASS IN YOUR HAND?
UH, TEO. YOUR NECK...

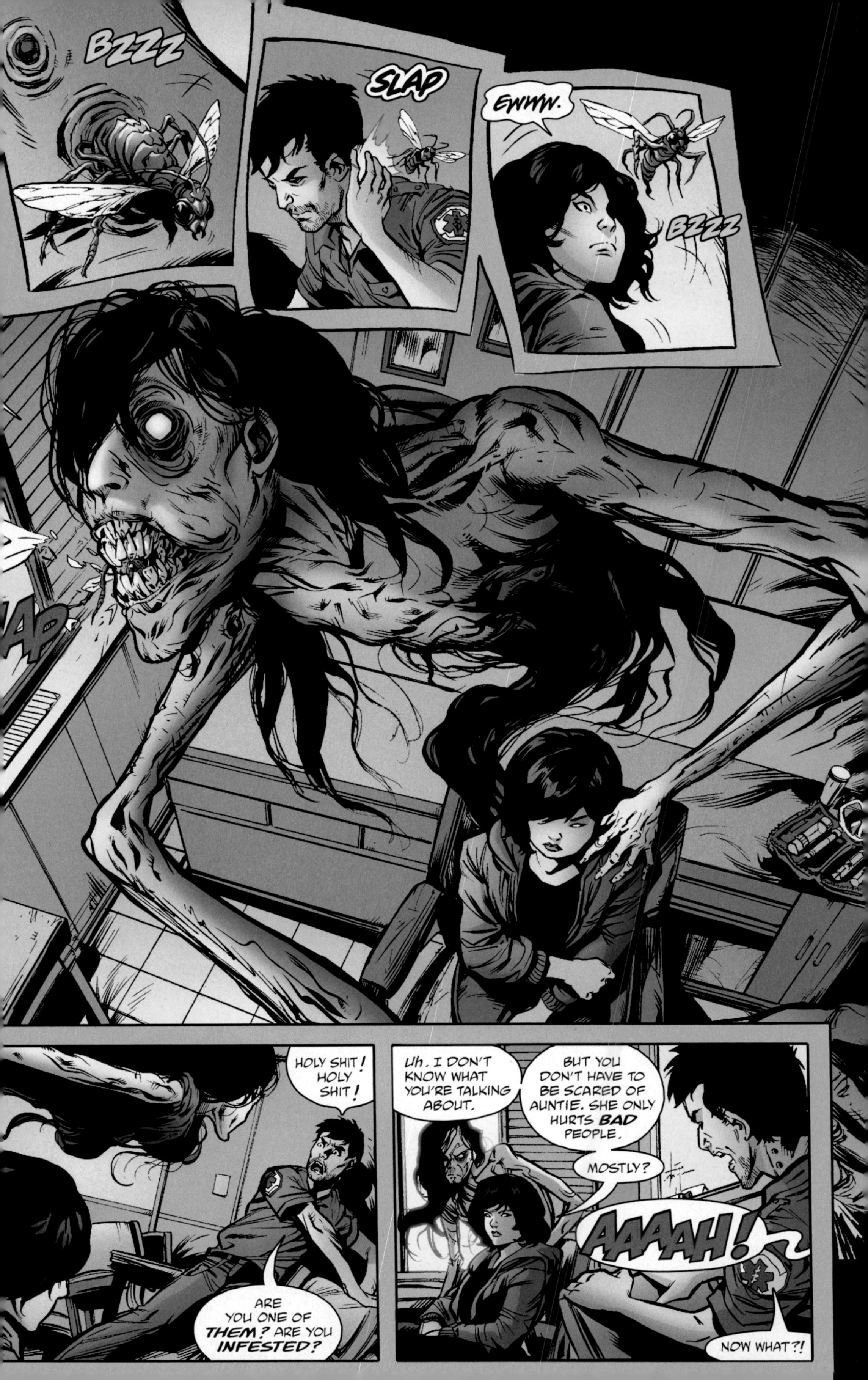
BZZZ
SLAP
EWWW.
BZZZ
AP
HOLY SHIT! HOLY SHIT!
ARE YOU ONE OF THEM? ARE YOU INFESTED?
UH. I DON'T KNOW WHAT YOU'RE TALKING ABOUT.
BUT YOU DON'T HAVE TO BE SCARED OF AUNTIE. SHE ONLY HURTS BAD PEOPLE.
MOSTLY?
AAAAH!
NOW WHAT?!

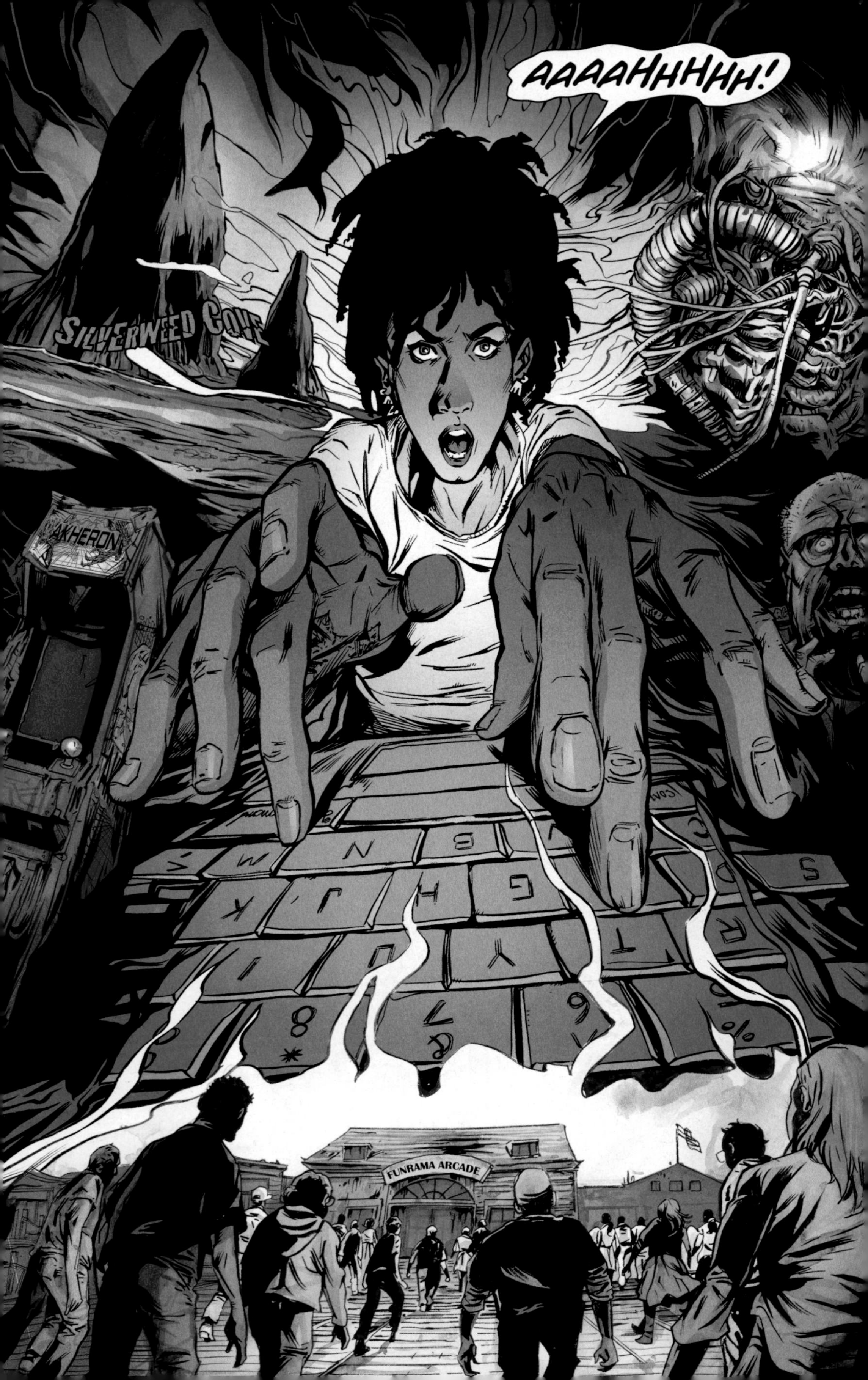
AAAAHHHHH!
SILVERWEED COVE
AKHERON
FUNRAMA ARCADE

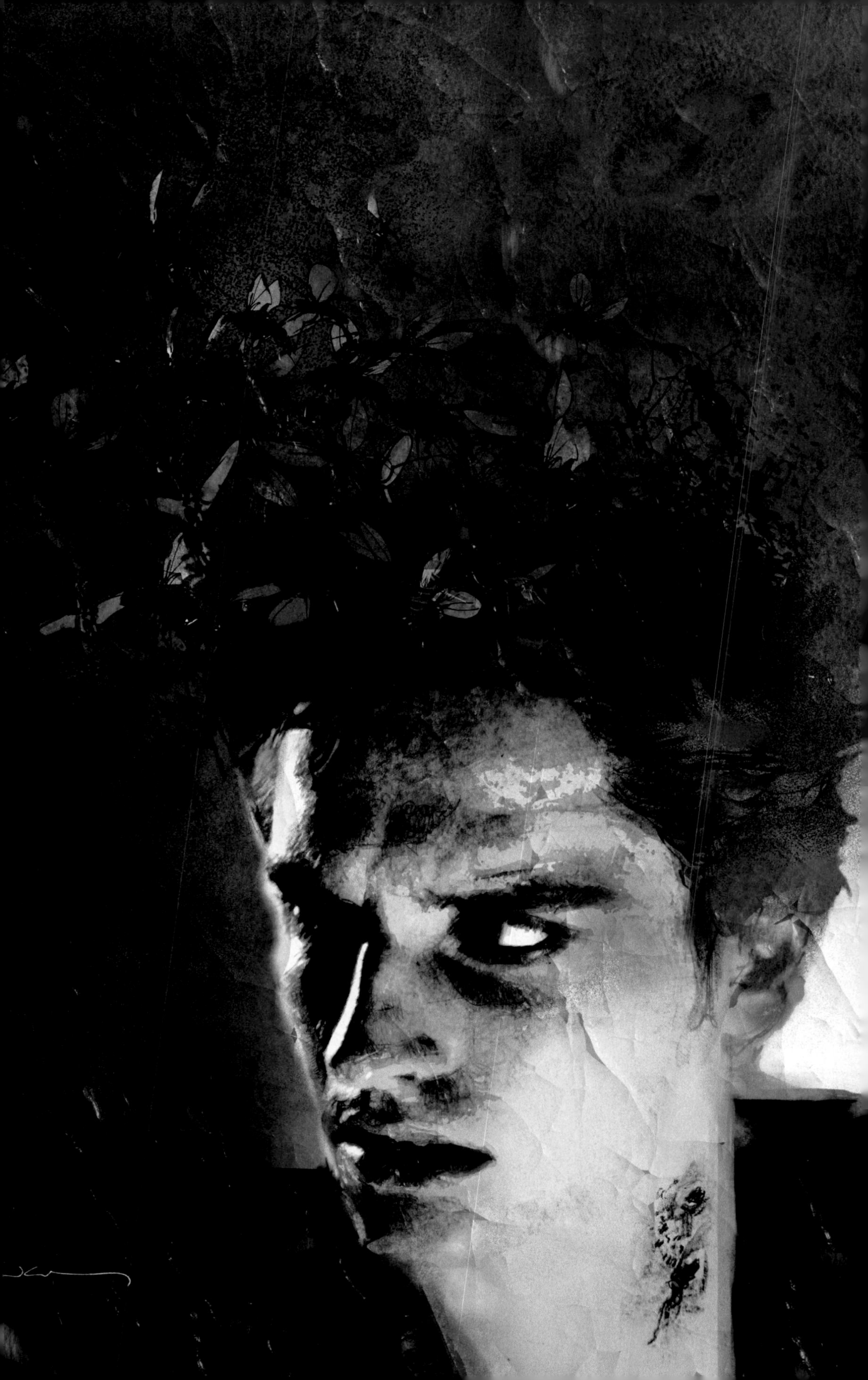

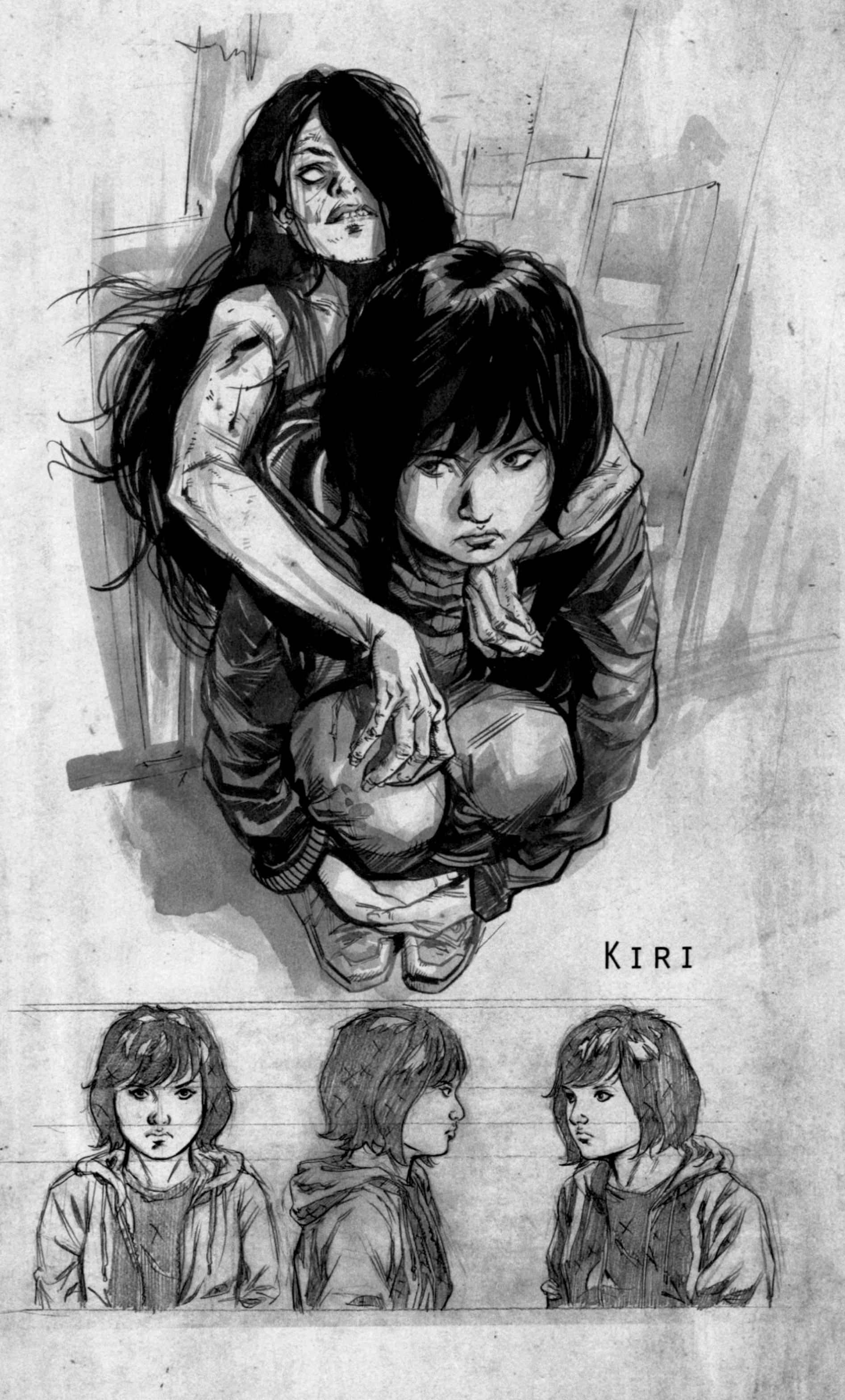
KIRI

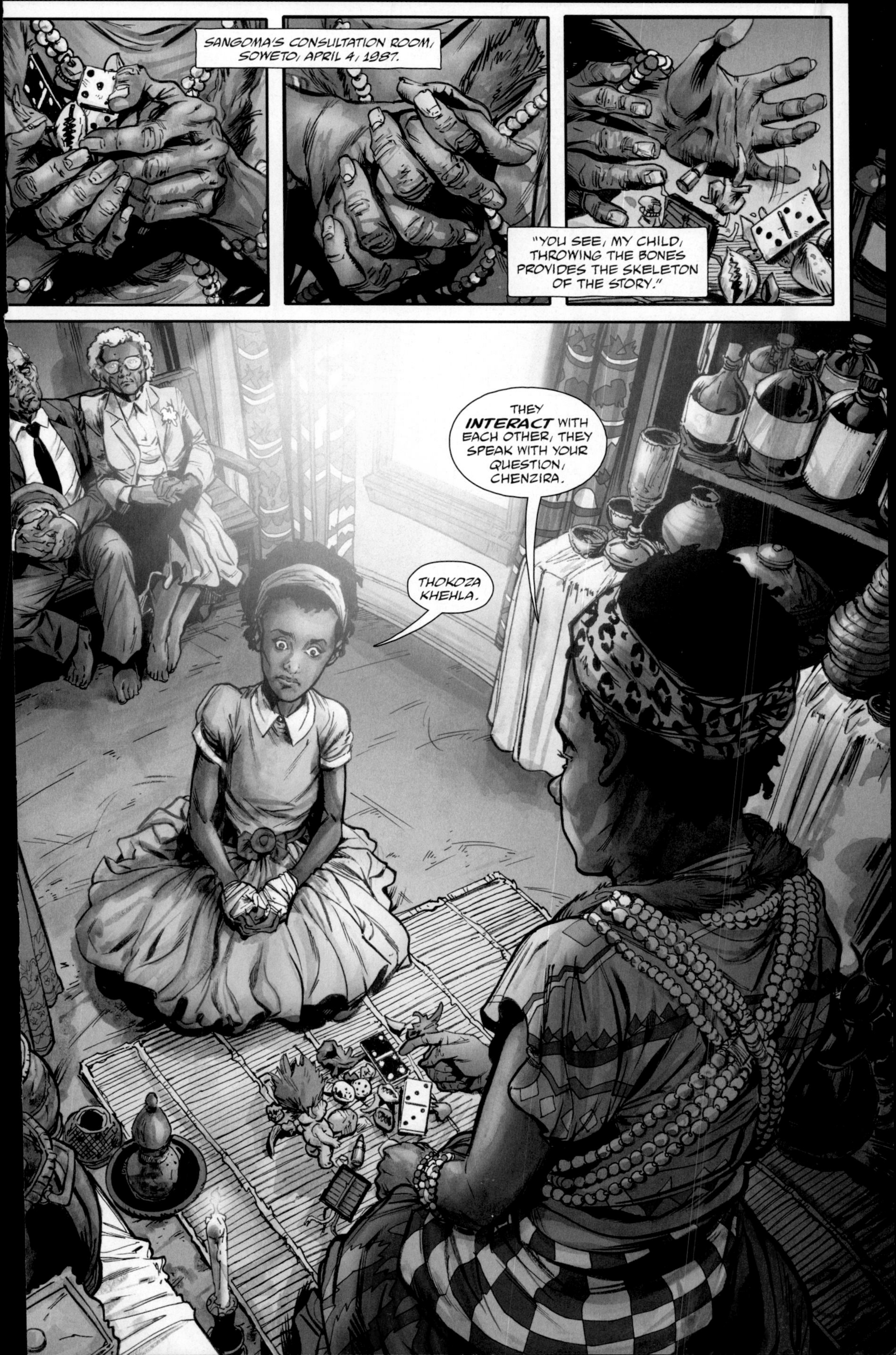
SANGOMA'S CONSULTATION ROOM, SOWETO, APRIL 4, 1987.
"YOU SEE, MY CHILD, THROWING THE BONES PROVIDES THE SKELETON OF THE STORY."
THEY **INTERACT** WITH EACH OTHER, THEY SPEAK WITH YOUR QUESTION, CHENZIRA.
THOKOZA KHEHLA.

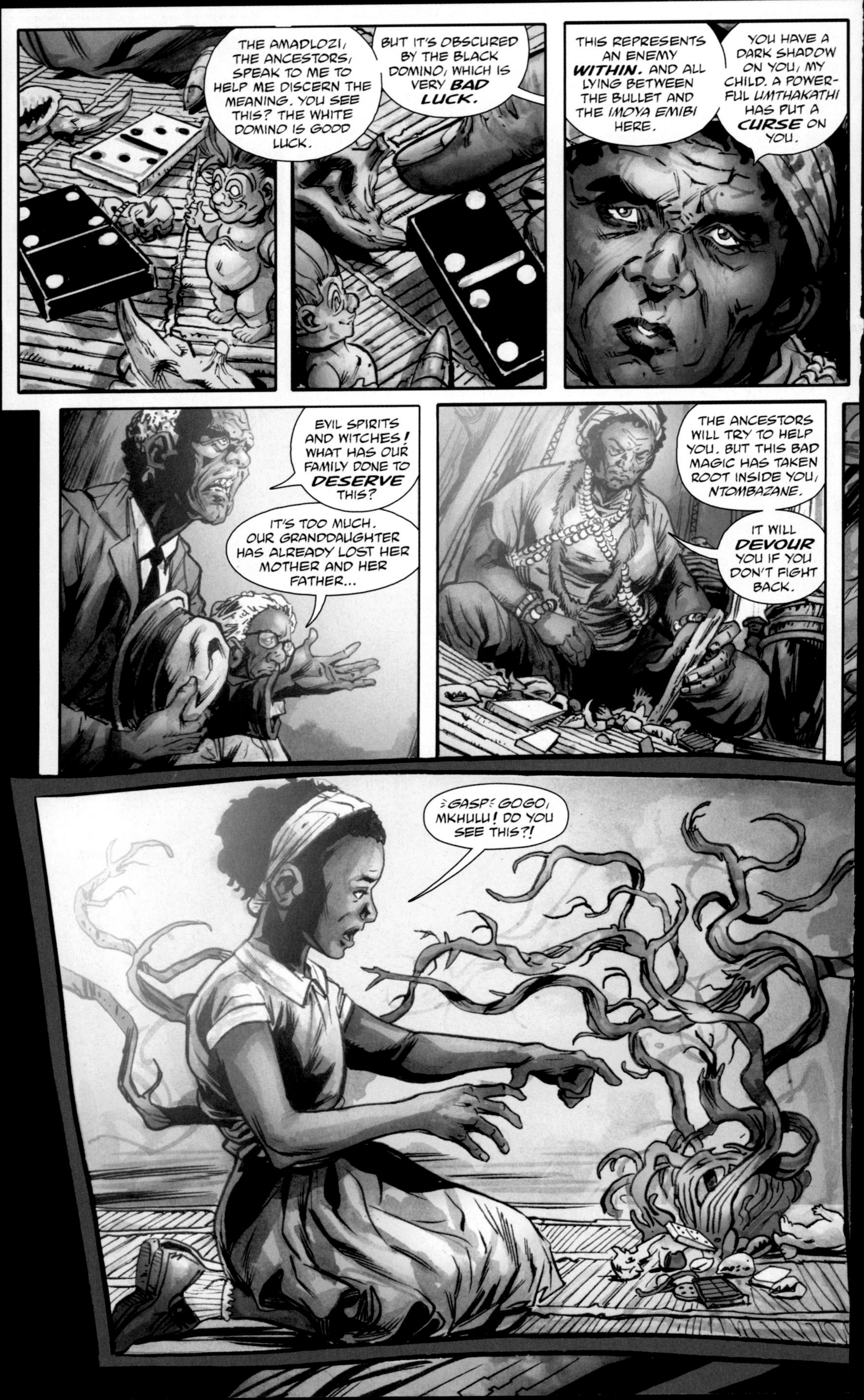
THE AMADLOZI, THE ANCESTORS, SPEAK TO ME TO HELP ME DISCERN THE MEANING. YOU SEE THIS? THE WHITE DOMINO IS GOOD LUCK.
BUT IT'S OBSCURED BY THE BLACK DOMINO, WHICH IS VERY BAD LUCK.
THIS REPRESENTS AN ENEMY WITHIN. AND ALL LYING BETWEEN THE BULLET AND THE IMOYA EMIBI HERE.
YOU HAVE A DARK SHADOW ON YOU, MY CHILD. A POWERFUL UMTHAKATHI HAS PUT A CURSE ON YOU.
EVIL SPIRITS AND WITCHES! WHAT HAS OUR FAMILY DONE TO DESERVE THIS?
IT'S TOO MUCH. OUR GRANDDAUGHTER HAS ALREADY LOST HER MOTHER AND HER FATHER...
THE ANCESTORS WILL TRY TO HELP YOU. BUT THIS BAD MAGIC HAS TAKEN ROOT INSIDE YOU, NTOMBAZANE.
IT WILL DEVOUR YOU IF YOU DON'T FIGHT BACK.
GASP GOGO, MKHULU! DO YOU SEE THIS?!

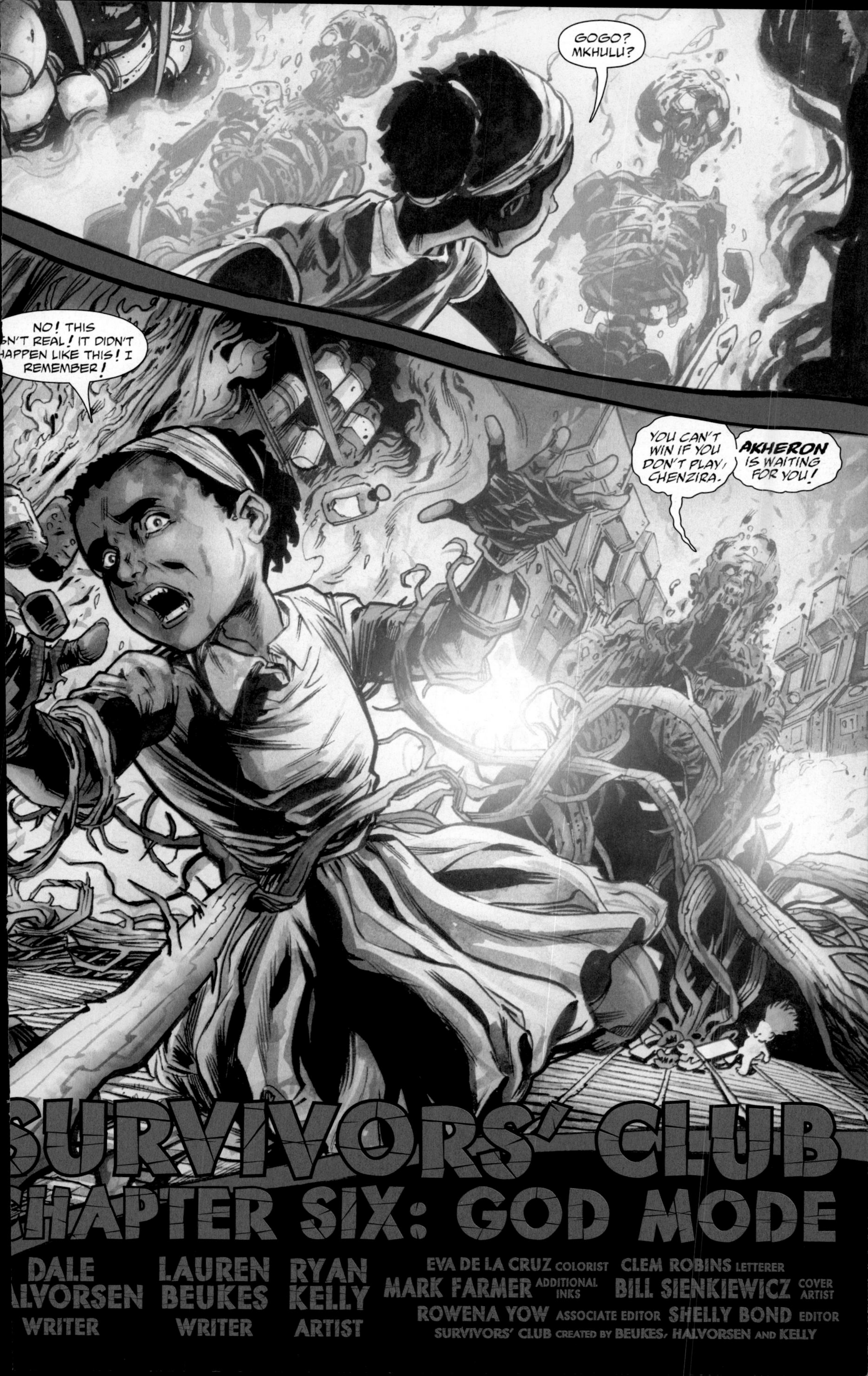
GOGO? MKHULU?
NO! THIS SN'T REAL! IT DIDN'T HAPPEN LIKE THIS! I REMEMBER!
YOU CAN'T WIN IF YOU DON'T PLAY, CHENZIRA.
AKHERON IS WAITING FOR YOU!
SURVIVORS' CLUB
HAPTER SIX: GOD MODE
DALE LVORSEN WRITER
LAUREN BEUKES WRITER
RYAN KELLY ARTIST
EVA DE LA CRUZ COLORIST
CLEM ROBINS LETTERER
MARK FARMER ADDITIONAL INKS
BILL SIENKIEWICZ COVER ARTIST
ROWENA YOW ASSOCIATE EDITOR
SHELLY BOND EDITOR
SURVIVORS' CLUB CREATED BY BEUKES, HALVORSEN AND KELLY

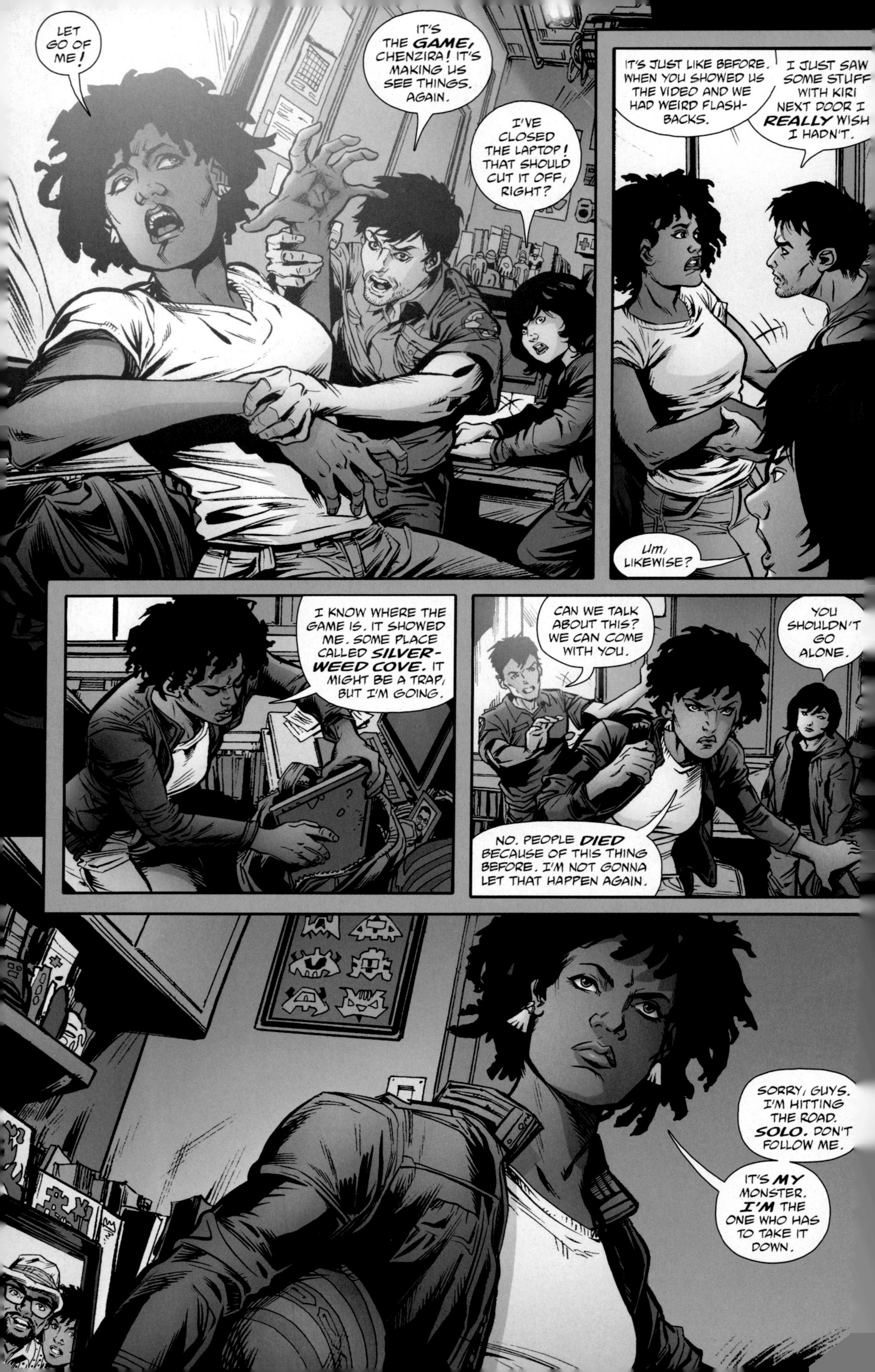
LET GO OF ME!
IT'S THE GAME, CHENZIRA! IT'S MAKING US SEE THINGS. AGAIN.
I'VE CLOSED THE LAPTOP! THAT SHOULD CUT IT OFF, RIGHT?
IT'S JUST LIKE BEFORE. WHEN YOU SHOWED US THE VIDEO AND WE HAD WEIRD FLASH-BACKS.
I JUST SAW SOME STUFF WITH KIRI NEXT DOOR I REALLY WISH I HADN'T.
UM, LIKEWISE?
I KNOW WHERE THE GAME IS. IT SHOWED ME. SOME PLACE CALLED SILVER-WEED COVE. IT MIGHT BE A TRAP, BUT I'M GOING.
CAN WE TALK ABOUT THIS? WE CAN COME WITH YOU.
YOU SHOULDN'T GO ALONE.
NO. PEOPLE DIED BECAUSE OF THIS THING BEFORE. I'M NOT GONNA LET THAT HAPPEN AGAIN.
SORRY, GUYS. I'M HITTING THE ROAD. SOLO. DON'T FOLLOW ME.
IT'S MY MONSTER. I'M THE ONE WHO HAS TO TAKE IT DOWN.

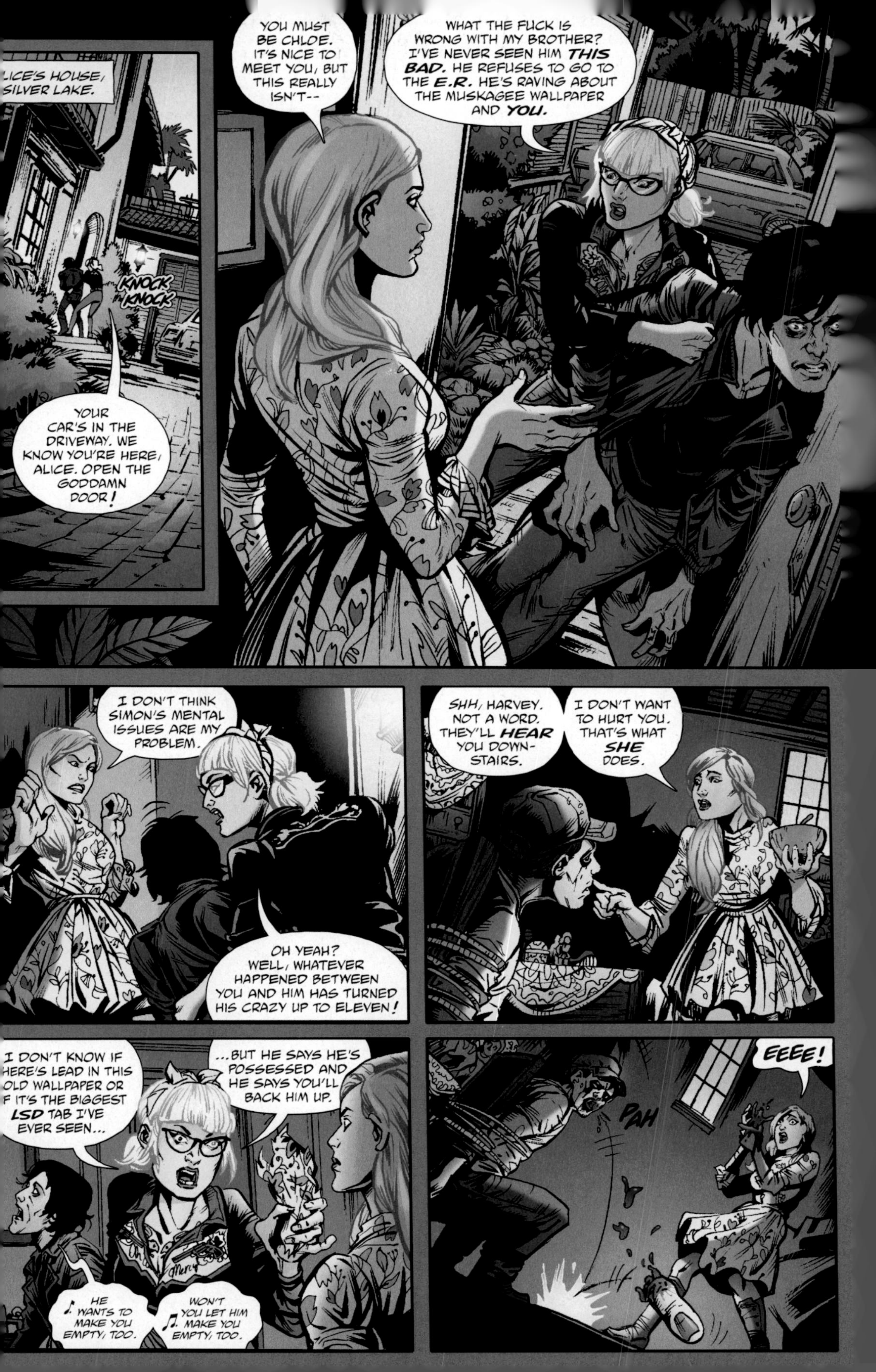
ALICE'S HOUSE, SILVER LAKE.
KNOCK KNOCK
YOUR CAR'S IN THE DRIVEWAY. WE KNOW YOU'RE HERE, ALICE. OPEN THE GODDAMN DOOR!
YOU MUST BE CHLOE. IT'S NICE TO MEET YOU, BUT THIS REALLY ISN'T--
WHAT THE FUCK IS WRONG WITH MY BROTHER? I'VE NEVER SEEN HIM THIS BAD. HE REFUSES TO GO TO THE E.R. HE'S RAVING ABOUT THE MUSKAGEE WALLPAPER AND YOU.
I DON'T THINK SIMON'S MENTAL ISSUES ARE MY PROBLEM.
OH YEAH? WELL, WHATEVER HAPPENED BETWEEN YOU AND HIM HAS TURNED HIS CRAZY UP TO ELEVEN!
SHH, HARVEY. NOT A WORD. THEY'LL HEAR YOU DOWNSTAIRS.
I DON'T WANT TO HURT YOU. THAT'S WHAT SHE DOES.
I DON'T KNOW IF THERE'S LEAD IN THIS OLD WALLPAPER OR IF IT'S THE BIGGEST LSD TAB I'VE EVER SEEN...
...BUT HE SAYS HE'S POSSESSED AND HE SAYS YOU'LL BACK HIM UP.
♪ HE WANTS TO MAKE YOU EMPTY, TOO.
♫ WON'T YOU LET HIM MAKE YOU EMPTY, TOO.
PAH
EEEE!

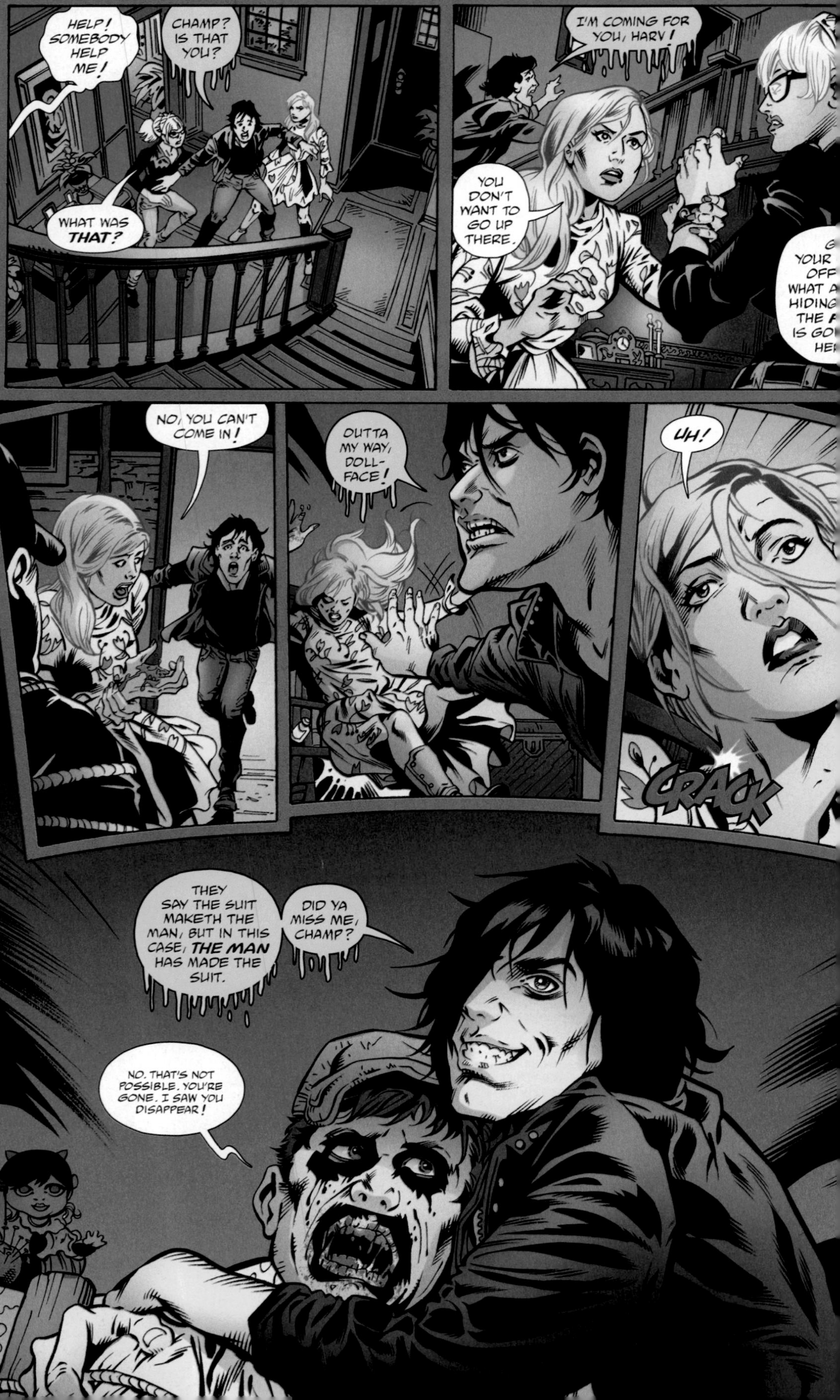
HELP! SOMEBODY HELP ME!
CHAMP? IS THAT YOU?
WHAT WAS THAT?
I'M COMING FOR YOU, HARV!
YOU DON'T WANT TO GO UP THERE.
NO, YOU CAN'T COME IN!
OUTTA MY WAY, DOLL-FACE!
UH!
CRACK
THEY SAY THE SUIT MAKETH THE MAN, BUT IN THIS CASE, THE MAN HAS MADE THE SUIT.
DID YA MISS ME, CHAMP?
NO. THAT'S NOT POSSIBLE. YOU'RE GONE. I SAW YOU DISAPPEAR!

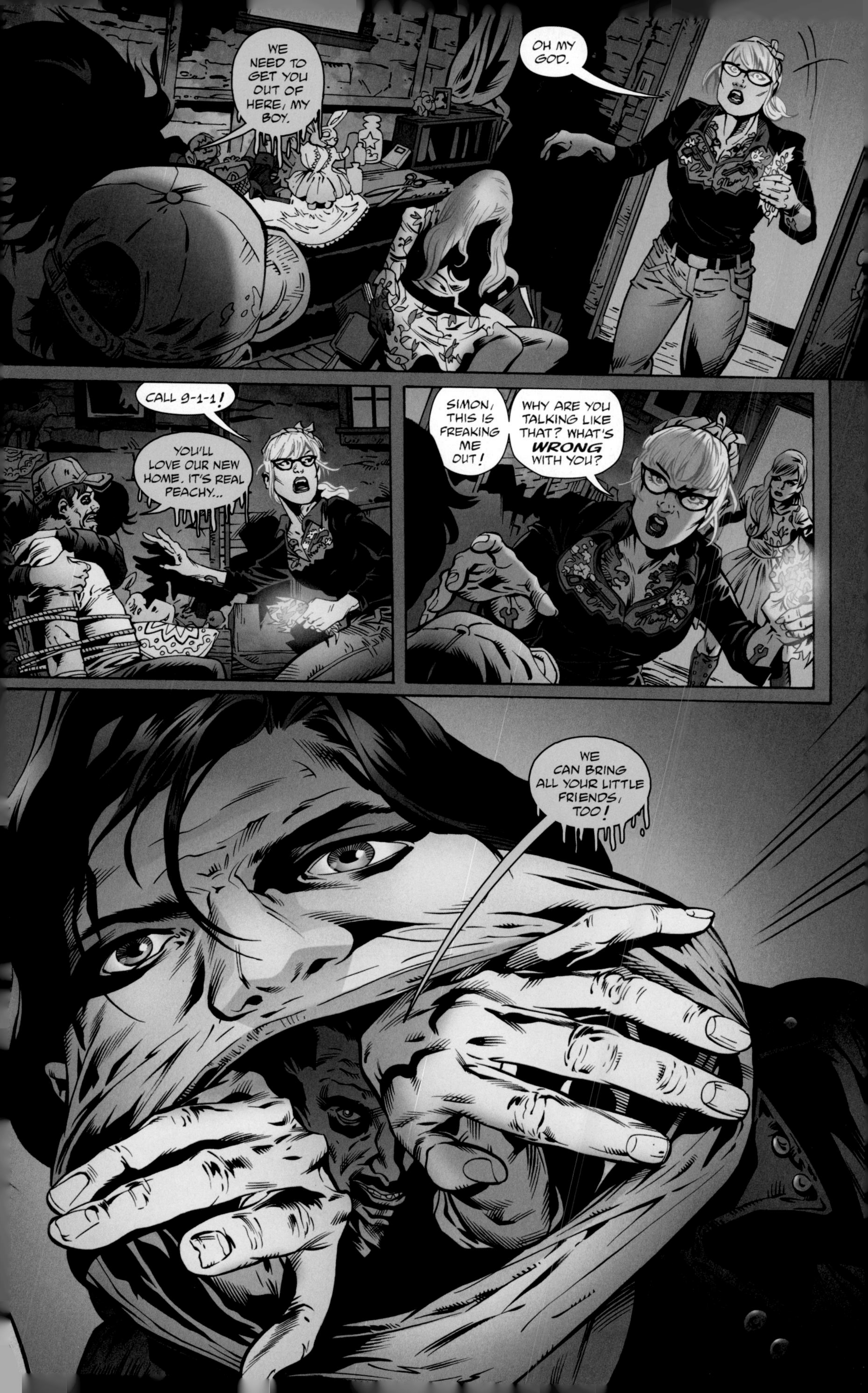
WE NEED TO GET YOU OUT OF HERE, MY BOY.
OH MY GOD.
CALL 9-1-1!
YOU'LL LOVE OUR NEW HOME. IT'S REAL PEACHY...
SIMON, THIS IS FREAKING ME OUT!
WHY ARE YOU TALKING LIKE THAT? WHAT'S **WRONG** WITH YOU?
WE CAN BRING ALL YOUR LITTLE FRIENDS, TOO!

PACIFIC COAST HIGHWAY.

"AT LEAST WE KNOW WHERE SHE'S GOING. BUT CHENZIRA PROBABLY HAS AN HOUR'S HEAD START ON US."

"HOW'S OUR BACKUP?"

YOU'VE REACHED **ALICE TAYLOR-NEWSOME.** LEAVE A MESSAGE AFTER THE BEEP.

NO ONE'S ANSWERING THEIR PHONES. BUT HEY, AT LEAST WE HAVE **AUNTIE.**

YEAH. ABOUT THAT...

YOU READY TO TELL ME YOUR 1987 STORY YET?

I WAS IN FIRST GRADE IN NAGASAKI. MY BEST FRIEND WAS MURDERED. IT WAS PRETTY HORRIBLE. THEY FOUND HER BODY IN THE GIRLS' RESTROOM. THAT'S WHEN **AUNTIE** CAME TO ME. SHE... HELPED.

I GUESS SHE'S LIKE A **YUREI?** A SPIRIT OF VENGEANCE.

IS SHE STILL VENGEFUL? CAN YOU CONTROL IT?

WELL, LET'S SAY I KEEP HER OCCUPIED. HOW ABOUT YOU?

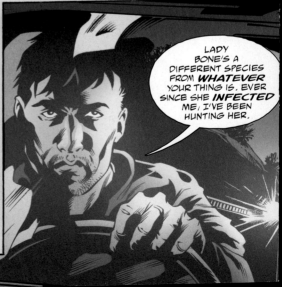

LADY BONE'S A DIFFERENT SPECIES FROM **WHATEVER** YOUR THING IS. EVER SINCE SHE **INFECTED** ME, I'VE BEEN HUNTING HER.

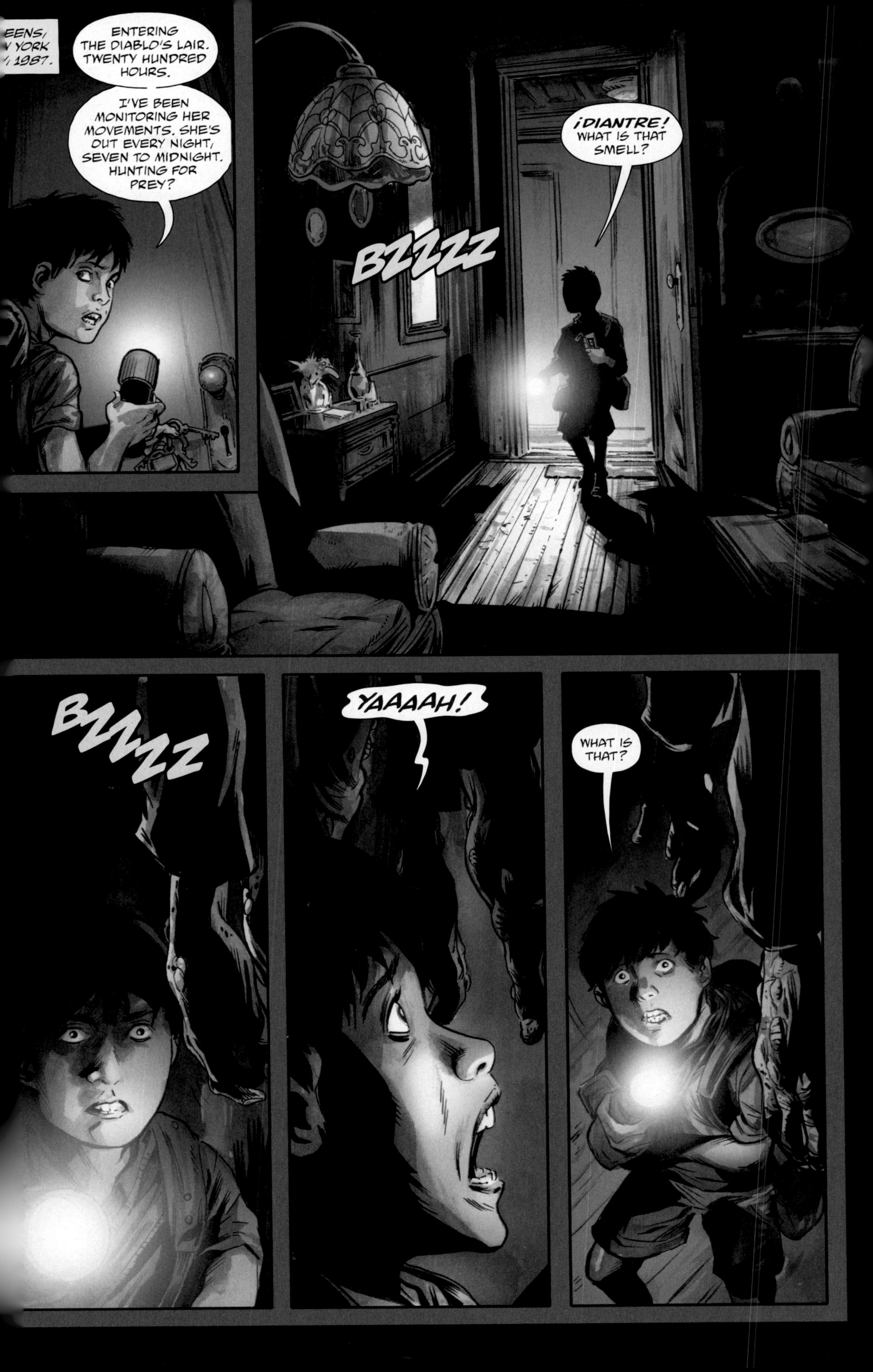
EENS,
Y YORK
, 1987.
ENTERING THE DIABLO'S LAIR. TWENTY HUNDRED HOURS.
I'VE BEEN MONITORING HER MOVEMENTS. SHE'S OUT EVERY NIGHT, SEVEN TO MIDNIGHT. HUNTING FOR PREY?
BZZZZ
¡DIANTRE! WHAT IS THAT SMELL?
BZZZZ
YAAAAH!
WHAT IS THAT?

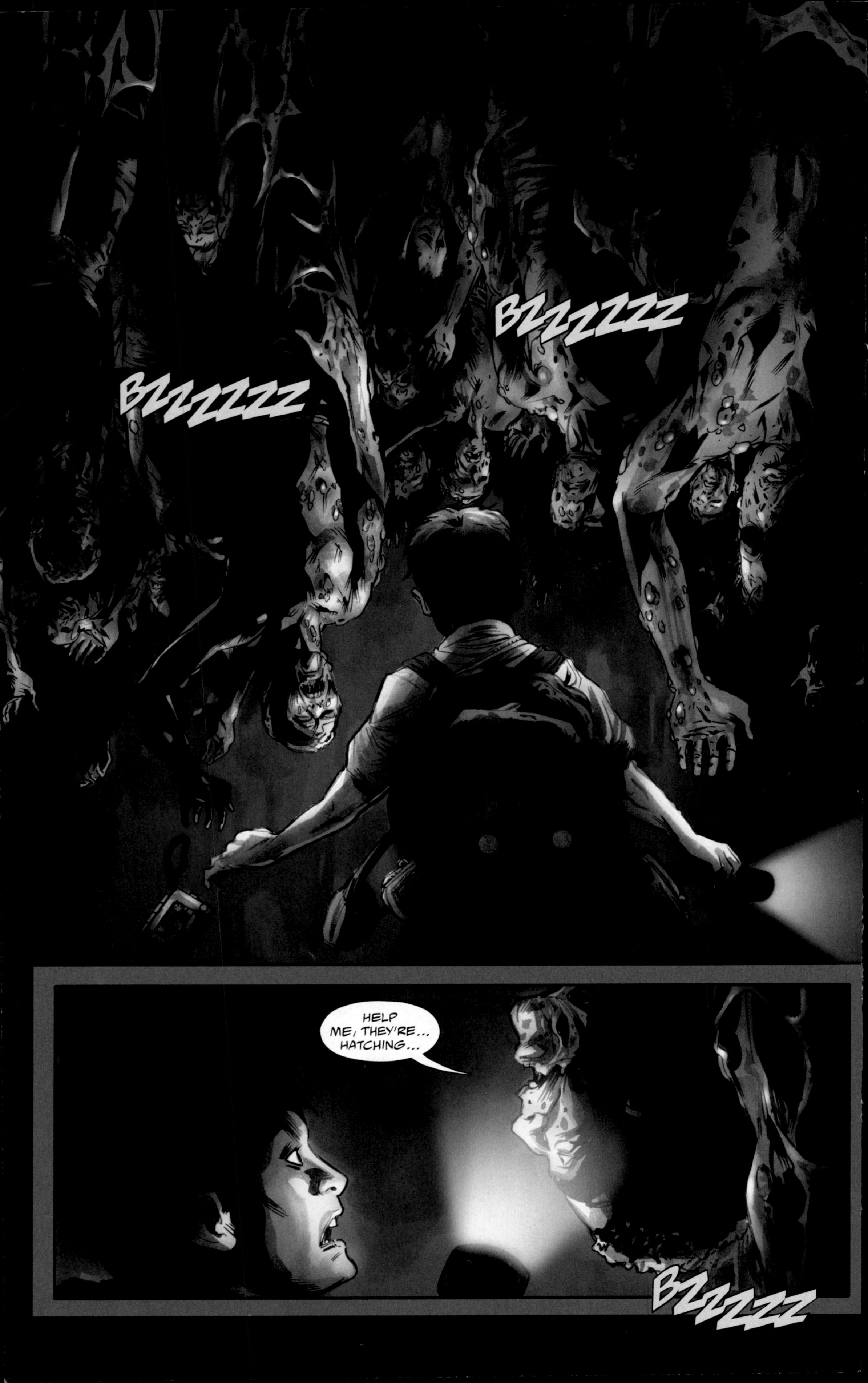
BZZZZZZ
BZZZZZZ
HELP ME, THEY'RE... HATCHING...
BZZZZZ

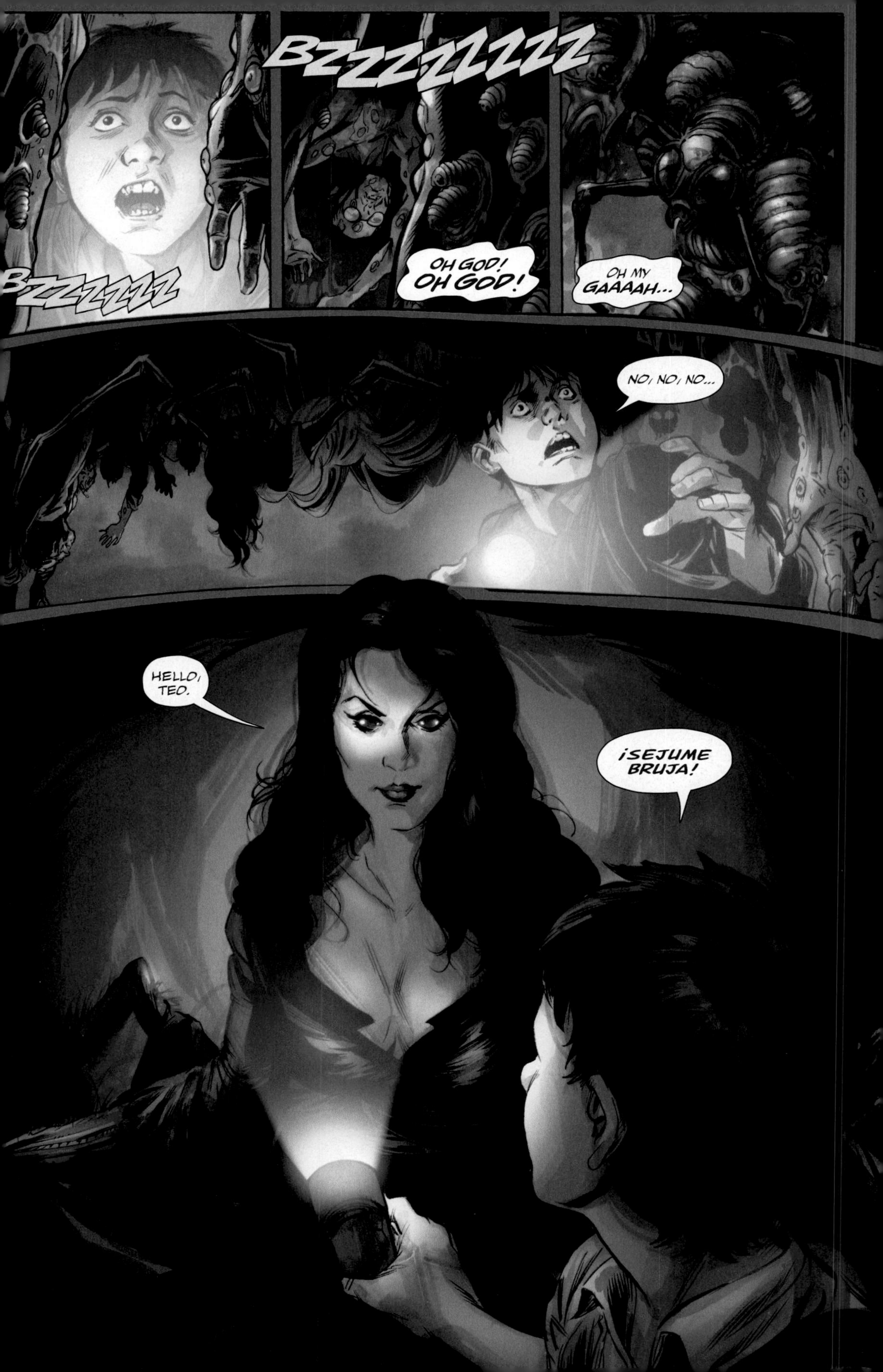
BZZZZZZZZZ
BZZZZZZZ
OH GOD! OH GOD!
OH MY GAAAAH...
NO, NO, NO...
HELLO, TEO.
¡SEJUME BRUJA!

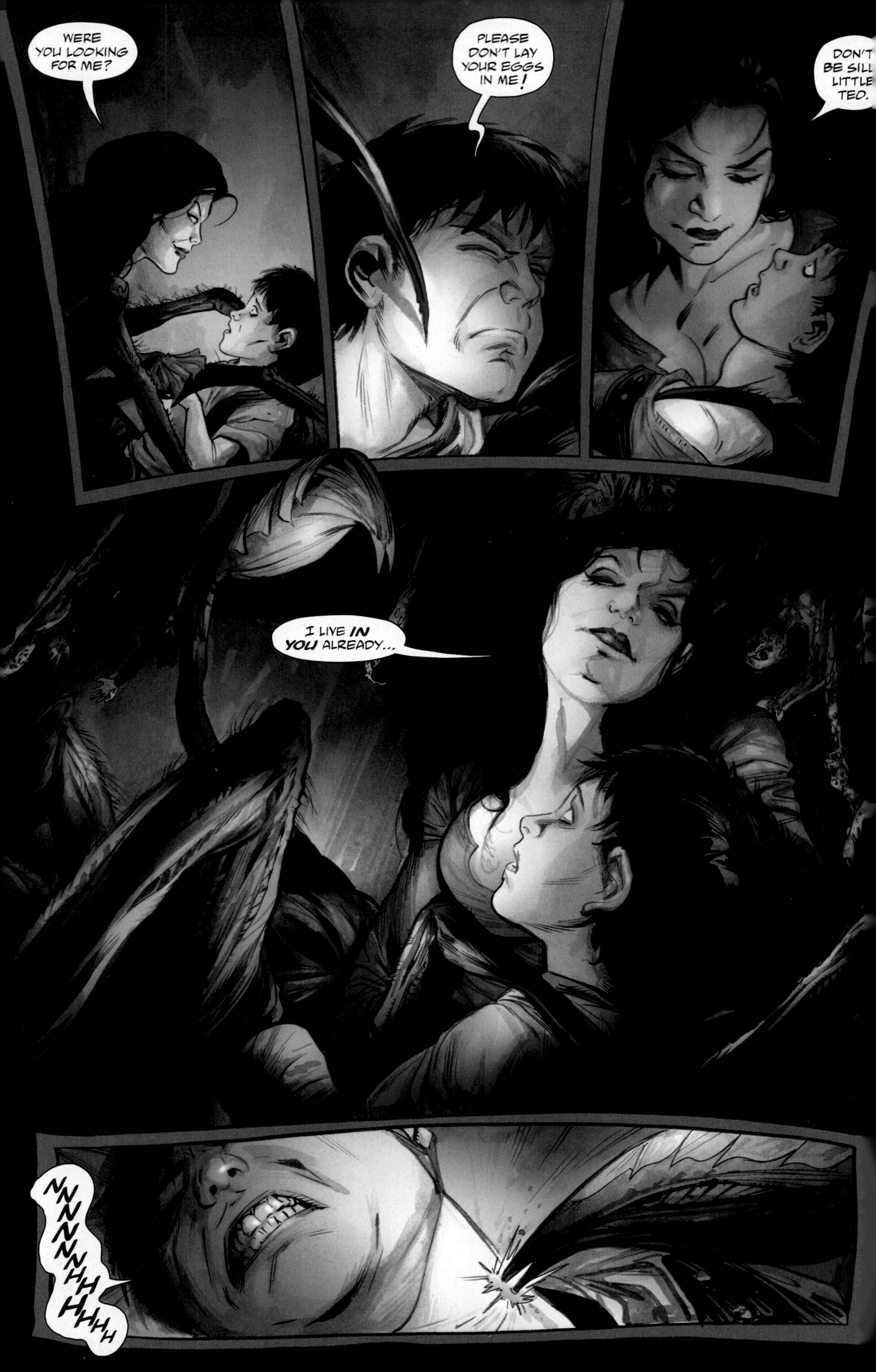
WERE YOU LOOKING FOR ME?
PLEASE DON'T LAY YOUR EGGS IN ME!
DON'T BE SILL LITTLE TEO.
I LIVE IN YOU ALREADY...
NNNNNHHHHH

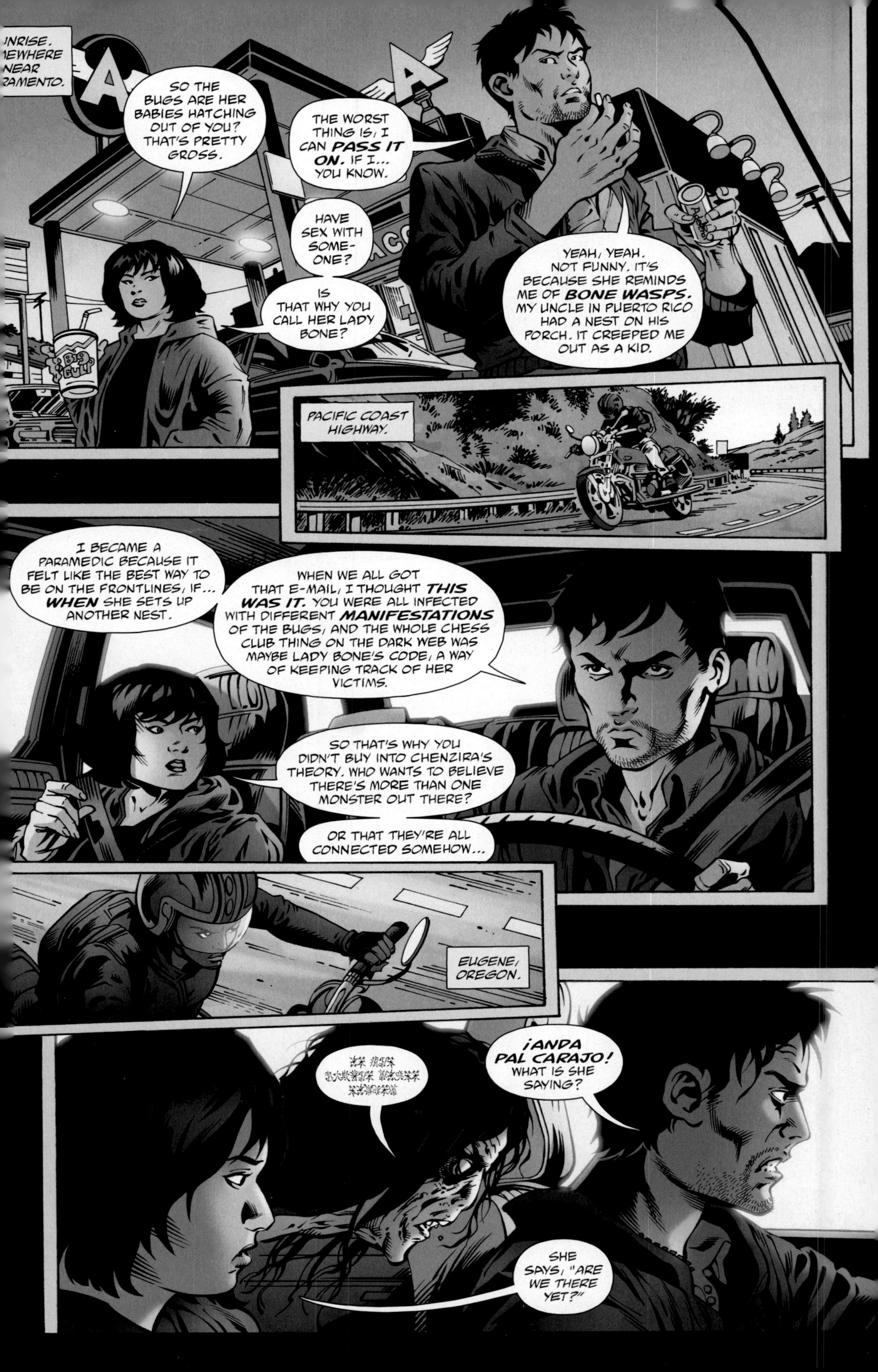

UNRISE.
MEWHERE
NEAR
RAMENTO.
SO THE BUGS ARE HER BABIES HATCHING OUT OF YOU? THAT'S PRETTY GROSS.
THE WORST THING IS, I CAN PASS IT ON. IF I... YOU KNOW.
HAVE SEX WITH SOME-ONE?
IS THAT WHY YOU CALL HER LADY BONE?
YEAH, YEAH. NOT FUNNY. IT'S BECAUSE SHE REMINDS ME OF BONE WASPS. MY UNCLE IN PUERTO RICO HAD A NEST ON HIS PORCH. IT CREEPED ME OUT AS A KID.
PACIFIC COAST HIGHWAY.
I BECAME A PARAMEDIC BECAUSE IT FELT LIKE THE BEST WAY TO BE ON THE FRONTLINES, IF... WHEN SHE SETS UP ANOTHER NEST.
WHEN WE ALL GOT THAT E-MAIL, I THOUGHT THIS WAS IT. YOU WERE ALL INFECTED WITH DIFFERENT MANIFESTATIONS OF THE BUGS, AND THE WHOLE CHESS CLUB THING ON THE DARK WEB WAS MAYBE LADY BONE'S CODE, A WAY OF KEEPING TRACK OF HER VICTIMS.
SO THAT'S WHY YOU DIDN'T BUY INTO CHENZIRA'S THEORY. WHO WANTS TO BELIEVE THERE'S MORE THAN ONE MONSTER OUT THERE?
OR THAT THEY'RE ALL CONNECTED SOMEHOW...
EUGENE, OREGON.
¡ANDA PAL CARAJO! WHAT IS SHE SAYING?
SHE SAYS, "ARE WE THERE YET?"

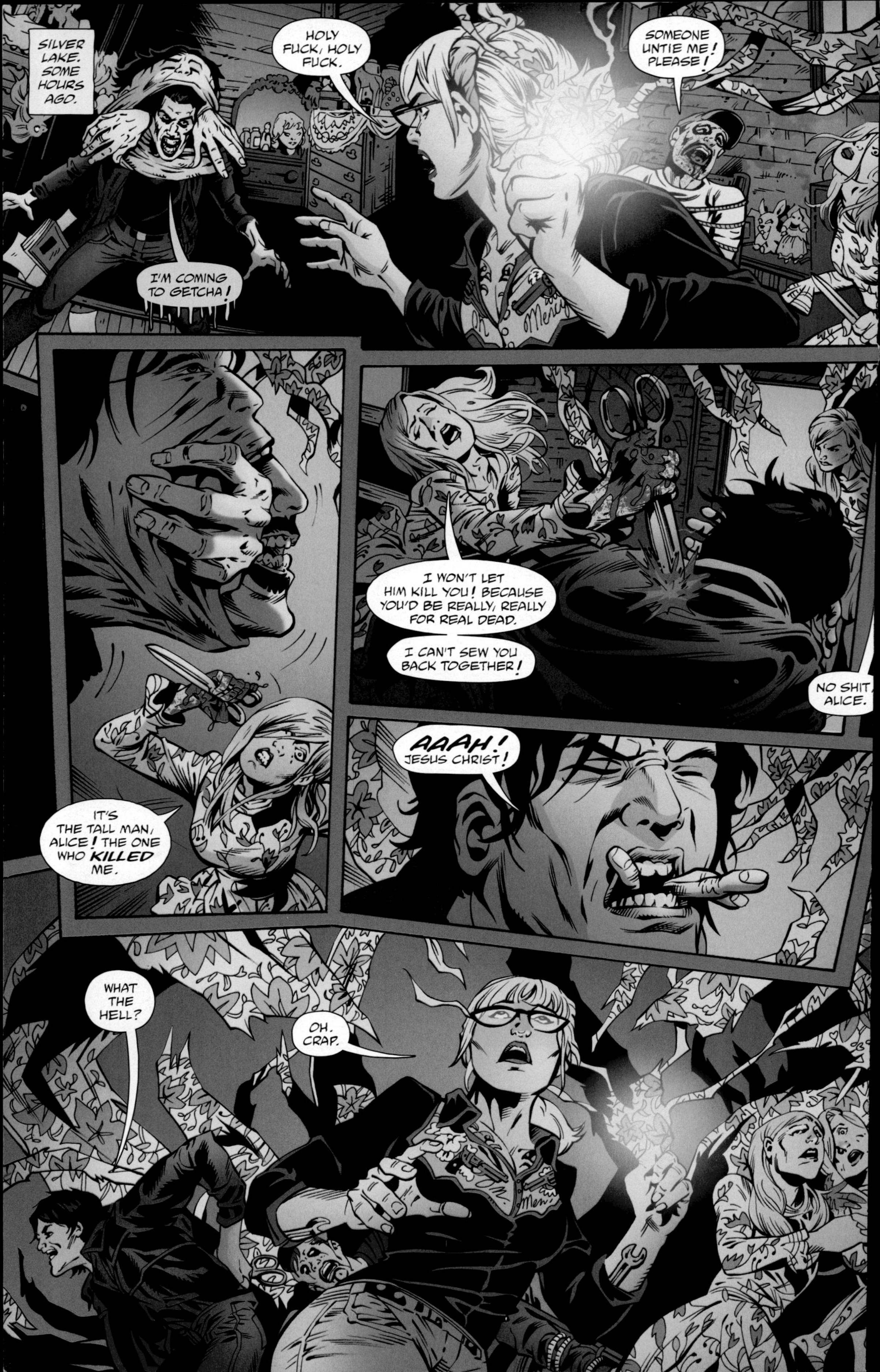
SILVER LAKE. SOME HOURS AGO.
HOLY FUCK, HOLY FUCK.
SOMEONE UNTIE ME! PLEASE!
I'M COMING TO GETCHA!
I WON'T LET HIM KILL YOU! BECAUSE YOU'D BE REALLY, REALLY FOR REAL DEAD.
I CAN'T SEW YOU BACK TOGETHER!
NO SHIT, ALICE.
IT'S THE TALL MAN, ALICE! THE ONE WHO KILLED ME.
AAAH! JESUS CHRIST!
WHAT THE HELL?
OH. CRAP.

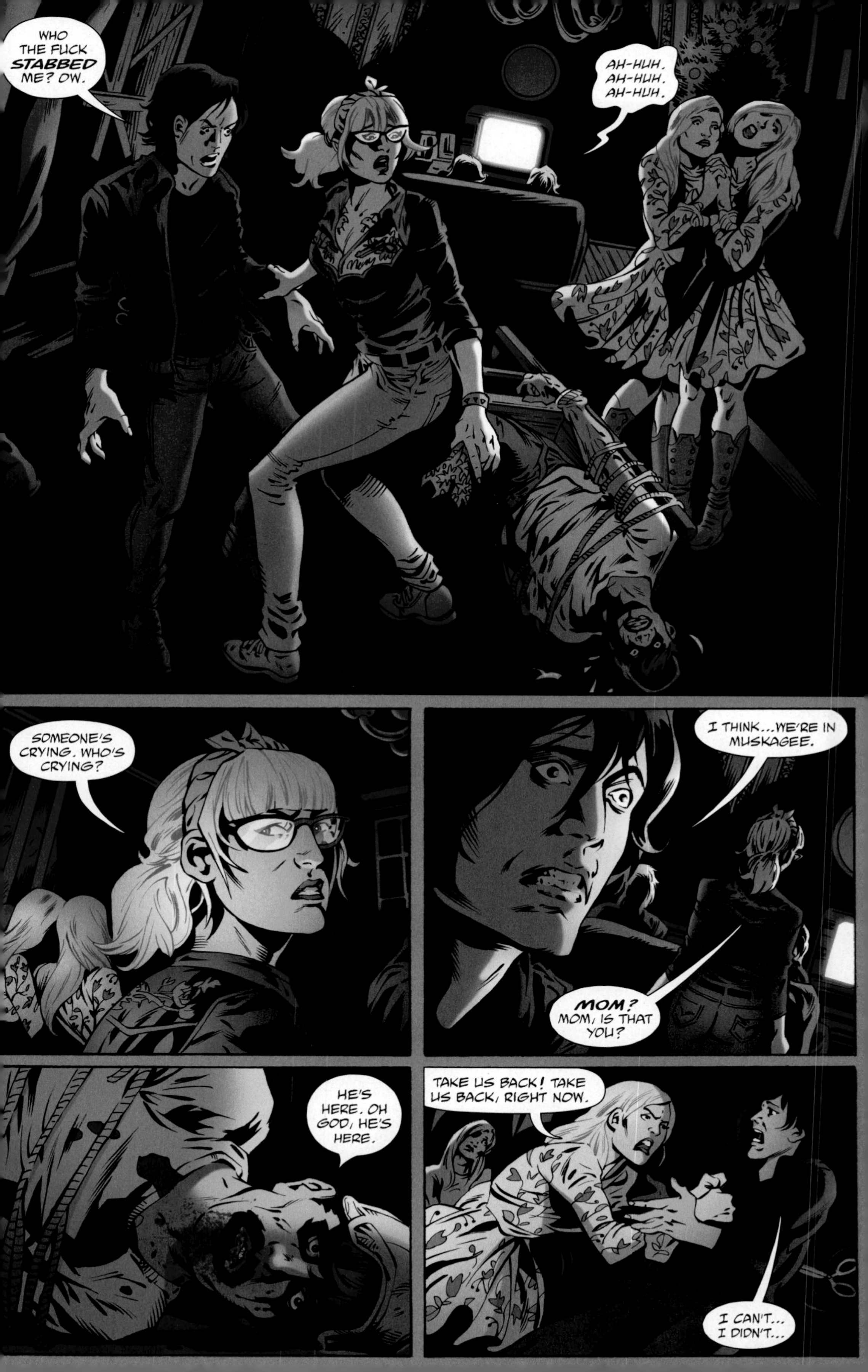
WHO THE FUCK **STABBED** ME? OW.
AH-HUH. AH-HUH. AH-HUH.
SOMEONE'S CRYING. WHO'S CRYING?
I THINK...WE'RE IN MUSKAGEE.
**MOM?** MOM, IS THAT YOU?
HE'S HERE. OH GOD, HE'S HERE.
TAKE US BACK! TAKE US BACK, RIGHT NOW.
I CAN'T... I DIDN'T...

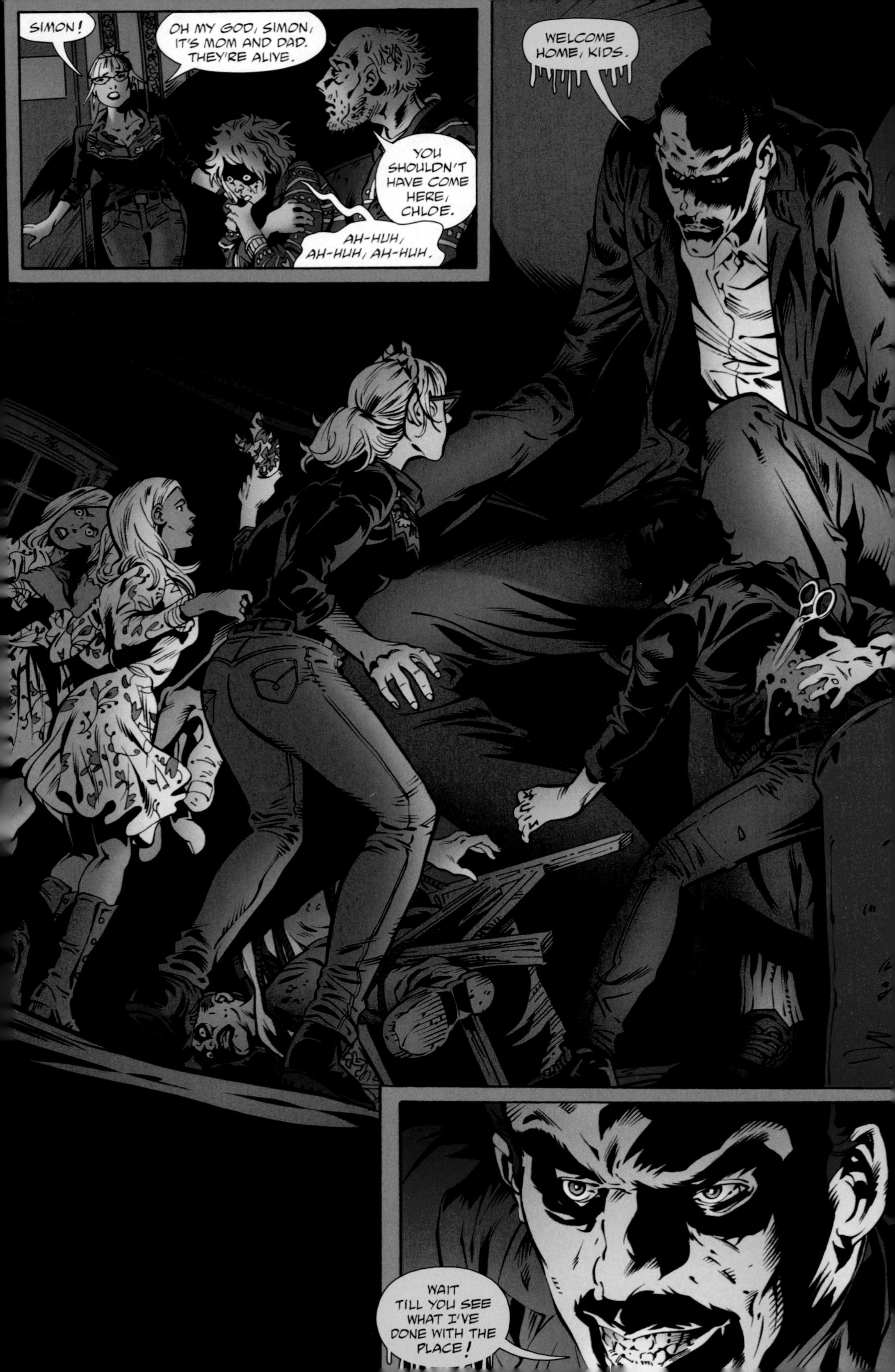
SIMON!
OH MY GOD, SIMON, IT'S MOM AND DAD. THEY'RE ALIVE.
YOU SHOULDN'T HAVE COME HERE, CHLOE.
AH-HUH, AH-HUH, AH-HUH.
WELCOME HOME, KIDS.
WAIT TILL YOU SEE WHAT I'VE DONE WITH THE PLACE!

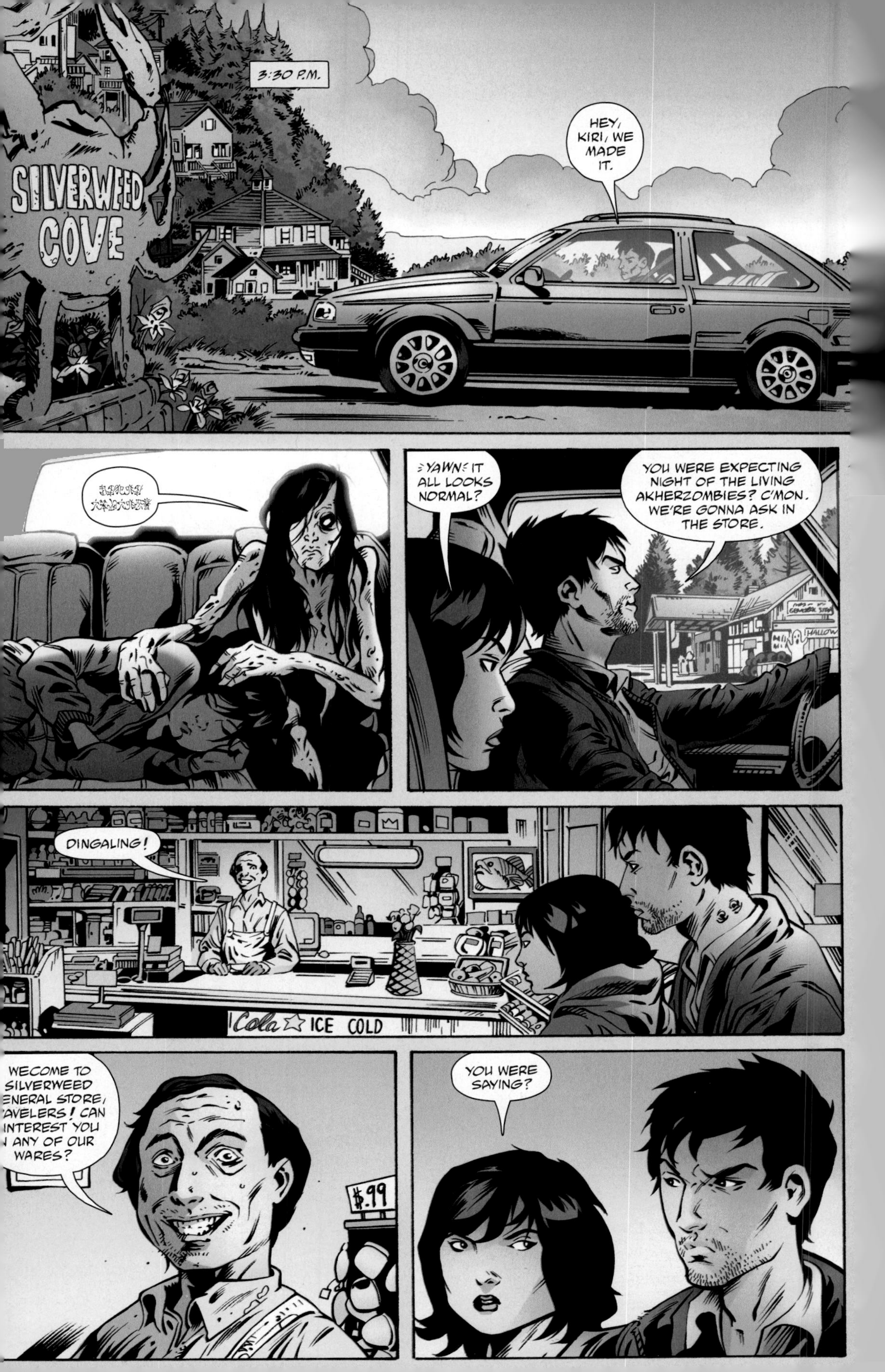

3:30 P.M.
SILVERWEED COVE
HEY, KIRI, WE MADE IT.
≷YAWN≶ IT ALL LOOKS NORMAL?
YOU WERE EXPECTING NIGHT OF THE LIVING AKHERZOMBIES? C'MON. WE'RE GONNA ASK IN THE STORE.
DINGALING!
Cola ICE COLD
WECOME TO SILVERWEED ENERAL STORE, AVELERS! CAN INTEREST YOU N ANY OF OUR WARES?
$.99
YOU WERE SAYING?

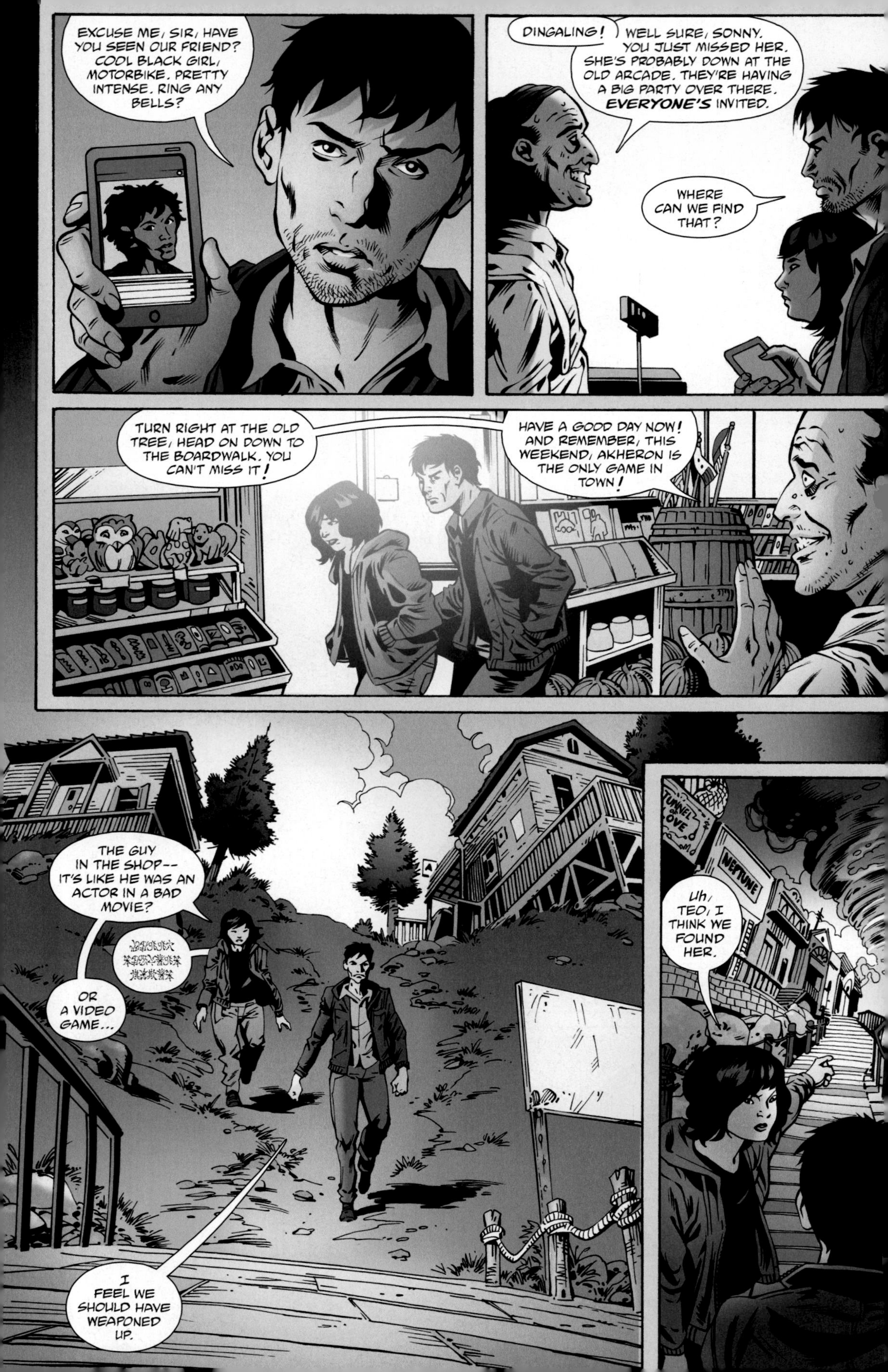
EXCUSE ME, SIR, HAVE YOU SEEN OUR FRIEND? COOL BLACK GIRL, MOTORBIKE. PRETTY INTENSE. RING ANY BELLS?
DINGALING!
WELL SURE, SONNY. YOU JUST MISSED HER. SHE'S PROBABLY DOWN AT THE OLD ARCADE. THEY'RE HAVING A BIG PARTY OVER THERE. EVERYONE'S INVITED.
WHERE CAN WE FIND THAT?
TURN RIGHT AT THE OLD TREE, HEAD ON DOWN TO THE BOARDWALK. YOU CAN'T MISS IT!
HAVE A GOOD DAY NOW! AND REMEMBER, THIS WEEKEND, AKHERON IS THE ONLY GAME IN TOWN!
THE GUY IN THE SHOP-- IT'S LIKE HE WAS AN ACTOR IN A BAD MOVIE?
OR A VIDEO GAME...
I FEEL WE SHOULD HAVE WEAPONED UP.
TUNNEL OF LOVE
NEPTUNE
UH, TEO, I THINK WE FOUND HER.

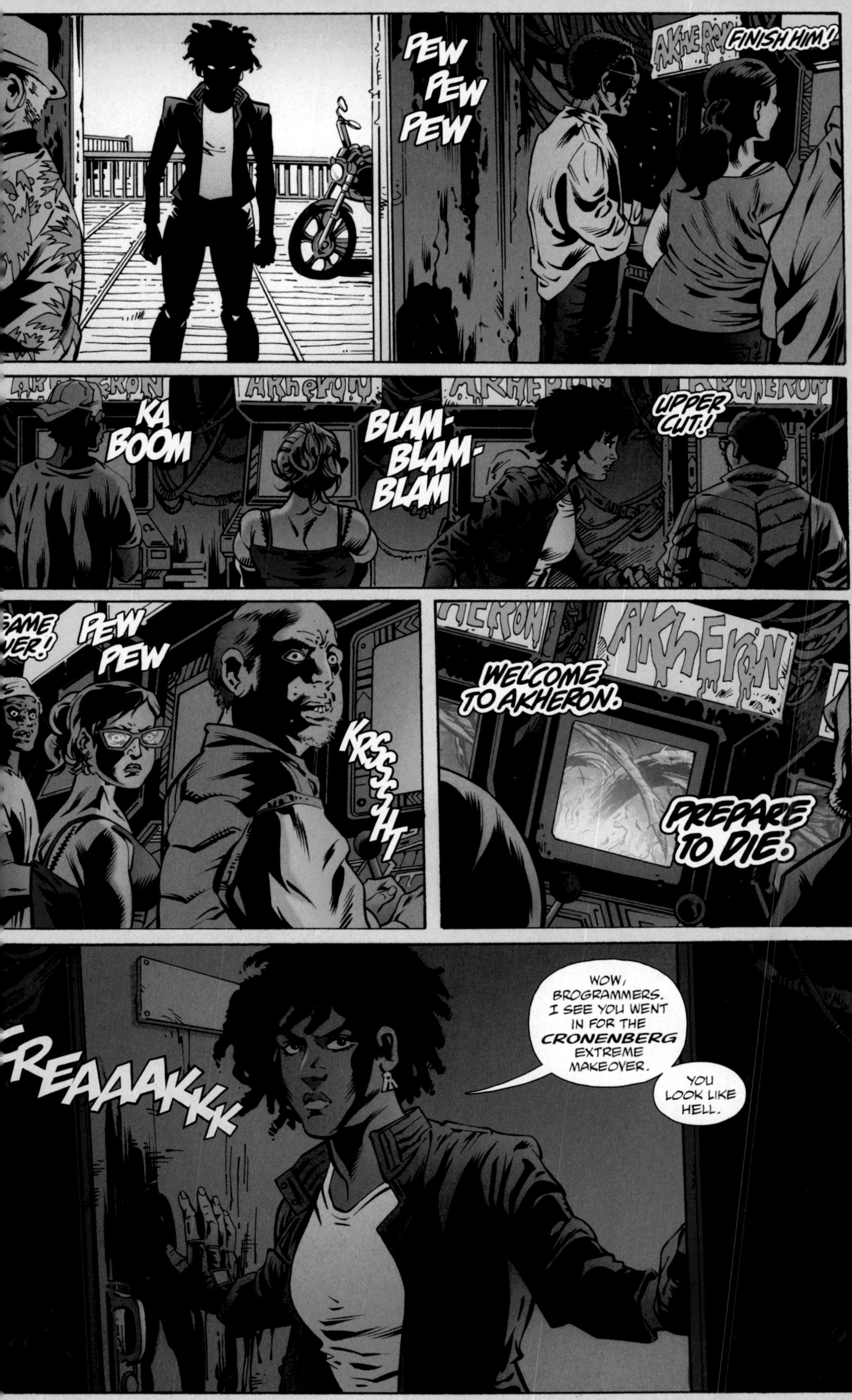
PEW PEW PEW
AKHERON
FINISH HIM!
KA BOOM
BLAM-BLAM-BLAM
UPPER CUT!
GAME VER!
PEW PEW
KRSSSHT
AKHERON
WELCOME TO AKHERON.
PREPARE TO DIE.
REAAAKKK
WOW, BROGRAMMERS. I SEE YOU WENT IN FOR THE CRONENBERG EXTREME MAKEOVER.
YOU LOOK LIKE HELL.

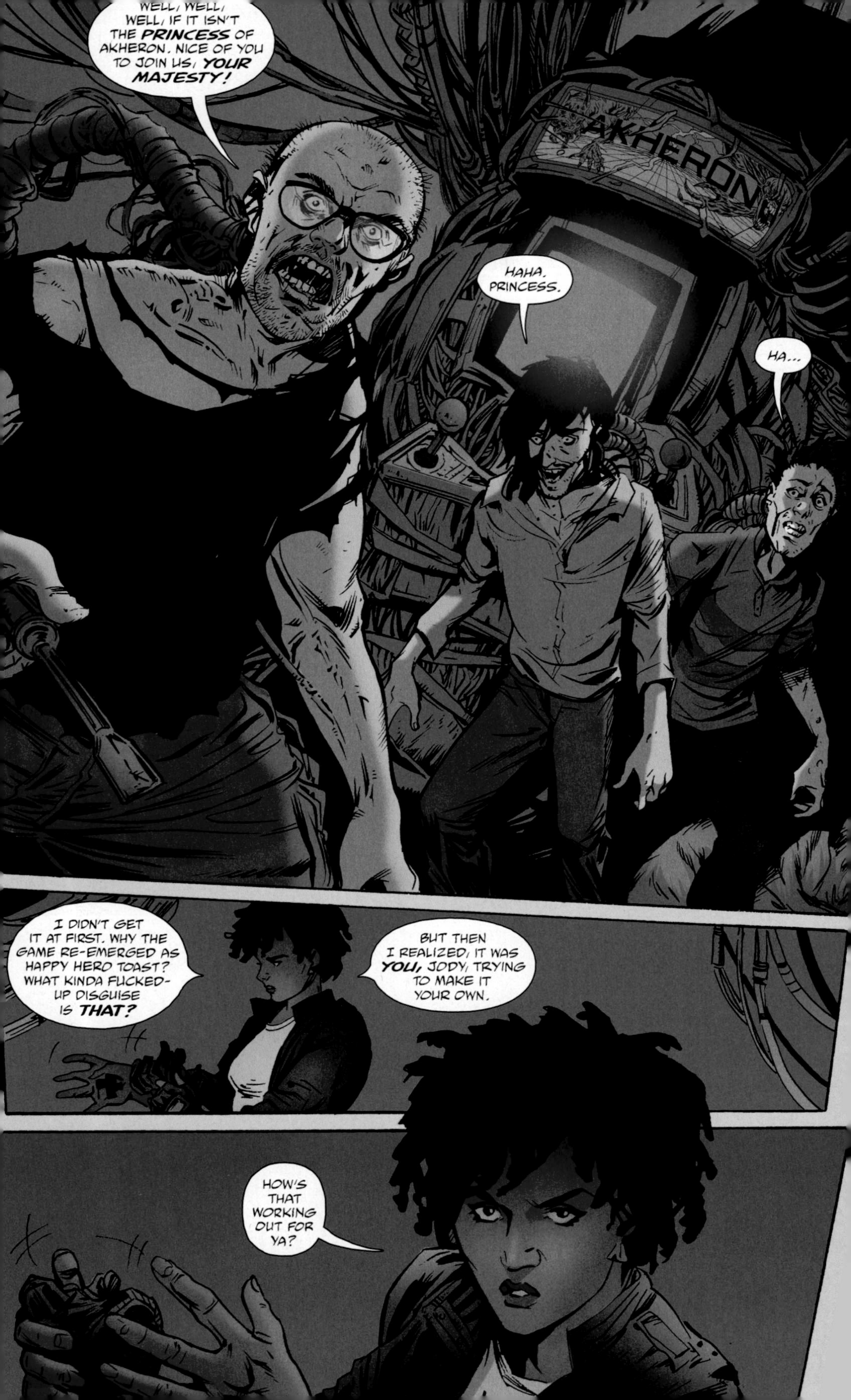
WELL, WELL, WELL, IF IT ISN'T THE PRINCESS OF AKHERON. NICE OF YOU TO JOIN US, YOUR MAJESTY!
AKHERON
HAHA. PRINCESS.
HA...
I DIDN'T GET IT AT FIRST. WHY THE GAME RE-EMERGED AS HAPPY HERO TOAST? WHAT KINDA FUCKED-UP DISGUISE IS THAT?
BUT THEN I REALIZED, IT WAS YOU, JODY, TRYING TO MAKE IT YOUR OWN.
HOW'S THAT WORKING OUT FOR YA?

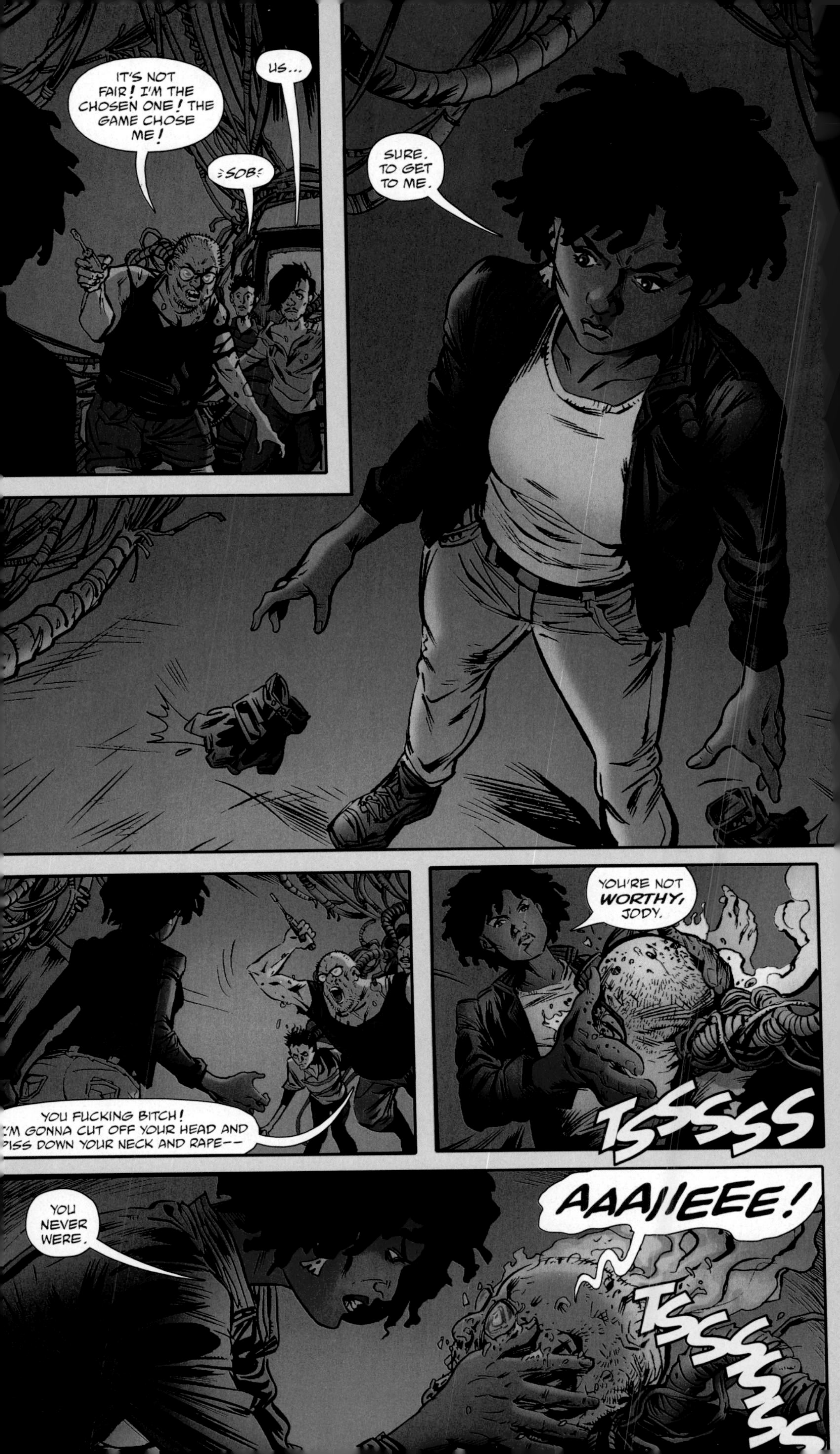
IT'S NOT FAIR! I'M THE CHOSEN ONE! THE GAME CHOSE ME!
US...
SOB
SURE. TO GET TO ME.
YOU FUCKING BITCH! I'M GONNA CUT OFF YOUR HEAD AND PISS DOWN YOUR NECK AND RAPE--
YOU'RE NOT WORTHY, JODY.
TSSSSS
YOU NEVER WERE.
AAAIIEEE!

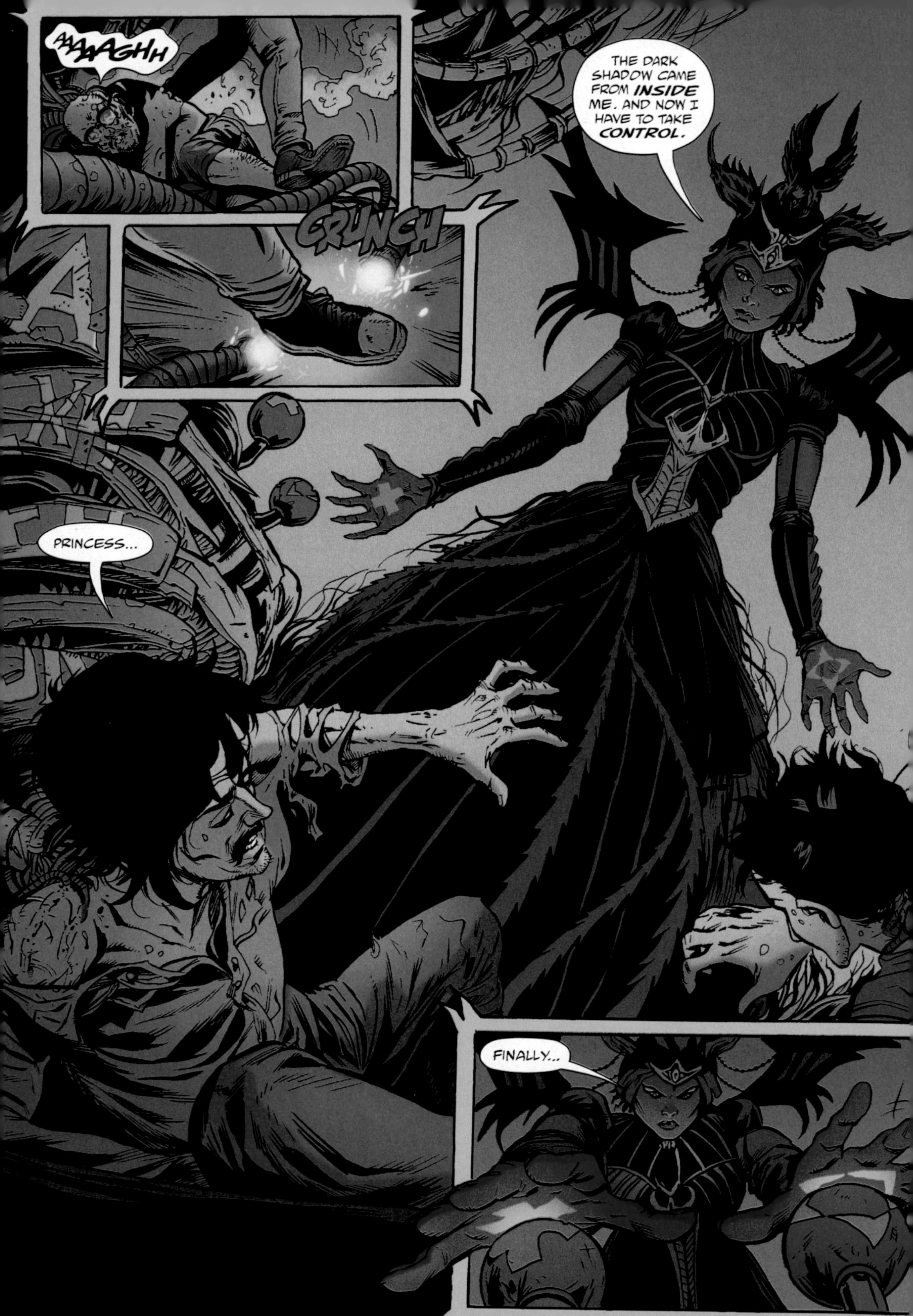
AAAAAGHH
CRUNCH
THE DARK SHADOW CAME FROM INSIDE ME. AND NOW I HAVE TO TAKE CONTROL.
PRINCESS...
FINALLY...

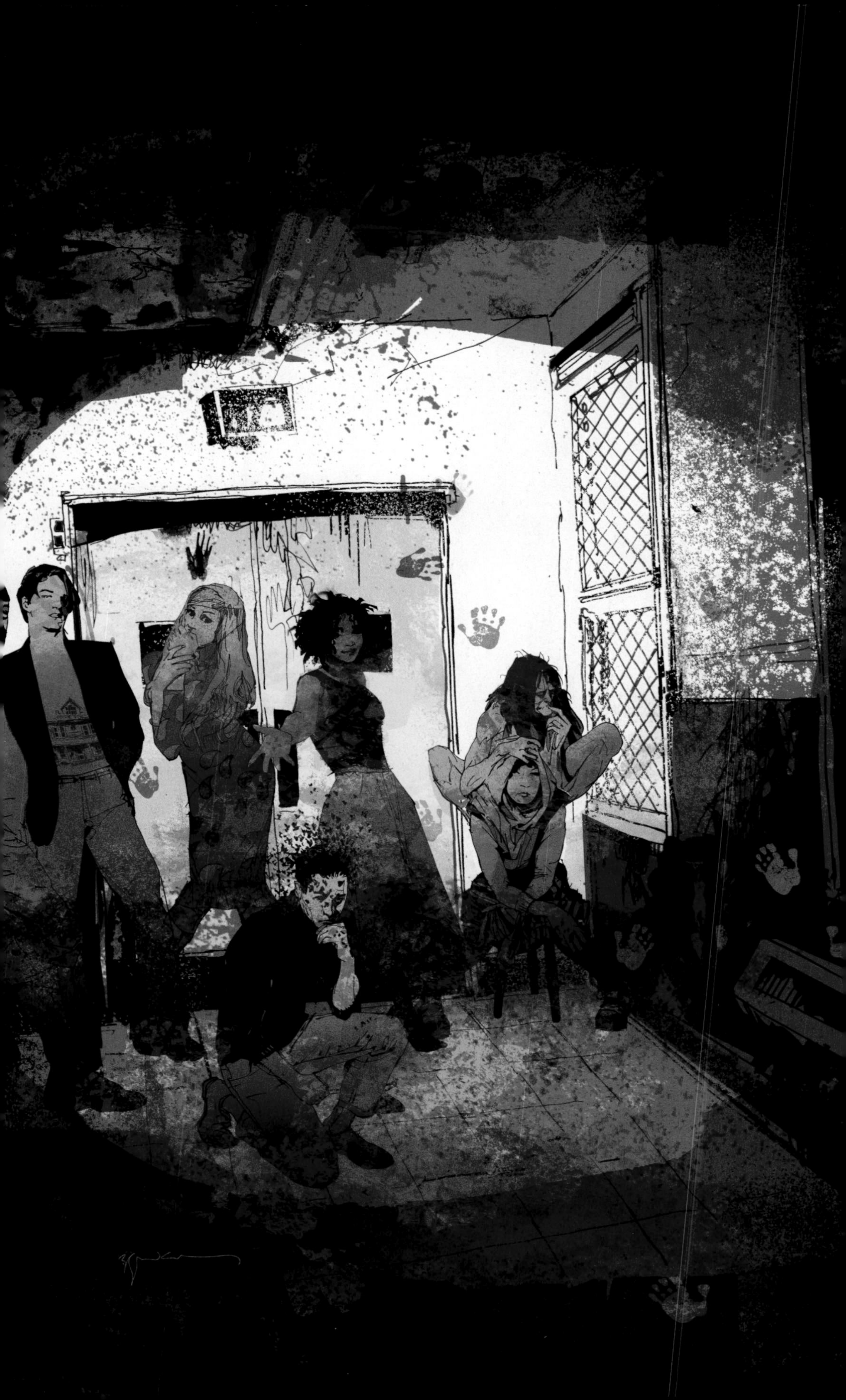

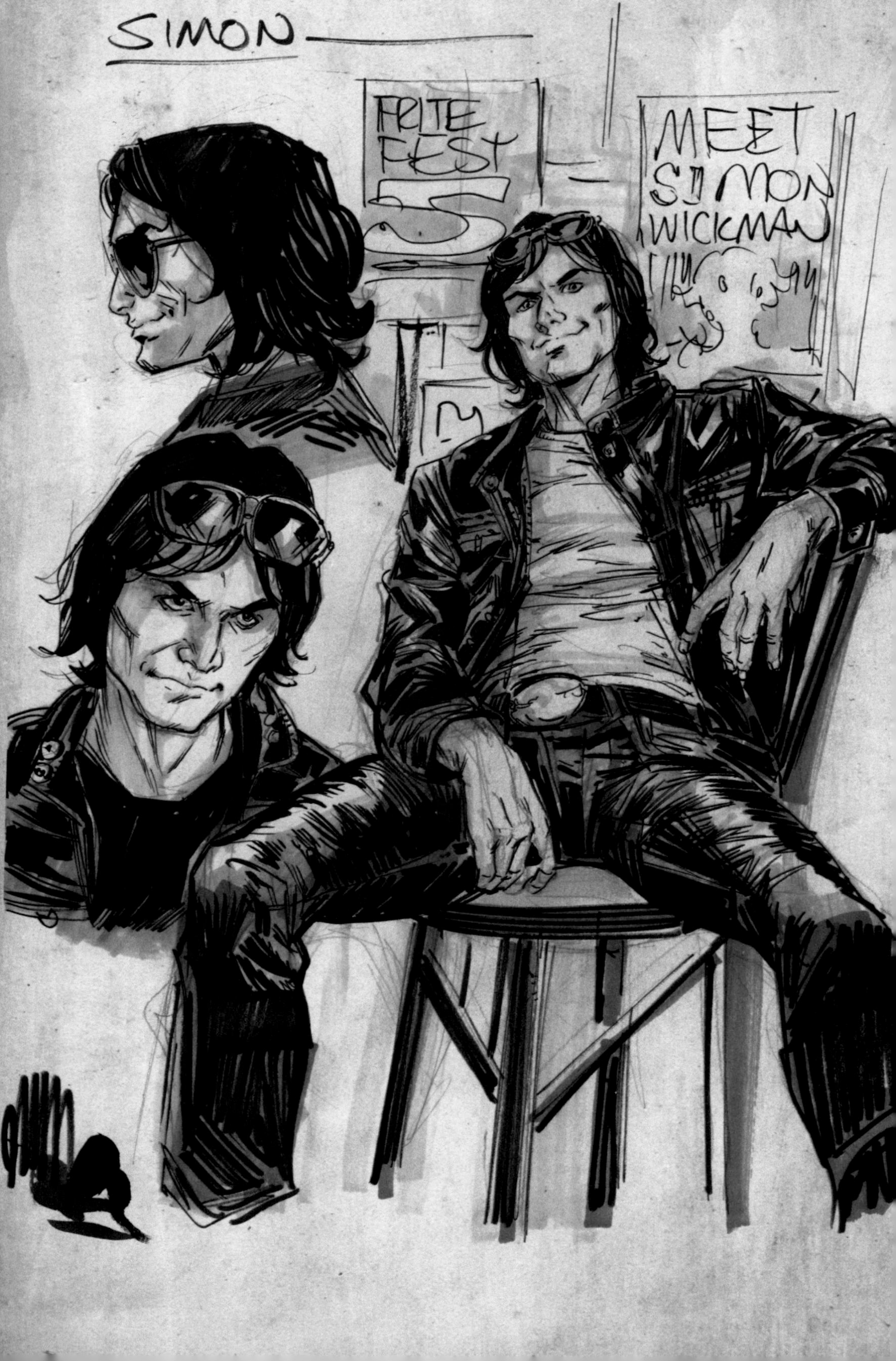
SIMON
FRITE FEST
MEET SIMON WICKMAN

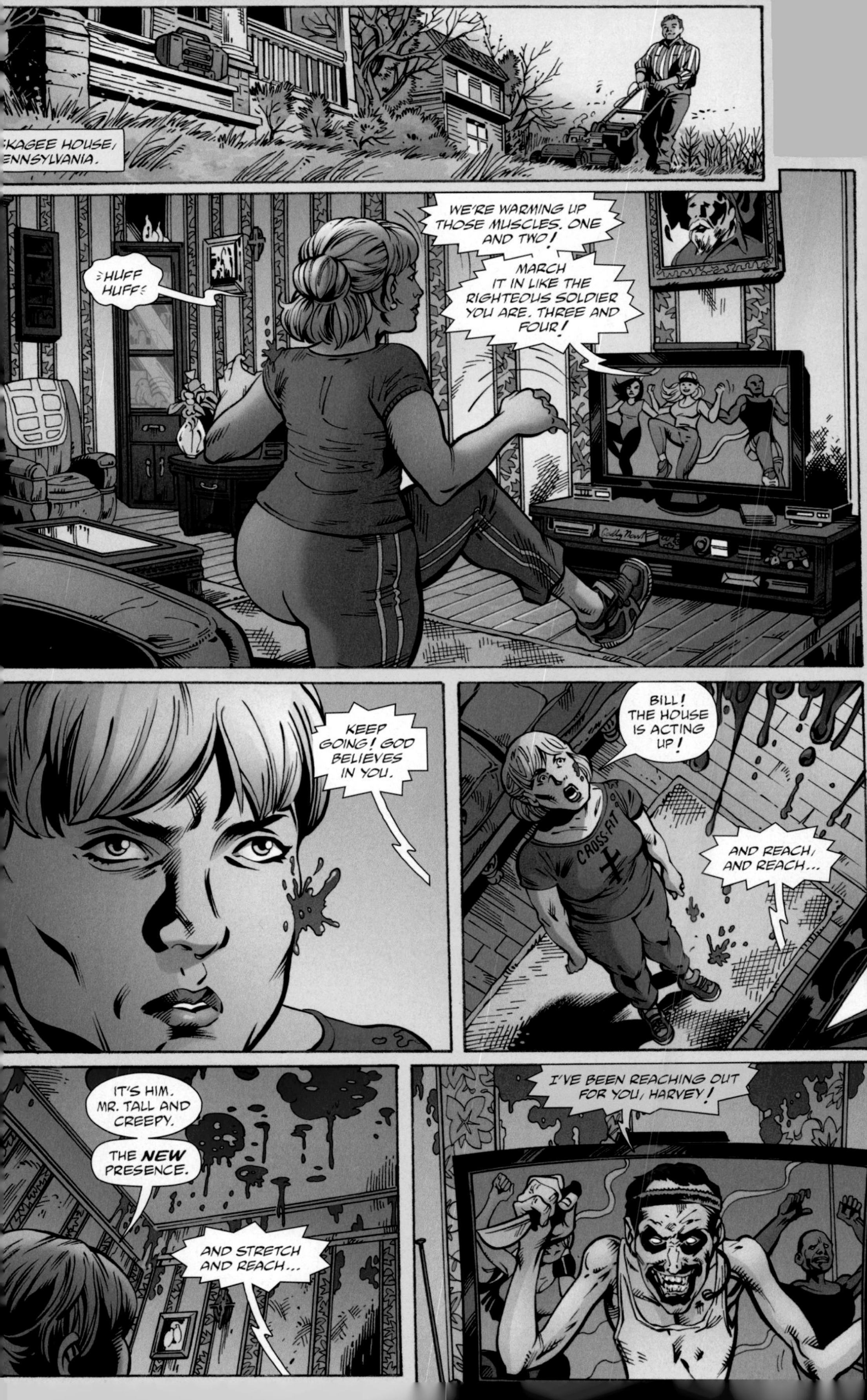

SKAGEE HOUSE, PENNSYLVANIA.
WE'RE WARMING UP THOSE MUSCLES. ONE AND TWO!
HUFF HUFF
MARCH IT IN LIKE THE RIGHTEOUS SOLDIER YOU ARE. THREE AND FOUR!
KEEP GOING! GOD BELIEVES IN YOU.
BILL! THE HOUSE IS ACTING UP!
AND REACH, AND REACH...
CROSS-FIT
IT'S HIM. MR. TALL AND CREEPY.
THE NEW PRESENCE.
AND STRETCH AND REACH...
I'VE BEEN REACHING OUT FOR YOU, HARVEY!

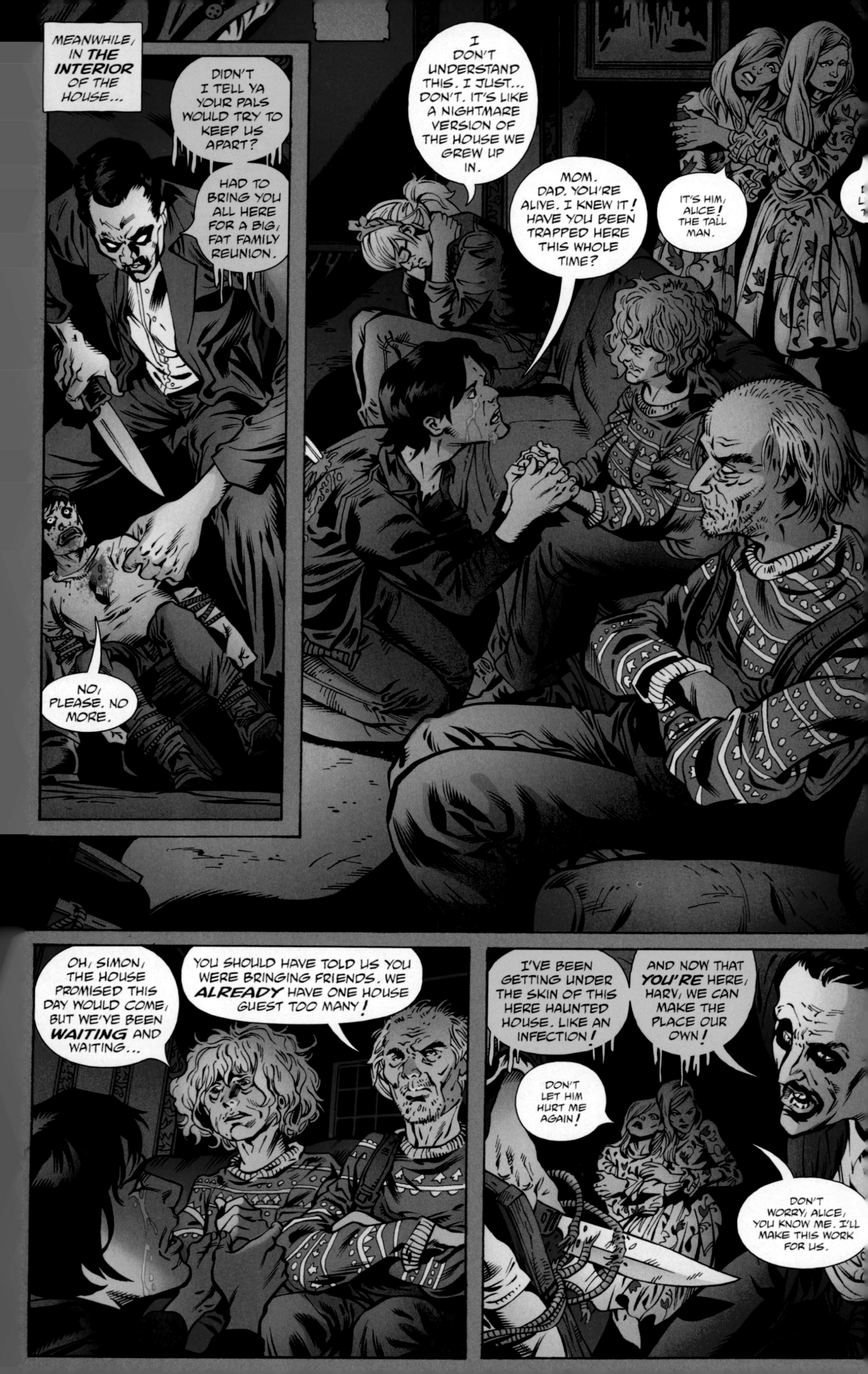
MEANWHILE, IN THE INTERIOR OF THE HOUSE...
DIDN'T I TELL YA YOUR PALS WOULD TRY TO KEEP US APART?
HAD TO BRING YOU ALL HERE FOR A BIG, FAT FAMILY REUNION.
NO, PLEASE. NO MORE.
I DON'T UNDERSTAND THIS. I JUST... DON'T. IT'S LIKE A NIGHTMARE VERSION OF THE HOUSE WE GREW UP IN.
MOM. DAD. YOU'RE ALIVE. I KNEW IT! HAVE YOU BEEN TRAPPED HERE THIS WHOLE TIME?
IT'S HIM, ALICE! THE TALL MAN.
OH, SIMON, THE HOUSE PROMISED THIS DAY WOULD COME, BUT WE'VE BEEN WAITING AND WAITING...
YOU SHOULD HAVE TOLD US YOU WERE BRINGING FRIENDS. WE ALREADY HAVE ONE HOUSE GUEST TOO MANY!
I'VE BEEN GETTING UNDER THE SKIN OF THIS HERE HAUNTED HOUSE. LIKE AN INFECTION!
AND NOW THAT YOU'RE HERE, HARV, WE CAN MAKE THE PLACE OUR OWN!
DON'T LET HIM HURT ME AGAIN!
DON'T WORRY, ALICE, YOU KNOW ME. I'LL MAKE THIS WORK FOR US.

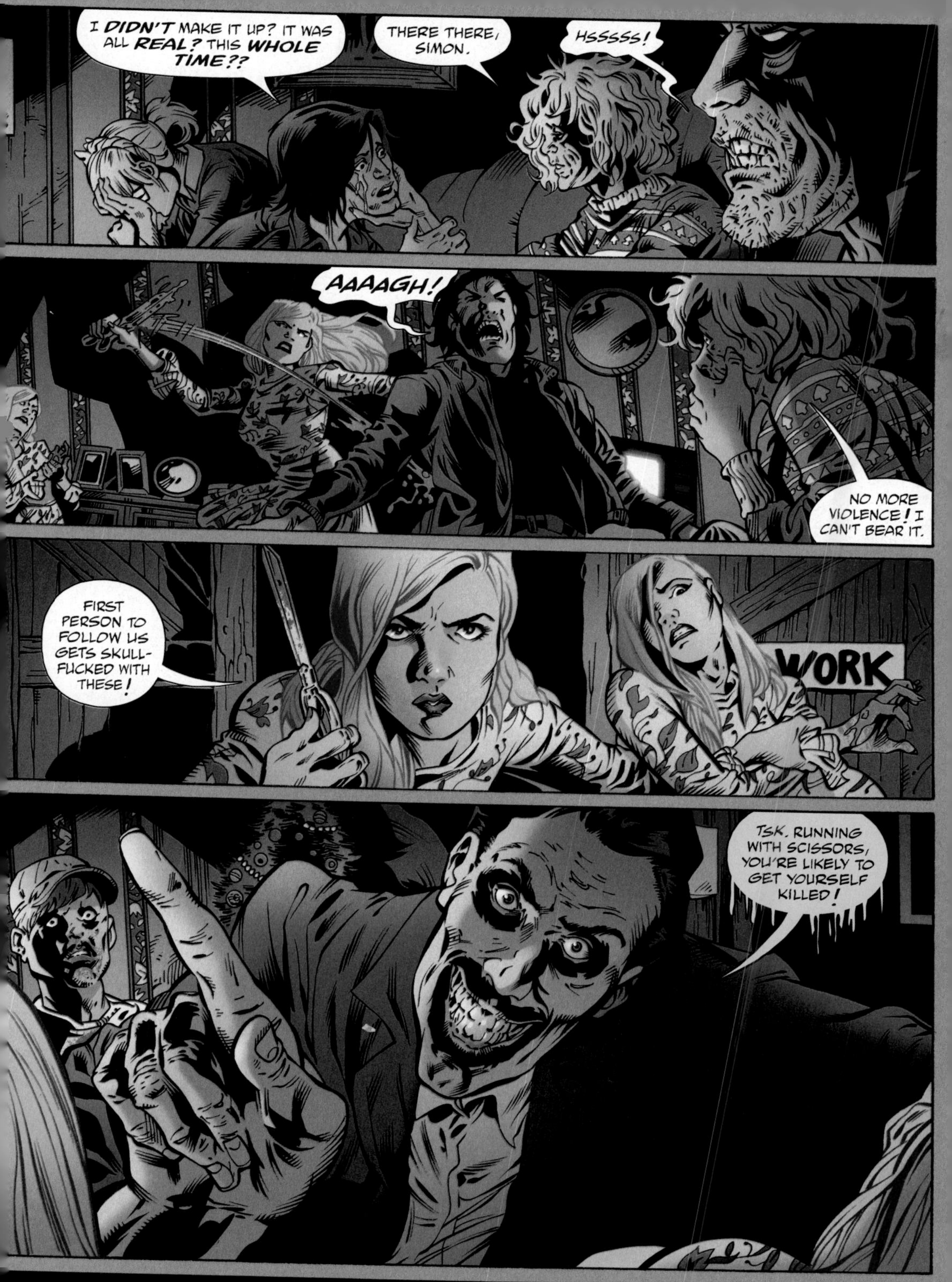
I DIDN'T MAKE IT UP? IT WAS ALL REAL? THIS WHOLE TIME??
THERE THERE, SIMON.
HSSSSS!
AAAAGH!
NO MORE VIOLENCE! I CAN'T BEAR IT.
FIRST PERSON TO FOLLOW US GETS SKULL-FUCKED WITH THESE!
WORK
TSK. RUNNING WITH SCISSORS, YOU'RE LIKELY TO GET YOURSELF KILLED!

# SURVIVORS' CLUB CHAPTER SEVEN: BOSS FIGHT

DALE HALVORSEN WRITER
LAUREN BEUKES WRITER
RYAN KELLY ARTIST

EVA DE LA CRUZ COLORIST CLEM ROBINS LETTERER
MARK FARMER ADDITIONAL INKS BILL SIENKIEWICZ COVER ARTIST
ROWENA YOW ASSOCIATE EDITOR SHELLY BOND EDITOR
SURVIVORS' CLUB CREATED BY BEUKES, HALVORSEN AND KELLY

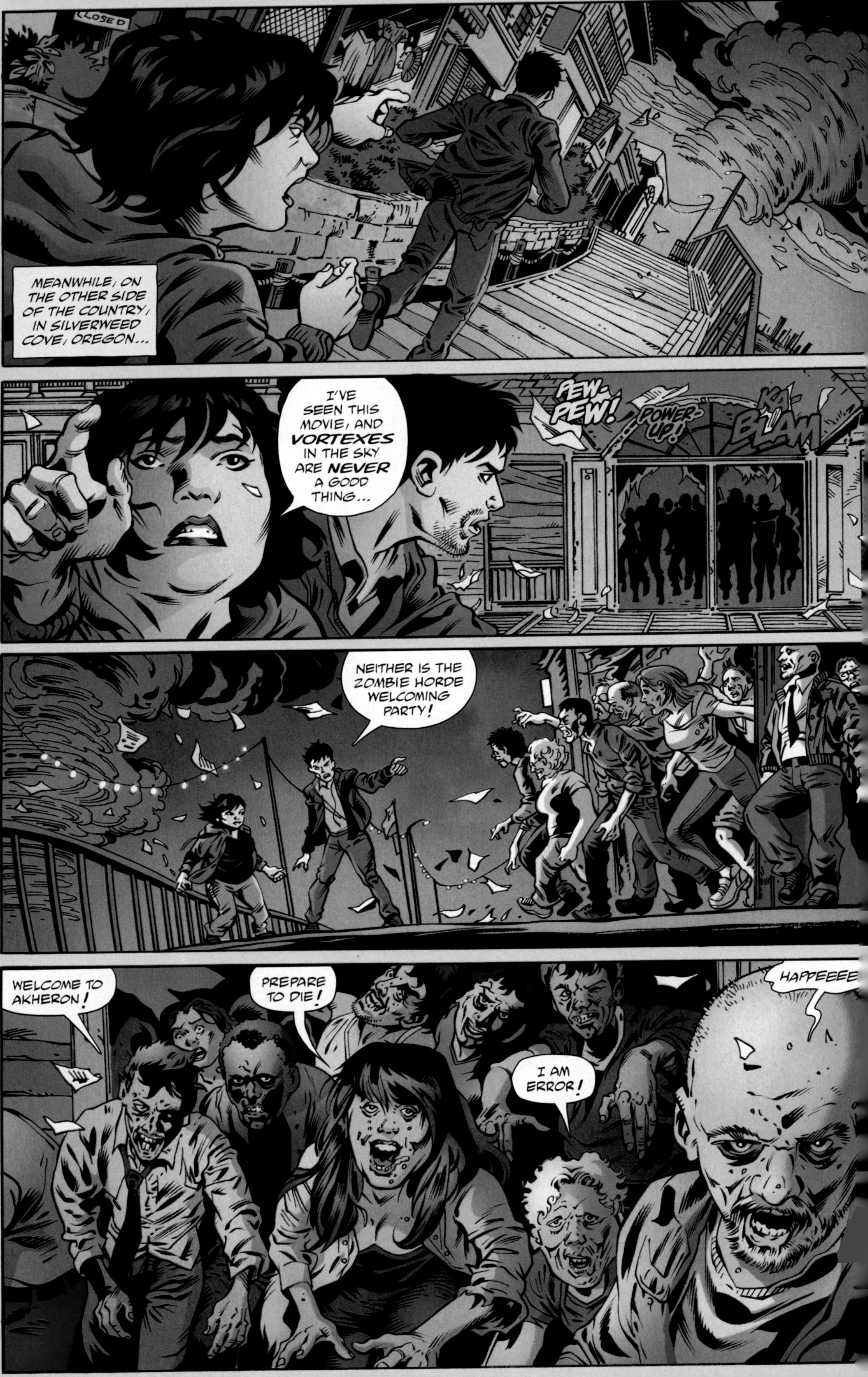
CLOSED
MEANWHILE, ON THE OTHER SIDE OF THE COUNTRY, IN SILVERWEED COVE, OREGON...
I'VE SEEN THIS MOVIE, AND VORTEXES IN THE SKY ARE NEVER A GOOD THING...
PEW-PEW!
POWER-UP!
KA-BLAM
NEITHER IS THE ZOMBIE HORDE WELCOMING PARTY!
WELCOME TO AKHERON!
PREPARE TO DIE!
HAPPEEEEE
I AM ERROR!

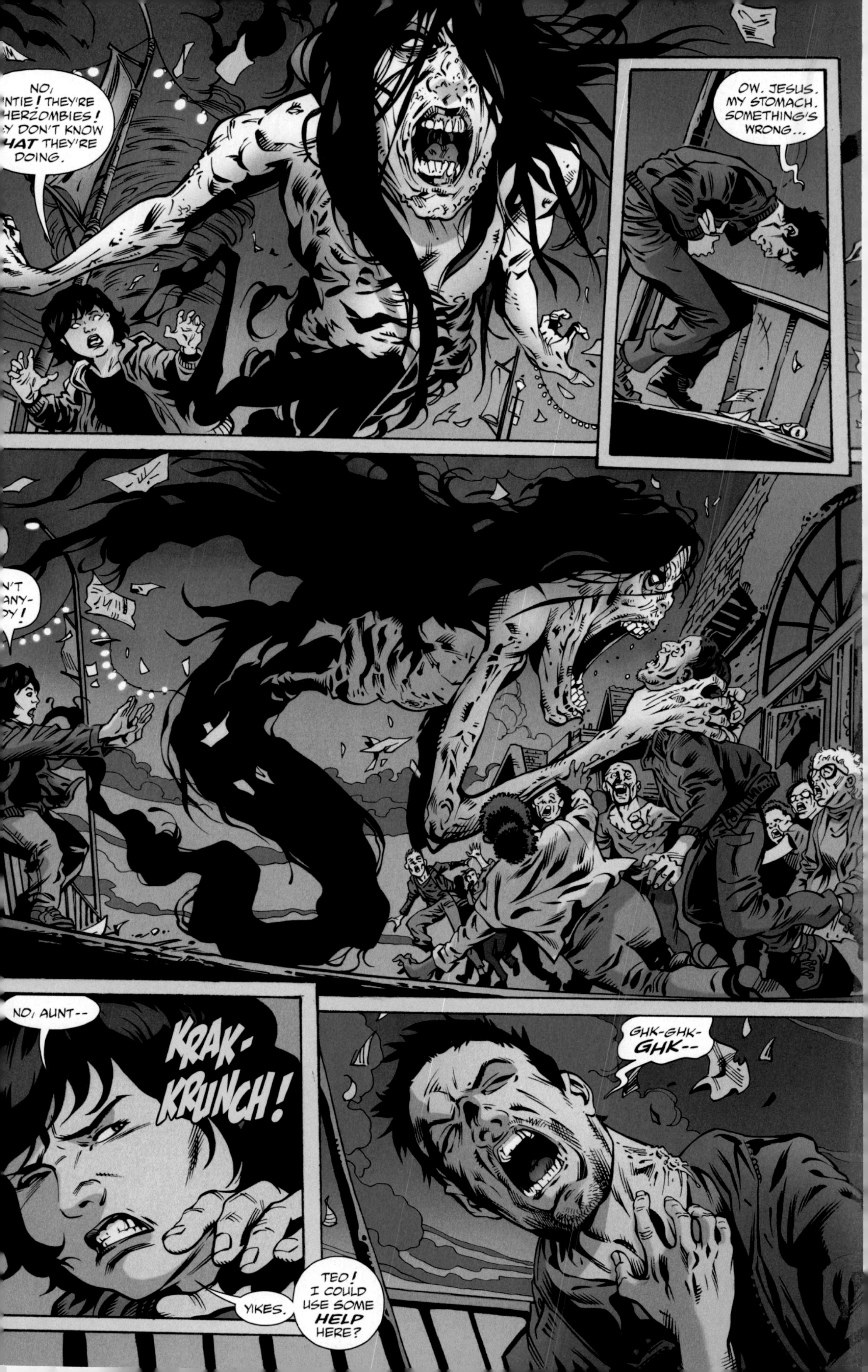

NO, ...NTIE! THEY'RE ...HERZOMBIES! ...Y DON'T KNOW ...HAT THEY'RE DOING.
OW. JESUS. MY STOMACH. SOMETHING'S WRONG...
...N'T ...ANY- ...DY!
NO, AUNT--
KRAK-KRUNCH!
GHK-GHK-GHK--
YIKES.
TEO! I COULD USE SOME HELP HERE?

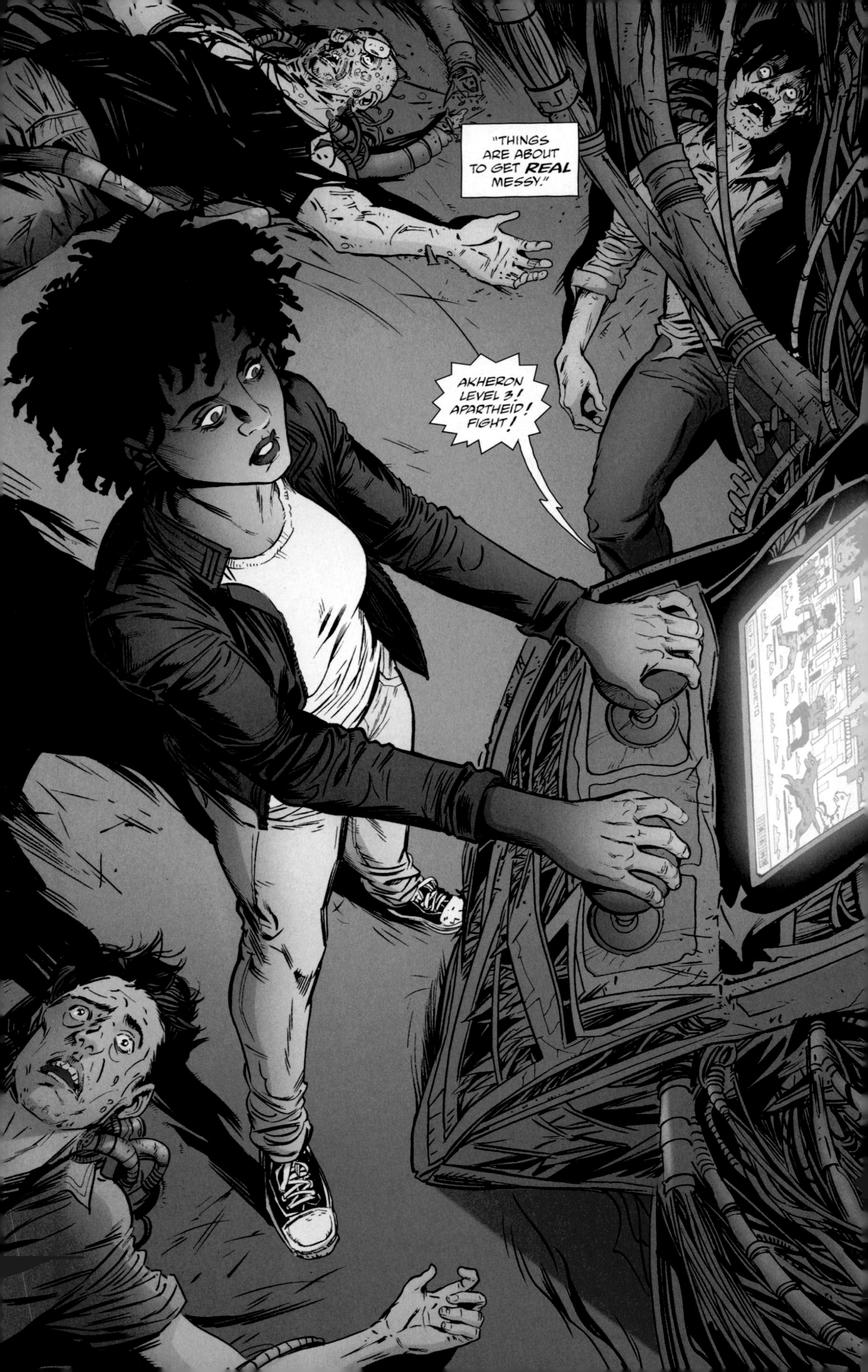
"THINGS ARE ABOUT TO GET REAL MESSY."
AKHERON LEVEL 3! APARTHEID! FIGHT!

YOU BLACKS ARE *ANIMALS*. YOU'LL *NEVER* GET THE VOTE! WE KILLED YOUR MOTHER FOR EVEN *THINKING* ABOUT IT!

WHUF? WHUF? WHUF!

W YOU. I LIVED GH THIS ONCE READY...

YELP!

...I'M *NOT* GOING THROUGH IT *AGAIN*.

EINA! MOER!

OW! STOP IT, DAD!

CLUNK

ENERGY

WILLPOWER

I *DIED* BECAUSE OF YOU, ZIRA! A BUNCH OF PEOPLE DID! YOU SHOULD HAVE BEEN LOOKING AFTER ME!

ENERGY

WILLPOWER

I WAS NINE YEARS OLD! YOU WERE DRUNK ALL THE TIME. I LOST MY MOM AND MY DAD ON THE SAME DAY!

I FORGIVE YOU, DAD.

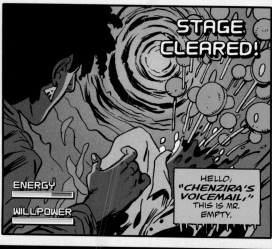

STAGE CLEARED!

ENERGY

WILLPOWER

HELLO, "CHENZIRA'S VOICEMAIL," THIS IS MR. EMPTY.

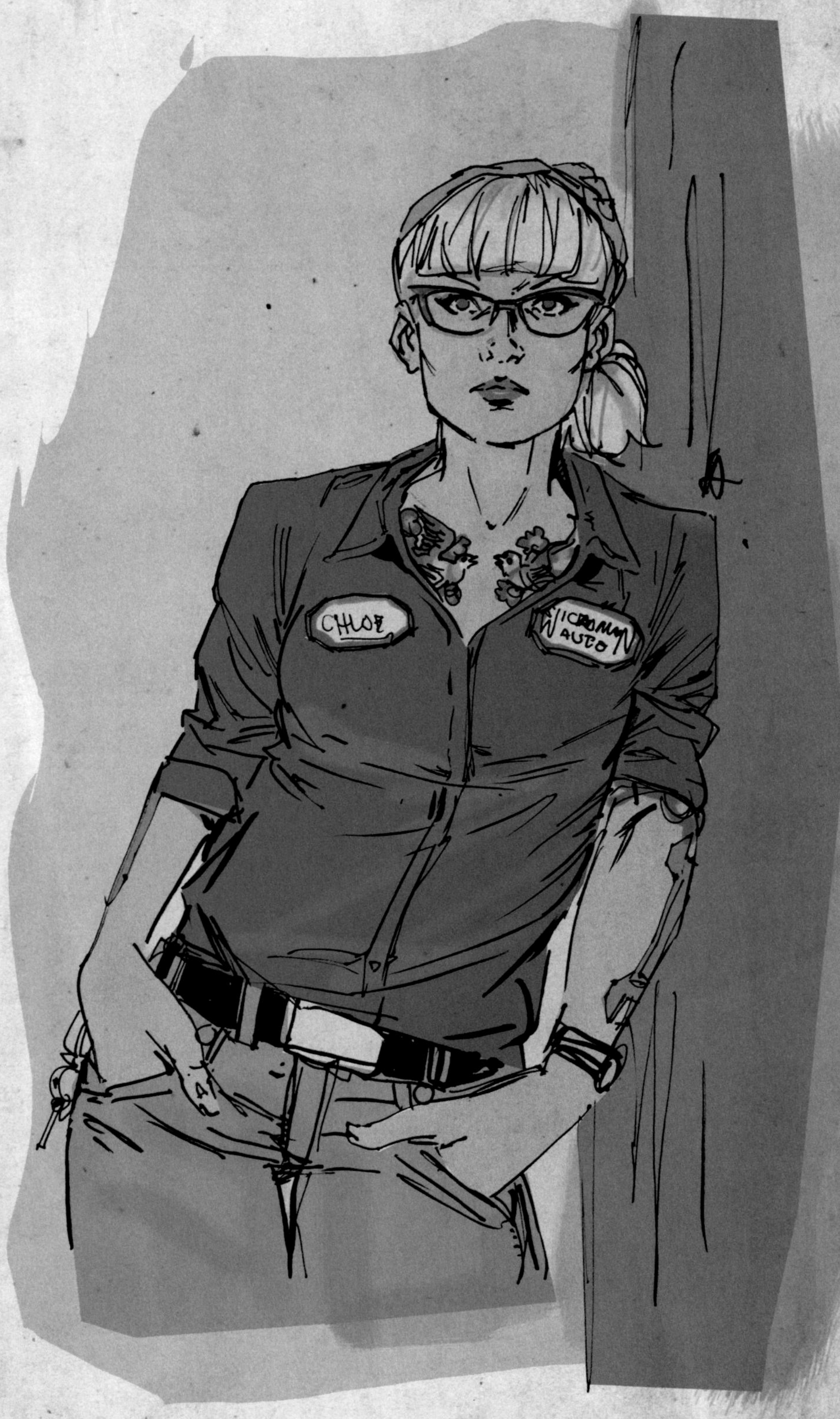
CHLOE
AUTO

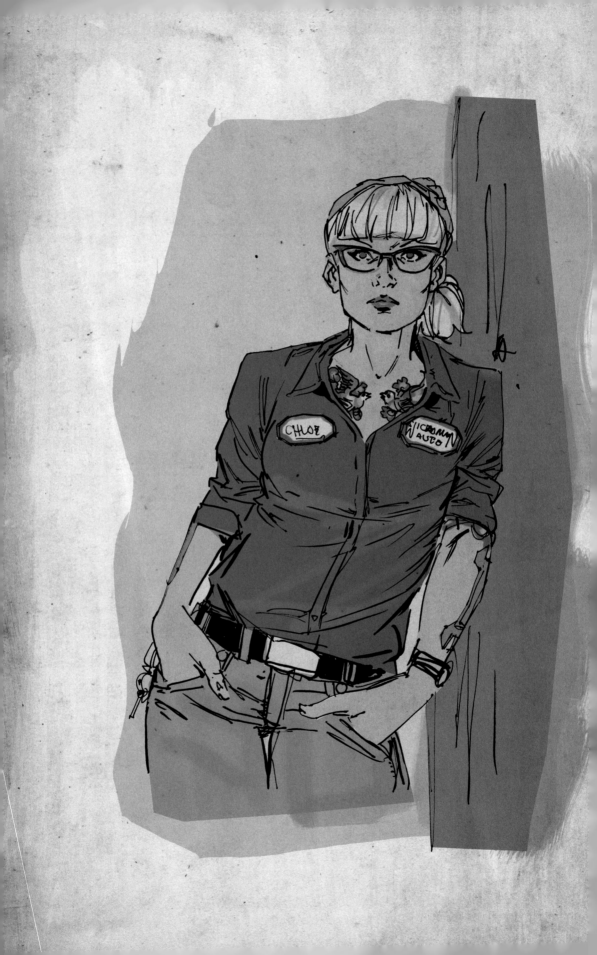

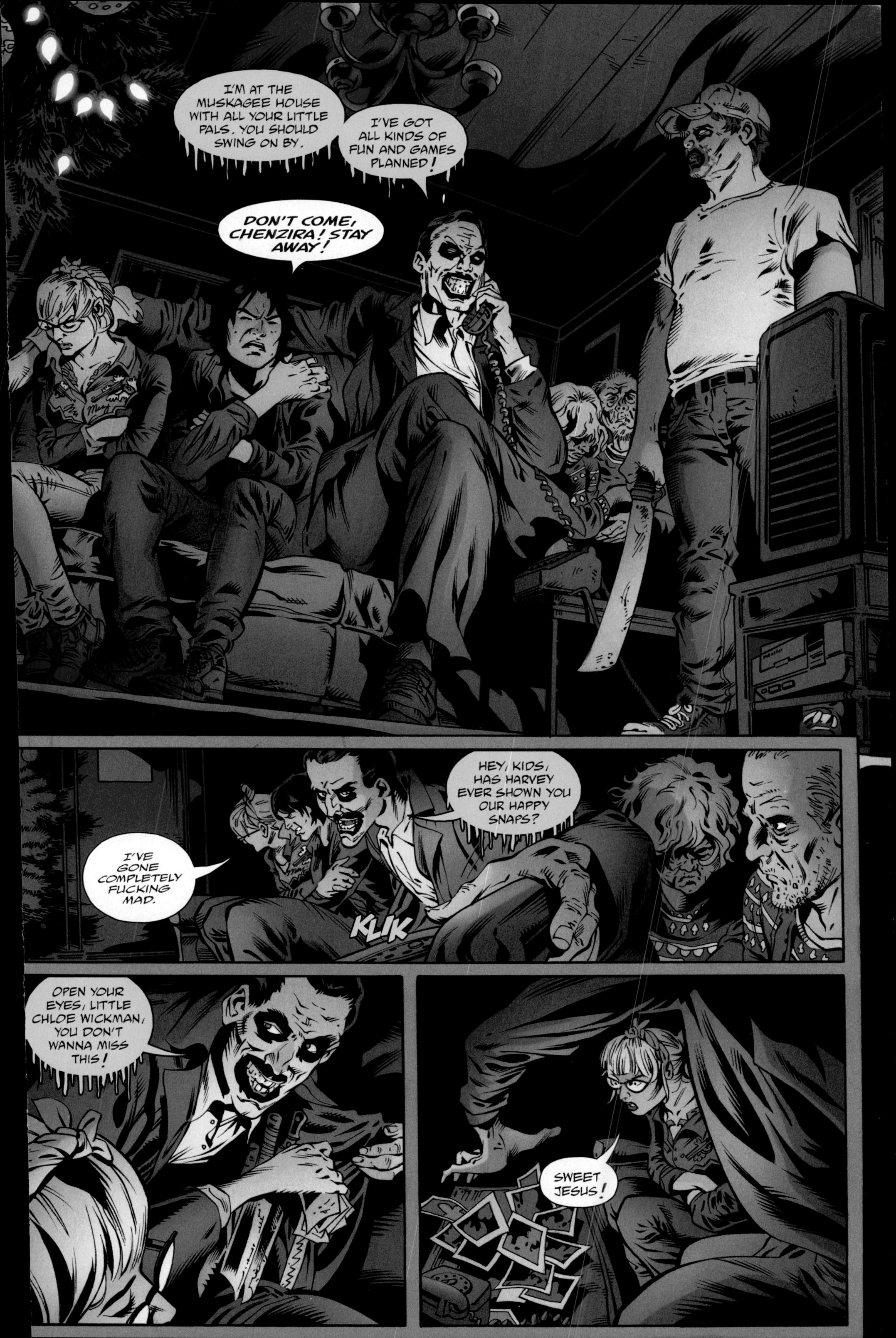
I'M AT THE MUSKAGEE HOUSE WITH ALL YOUR LITTLE PALS. YOU SHOULD SWING ON BY.
I'VE GOT ALL KINDS OF FUN AND GAMES PLANNED!
DON'T COME, CHENZIRA! STAY AWAY!
HEY, KIDS, HAS HARVEY EVER SHOWN YOU OUR HAPPY SNAPS?
I'VE GONE COMPLETELY FUCKING MAD.
KLIK
OPEN YOUR EYES, LITTLE CHLOE WICKMAN, YOU DON'T WANNA MISS THIS!
SWEET JESUS!

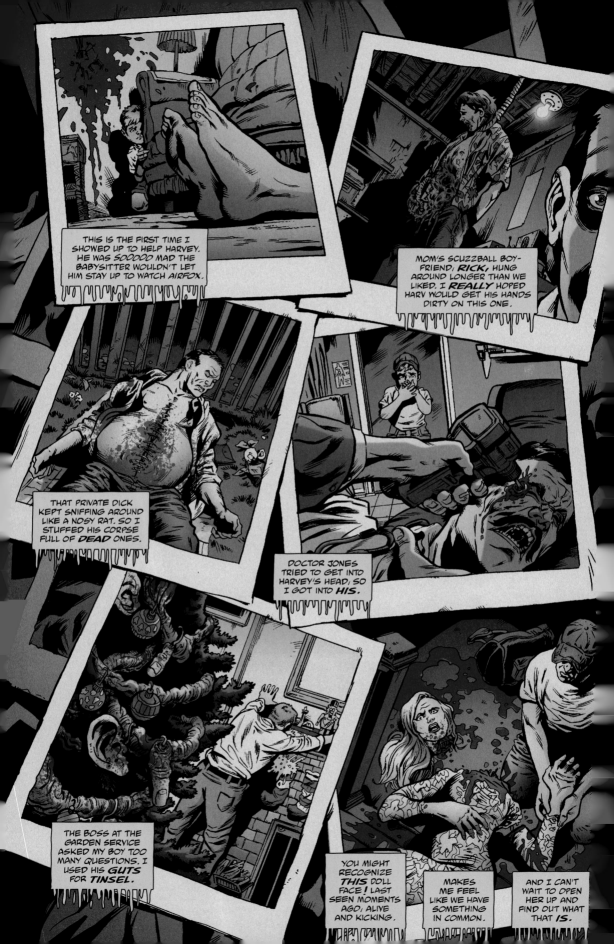

THIS IS THE FIRST TIME I SHOWED UP TO HELP HARVEY. HE WAS SOOOOO MAD THE BABYSITTER WOULDN'T LET HIM STAY UP TO WATCH *AIRFOX.*

MOM'S SCUZZBALL BOY-FRIEND, *RICK,* HUNG AROUND LONGER THAN WE LIKED. I *REALLY* HOPED HARV WOULD GET HIS HANDS DIRTY ON THIS ONE.

THAT PRIVATE DICK KEPT SNIFFING AROUND LIKE A NOSY RAT. SO I STUFFED HIS CORPSE FULL OF *DEAD* ONES.

DOCTOR JONES TRIED TO GET INTO HARVEY'S HEAD, SO I GOT INTO *HIS.*

THE BOSS AT THE GARDEN SERVICE ASKED MY BOY TOO MANY QUESTIONS. I USED HIS *GUTS* FOR *TINSEL.*

YOU MIGHT RECOGNIZE *THIS* DOLL FACE! LAST SEEN MOMENTS AGO, ALIVE AND KICKING.

MAKES ME FEEL LIKE WE HAVE SOMETHING IN COMMON.

AND I CAN'T WAIT TO OPEN HER UP AND FIND OUT WHAT THAT *IS.*

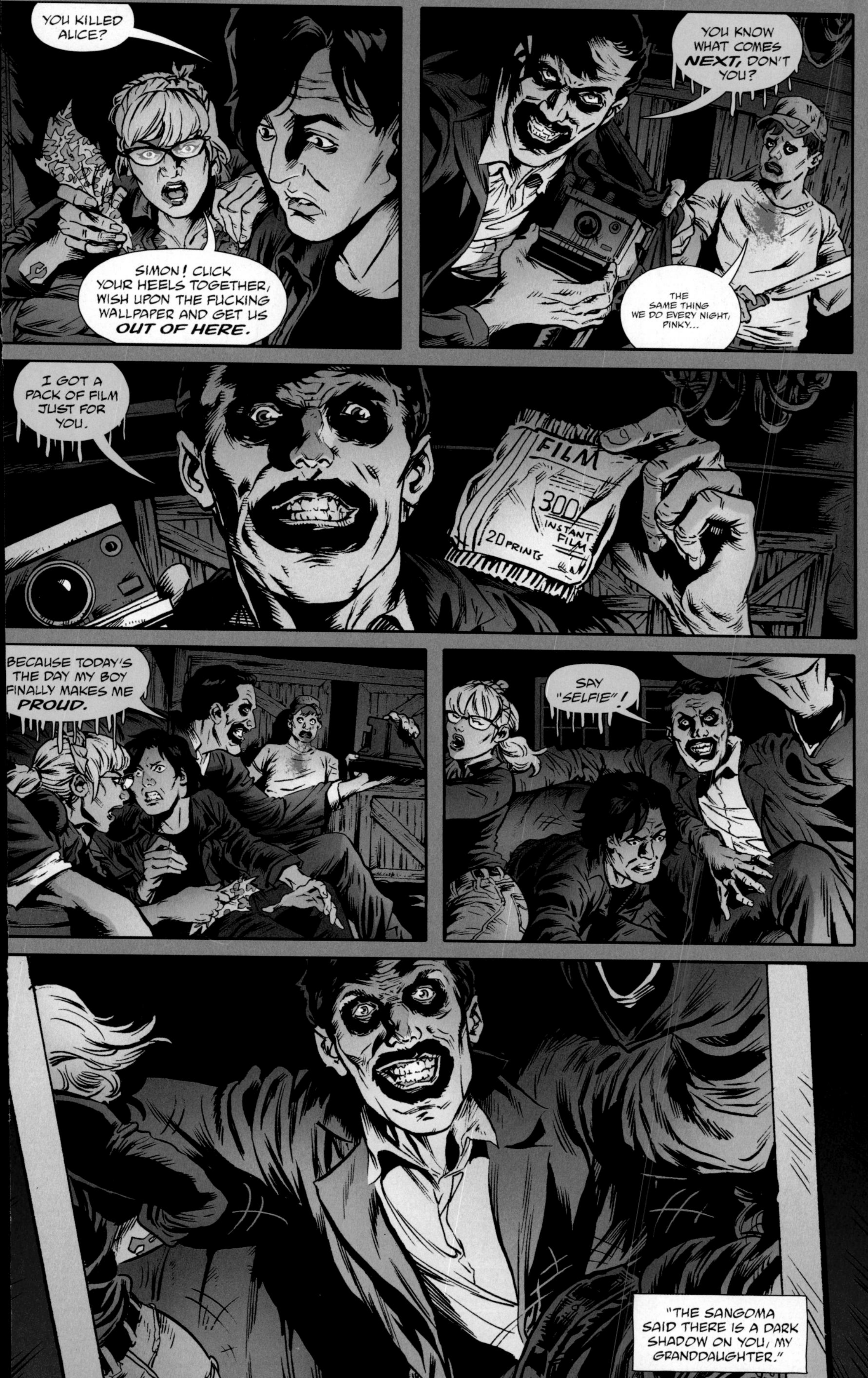
YOU KILLED ALICE?
SIMON! CLICK YOUR HEELS TOGETHER, WISH UPON THE FUCKING WALLPAPER AND GET US OUT OF HERE.
YOU KNOW WHAT COMES NEXT, DON'T YOU?
THE SAME THING WE DO EVERY NIGHT, PINKY...
I GOT A PACK OF FILM JUST FOR YOU.
FILM
300
INSTANT FILM
20 PRINTS
BECAUSE TODAY'S THE DAY MY BOY FINALLY MAKES ME PROUD.
SAY "SELFIE"!
"THE SANGOMA SAID THERE IS A DARK SHADOW ON YOU, MY GRANDDAUGHTER."

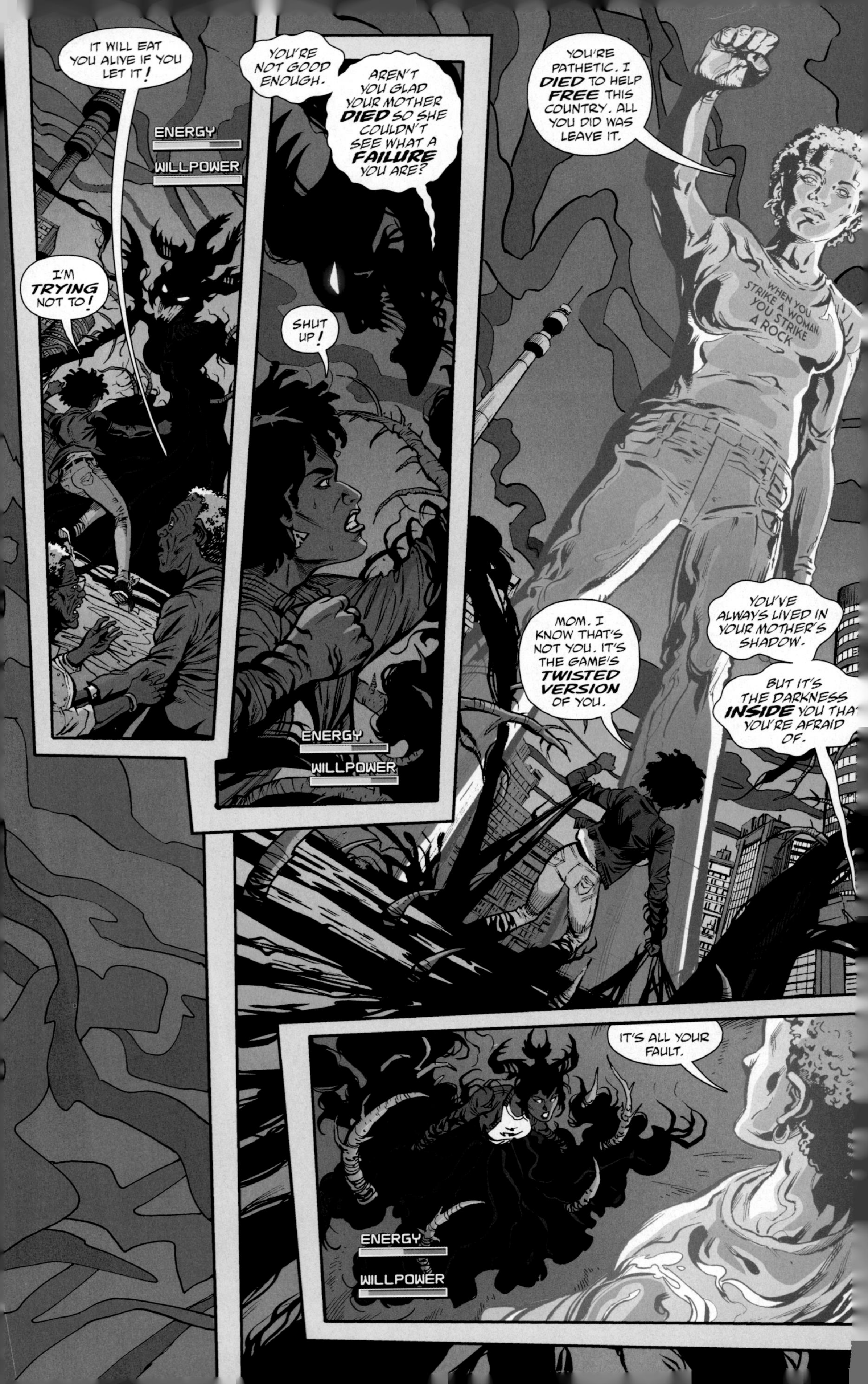
IT WILL EAT YOU ALIVE IF YOU LET IT!
ENERGY
WILLPOWER
I'M TRYING NOT TO!
YOU'RE NOT GOOD ENOUGH.
AREN'T YOU GLAD YOUR MOTHER DIED SO SHE COULDN'T SEE WHAT A FAILURE YOU ARE?
SHUT UP!
ENERGY
WILLPOWER
YOU'RE PATHETIC. I DIED TO HELP FREE THIS COUNTRY. ALL YOU DID WAS LEAVE IT.
WHEN YOU STRIKE A WOMAN, YOU STRIKE A ROCK
MOM. I KNOW THAT'S NOT YOU. IT'S THE GAME'S TWISTED VERSION OF YOU.
YOU'VE ALWAYS LIVED IN YOUR MOTHER'S SHADOW.
BUT IT'S THE DARKNESS INSIDE YOU THA' YOU'RE AFRAID OF.
IT'S ALL YOUR FAULT.
ENERGY
WILLPOWER

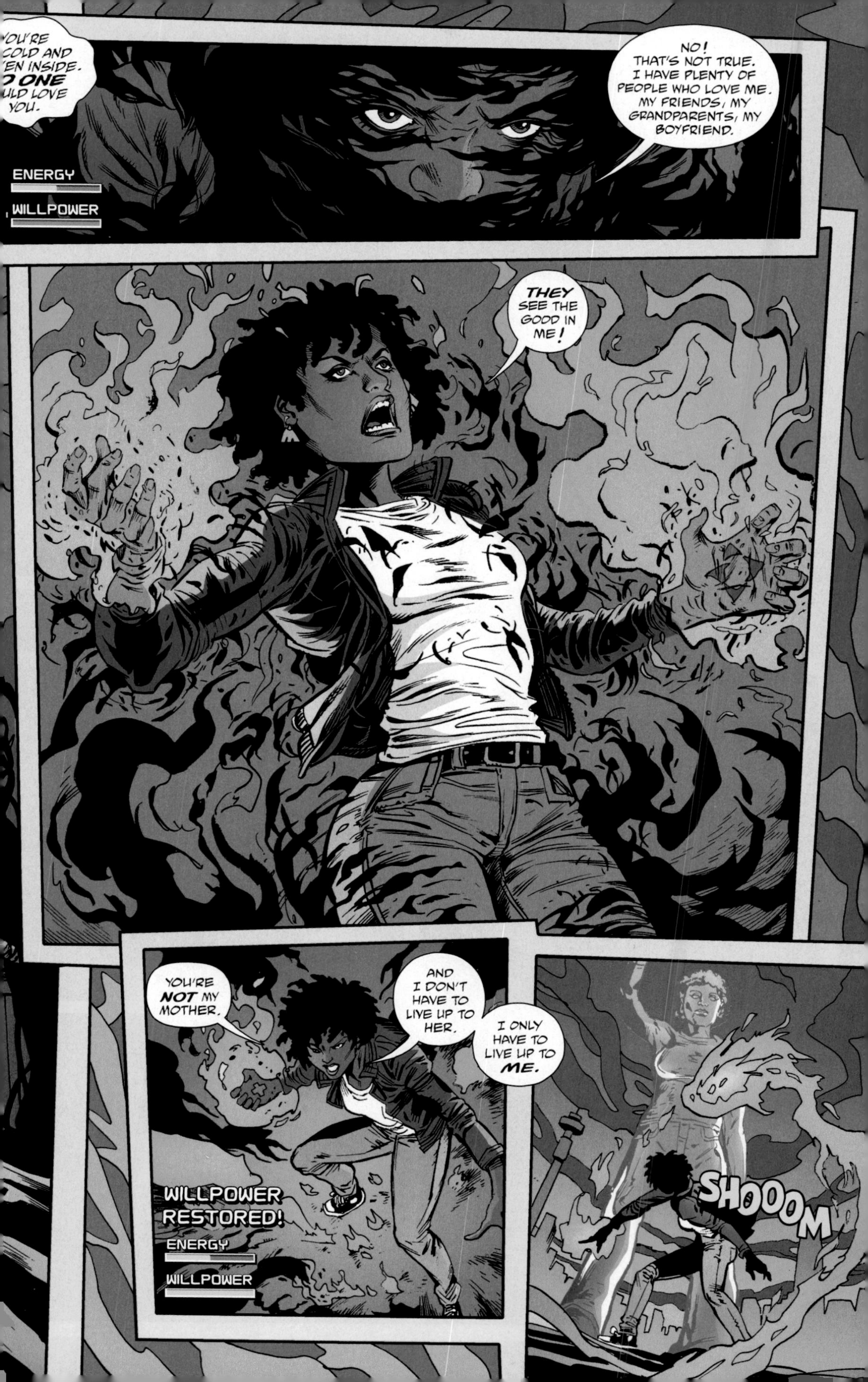

YOU'RE COLD AND ...EN INSIDE. ...O ONE ...ULD LOVE YOU.
NO! THAT'S NOT TRUE. I HAVE PLENTY OF PEOPLE WHO LOVE ME. MY FRIENDS, MY GRANDPARENTS, MY BOYFRIEND.
ENERGY
WILLPOWER
THEY SEE THE GOOD IN ME!
YOU'RE NOT MY MOTHER.
AND I DON'T HAVE TO LIVE UP TO HER.
I ONLY HAVE TO LIVE UP TO ME.
WILLPOWER RESTORED!
ENERGY
WILLPOWER
SHOOOM

Mr. Empty

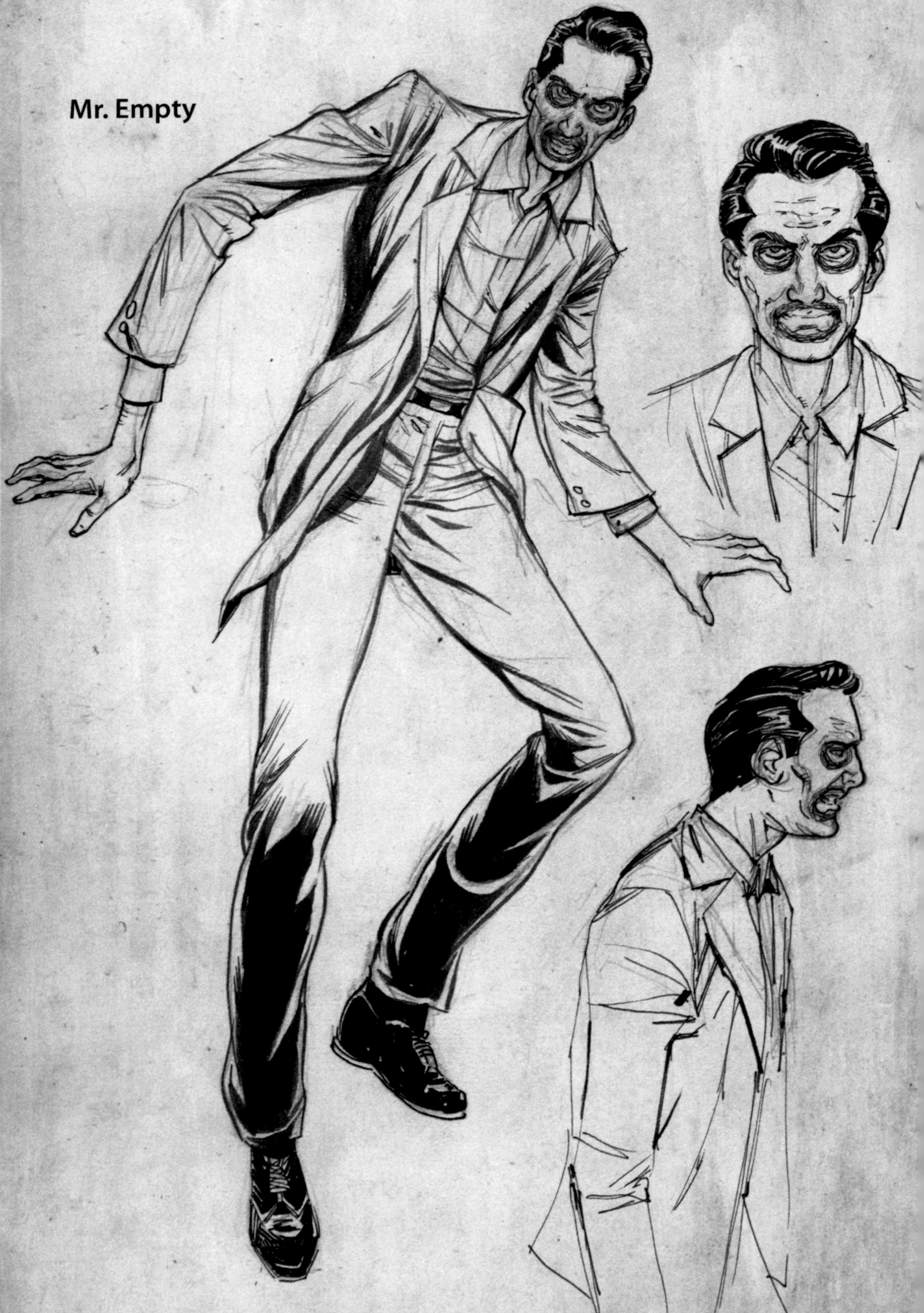

BACK IN SILVERWEED COVE...

GHK-GHK-GHK...

BLAAUGH

SHPLUK

STOP IT! YOU CAN'T EAT THESE PEOPLE! I DIDN'T GIVE YOU PERMISSION!

TEO! HELP ME, SHE WON'T LISTEN!

WELCOME TO AKHER-- AAAGH!

EEUGH

OH MY GOSH, TEO!

NO...STAY AWAY, KIRI...

RRRRRRRIIIIP

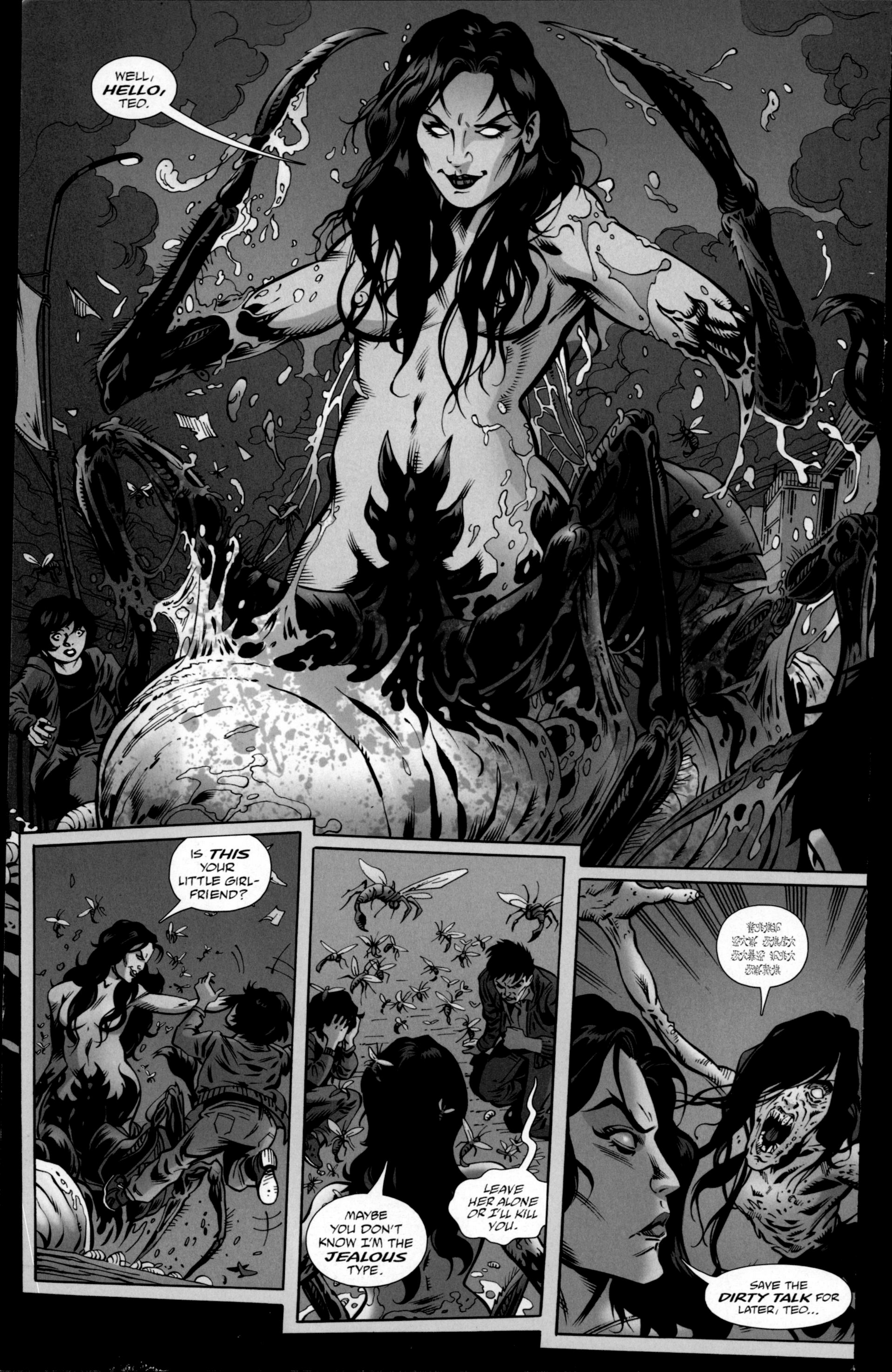
WELL, HELLO, TEO.
IS THIS YOUR LITTLE GIRL-FRIEND?
MAYBE YOU DON'T KNOW I'M THE JEALOUS TYPE.
LEAVE HER ALONE OR I'LL KILL YOU.
SAVE THE DIRTY TALK FOR LATER, TEO...

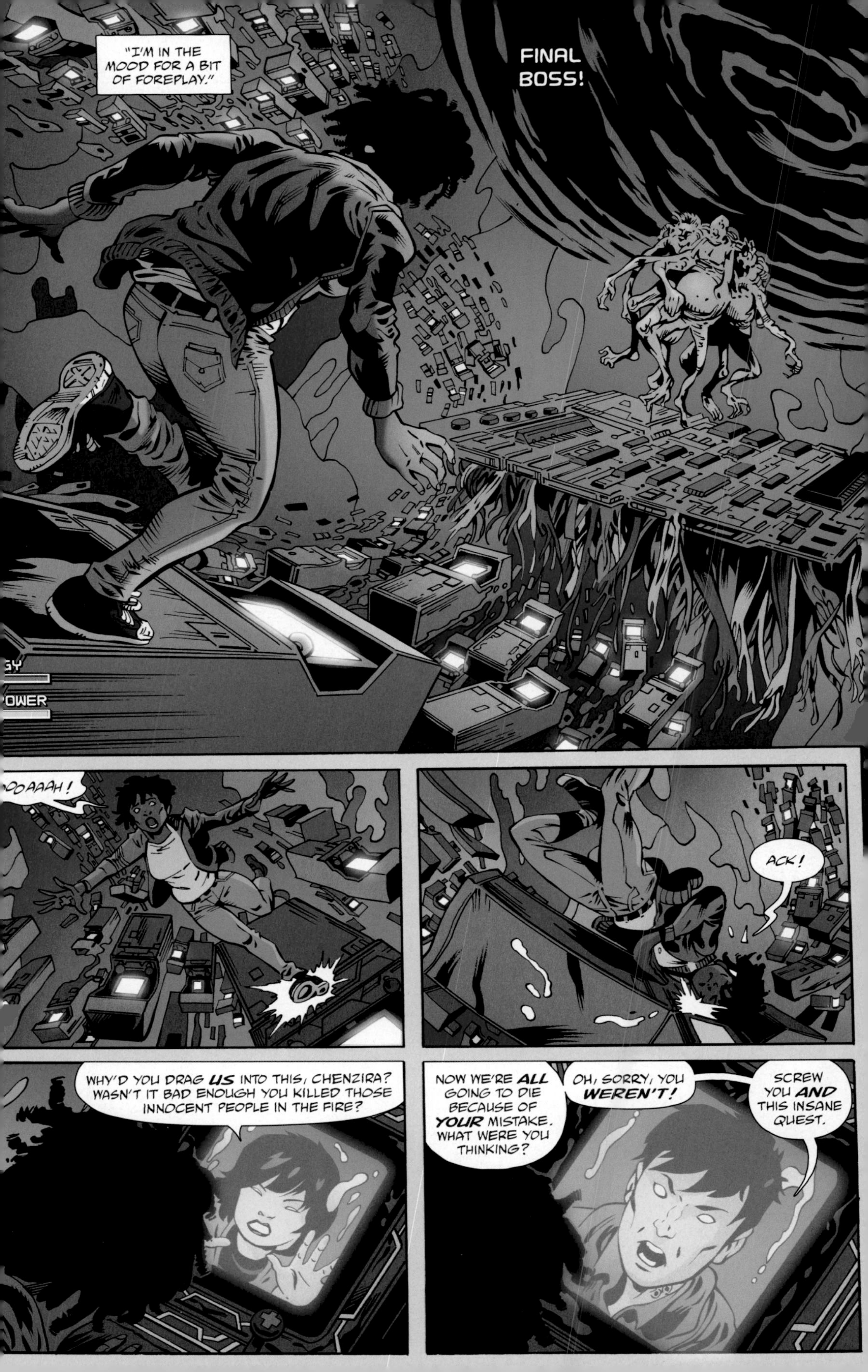
"I'M IN THE MOOD FOR A BIT OF FOREPLAY."
FINAL BOSS!
OOAAAH!
ACK!
WHY'D YOU DRAG **US** INTO THIS, CHENZIRA? WASN'T IT BAD ENOUGH YOU KILLED THOSE INNOCENT PEOPLE IN THE FIRE?
NOW WE'RE **ALL** GOING TO DIE BECAUSE OF **YOUR** MISTAKE. WHAT WERE YOU THINKING?
OH, SORRY, YOU **WEREN'T!**
SCREW YOU **AND** THIS INSANE QUEST.

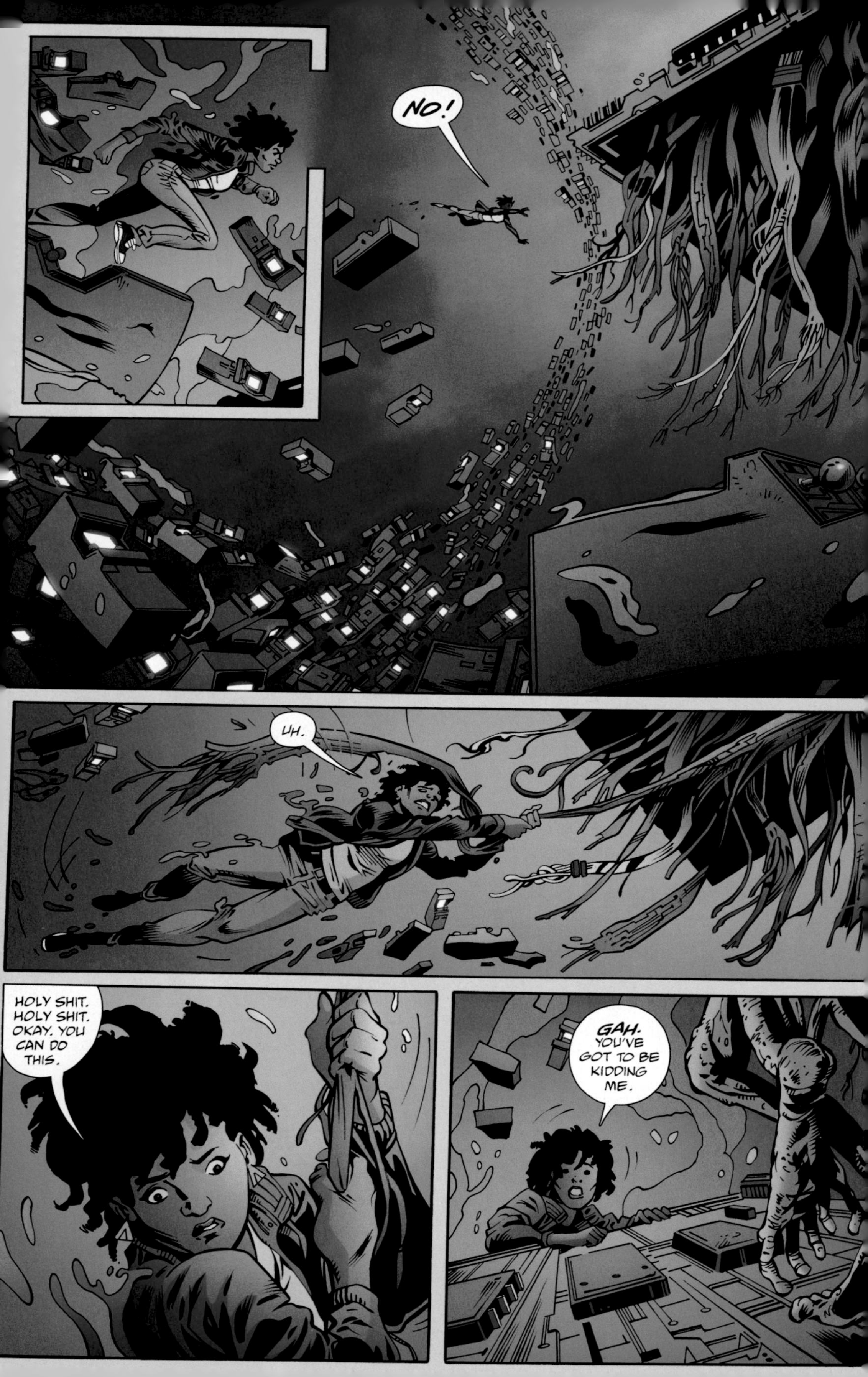
NO!
UH.
HOLY SHIT. HOLY SHIT. OKAY. YOU CAN DO THIS.
GAH. YOU'VE GOT TO BE KIDDING ME.

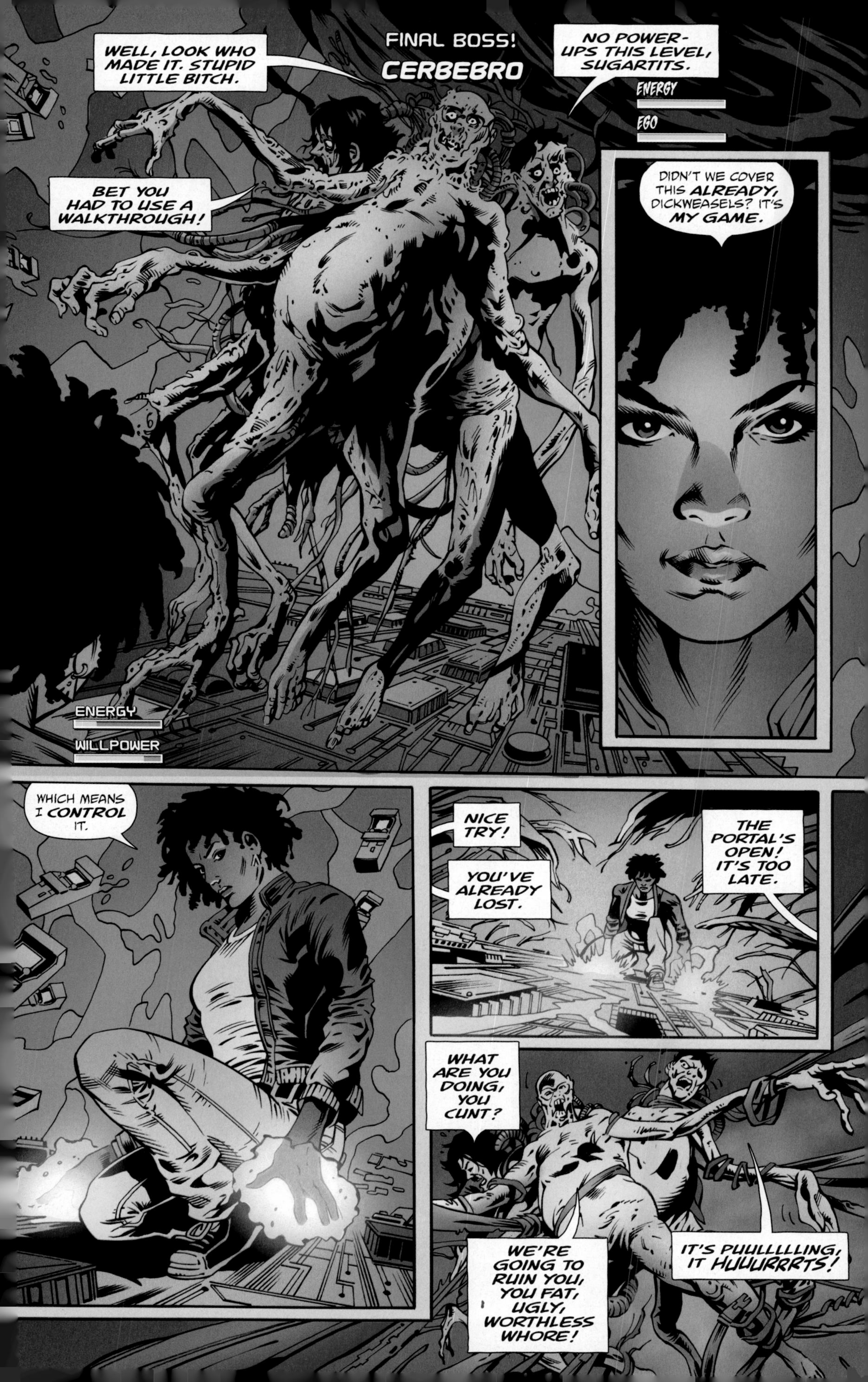
FINAL BOSS!
CERBEBRO
WELL, LOOK WHO MADE IT. STUPID LITTLE BITCH.
NO POWER-UPS THIS LEVEL, SUGARTITS.
ENERGY
EGO
BET YOU HAD TO USE A WALKTHROUGH!
DIDN'T WE COVER THIS ALREADY, DICKWEASELS? IT'S MY GAME.
ENERGY
WILLPOWER
WHICH MEANS I CONTROL IT.
NICE TRY!
YOU'VE ALREADY LOST.
THE PORTAL'S OPEN! IT'S TOO LATE.
WHAT ARE YOU DOING, YOU CUNT?
WE'RE GOING TO RUIN YOU, YOU FAT, UGLY, WORTHLESS WHORE!
IT'S PUUULLLLING, IT HUUURRRTS!

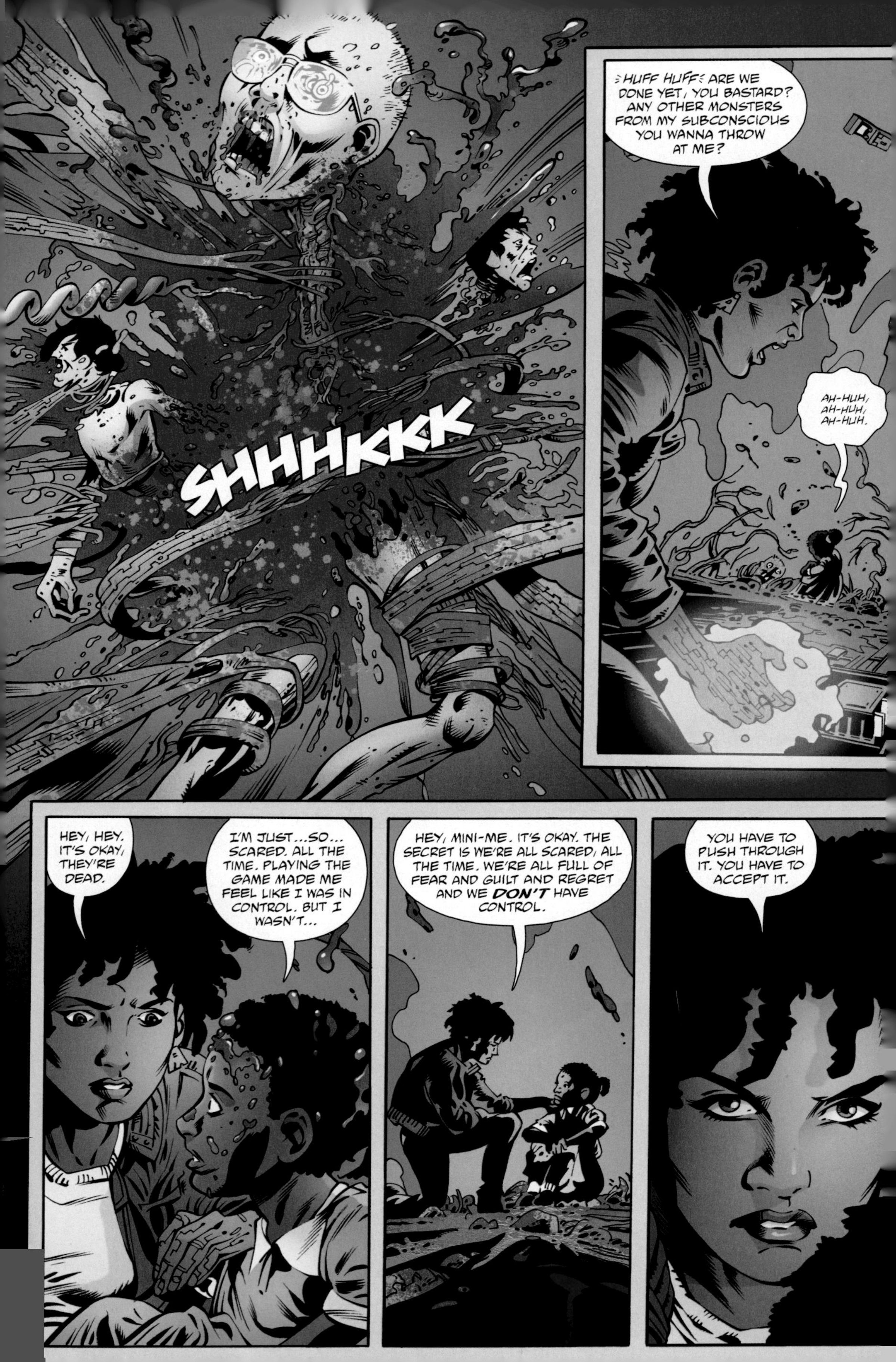
SHHHKKK
HUFF HUFF ARE WE DONE YET, YOU BASTARD? ANY OTHER MONSTERS FROM MY SUBCONSCIOUS YOU WANNA THROW AT ME?
AH-HUH, AH-HUH, AH-HUH.
HEY, HEY. IT'S OKAY, THEY'RE DEAD.
I'M JUST...SO... SCARED. ALL THE TIME. PLAYING THE GAME MADE ME FEEL LIKE I WAS IN CONTROL. BUT I WASN'T...
HEY, MINI-ME. IT'S OKAY. THE SECRET IS WE'RE ALL SCARED, ALL THE TIME. WE'RE ALL FULL OF FEAR AND GUILT AND REGRET AND WE DON'T HAVE CONTROL.
YOU HAVE TO PUSH THROUGH IT. YOU HAVE TO ACCEPT IT.

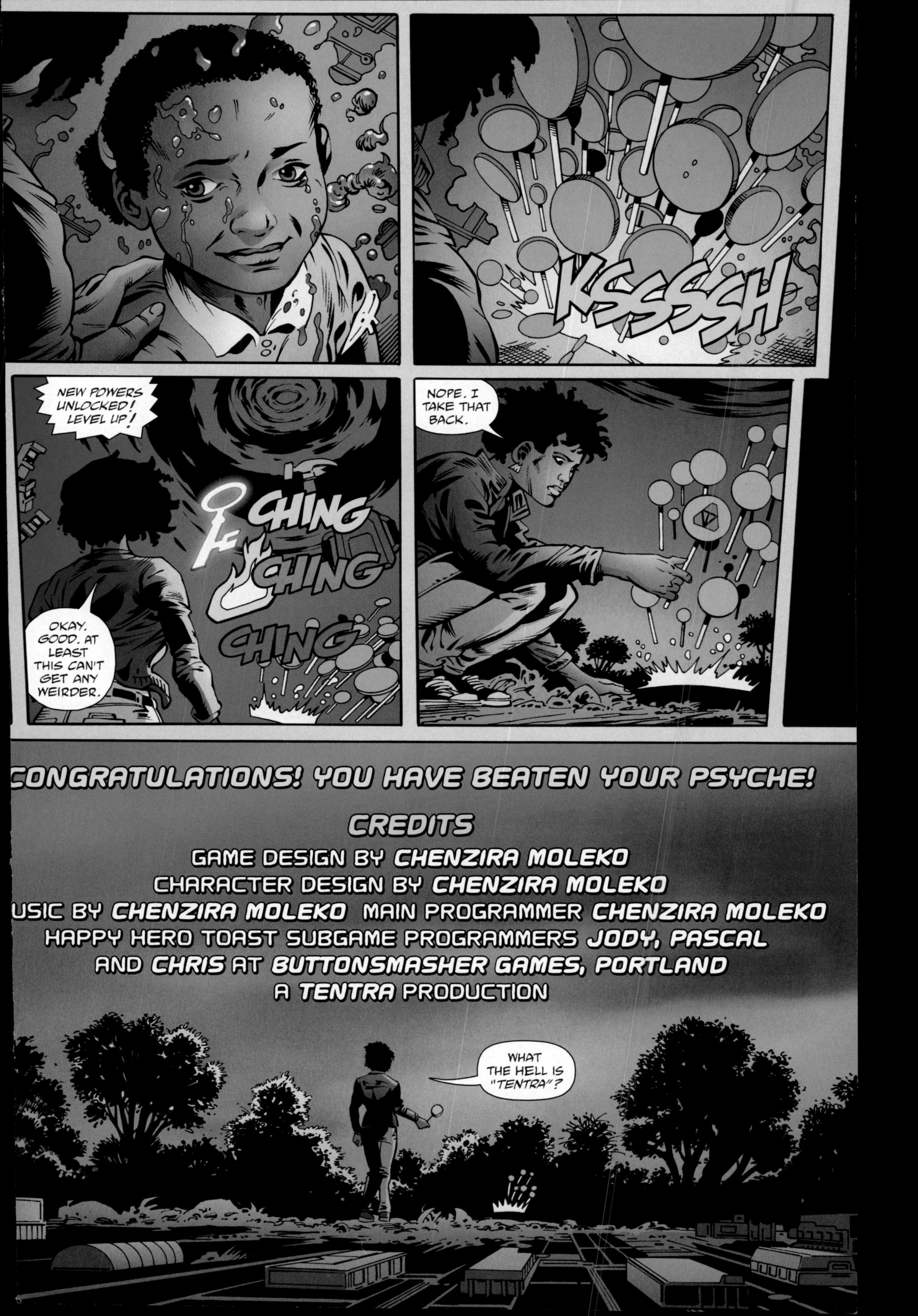
KSSSSH
NEW POWERS UNLOCKED! LEVEL UP!
CHING
CHING
CHING
OKAY. GOOD. AT LEAST THIS CAN'T GET ANY WEIRDER.
NOPE. I TAKE THAT BACK.
CONGRATULATIONS! YOU HAVE BEATEN YOUR PSYCHE!
CREDITS
GAME DESIGN BY CHENZIRA MOLEKO
CHARACTER DESIGN BY CHENZIRA MOLEKO
USIC BY CHENZIRA MOLEKO MAIN PROGRAMMER CHENZIRA MOLEKO
HAPPY HERO TOAST SUBGAME PROGRAMMERS JODY, PASCAL
AND CHRIS AT BUTTONSMASHER GAMES, PORTLAND
A TENTRA PRODUCTION
WHAT THE HELL IS "TENTRA"?

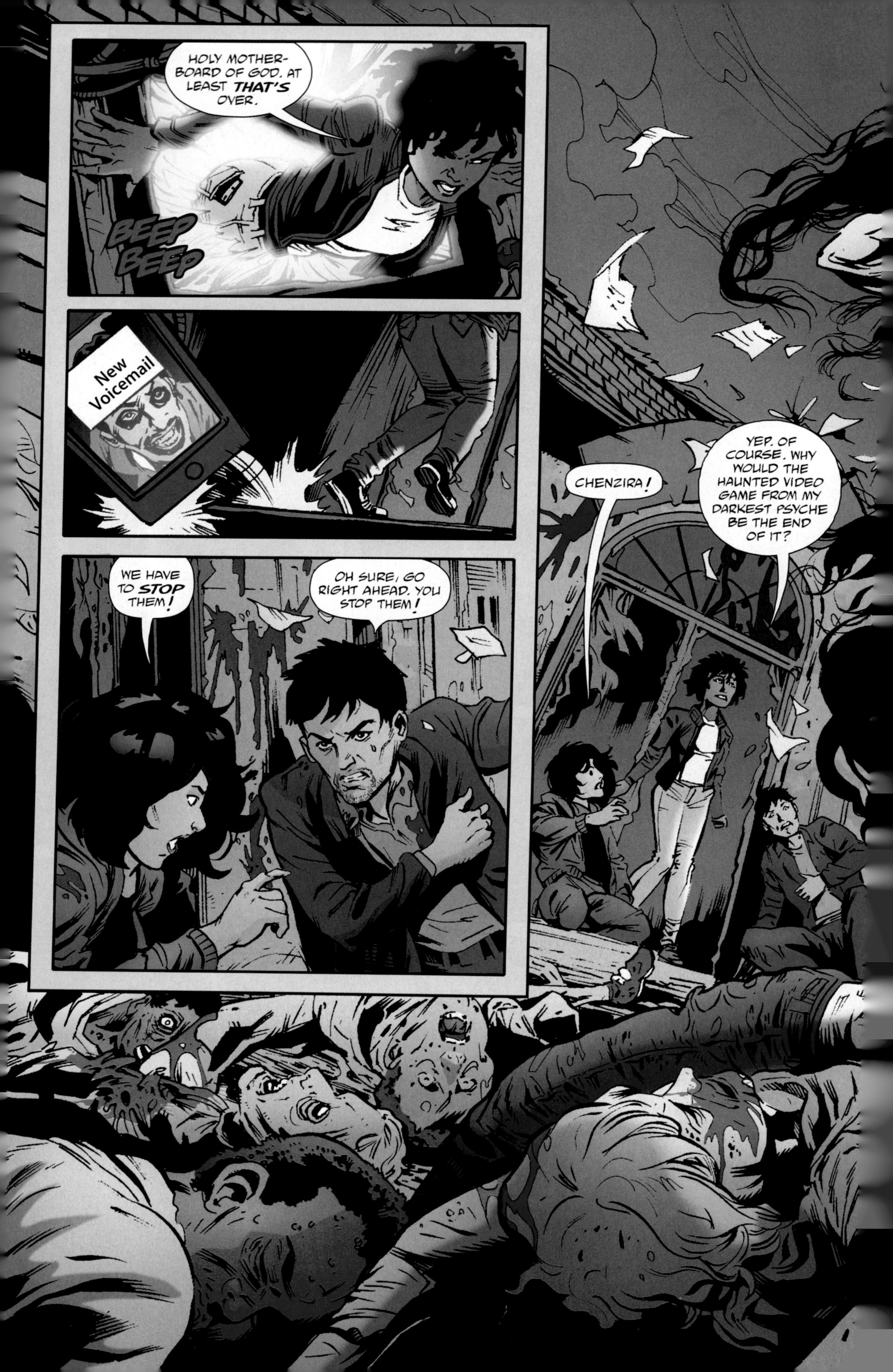
HOLY MOTHER-BOARD OF GOD. AT LEAST THAT'S OVER.
BEEP BEEP
New Voicemail
WE HAVE TO STOP THEM!
OH SURE, GO RIGHT AHEAD. YOU STOP THEM!
CHENZIRA!
YEP. OF COURSE. WHY WOULD THE HAUNTED VIDEO GAME FROM MY DARKEST PSYCHE BE THE END OF IT?

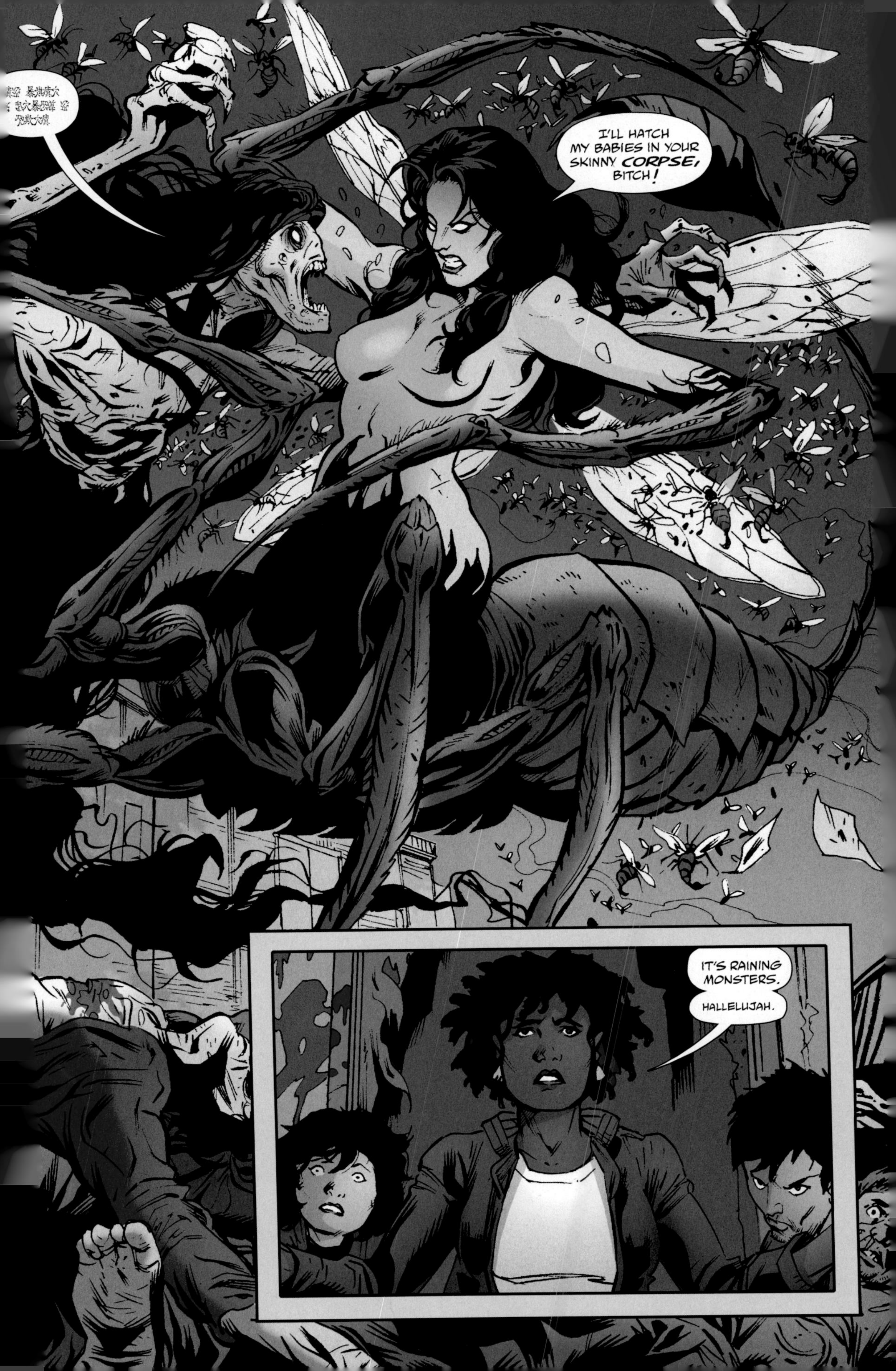
I'LL HATCH MY BABIES IN YOUR SKINNY CORPSE, BITCH!
IT'S RAINING MONSTERS.
HALLELUJAH.

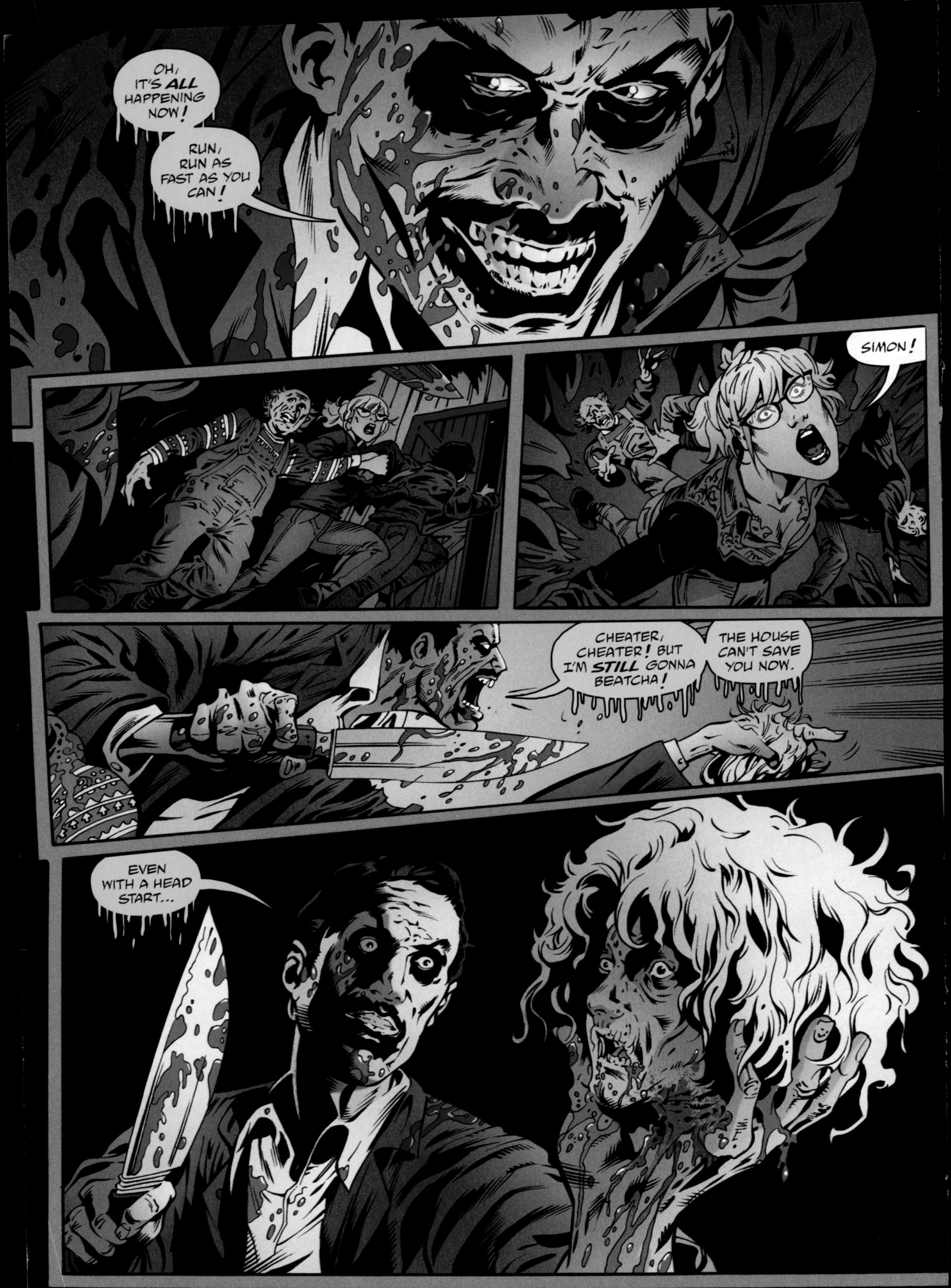
OH, IT'S ALL HAPPENING NOW!
RUN, RUN AS FAST AS YOU CAN!
SIMON!
CHEATER, CHEATER! BUT I'M STILL GONNA BEATCHA!
THE HOUSE CAN'T SAVE YOU NOW.
EVEN WITH A HEAD START...

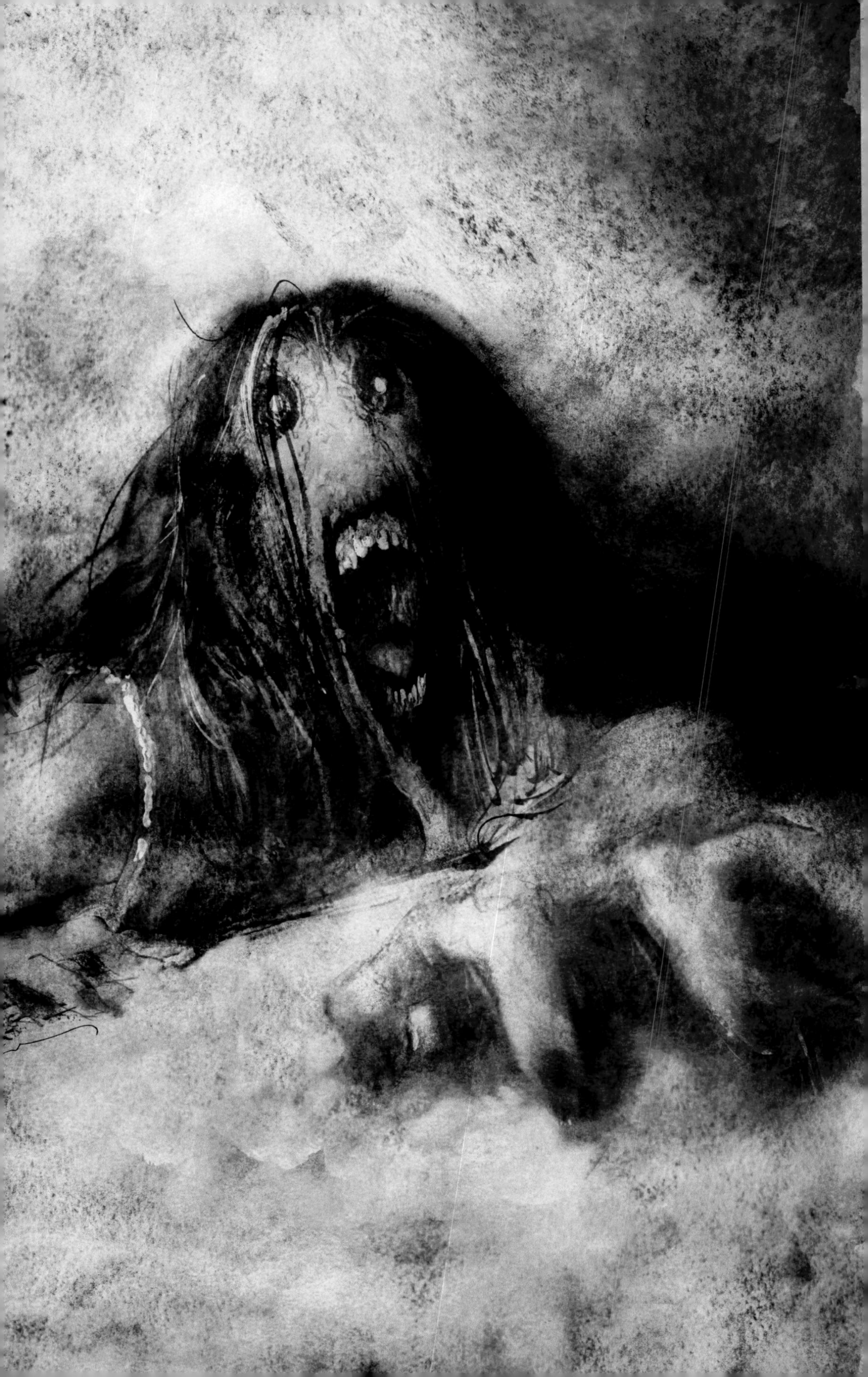

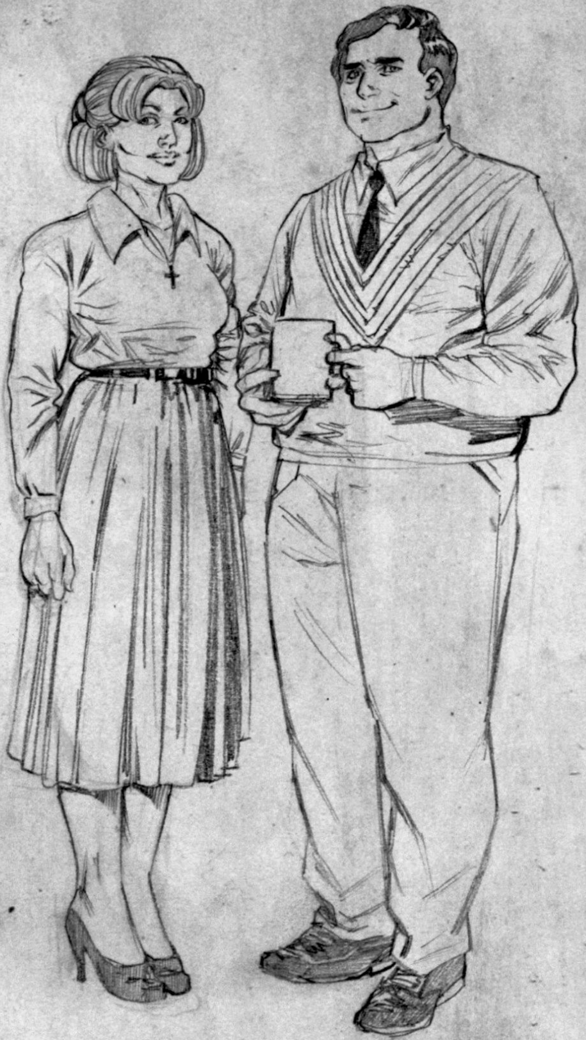

Bill and Faith Hinkel

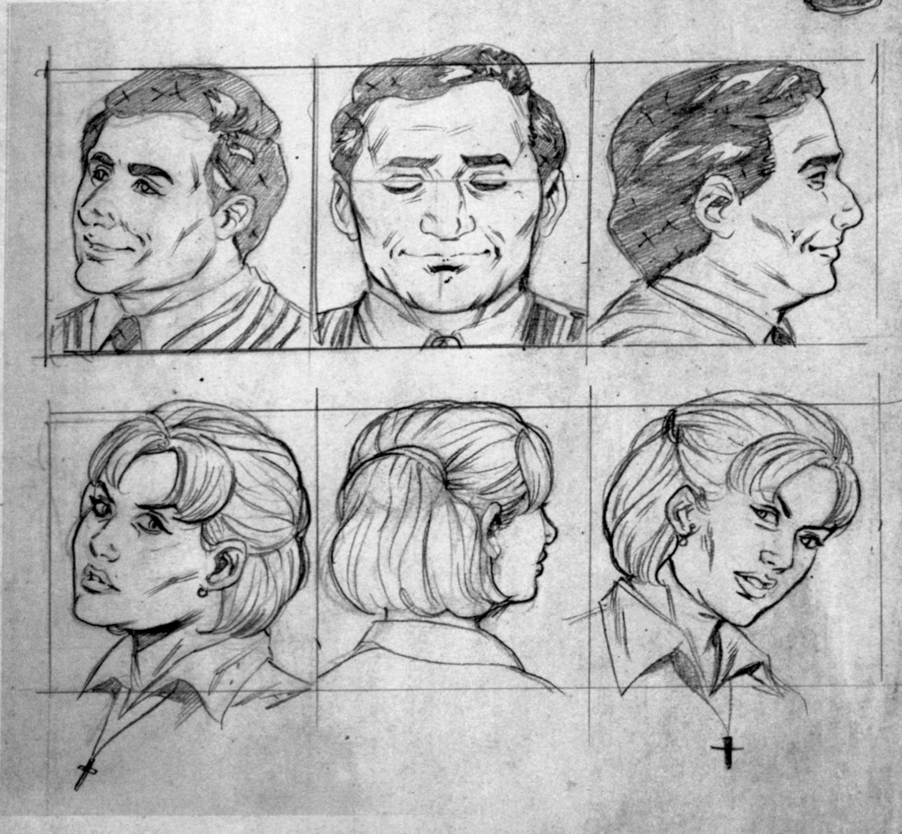

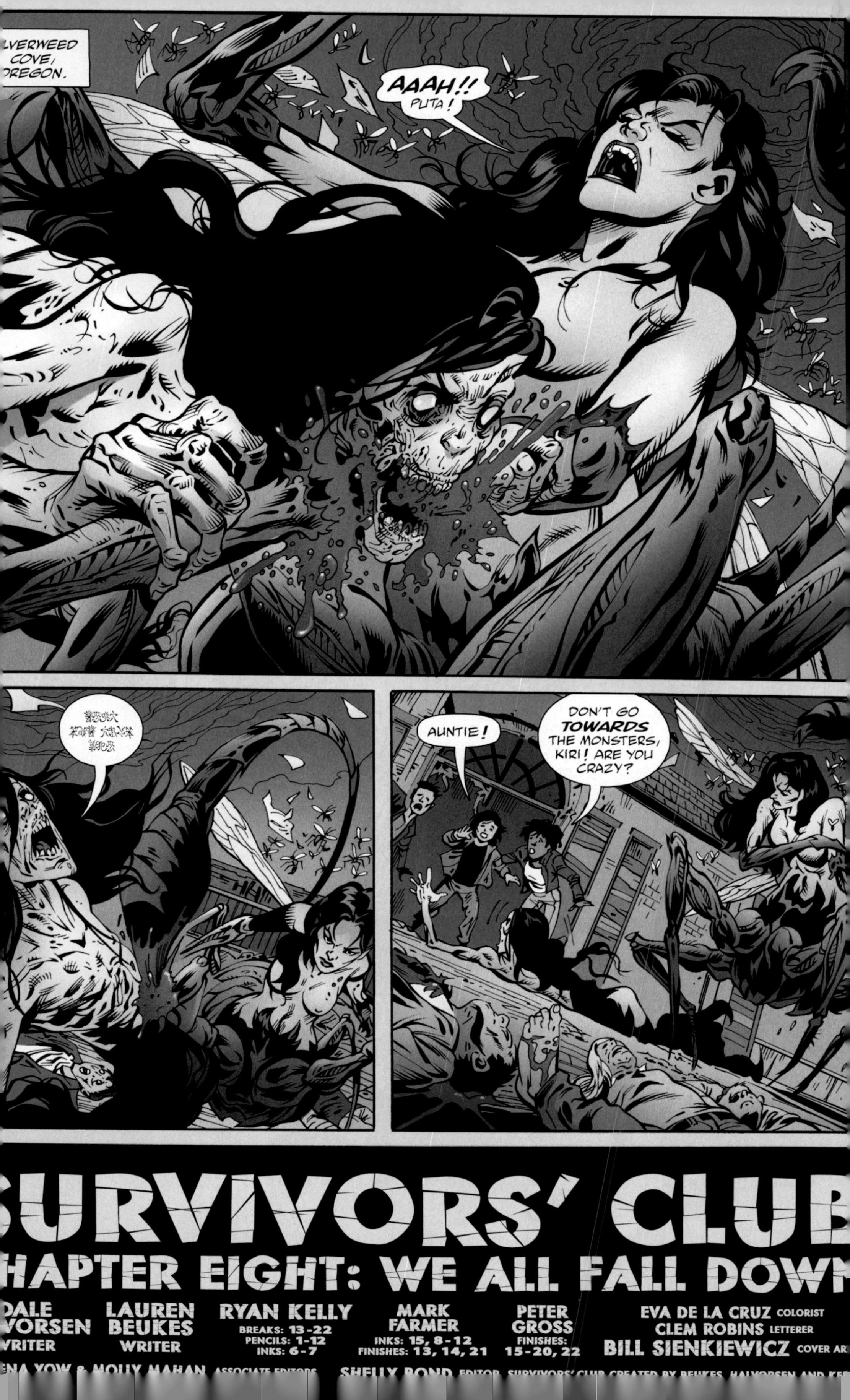
LVERWEED COVE, OREGON.
AAAH!! PUTA!
AUNTIE!
DON'T GO TOWARDS THE MONSTERS, KIRI! ARE YOU CRAZY?
SURVIVORS' CLUB
HAPTER EIGHT: WE ALL FALL DOWN
DALE VORSEN WRITER
LAUREN BEUKES WRITER
RYAN KELLY BREAKS: 13-22 PENCILS: 1-12 INKS: 6-7
MARK FARMER INKS: 15, 8-12 FINISHES: 13, 14, 21
PETER GROSS FINISHES: 15-20, 22
EVA DE LA CRUZ COLORIST
CLEM ROBINS LETTERER
BILL SIENKIEWICZ COVER AR
ENA YOW & MOLLY MAHAN ASSOCIATE EDITORS
SHELLY BOND EDITOR

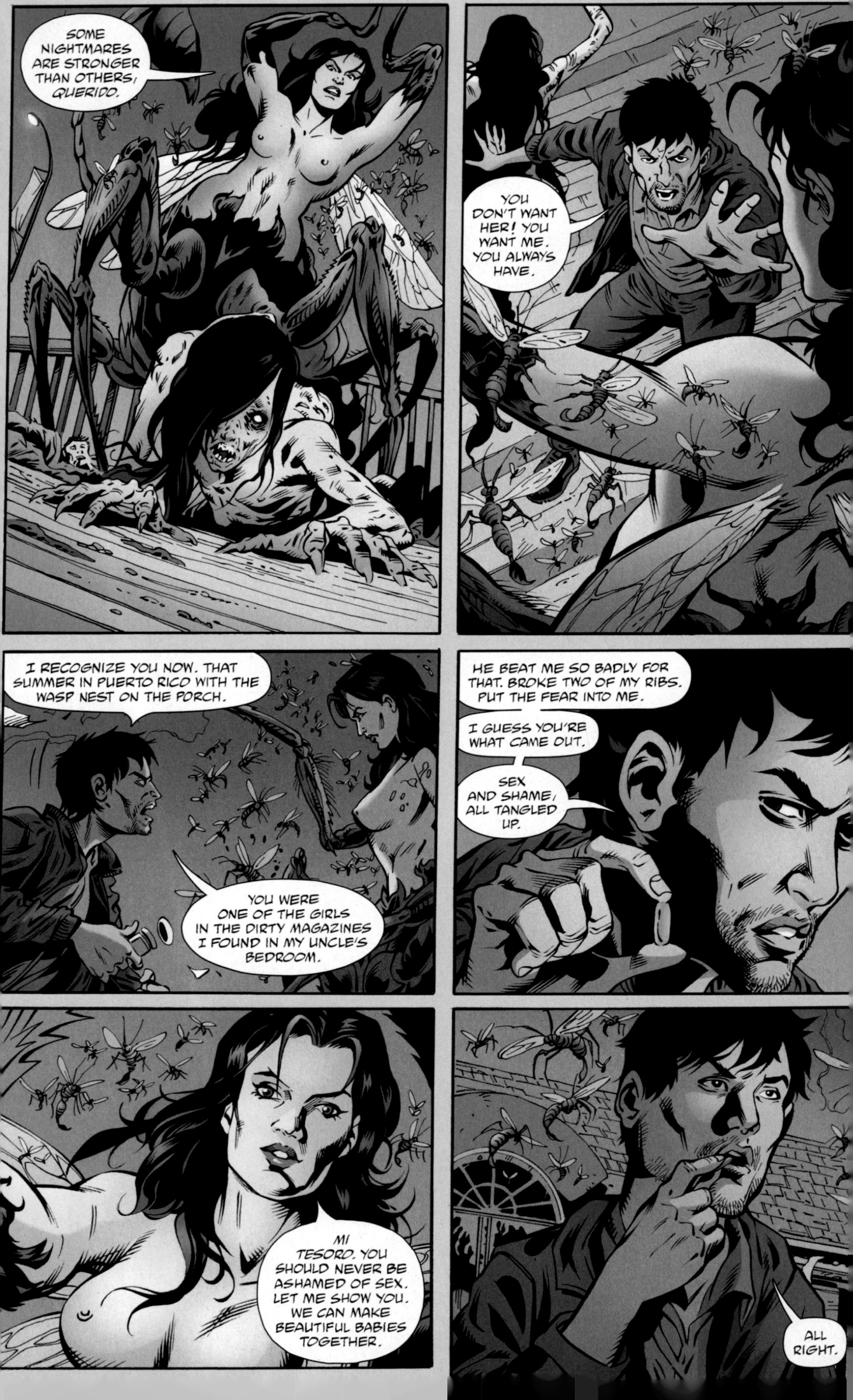
SOME NIGHTMARES ARE STRONGER THAN OTHERS, QUERIDO.
YOU DON'T WANT HER! YOU WANT ME. YOU ALWAYS HAVE.
I RECOGNIZE YOU NOW. THAT SUMMER IN PUERTO RICO WITH THE WASP NEST ON THE PORCH.
YOU WERE ONE OF THE GIRLS IN THE DIRTY MAGAZINES I FOUND IN MY UNCLE'S BEDROOM.
HE BEAT ME SO BADLY FOR THAT. BROKE TWO OF MY RIBS. PUT THE FEAR INTO ME.
I GUESS YOU'RE WHAT CAME OUT.
SEX AND SHAME, ALL TANGLED UP.
MI TESORO. YOU SHOULD NEVER BE ASHAMED OF SEX. LET ME SHOW YOU. WE CAN MAKE BEAUTIFUL BABIES TOGETHER.
ALL RIGHT.

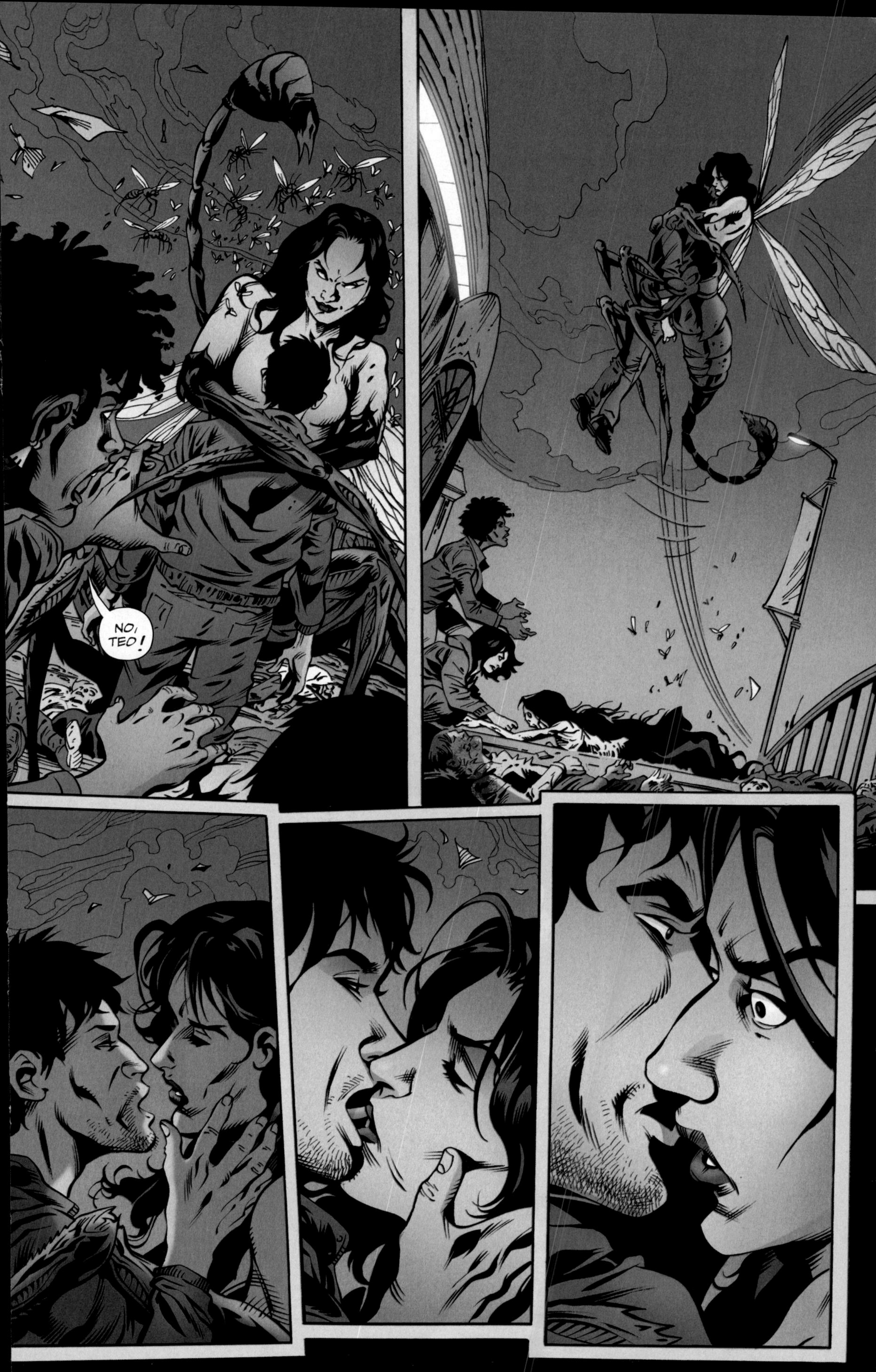
NO, TEO!

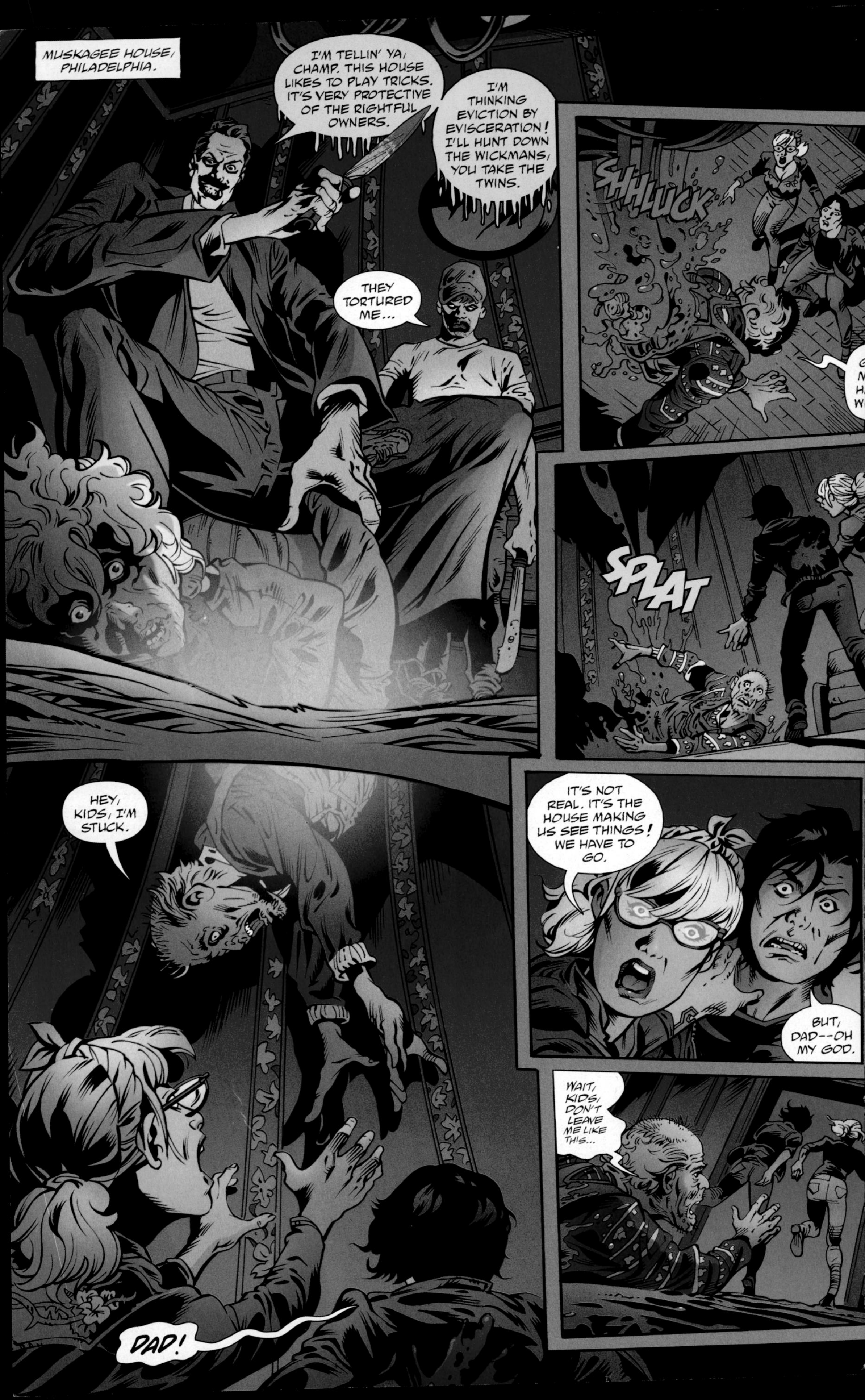
MUSKAGEE HOUSE, PHILADELPHIA.
I'M TELLIN' YA, CHAMP. THIS HOUSE LIKES TO PLAY TRICKS. IT'S VERY PROTECTIVE OF THE RIGHTFUL OWNERS.
I'M THINKING EVICTION BY EVISCERATION! I'LL HUNT DOWN THE WICKMANS, YOU TAKE THE TWINS.
THEY TORTURED ME...
SHHLUCK
SPLAT
HEY, KIDS, I'M STUCK.
DAD!
IT'S NOT REAL. IT'S THE HOUSE MAKING US SEE THINGS! WE HAVE TO GO.
BUT, DAD--OH MY GOD.
WAIT, KIDS, DON'T LEAVE ME LIKE THIS...

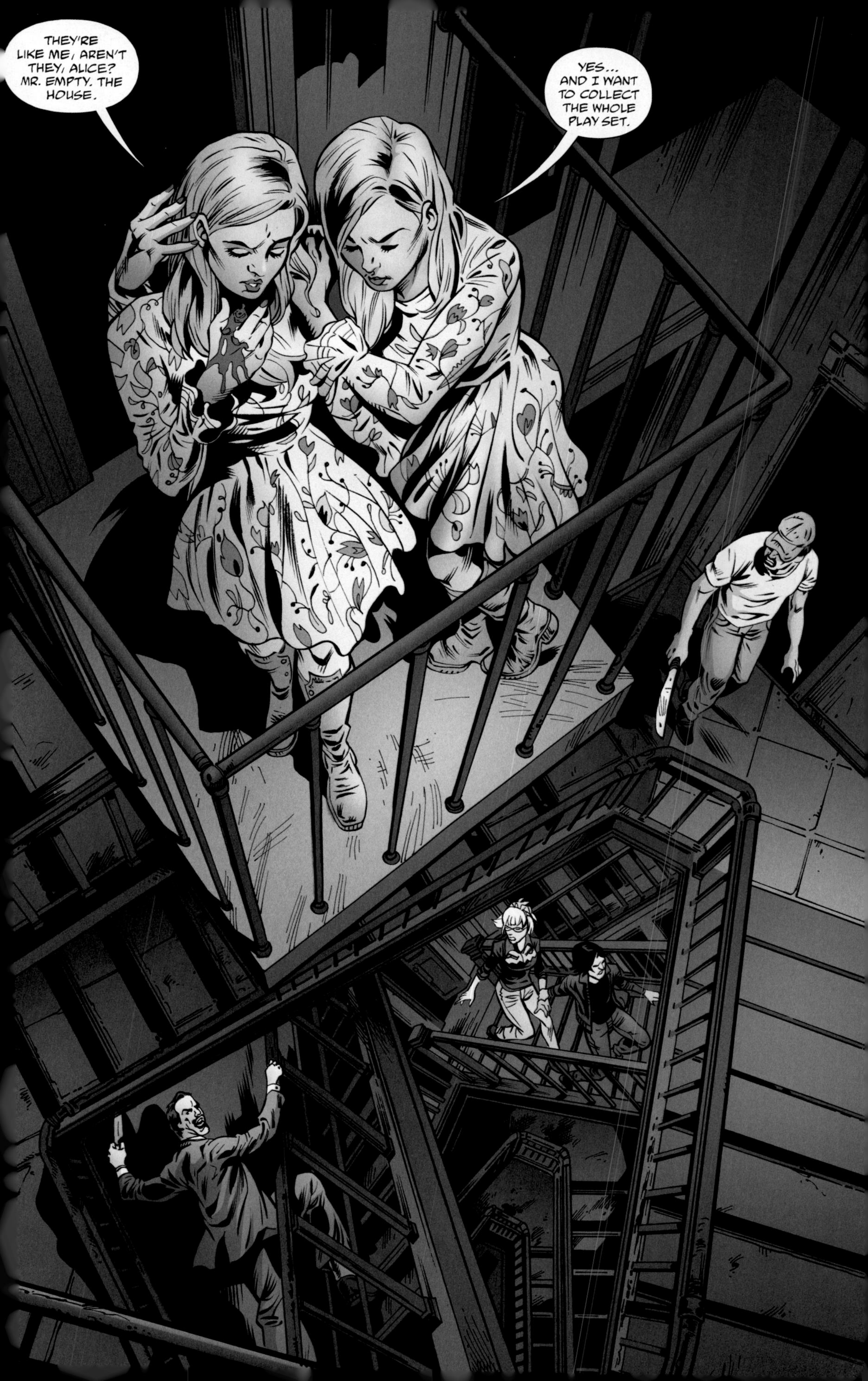
THEY'RE LIKE ME, AREN'T THEY, ALICE? MR. EMPTY. THE HOUSE.
YES... AND I WANT TO COLLECT THE WHOLE PLAY SET.

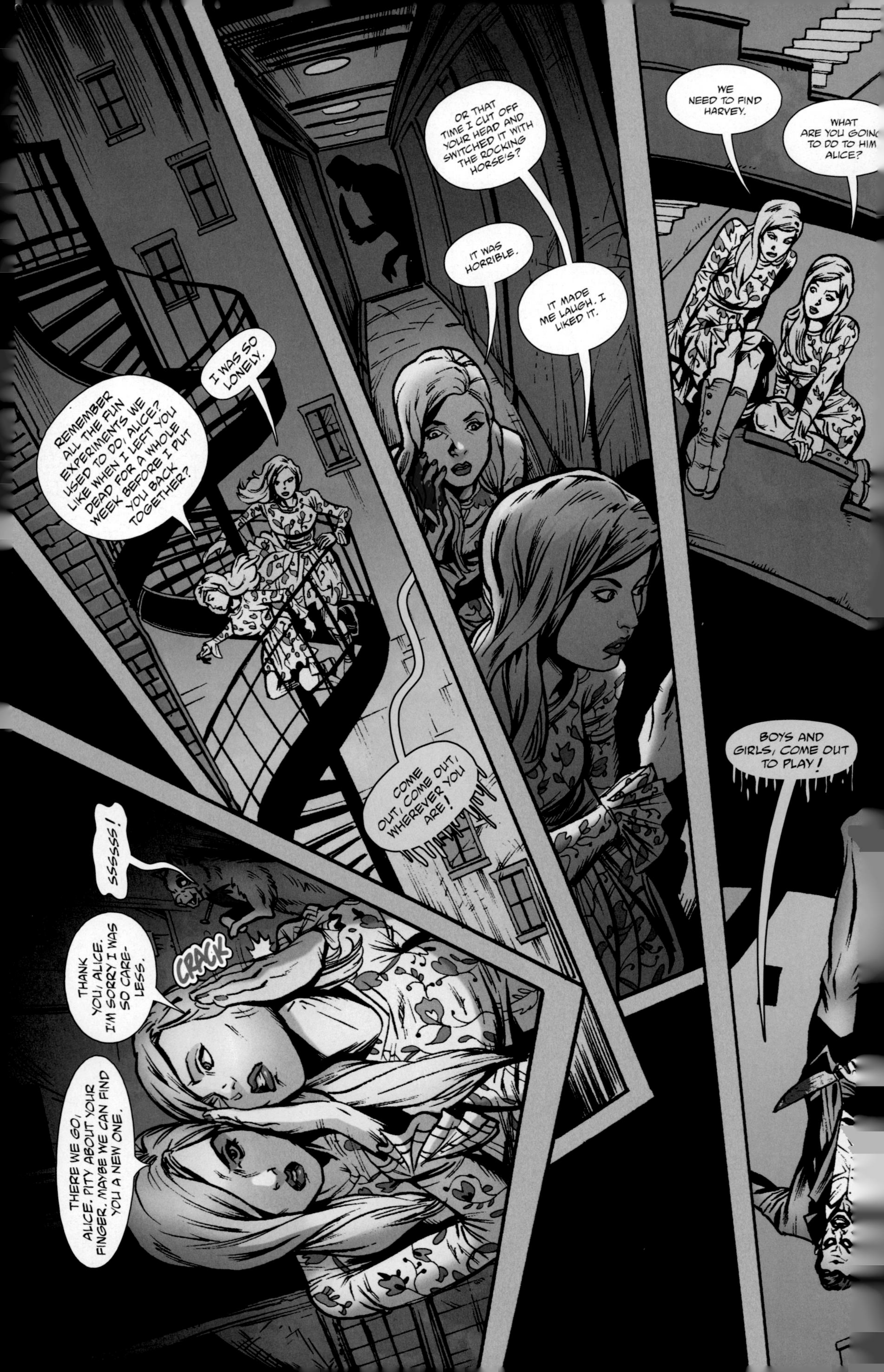
REMEMBER ALL THE FUN EXPERIMENTS WE USED TO DO, ALICE? LIKE WHEN I LEFT YOU DEAD FOR A WHOLE WEEK BEFORE I PUT YOU BACK TOGETHER?
I WAS SO LONELY.
OR THAT TIME I CUT OFF YOUR HEAD AND SWITCHED IT WITH THE ROCKING HORSE'S?
IT WAS HORRIBLE.
IT MADE ME LAUGH. I LIKED IT.
WE NEED TO FIND HARVEY.
WHAT ARE YOU GOING TO DO TO HIM ALICE?
COME OUT, COME OUT, WHEREVER YOU ARE!
BOYS AND GIRLS, COME OUT TO PLAY!
SSSSSS!
CRACK
THANK YOU, ALICE. I'M SORRY I WAS SO CARE-LESS.
THERE WE GO, ALICE. PITY ABOUT YOUR FINGER. MAYBE WE CAN FIND YOU A NEW ONE.

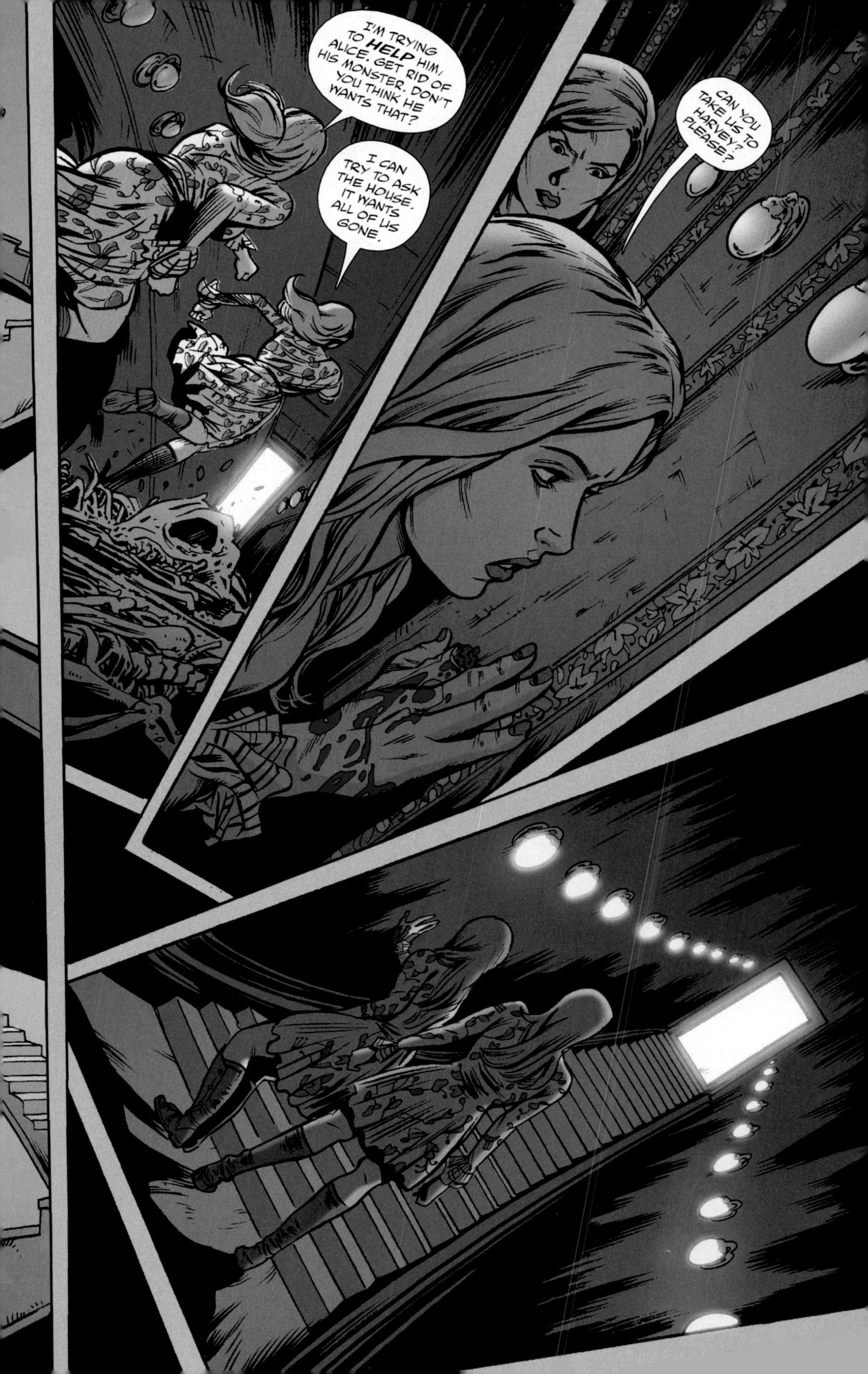
I'M TRYING TO HELP HIM, ALICE. GET RID OF HIS MONSTER. DON'T YOU THINK HE WANTS THAT?
I CAN TRY TO ASK THE HOUSE. IT WANTS ALL OF US GONE.
CAN YOU TAKE US TO HARVEY? PLEASE?

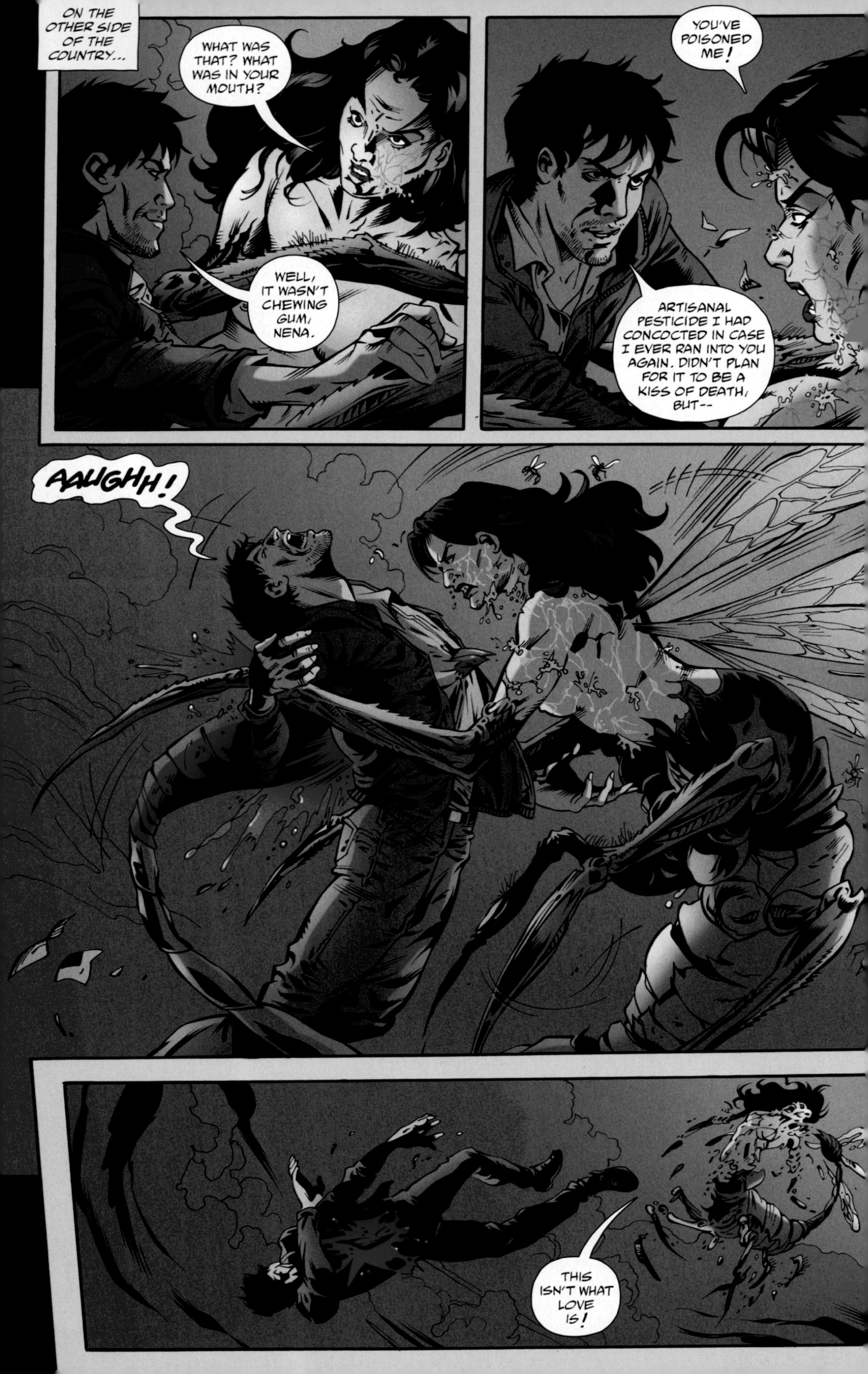
ON THE OTHER SIDE OF THE COUNTRY...
WHAT WAS THAT? WHAT WAS IN YOUR MOUTH?
WELL, IT WASN'T CHEWING GUM, NENA.
YOU'VE POISONED ME!
ARTISANAL PESTICIDE I HAD CONCOCTED IN CASE I EVER RAN INTO YOU AGAIN. DIDN'T PLAN FOR IT TO BE A KISS OF DEATH, BUT--
AAUGHH!
THIS ISN'T WHAT LOVE IS!

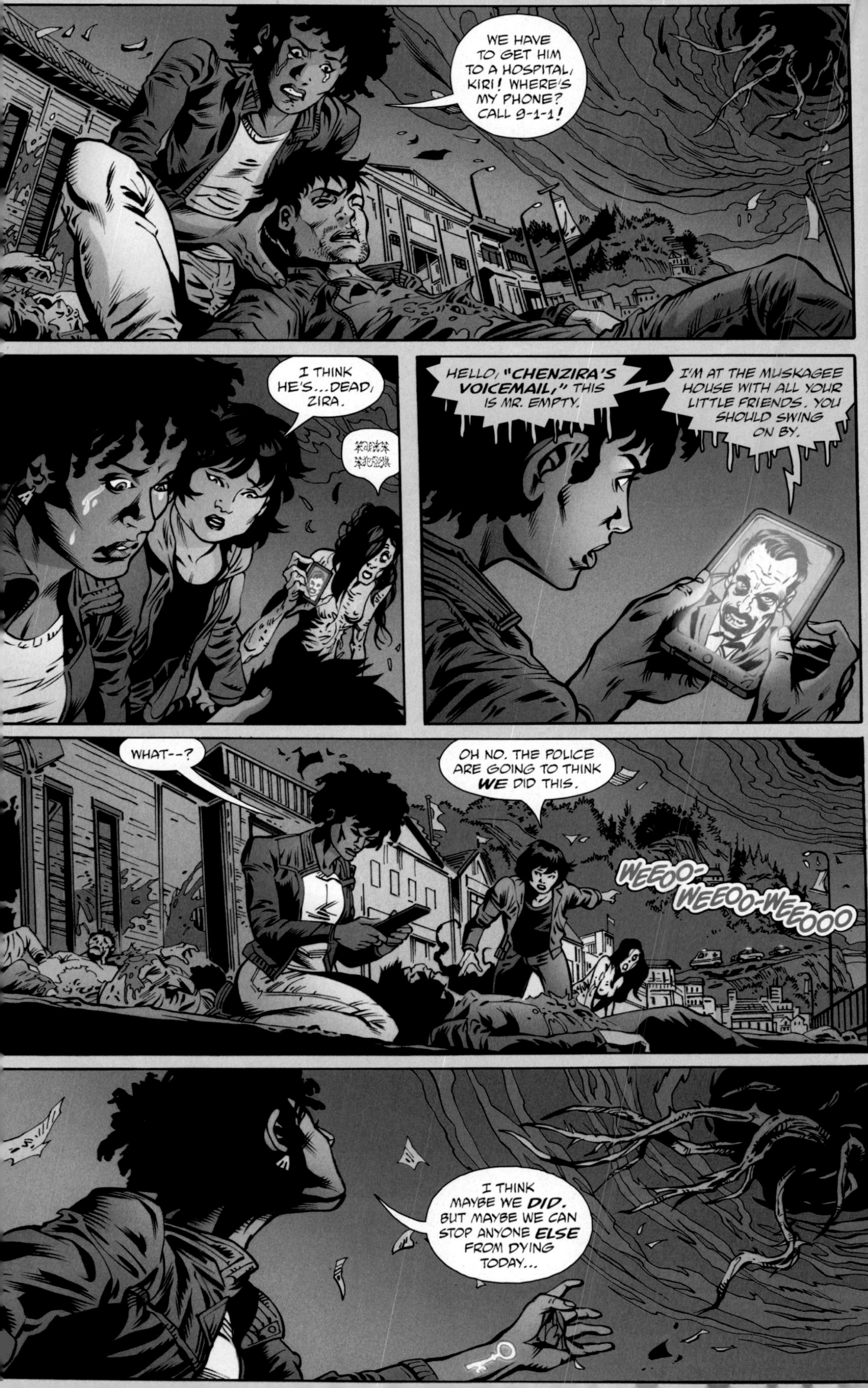
WE HAVE TO GET HIM TO A HOSPITAL, KIRI! WHERE'S MY PHONE? CALL 9-1-1!
I THINK HE'S...DEAD, ZIRA.
HELLO, "CHENZIRA'S VOICEMAIL," THIS IS MR. EMPTY.
I'M AT THE MUSKAGEE HOUSE WITH ALL YOUR LITTLE FRIENDS. YOU SHOULD SWING ON BY.
WHAT--?
OH NO. THE POLICE ARE GOING TO THINK WE DID THIS.
WEEOO-WEEOO-WEEOOO
I THINK MAYBE WE DID. BUT MAYBE WE CAN STOP ANYONE ELSE FROM DYING TODAY...

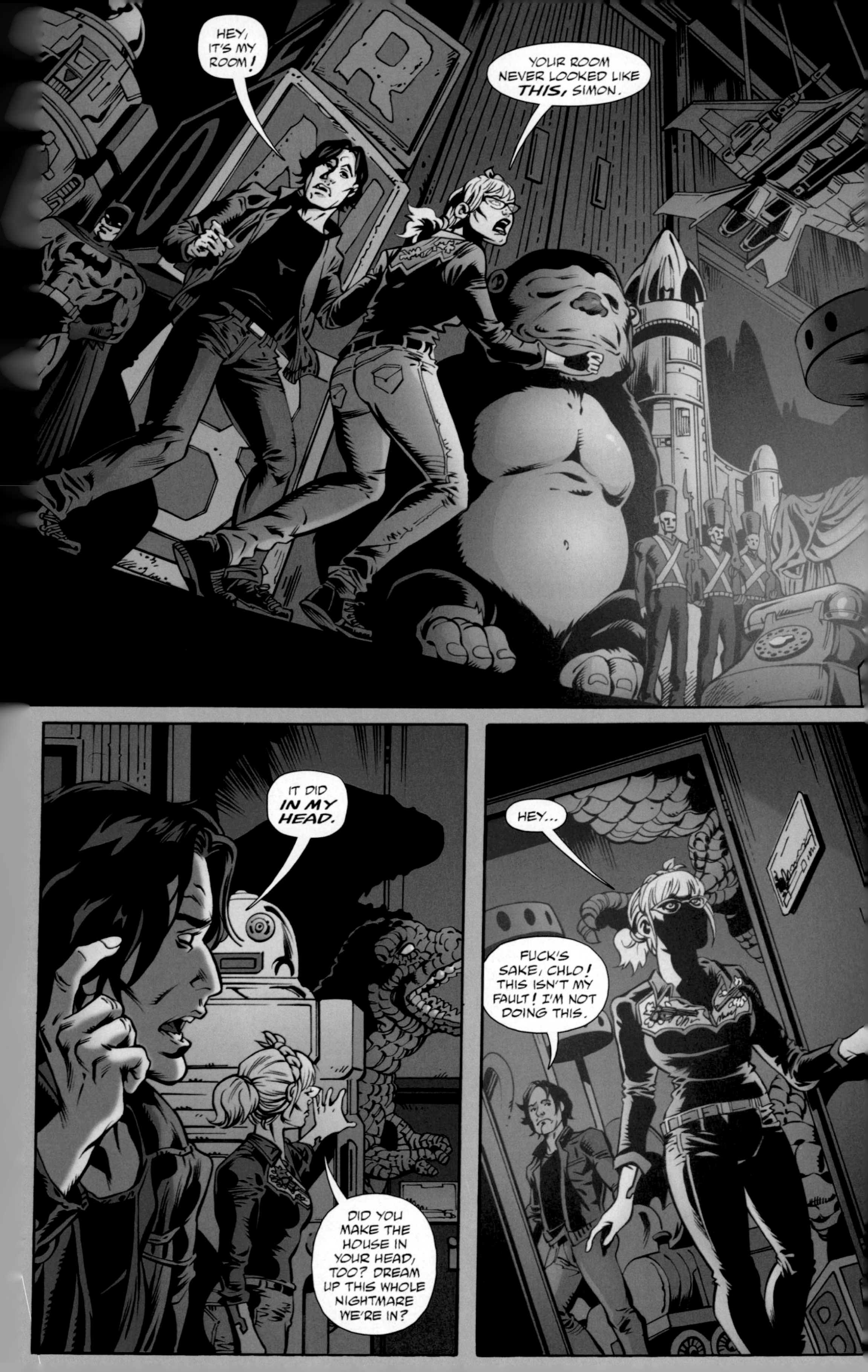
HEY, IT'S MY ROOM!
YOUR ROOM NEVER LOOKED LIKE THIS, SIMON.
IT DID IN MY HEAD.
DID YOU MAKE THE HOUSE IN YOUR HEAD, TOO? DREAM UP THIS WHOLE NIGHTMARE WE'RE IN?
HEY...
FUCK'S SAKE, CHLO! THIS ISN'T MY FAULT! I'M NOT DOING THIS.

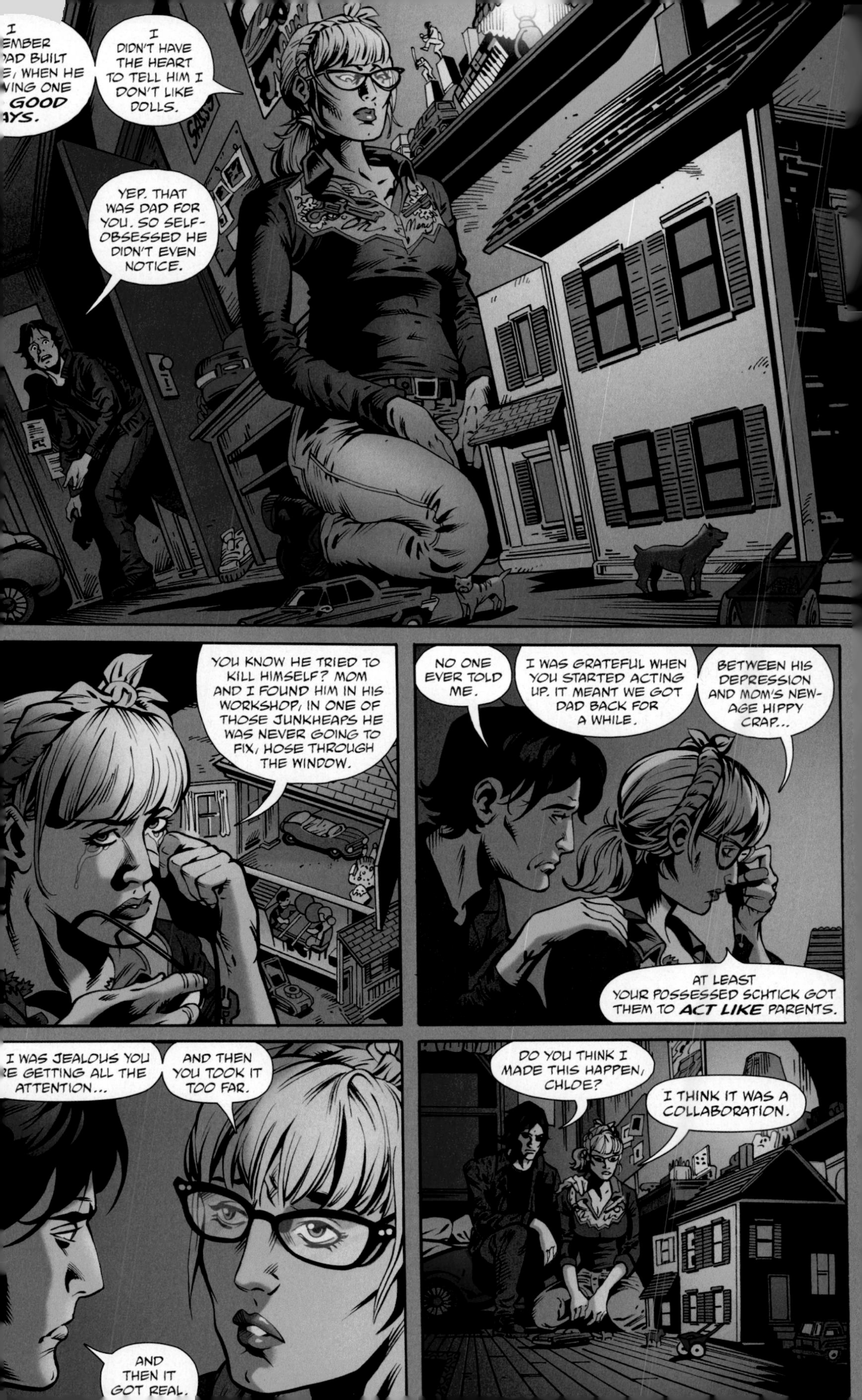
I EMBER AD BUILT E, WHEN HE VING ONE GOOD AYS.
I DIDN'T HAVE THE HEART TO TELL HIM I DON'T LIKE DOLLS.
YEP. THAT WAS DAD FOR YOU. SO SELF-OBSESSED HE DIDN'T EVEN NOTICE.
YOU KNOW HE TRIED TO KILL HIMSELF? MOM AND I FOUND HIM IN HIS WORKSHOP, IN ONE OF THOSE JUNKHEAPS HE WAS NEVER GOING TO FIX, HOSE THROUGH THE WINDOW.
NO ONE EVER TOLD ME.
I WAS GRATEFUL WHEN YOU STARTED ACTING UP. IT MEANT WE GOT DAD BACK FOR A WHILE.
BETWEEN HIS DEPRESSION AND MOM'S NEW-AGE HIPPY CRAP...
AT LEAST YOUR POSSESSED SCHTICK GOT THEM TO ACT LIKE PARENTS.
I WAS JEALOUS YOU RE GETTING ALL THE ATTENTION...
AND THEN YOU TOOK IT TOO FAR.
AND THEN IT GOT REAL.
DO YOU THINK I MADE THIS HAPPEN, CHLOE?
I THINK IT WAS A COLLABORATION.

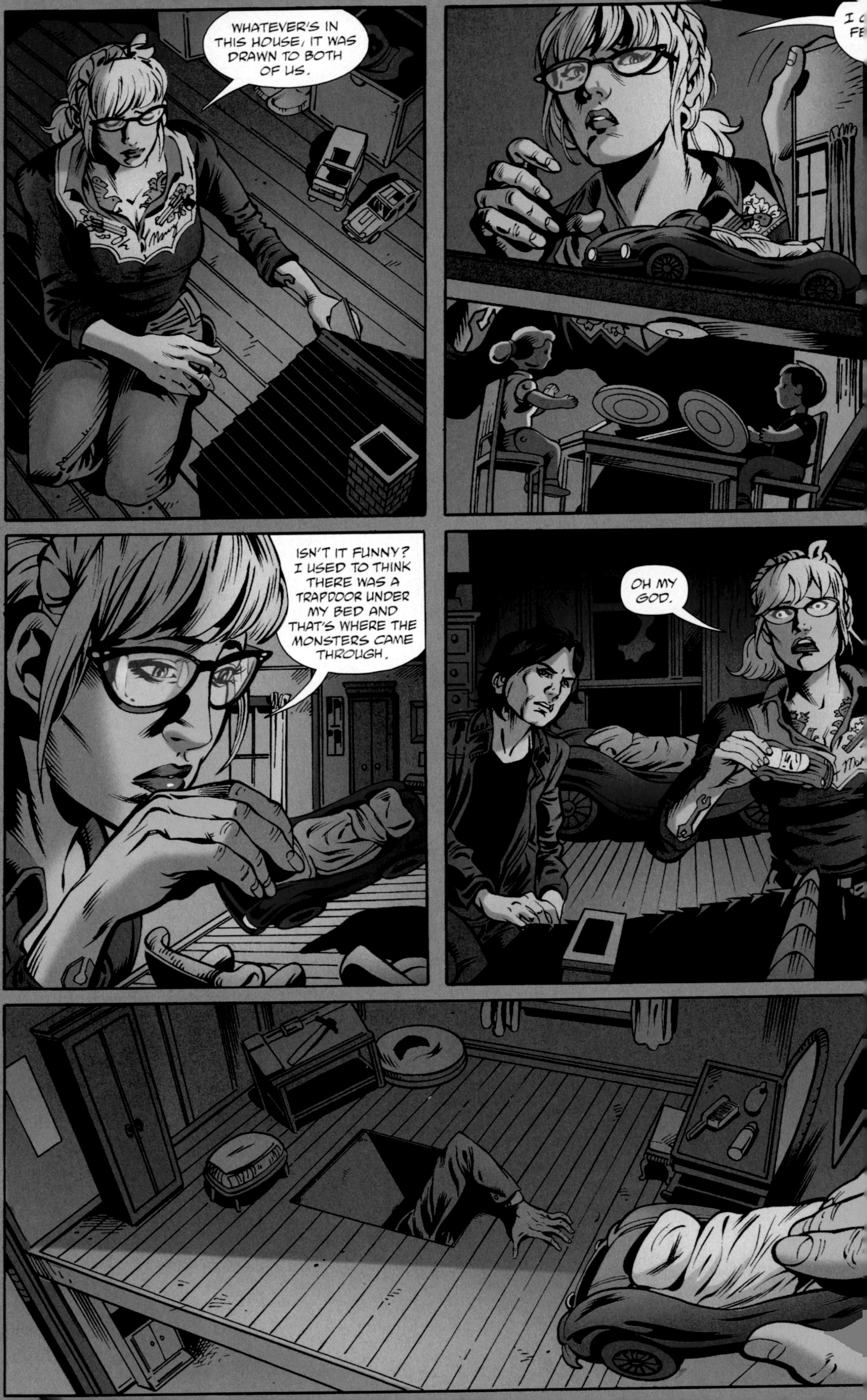
WHATEVER'S IN THIS HOUSE, IT WAS DRAWN TO BOTH OF US.
ISN'T IT FUNNY? I USED TO THINK THERE WAS A TRAPDOOR UNDER MY BED AND THAT'S WHERE THE MONSTERS CAME THROUGH.
OH MY GOD.

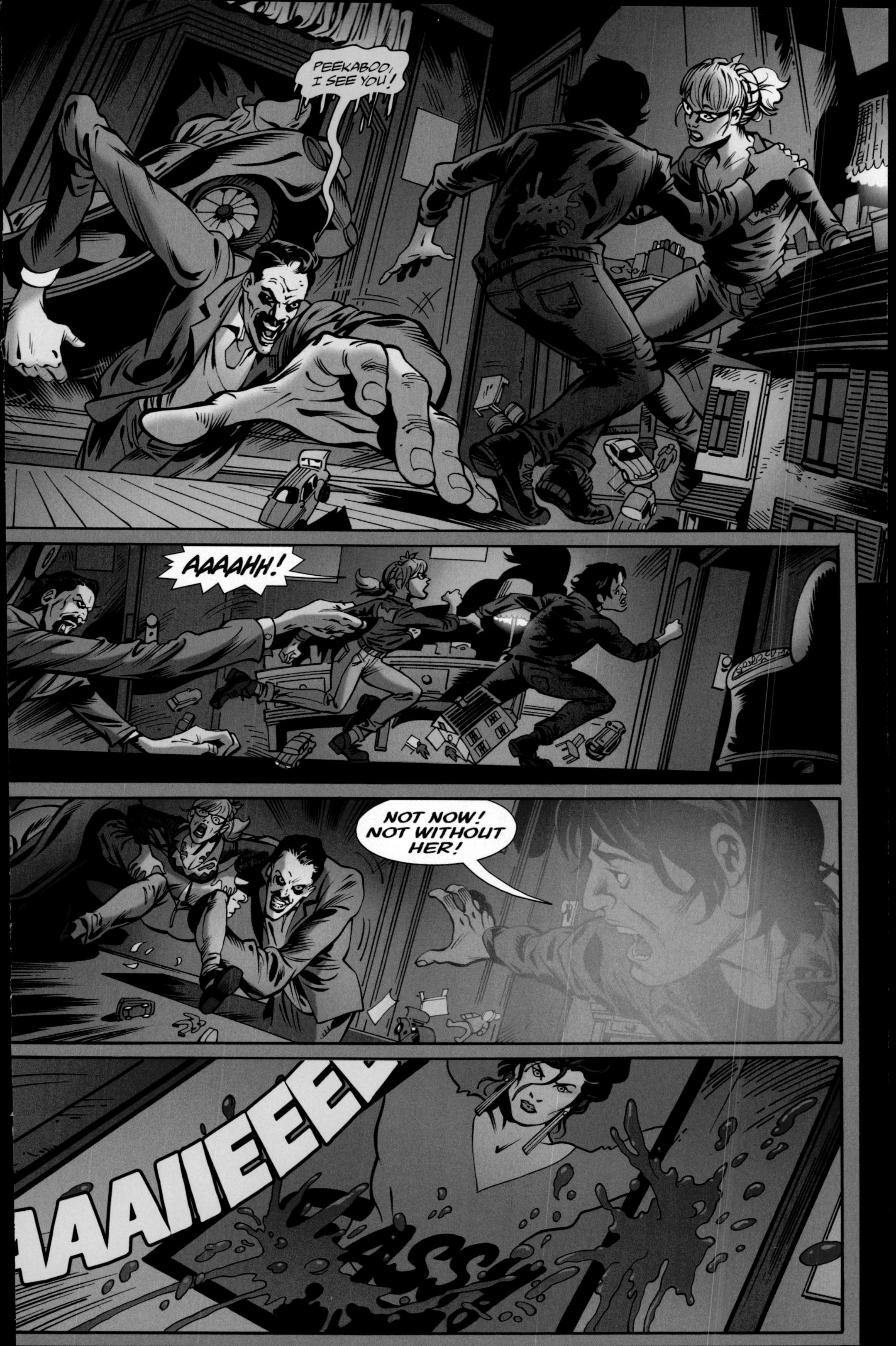
PEEKABOO, I SEE YOU!
AAAAHH!
NOT NOW! NOT WITHOUT HER!
HAAIIEEEE

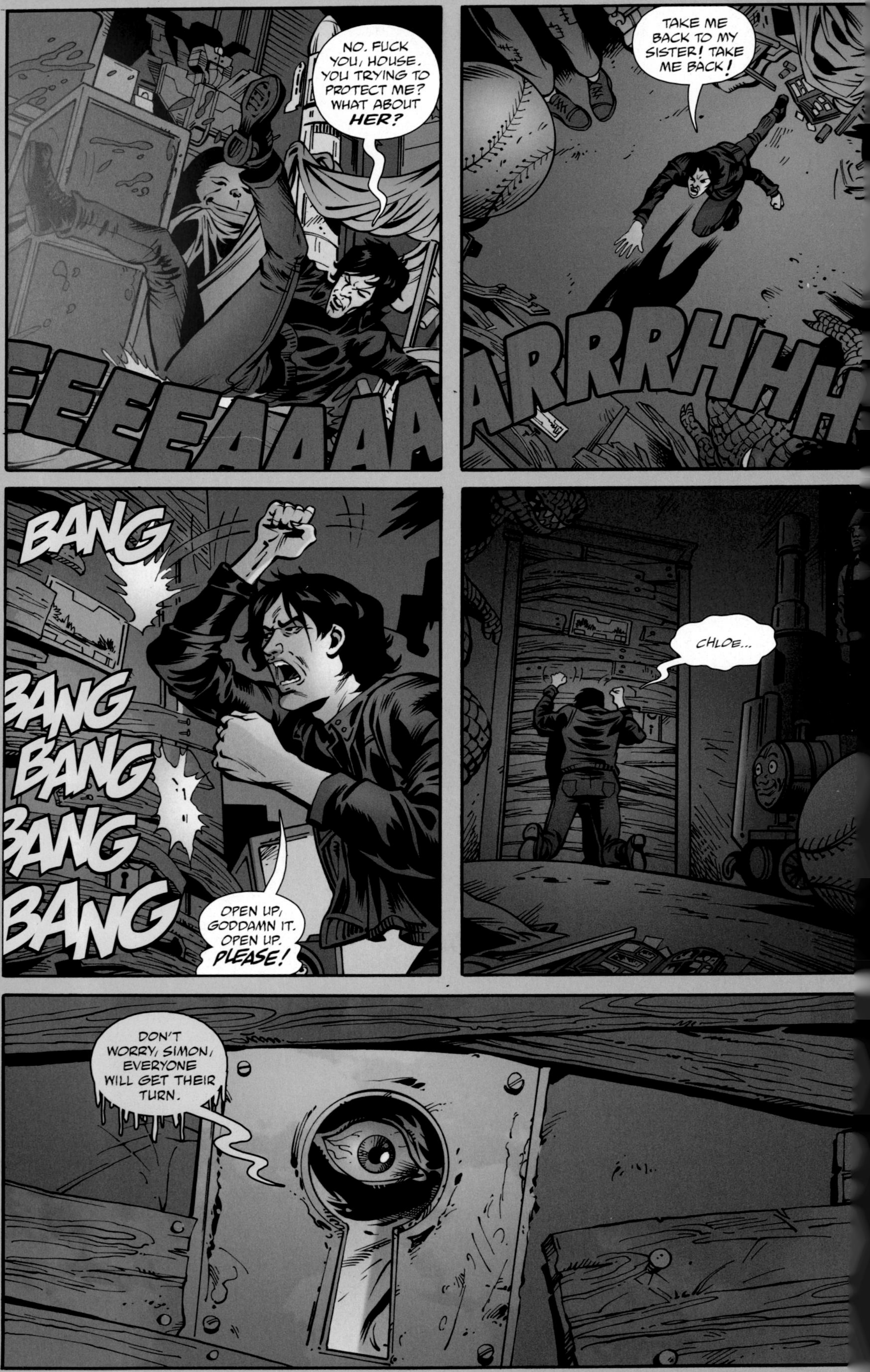
NO. FUCK YOU, HOUSE. YOU TRYING TO PROTECT ME? WHAT ABOUT HER?
TAKE ME BACK TO MY SISTER! TAKE ME BACK!
EEEEAAAAARRRRHHH
BANG
BANG
BANG
BANG
BANG
OPEN UP, GODDAMN IT. OPEN UP. PLEASE!
CHLOE...
DON'T WORRY, SIMON, EVERYONE WILL GET THEIR TURN.

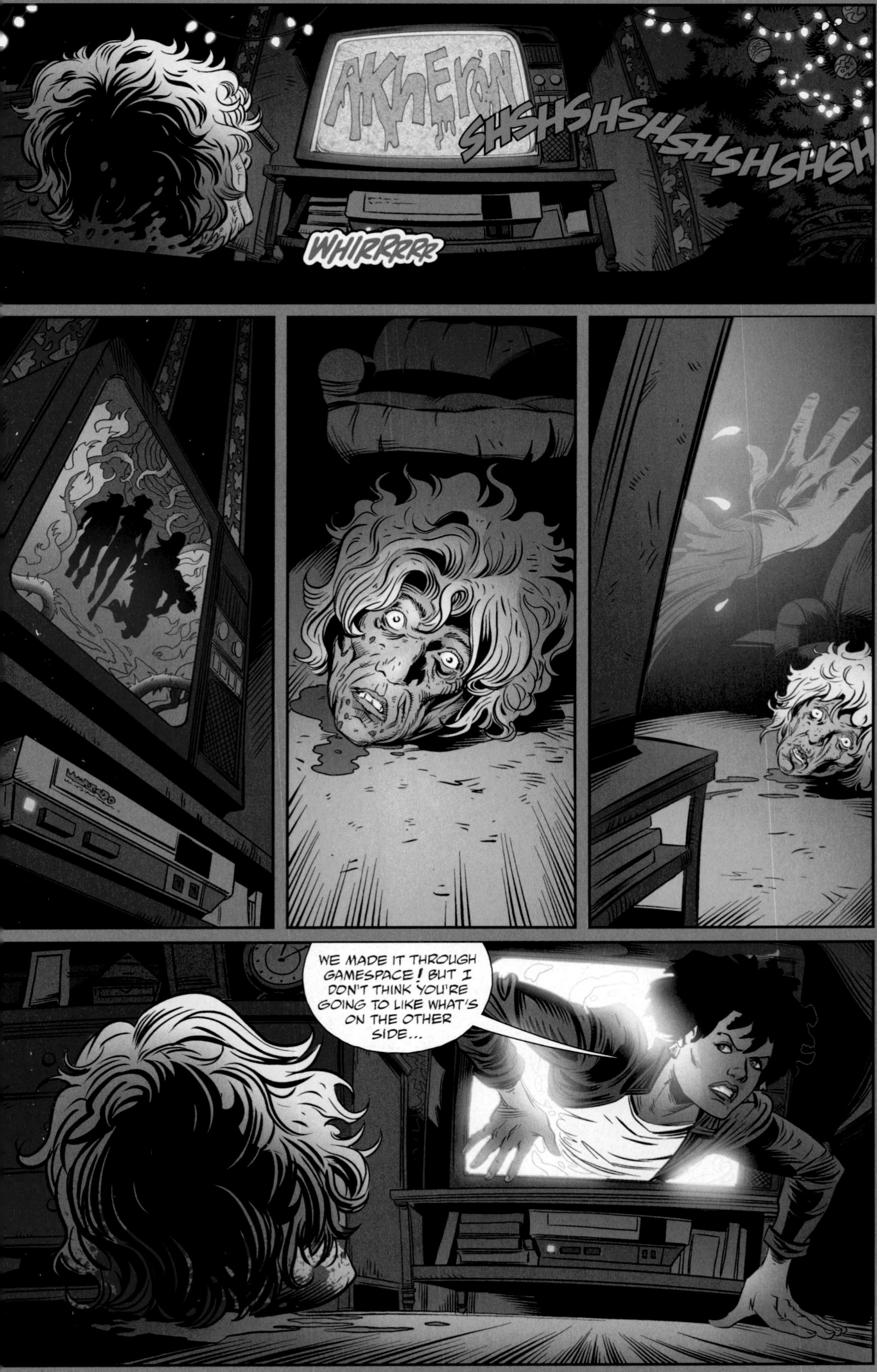
SHSHSHSHSHSHSHSHSH
WHIRRRRR
WE MADE IT THROUGH GAMESPACE! BUT I DON'T THINK YOU'RE GOING TO LIKE WHAT'S ON THE OTHER SIDE...

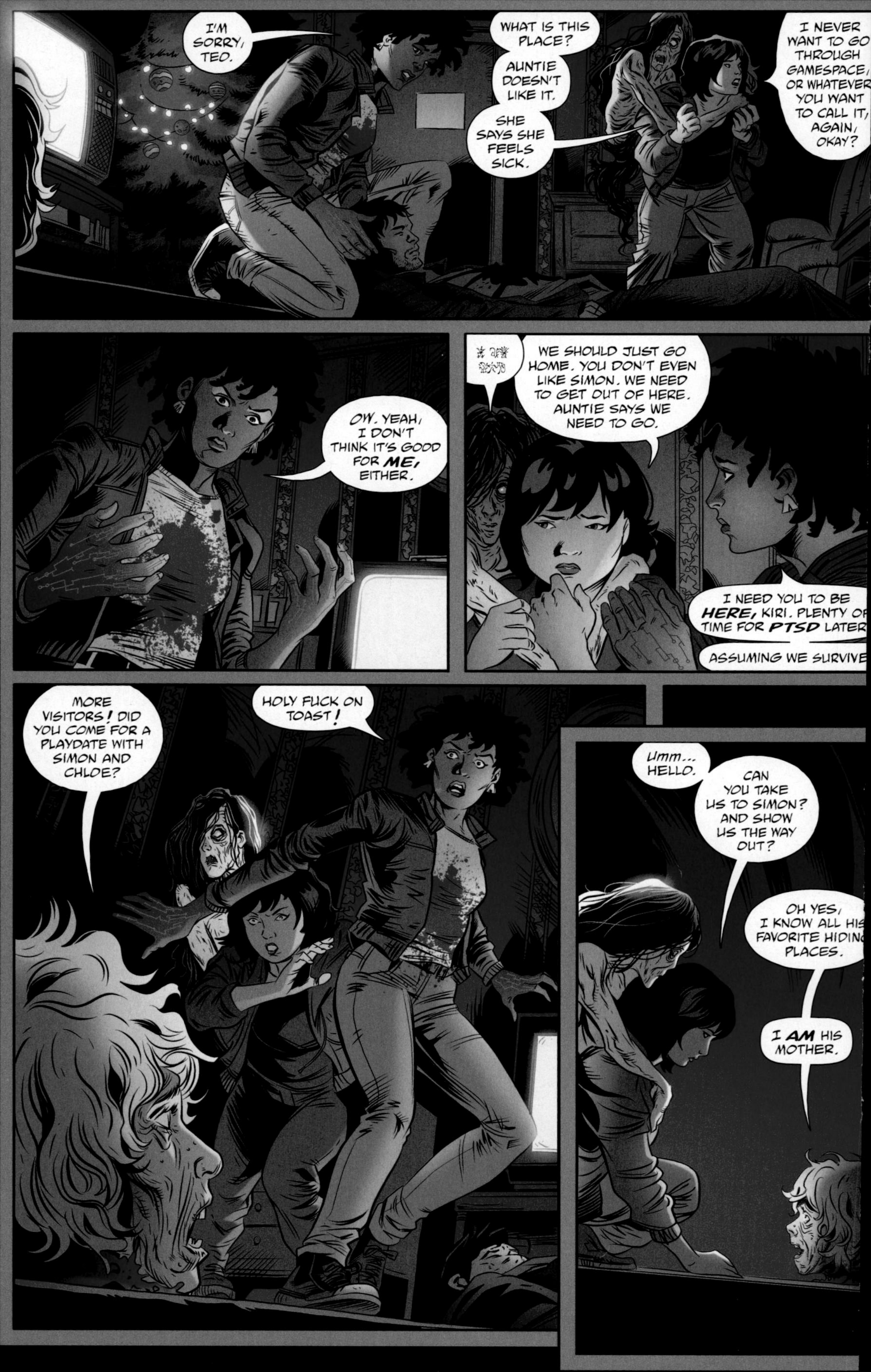
I'M SORRY, TEO.
WHAT IS THIS PLACE?
AUNTIE DOESN'T LIKE IT.
SHE SAYS SHE FEELS SICK.
I NEVER WANT TO GO THROUGH GAMESPACE, OR WHATEVER YOU WANT TO CALL IT, AGAIN, OKAY?
OW. YEAH, I DON'T THINK IT'S GOOD FOR ME, EITHER.
WE SHOULD JUST GO HOME. YOU DON'T EVEN LIKE SIMON. WE NEED TO GET OUT OF HERE. AUNTIE SAYS WE NEED TO GO.
I NEED YOU TO BE HERE, KIRI. PLENTY OF TIME FOR PTSD LATER
ASSUMING WE SURVIVE
MORE VISITORS! DID YOU COME FOR A PLAYDATE WITH SIMON AND CHLOE?
HOLY FUCK ON TOAST!
Umm... HELLO.
CAN YOU TAKE US TO SIMON? AND SHOW US THE WAY OUT?
OH YES, I KNOW ALL HIS FAVORITE HIDING PLACES.
I AM HIS MOTHER.

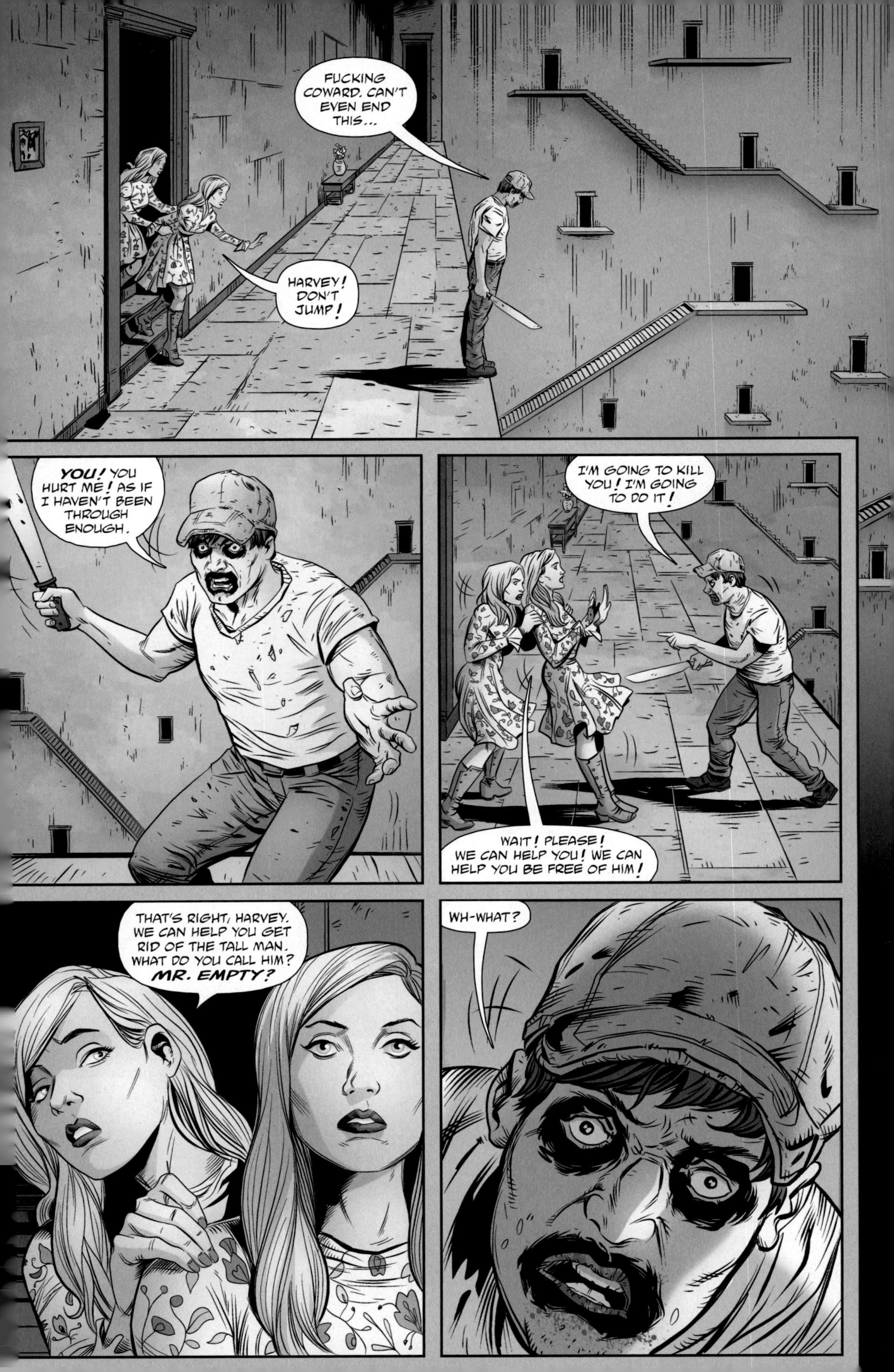
FUCKING COWARD. CAN'T EVEN END THIS...
HARVEY! DON'T JUMP!
YOU! YOU HURT ME! AS IF I HAVEN'T BEEN THROUGH ENOUGH.
I'M GOING TO KILL YOU! I'M GOING TO DO IT!
WAIT! PLEASE! WE CAN HELP YOU! WE CAN HELP YOU BE FREE OF HIM!
THAT'S RIGHT, HARVEY. WE CAN HELP YOU GET RID OF THE TALL MAN. WHAT DO YOU CALL HIM? MR. EMPTY?
WH-WHAT?

ISN'T THAT WHAT YOU WANT? A LIFE WITHOUT HIM? A NORMAL LIFE? WHERE YOU CAN GO FOR PIZZA AND A BEER AND A MOVIE? MAYBE EVEN WITH A GIRL?

AND NO MR. EMPTY.

NO MR. EMPTY...

I'VE LIVED WITH *OTHER ALICE* SINCE I WAS SIX.

I KNOW HOW THIS WORKS, HARVEY, YOU HAVE TO TRUST ME.

I KNO HOW T WORK HARVE YOU H TO TR ME

HE'S A DEMON! I'VE TRIED TO RUN AWAY. I WENT TO THE POLICE, THE CHURCH, DOCTORS...I WAS IN A MENTAL FACILITY FOR THREE YEARS. NO ONE BELIEVED ME.

AND HE STILL FOUND ME!

IT FEELS LIKE I HAVE SO MUCH BLOOD ON MY HANDS EVEN THOUGH I NEVER...

WELL, YOU MIGHT HAVE TO GET YOU HANDS DIRT THIS TIME

DIRT THIS TIME

ONE THING I'VE LEARNED ABOUT HAVING MY OWN "DEMON" IS THAT I CAN KILL HER IF I WANT TO, OR BRING HER BACK.

*YOU* HAVE ALL THE POWER, HARVEY.

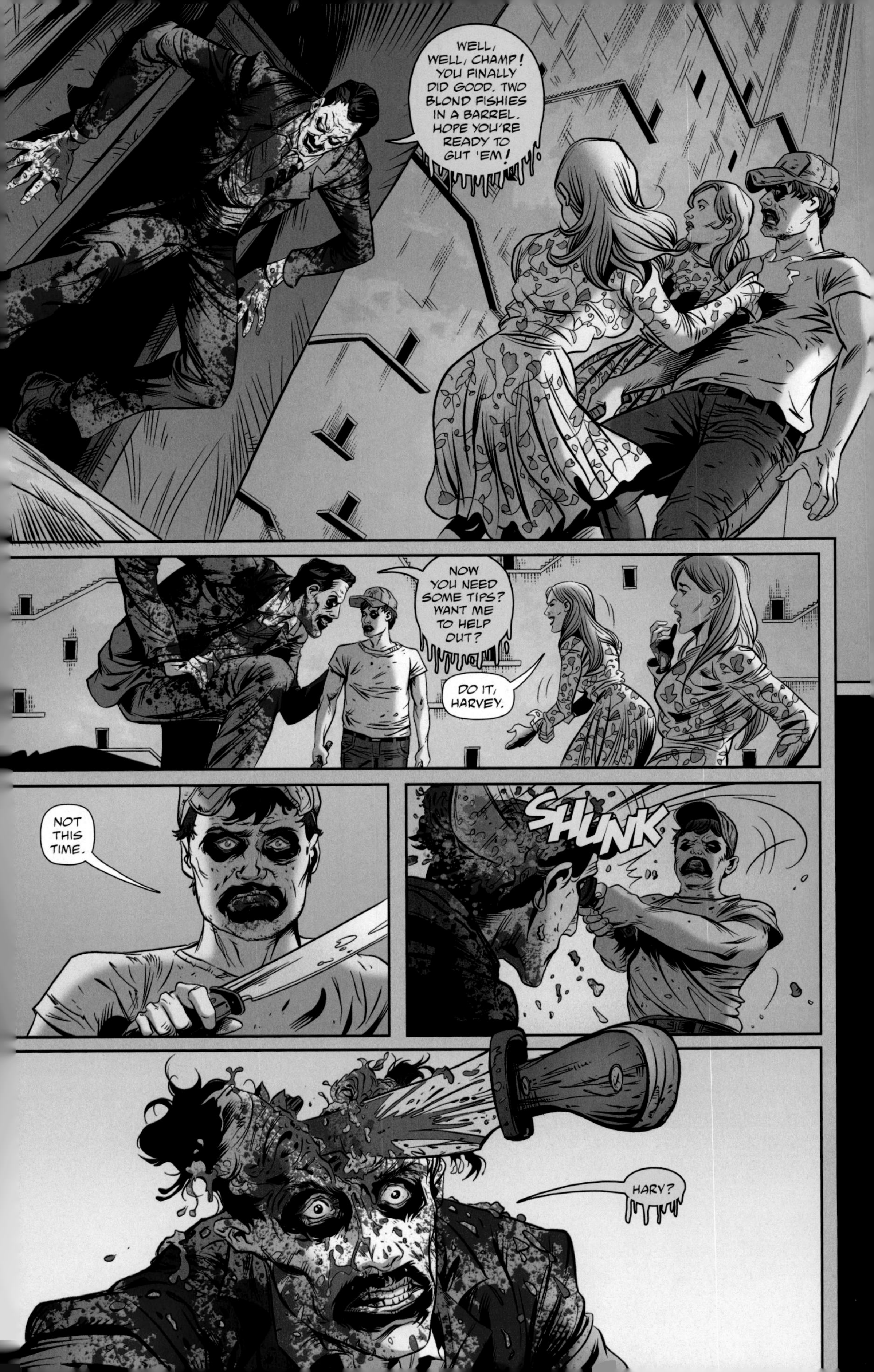
WELL, WELL, CHAMP! YOU FINALLY DID GOOD. TWO BLOND FISHIES IN A BARREL. HOPE YOU'RE READY TO GUT 'EM!
NOW YOU NEED SOME TIPS? WANT ME TO HELP OUT?
DO IT, HARVEY.
NOT THIS TIME.
SHUNK
HARV?

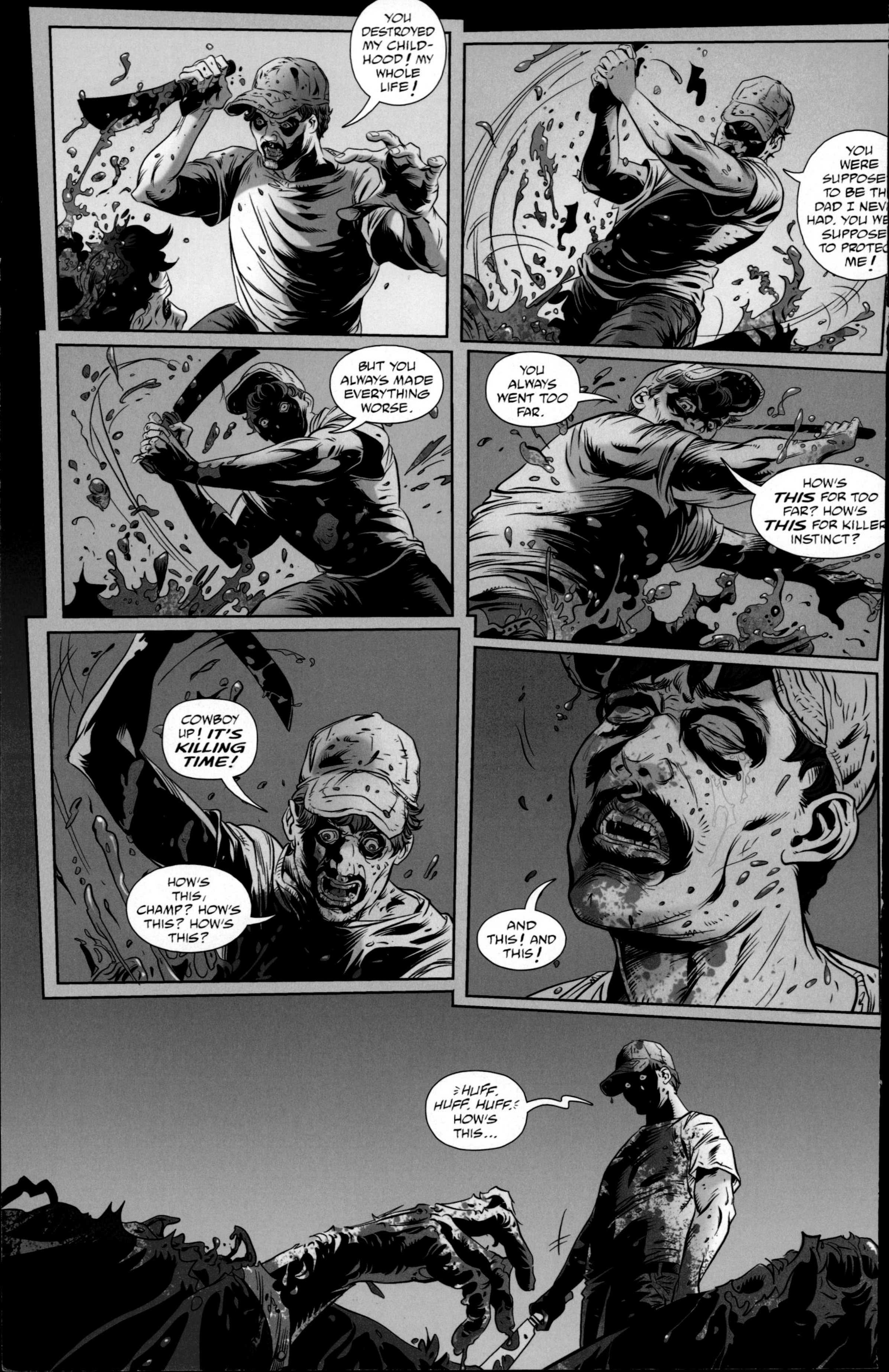
YOU DESTROYED MY CHILD-HOOD! MY WHOLE LIFE!
YOU WERE SUPPOSE TO BE TH DAD I NEV HAD. YOU WE SUPPOSE TO PROTEC ME!
BUT YOU ALWAYS MADE EVERYTHING WORSE.
YOU ALWAYS WENT TOO FAR.
HOW'S THIS FOR TOO FAR? HOW'S THIS FOR KILLER INSTINCT?
COWBOY UP! IT'S KILLING TIME!
HOW'S THIS, CHAMP? HOW'S THIS? HOW'S THIS?
AND THIS! AND THIS!
HUFF. HUFF. HUFF. HOW'S THIS...

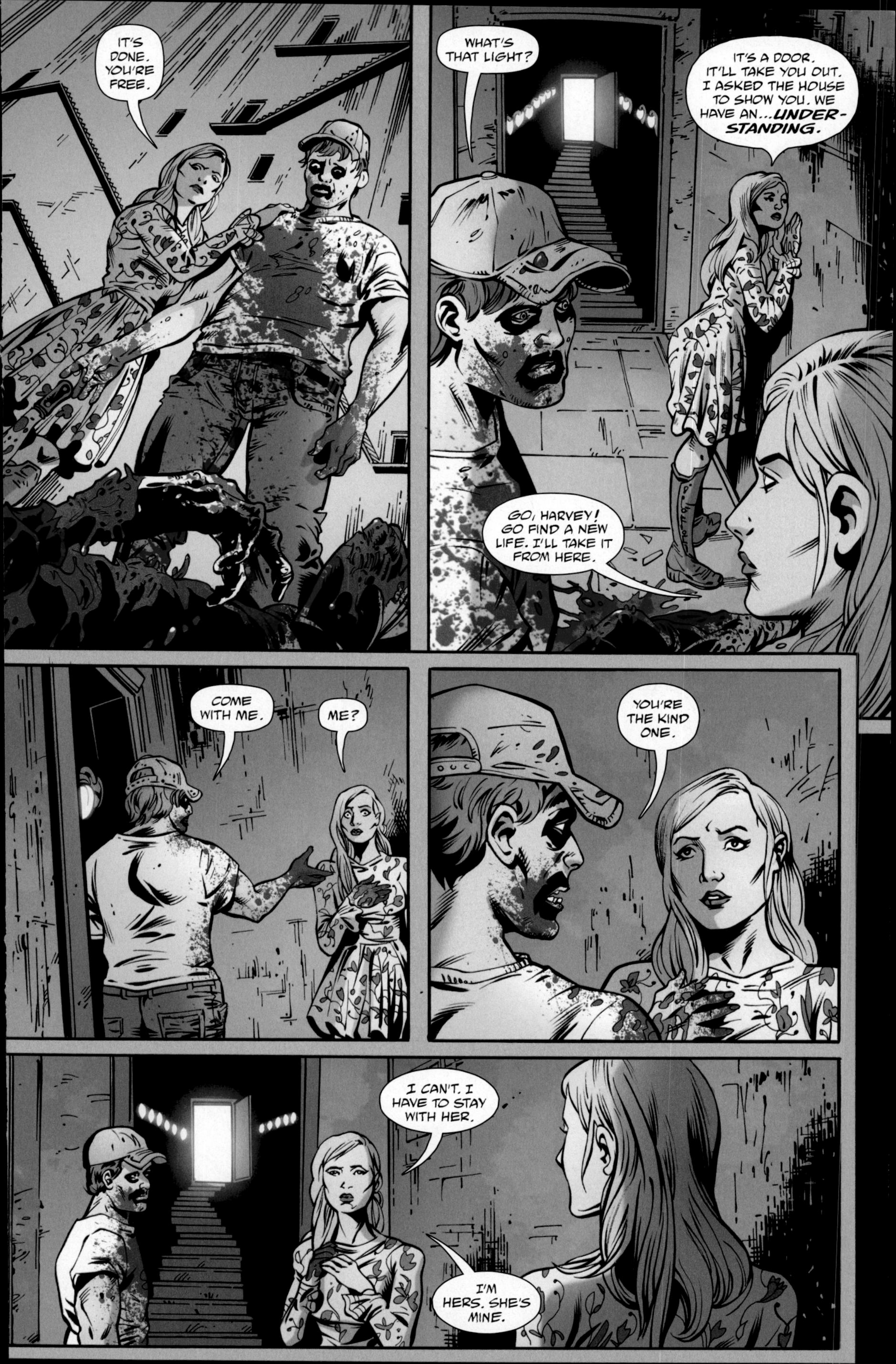
IT'S DONE. YOU'RE FREE.
WHAT'S THAT LIGHT?
IT'S A DOOR. IT'LL TAKE YOU OUT. I ASKED THE HOUSE TO SHOW YOU. WE HAVE AN... UNDER-STANDING.
GO, HARVEY! GO FIND A NEW LIFE. I'LL TAKE IT FROM HERE.
COME WITH ME.
ME?
YOU'RE THE KIND ONE.
I CAN'T. I HAVE TO STAY WITH HER.
I'M HERS. SHE'S MINE.

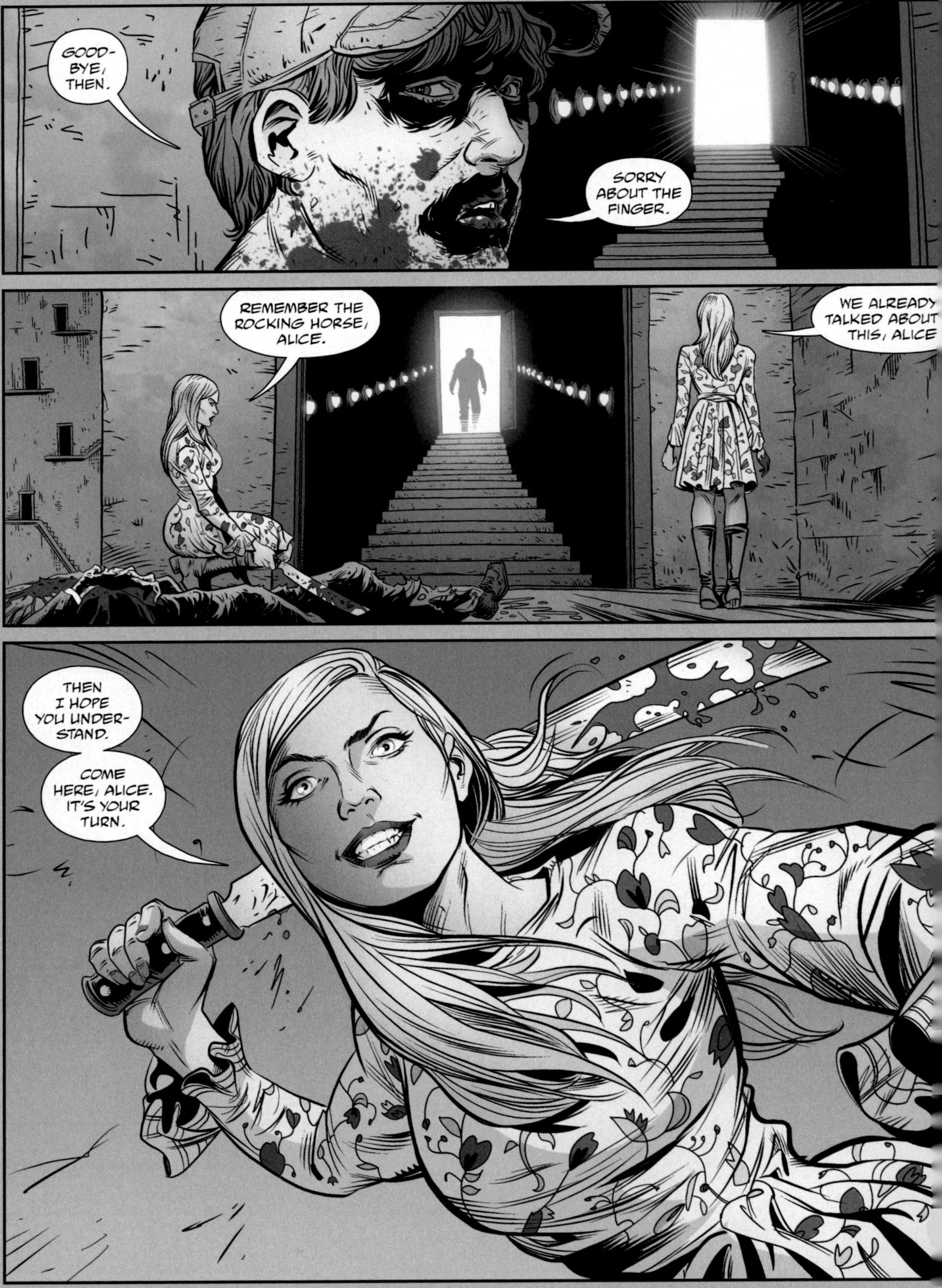
GOOD-BYE, THEN.
SORRY ABOUT THE FINGER.
REMEMBER THE ROCKING HORSE, ALICE.
WE ALREADY TALKED ABOUT THIS, ALICE
THEN I HOPE YOU UNDER-STAND.
COME HERE, ALICE. IT'S YOUR TURN.

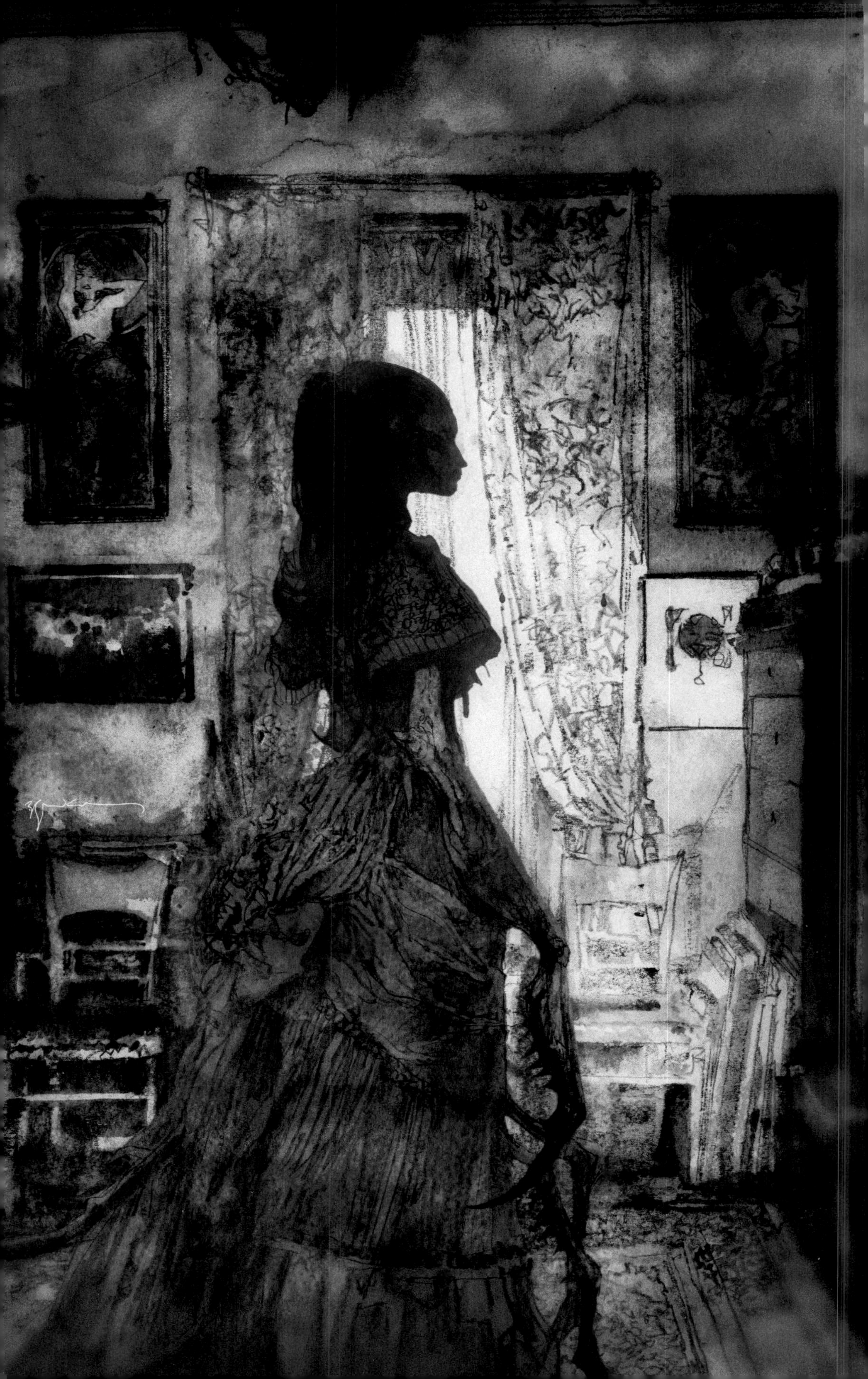

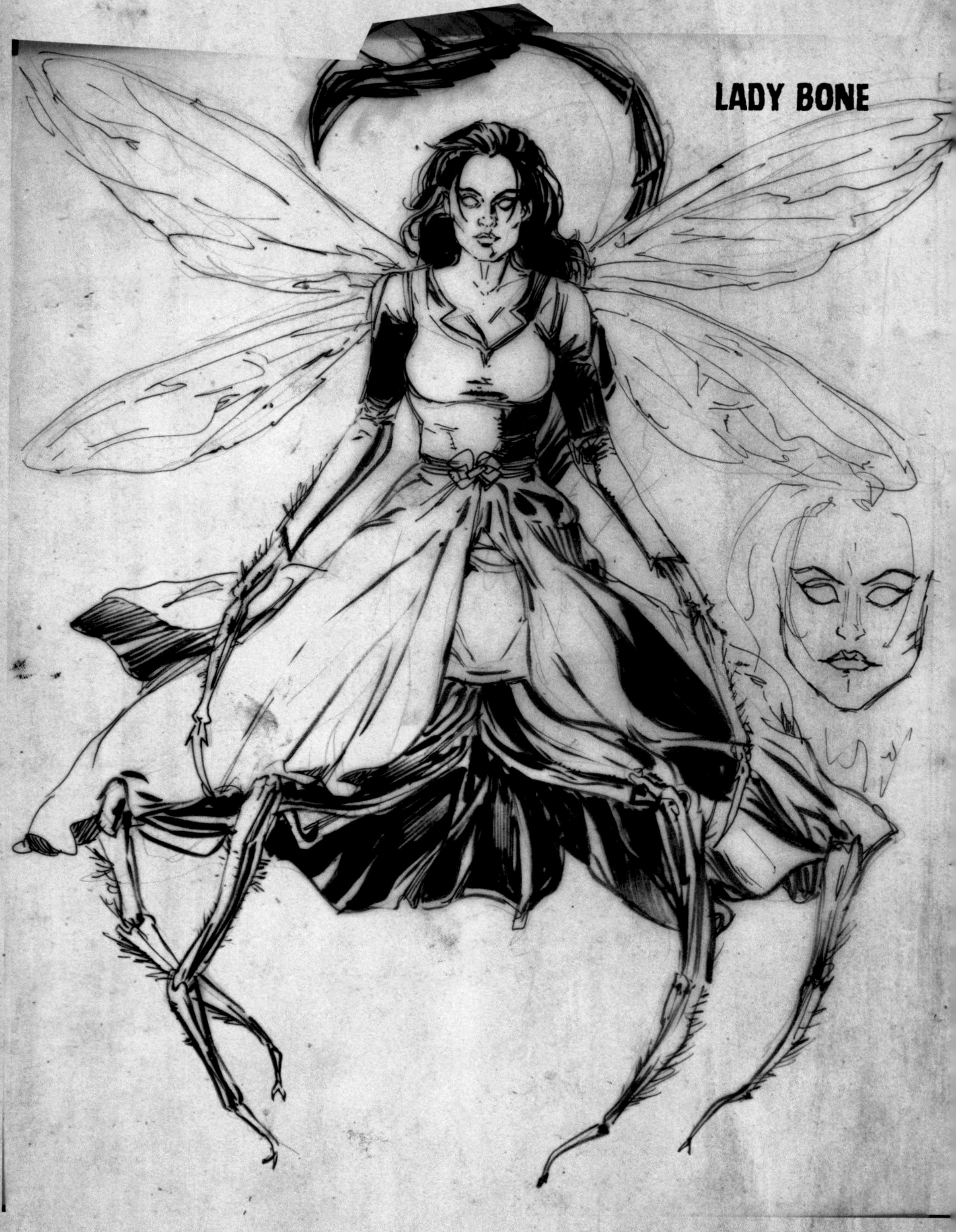
LADY BONE

SOMEWHERE...

WHAT SAY WE GIVE YOU A **BOLD NEW LOOK,** MR. EMPTY?

OH, WE CAN DEFINITELY USE THIS. DON'T YOU THINK, ALICE?

I DON'T LIKE THIS GAME. I DON'T WANT TO PLAY ANYMORE, ALICE.

YOU SHOULD BE HAPPY. I'M MAKING YOU INTO THE **REAL** REFLECTION OF ME.

# SURVIVORS' CLUB
## CHAPTER NINE: THE MONSTERS INSIDE

DALE HALVORSEN WRITER

LAUREN BEUKES WRITER

RYAN KELLY LAYOUTS

RYAN KELLY FINISHES 4-5
MARK FARMER FINISHES 6-8, 10-13, 17-19
PETER GROSS FINISHES 1-3, 9, 14-16, 20-22

EVA DE LA CRUZ COLORI

CLEM ROBINS LETTER

BILL SIENKIEWICZ COV

MOLLY MAHAN ASSOCIATE EDITOR

SHELLY BOND EDITOR SURVIVORS' CLUB CREATED BY BEUKES, HALVORSEN AND KELLY

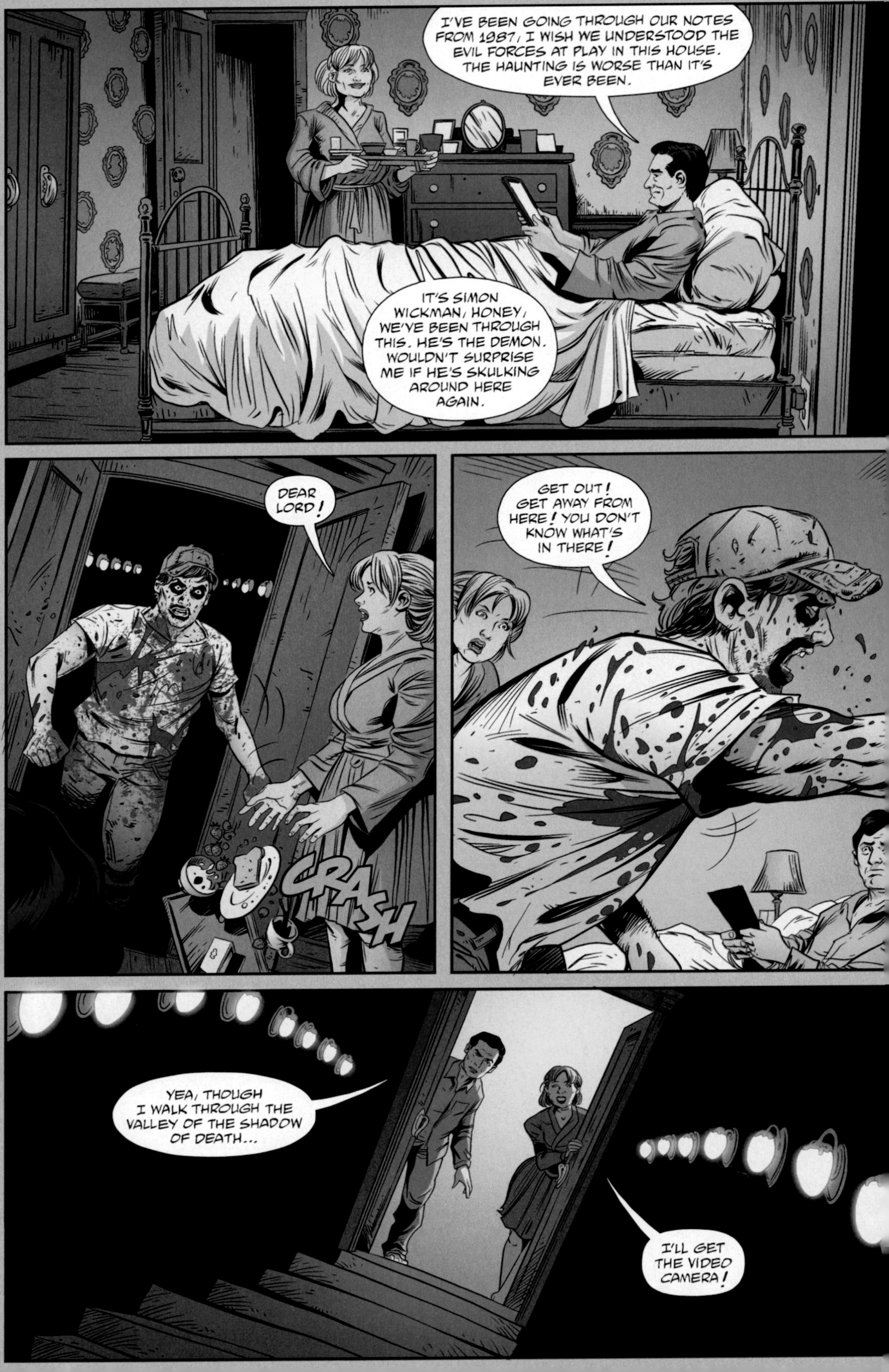

I'VE BEEN GOING THROUGH OUR NOTES FROM 1987, I WISH WE UNDERSTOOD THE EVIL FORCES AT PLAY IN THIS HOUSE. THE HAUNTING IS WORSE THAN IT'S EVER BEEN.
IT'S SIMON WICKMAN, HONEY, WE'VE BEEN THROUGH THIS. HE'S THE DEMON. WOULDN'T SURPRISE ME IF HE'S SKULKING AROUND HERE AGAIN.
DEAR LORD!
CRASH
GET OUT! GET AWAY FROM HERE! YOU DON'T KNOW WHAT'S IN THERE!
YEA, THOUGH I WALK THROUGH THE VALLEY OF THE SHADOW OF DEATH...
I'LL GET THE VIDEO CAMERA!

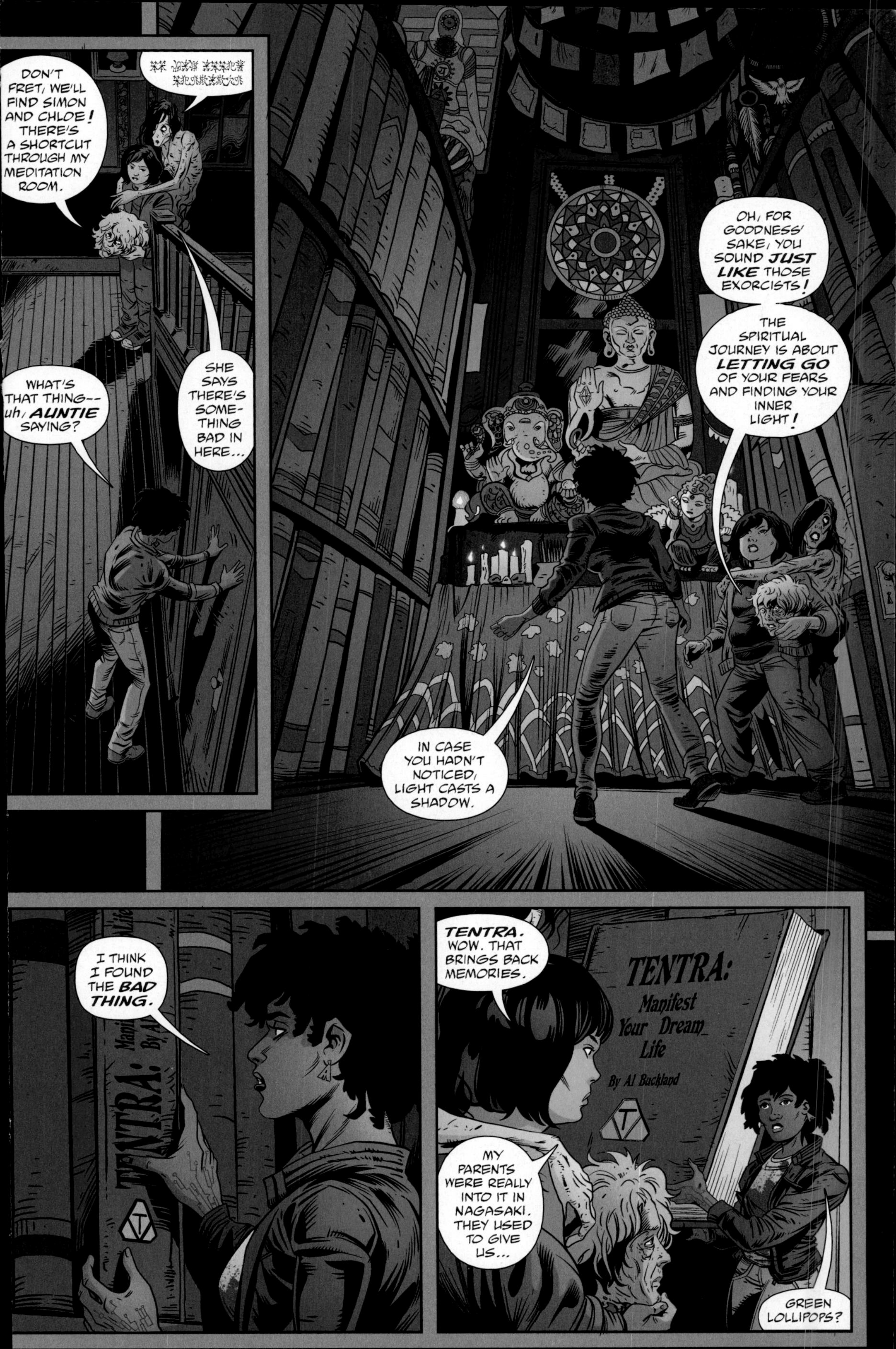
DON'T FRET, WE'LL FIND SIMON AND CHLOE! THERE'S A SHORTCUT THROUGH MY MEDITATION ROOM.
WHAT'S THAT THING--uh, AUNTIE SAYING?
SHE SAYS THERE'S SOME-THING BAD IN HERE...
OH, FOR GOODNESS' SAKE, YOU SOUND JUST LIKE THOSE EXORCISTS!
THE SPIRITUAL JOURNEY IS ABOUT LETTING GO OF YOUR FEARS AND FINDING YOUR INNER LIGHT!
IN CASE YOU HADN'T NOTICED, LIGHT CASTS A SHADOW.
I THINK I FOUND THE BAD THING.
TENTRA:
TENTRA. WOW. THAT BRINGS BACK MEMORIES.
TENTRA: Manifest Your Dream Life
By Al Buckland
MY PARENTS WERE REALLY INTO IT IN NAGASAKI. THEY USED TO GIVE US...
GREEN LOLLIPOPS?

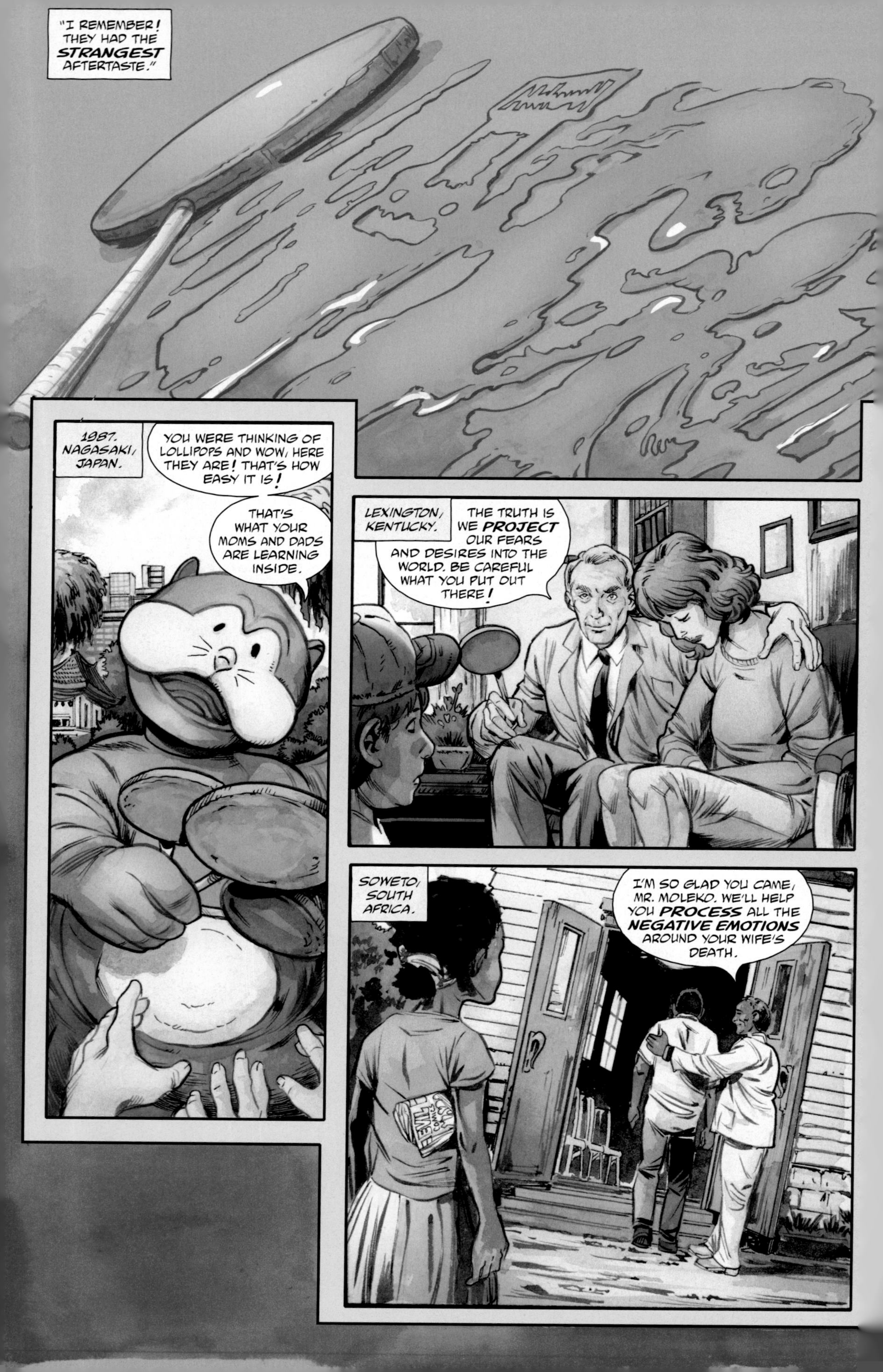
"I REMEMBER! THEY HAD THE STRANGEST AFTERTASTE."
1987. NAGASAKI, JAPAN.
YOU WERE THINKING OF LOLLIPOPS AND WOW, HERE THEY ARE! THAT'S HOW EASY IT IS!
THAT'S WHAT YOUR MOMS AND DADS ARE LEARNING INSIDE.
LEXINGTON, KENTUCKY.
THE TRUTH IS WE PROJECT OUR FEARS AND DESIRES INTO THE WORLD. BE CAREFUL WHAT YOU PUT OUT THERE!
SOWETO, SOUTH AFRICA.
I'M SO GLAD YOU CAME, MR. MOLEKO. WE'LL HELP YOU PROCESS ALL THE NEGATIVE EMOTIONS AROUND YOUR WIFE'S DEATH.

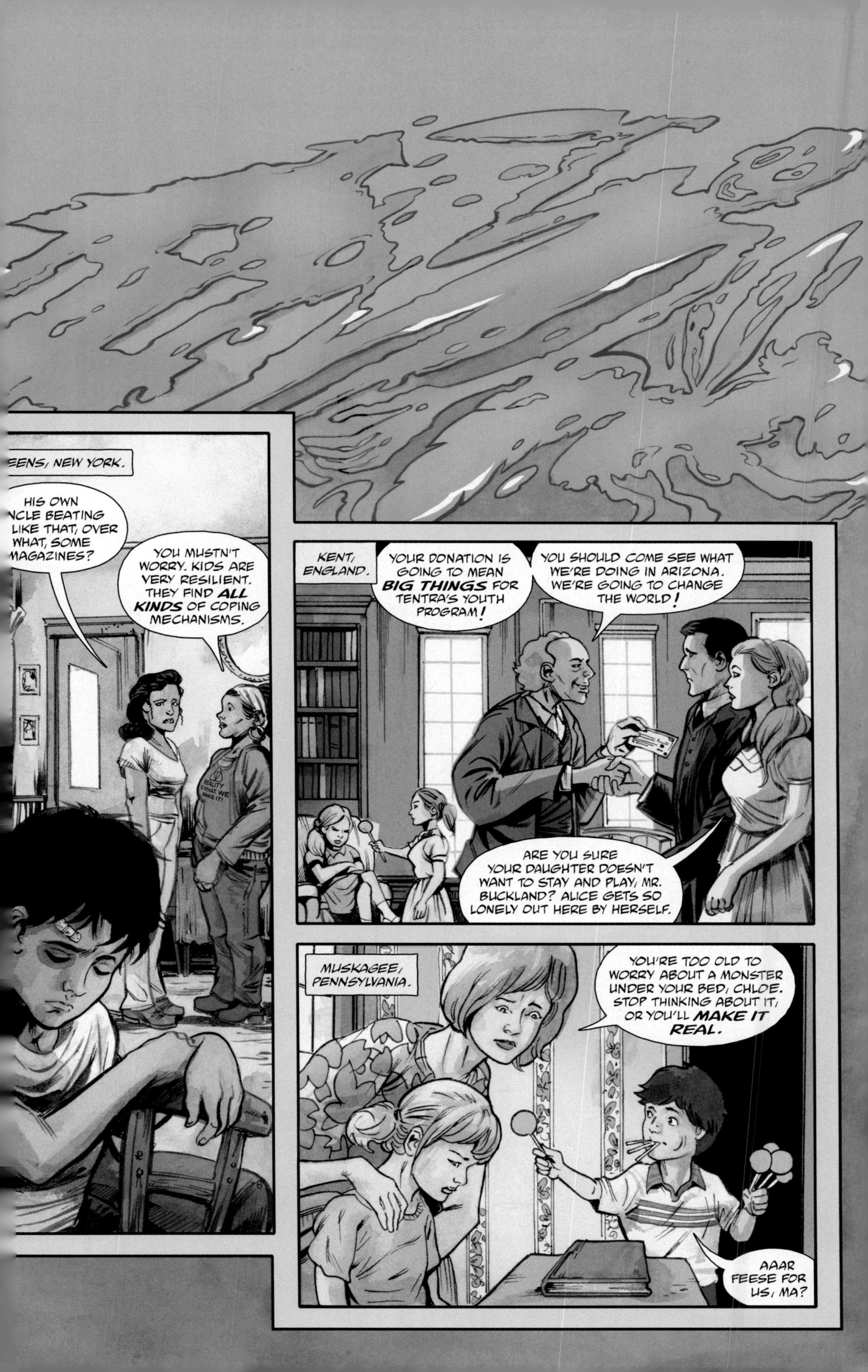
EENS, NEW YORK.
HIS OWN NCLE BEATING LIKE THAT, OVER WHAT, SOME MAGAZINES?
YOU MUSTN'T WORRY. KIDS ARE VERY RESILIENT. THEY FIND ALL KINDS OF COPING MECHANISMS.
REALITY IS WHAT WE MAKE IT!
KENT, ENGLAND.
YOUR DONATION IS GOING TO MEAN BIG THINGS FOR TENTRA'S YOUTH PROGRAM!
YOU SHOULD COME SEE WHAT WE'RE DOING IN ARIZONA. WE'RE GOING TO CHANGE THE WORLD!
ARE YOU SURE YOUR DAUGHTER DOESN'T WANT TO STAY AND PLAY, MR. BUCKLAND? ALICE GETS SO LONELY OUT HERE BY HERSELF.
MUSKAGEE, PENNSYLVANIA.
YOU'RE TOO OLD TO WORRY ABOUT A MONSTER UNDER YOUR BED, CHLOE. STOP THINKING ABOUT IT, OR YOU'LL MAKE IT REAL.
AAAR FEESE FOR US, MA?

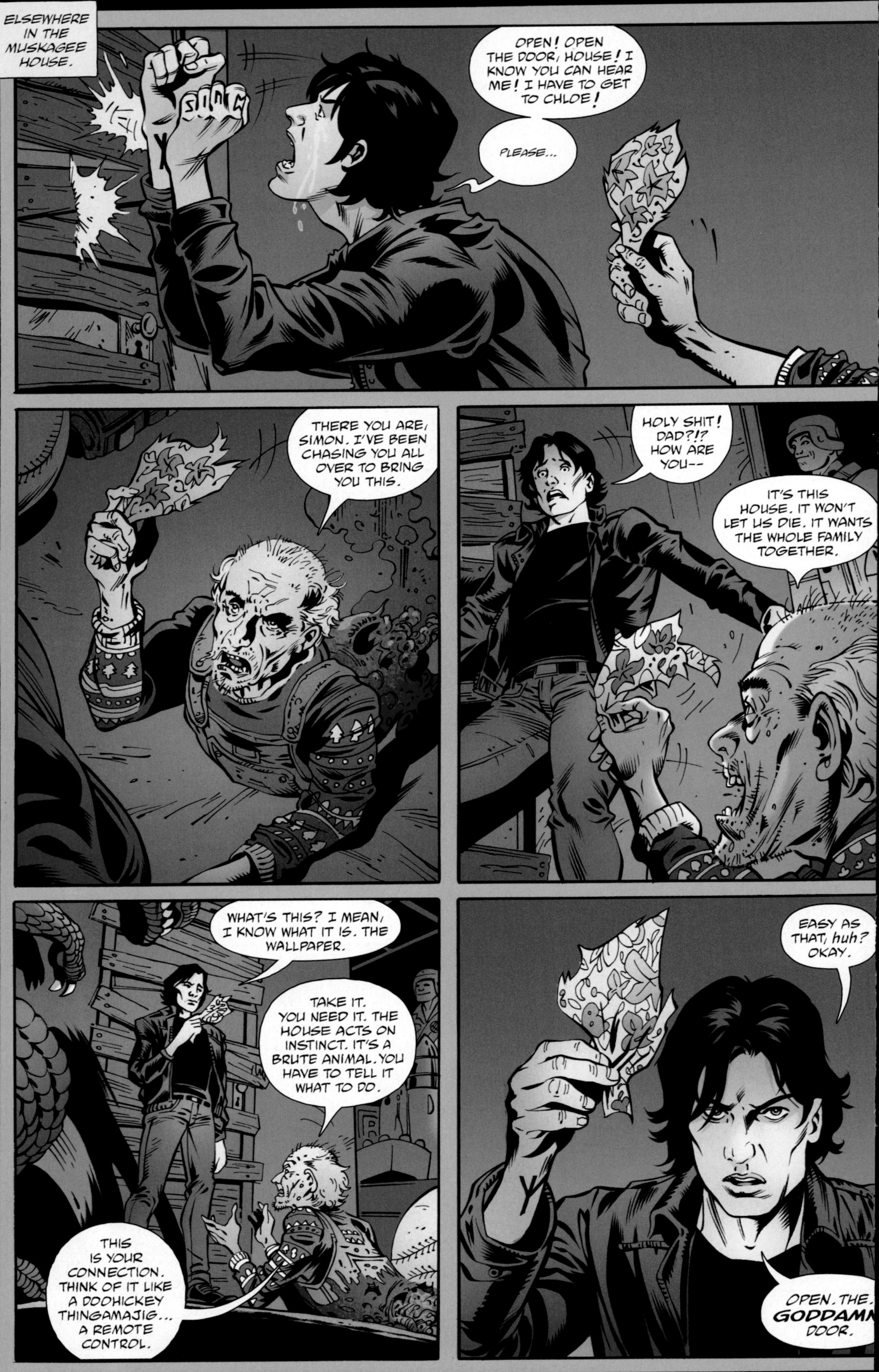
ELSEWHERE IN THE MUSKAGEE HOUSE.
OPEN! OPEN THE DOOR, HOUSE! I KNOW YOU CAN HEAR ME! I HAVE TO GET TO CHLOE!
PLEASE...
THERE YOU ARE, SIMON. I'VE BEEN CHASING YOU ALL OVER TO BRING YOU THIS.
HOLY SHIT! DAD?!? HOW ARE YOU--
IT'S THIS HOUSE. IT WON'T LET US DIE. IT WANTS THE WHOLE FAMILY TOGETHER.
WHAT'S THIS? I MEAN, I KNOW WHAT IT IS. THE WALLPAPER.
TAKE IT. YOU NEED IT. THE HOUSE ACTS ON INSTINCT. IT'S A BRUTE ANIMAL. YOU HAVE TO TELL IT WHAT TO DO.
THIS IS YOUR CONNECTION. THINK OF IT LIKE A DOOHICKEY THINGAMAJIG... A REMOTE CONTROL.
EASY AS THAT, *huh*? OKAY.
OPEN. THE. **GODDAMN** DOOR.

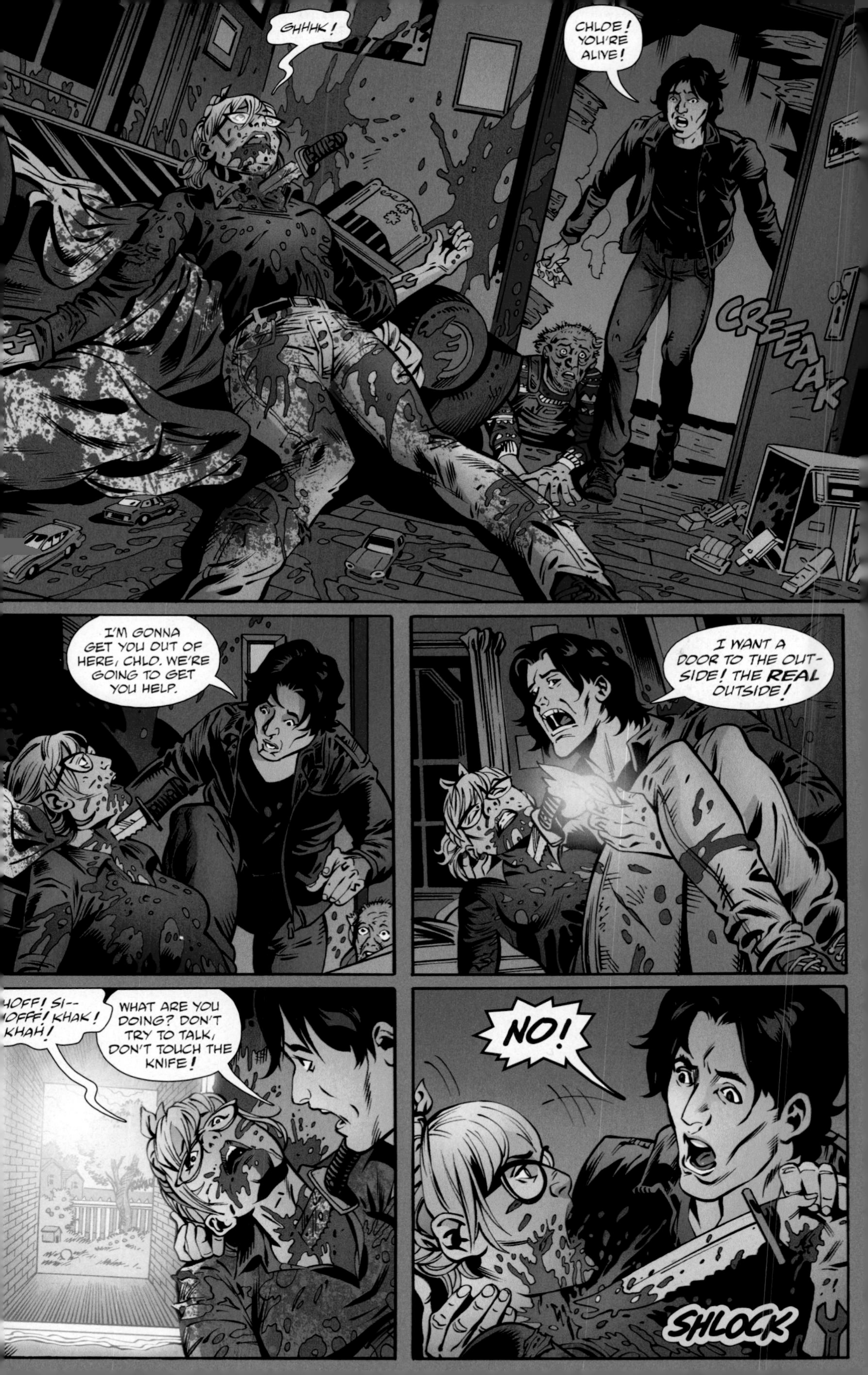
GHHHK!
CHLOE! YOU'RE ALIVE!
CREEAAK
I'M GONNA GET YOU OUT OF HERE, CHLO. WE'RE GOING TO GET YOU HELP.
I WANT A DOOR TO THE OUT-SIDE! THE REAL OUTSIDE!
HOFF! SI-- HOFF! KHAK! KHAH!
WHAT ARE YOU DOING? DON'T TRY TO TALK, DON'T TOUCH THE KNIFE!
NO!
SHLOCK

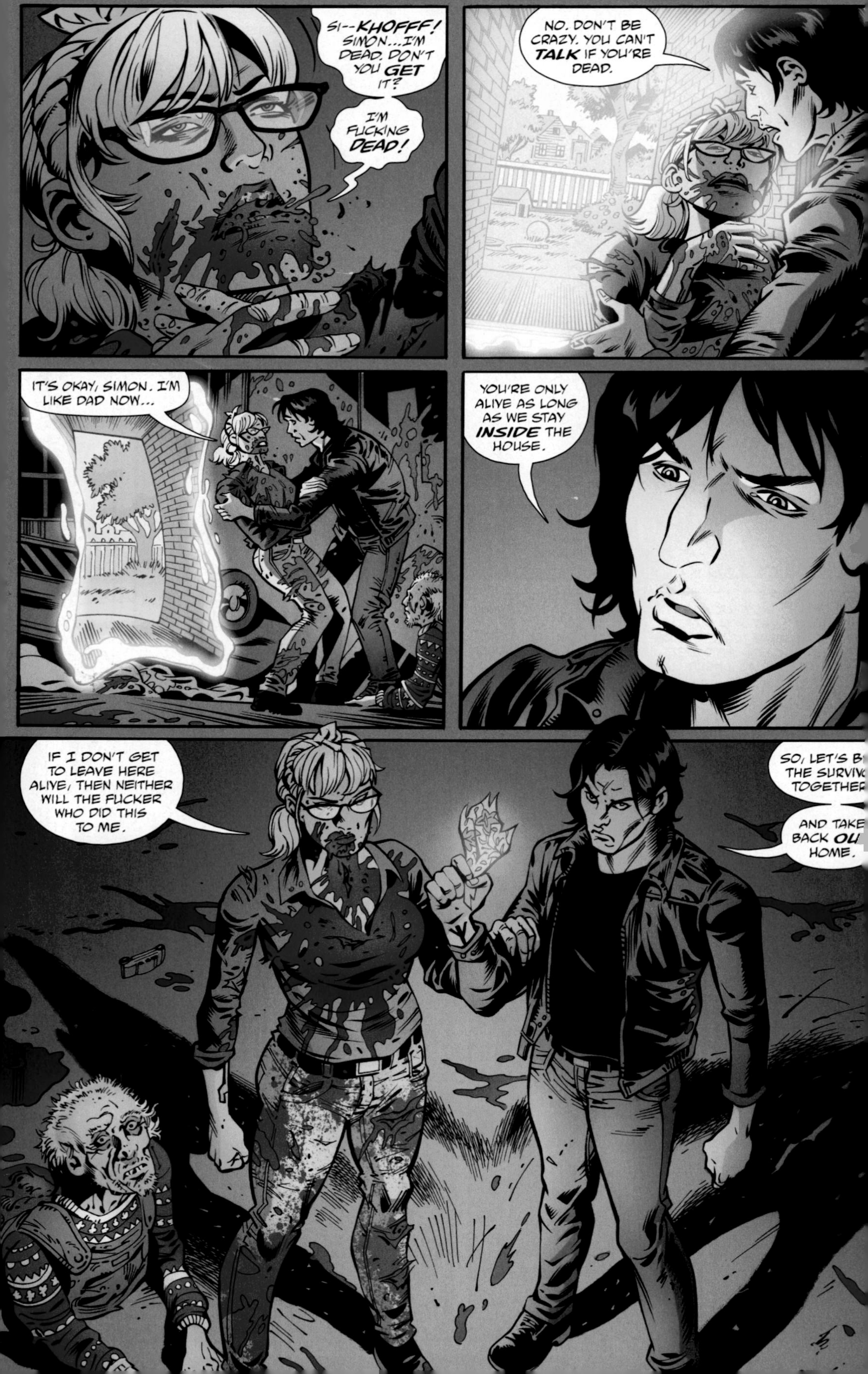
SI--KHOFFF! SIMON...I'M DEAD. DON'T YOU GET IT?
I'M FUCKING DEAD!
NO. DON'T BE CRAZY. YOU CAN'T TALK IF YOU'RE DEAD.
IT'S OKAY, SIMON. I'M LIKE DAD NOW...
YOU'RE ONLY ALIVE AS LONG AS WE STAY INSIDE THE HOUSE.
IF I DON'T GET TO LEAVE HERE ALIVE, THEN NEITHER WILL THE FUCKER WHO DID THIS TO ME.
SO, LET'S B THE SURVIVO TOGETHER
AND TAKE BACK OU HOME.

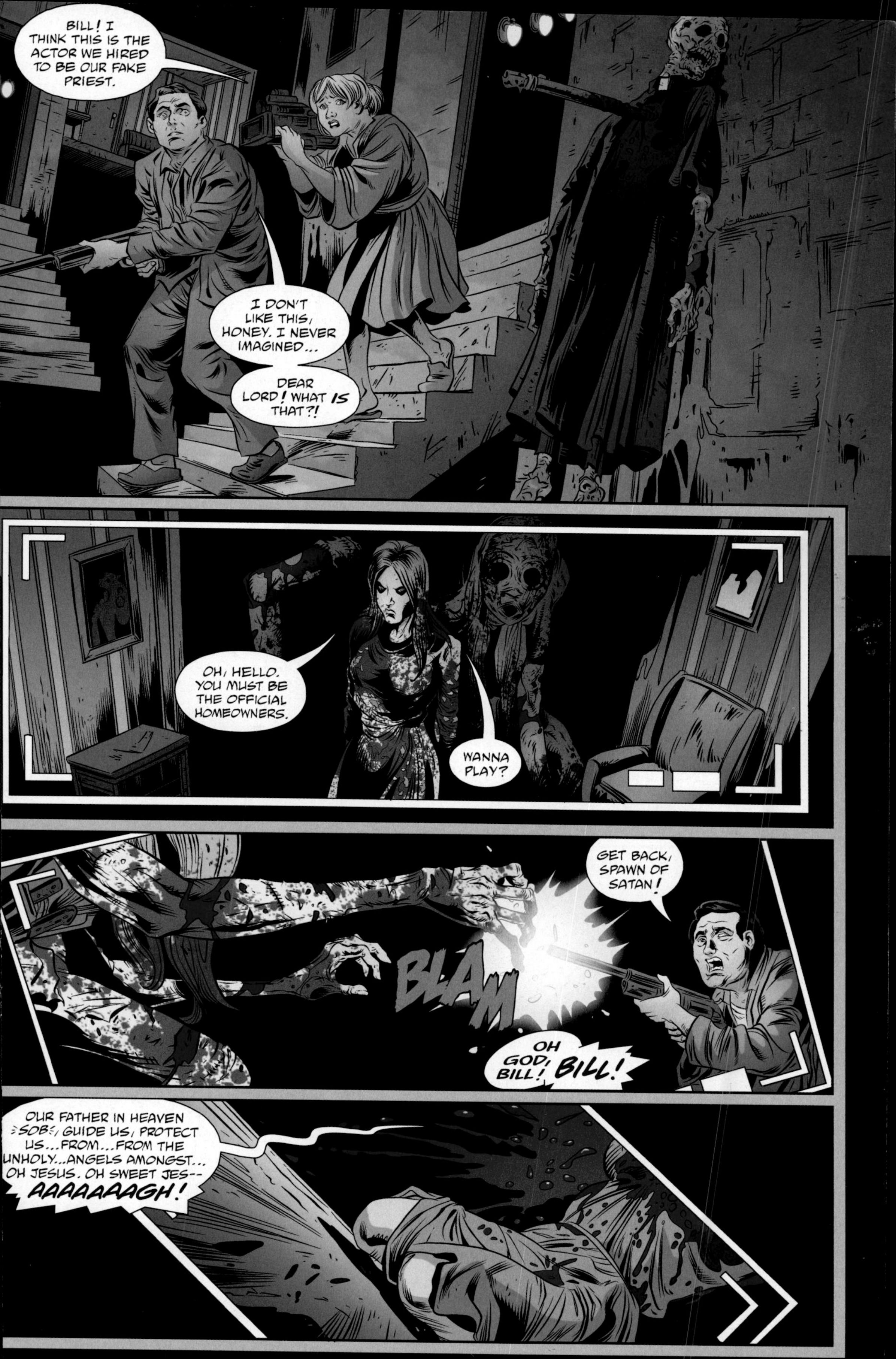
BILL! I THINK THIS IS THE ACTOR WE HIRED TO BE OUR FAKE PRIEST.
I DON'T LIKE THIS, HONEY. I NEVER IMAGINED...
DEAR LORD! WHAT IS THAT?!
OH, HELLO. YOU MUST BE THE OFFICIAL HOMEOWNERS.
WANNA PLAY?
GET BACK, SPAWN OF SATAN!
BLAM
OH GOD, BILL! BILL!
OUR FATHER IN HEAVEN =SOB= GUIDE US, PROTECT US...FROM...FROM THE UNHOLY...ANGELS AMONGST... OH JESUS. OH SWEET JES--
AAAAAAAGH!

WHOA! THE FLOOR'S MOVING! WHAT'S GOING ON?

OH, IT'S JUST THE HOUSE REARRANGING ITSELF.

LIKE A DOG, AFTER A NAP.

THANK GOD, YOU'RE ALIVE!

CHENZIRA? HOW ARE YOU IN PENNSYLVANIA? IS TEO HERE TOO? AND WHAT IS THAT *THING* ON KIRI'S BACK?

IT'S JUST AUNTIE. BUT THERE'S SOMETHING WRONG WITH HER.

LISTEN! WE KNOW WHAT'S GOING ON! DO YOU REMEMBER TENTRA AND THE GREEN LOLLIPOPS?

THAT DUMB CULT MOM WAS INTO?

ALL OUR PARENTS WERE GOING TO THE MEETINGS. THAT'S WHAT CONNECTS US!

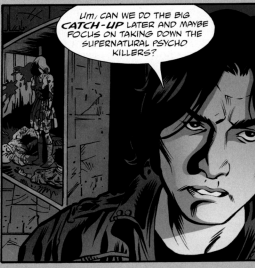
*Um,* CAN WE DO THE BIG *CATCH-UP* LATER AND MAYBE FOCUS ON TAKING DOWN THE SUPERNATURAL PSYCHO KILLERS?

DON'T WORRY, IT'S ALREADY TAKEN CARE OF.

YOU'RE ALL SO SCARED TO *CLAIM* YOUR DARKNESS, LET ALONE *CONTROL* IT.

YOU WASTED YO GIFTS.

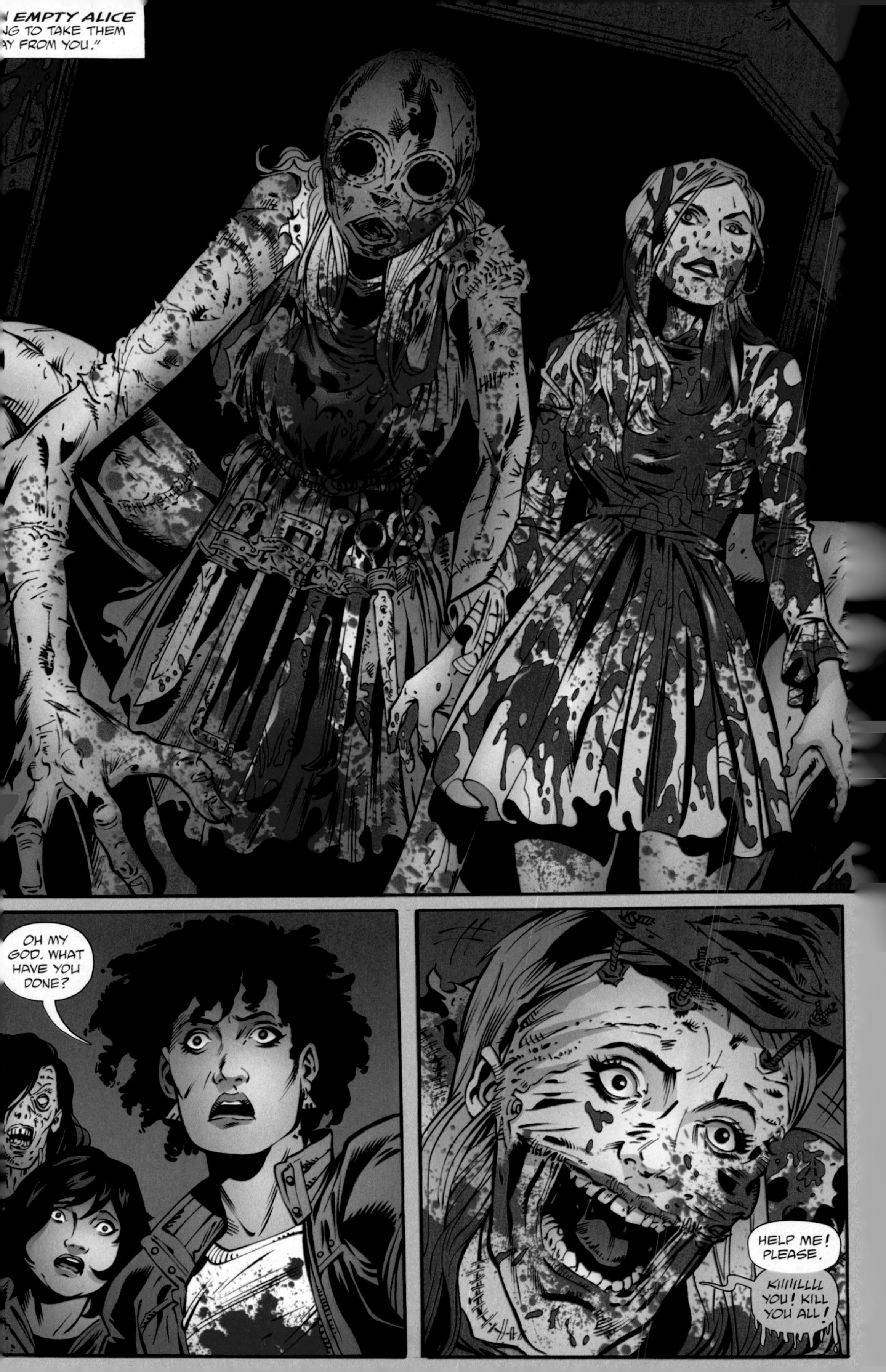

EMPTY ALICE
NG TO TAKE THEM
AY FROM YOU."
OH MY GOD. WHAT HAVE YOU DONE?
HELP ME! PLEASE.
KIIIILLLL YOU! KILL YOU ALL!

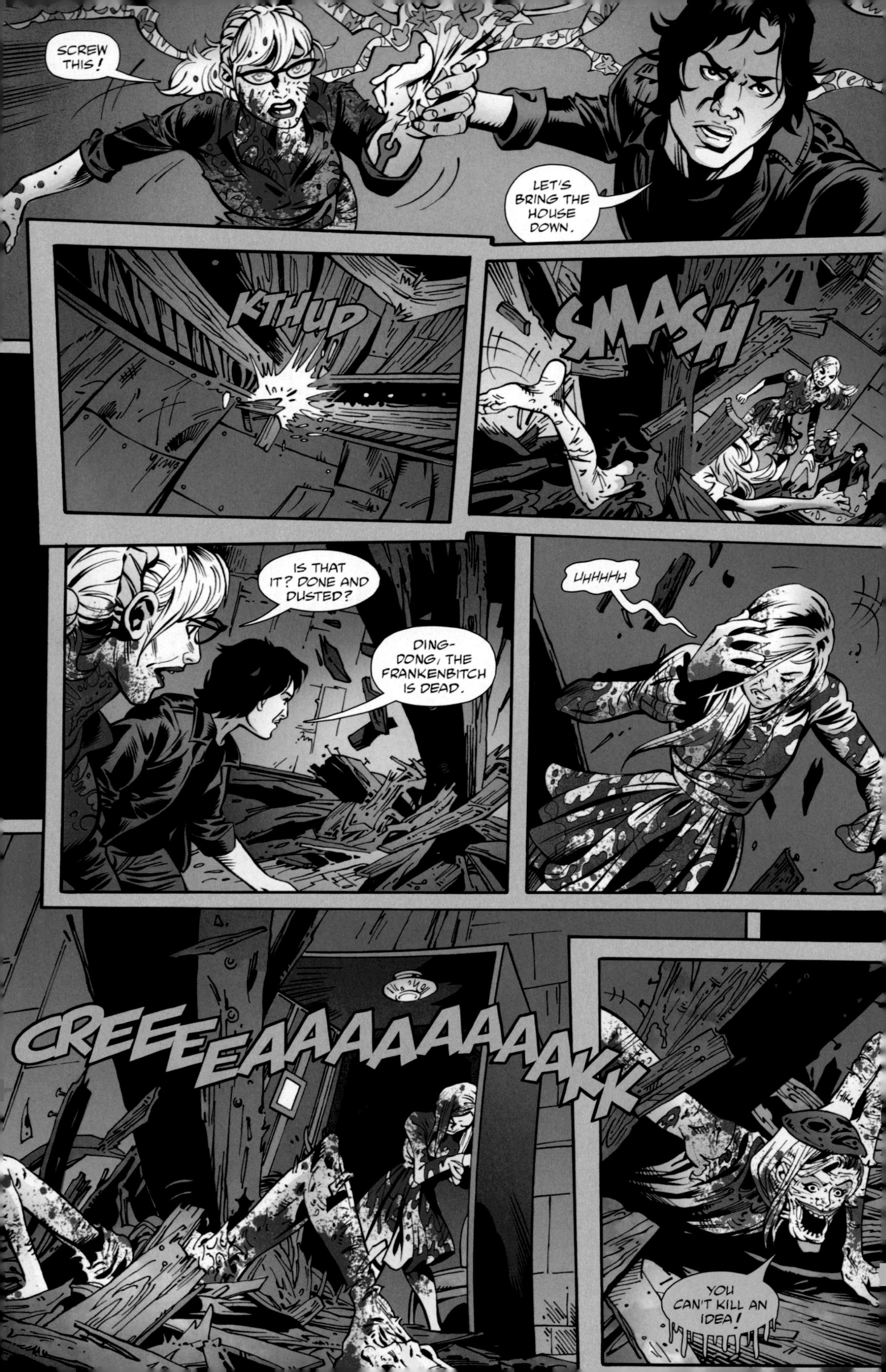
SCREW THIS!
LET'S BRING THE HOUSE DOWN.
KTHUD
SMASH
IS THAT IT? DONE AND DUSTED?
DING-DONG, THE FRANKENBITCH IS DEAD.
UHHHHH
CREEEEAAAAAAAAAKK
YOU CAN'T KILL AN IDEA!

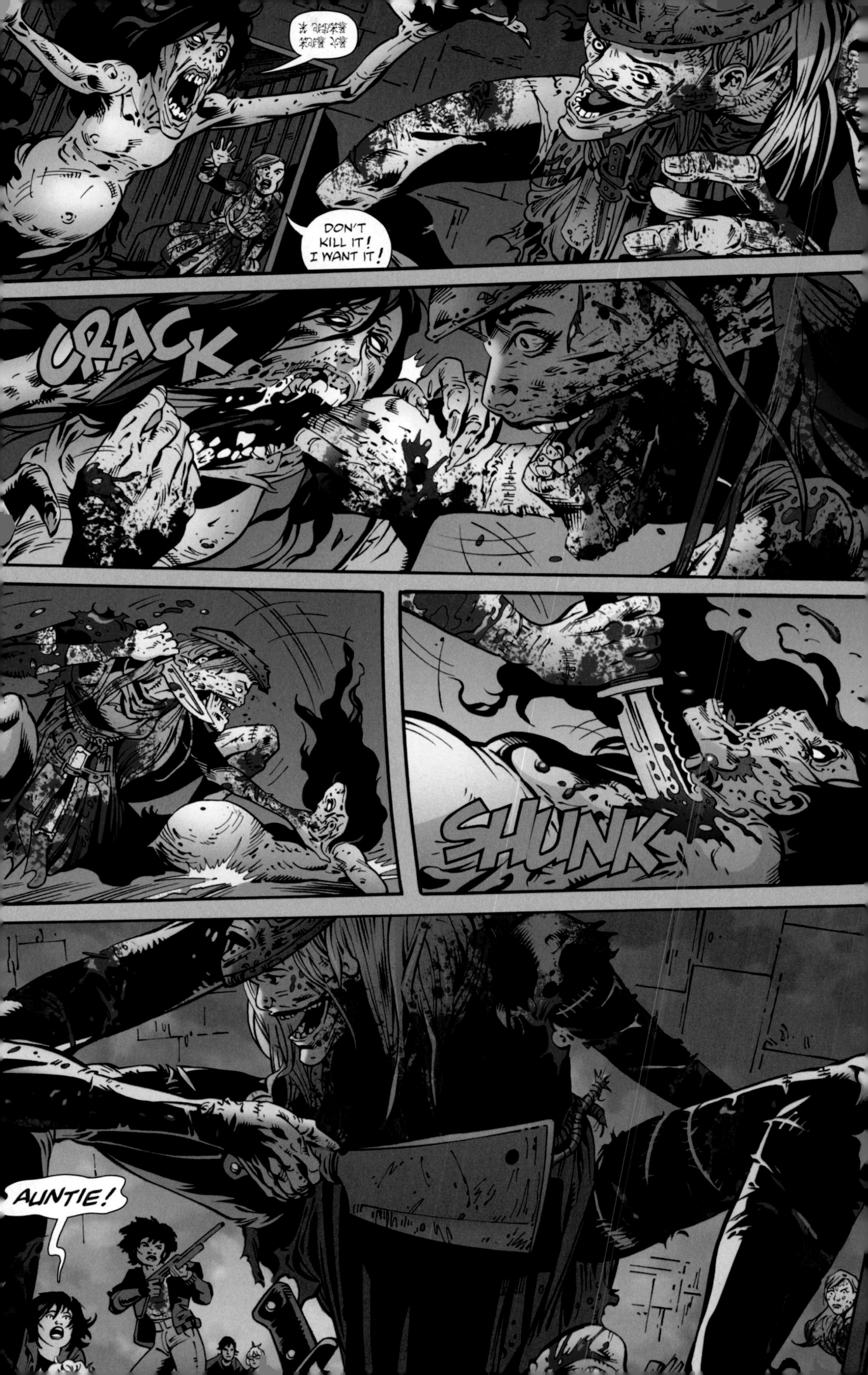
DON'T KILL IT! I WANT IT!
CRACK
SHUNK
AUNTIE!

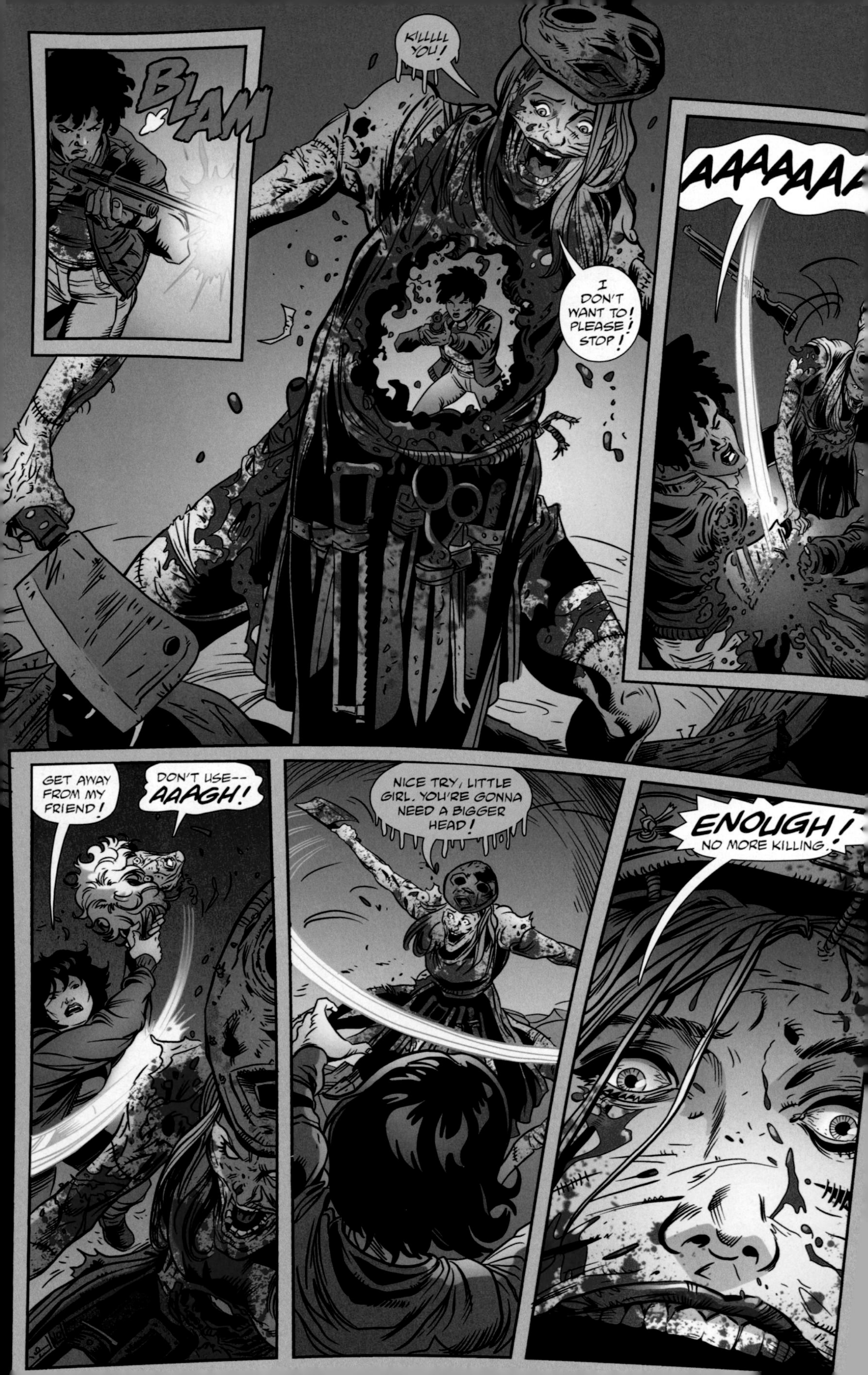

BLAM
KILLLLL YOU!
AAAAAAA
I DON'T WANT TO! PLEASE! STOP!
GET AWAY FROM MY FRIEND!
DON'T USE-- AAAGH!
NICE TRY, LITTLE GIRL. YOU'RE GONNA NEED A BIGGER HEAD!
ENOUGH! NO MORE KILLING.

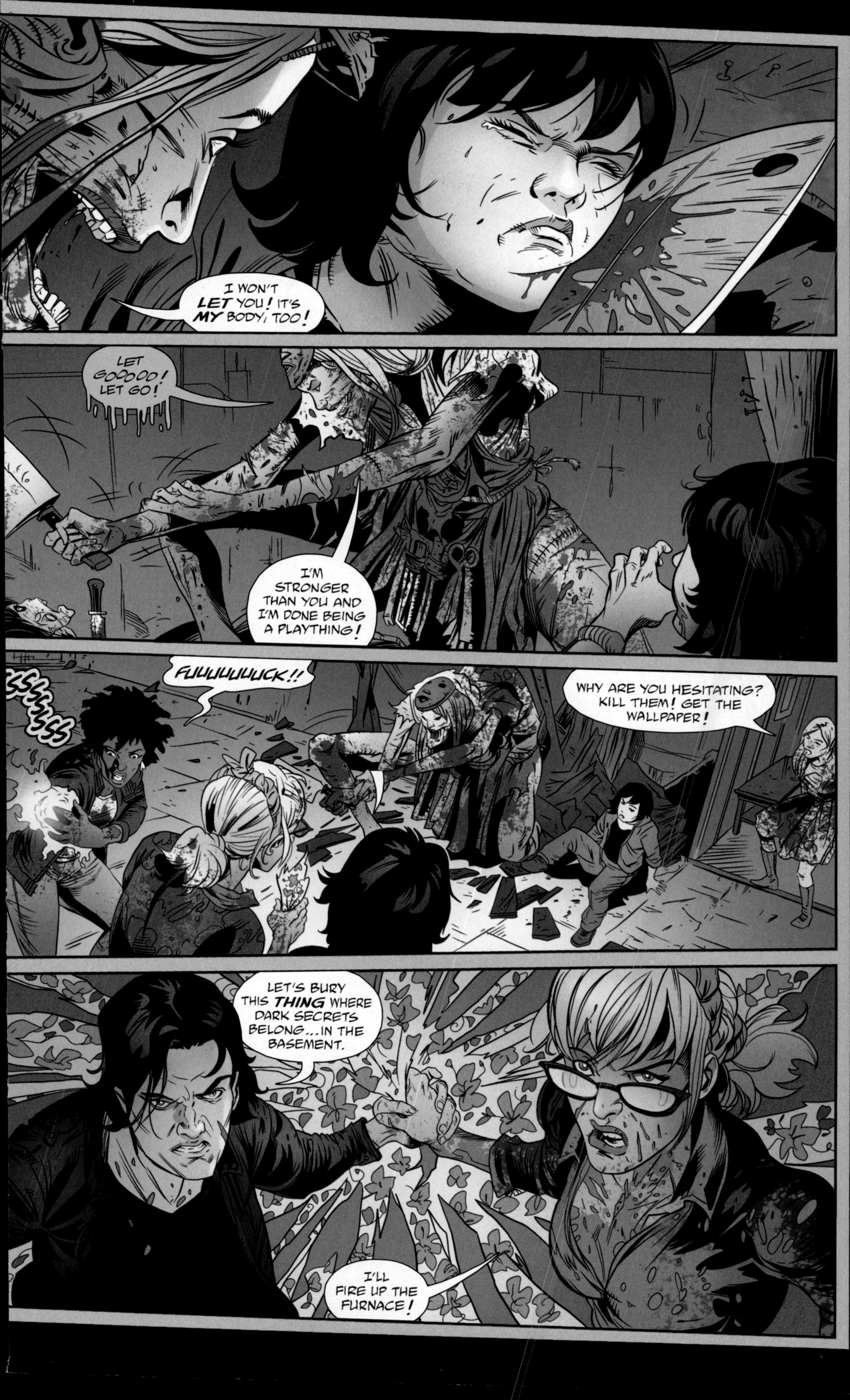
I WON'T LET YOU! IT'S MY BODY, TOO!
LET GOOOOO! LET GO!
I'M STRONGER THAN YOU AND I'M DONE BEING A PLAYTHING!
FUUUUUUUCK!!
SSSSSSSSS
WHY ARE YOU HESITATING? KILL THEM! GET THE WALLPAPER!
LET'S BURY THIS THING WHERE DARK SECRETS BELONG...IN THE BASEMENT.
I'LL FIRE UP THE FURNACE!

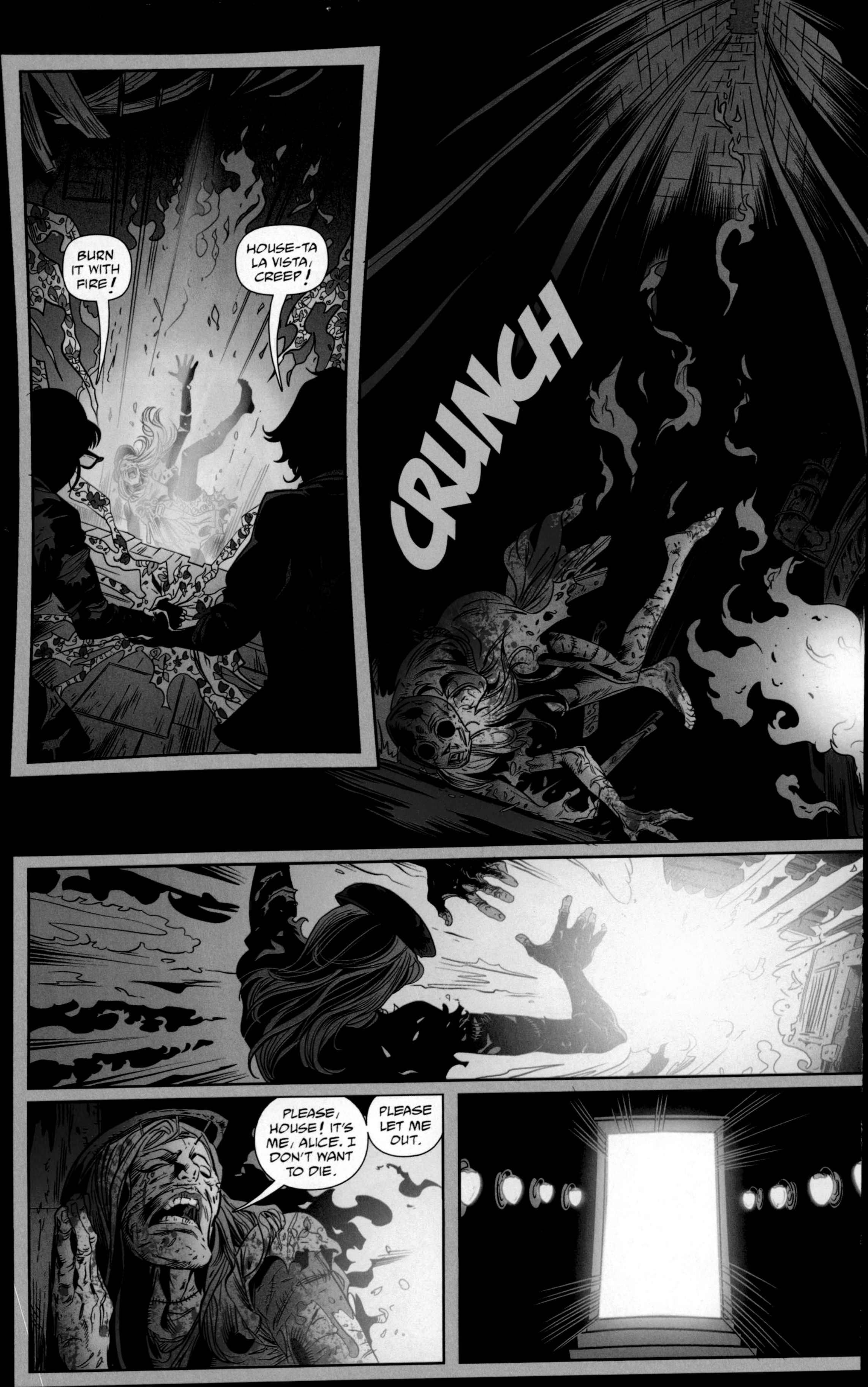
BURN IT WITH FIRE!
HOUSE-TA LA VISTA, CREEP!
CRUNCH
PLEASE, HOUSE! IT'S ME, ALICE. I DON'T WANT TO DIE.
PLEASE LET ME OUT.

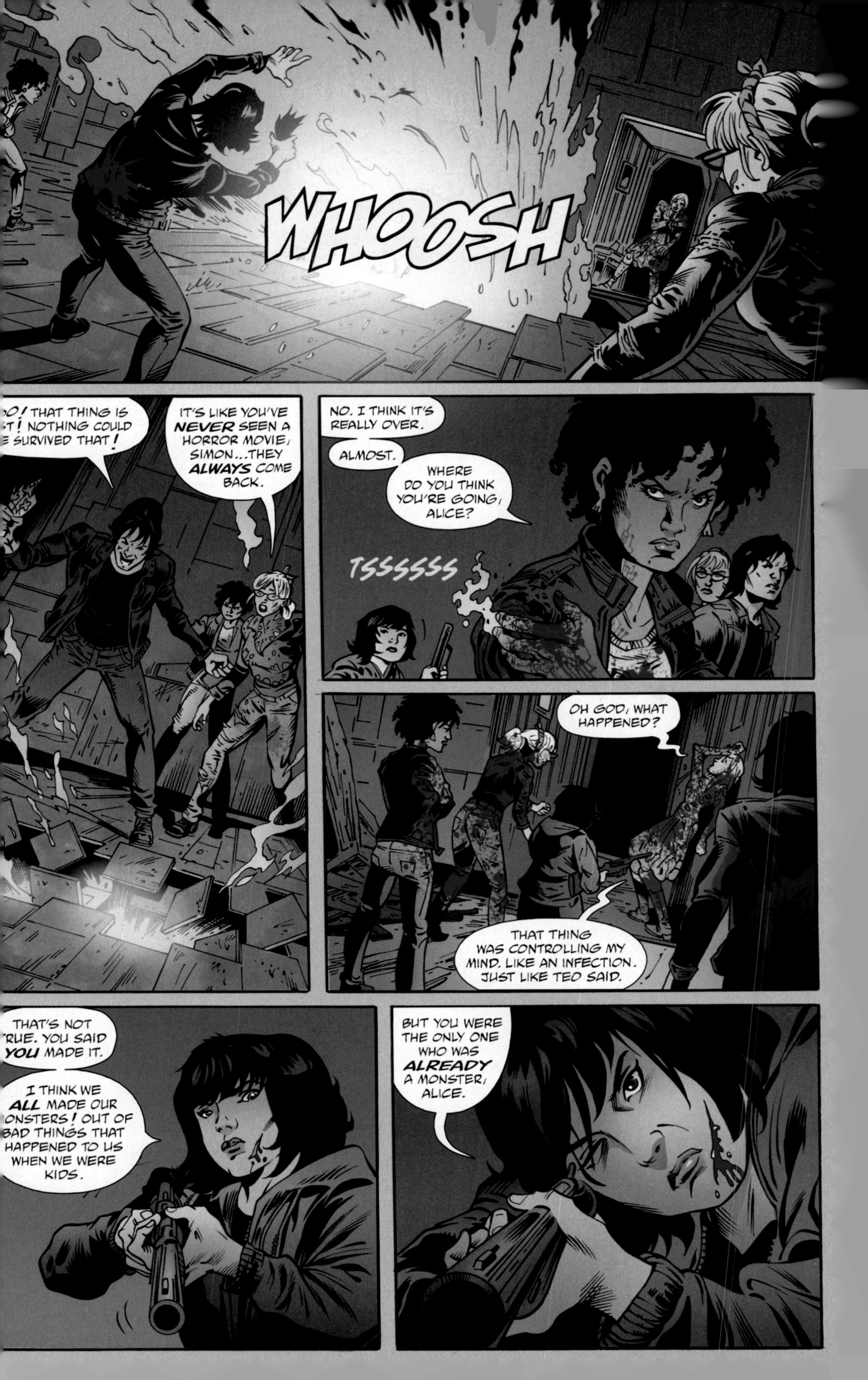
WHOOSH
…O! THAT THING IS …T! NOTHING COULD …E SURVIVED THAT!
IT'S LIKE YOU'VE NEVER SEEN A HORROR MOVIE, SIMON... THEY ALWAYS COME BACK.
NO. I THINK IT'S REALLY OVER.
ALMOST.
WHERE DO YOU THINK YOU'RE GOING, ALICE?
TSSSSSS
OH GOD, WHAT HAPPENED?
THAT THING WAS CONTROLLING MY MIND. LIKE AN INFECTION. JUST LIKE TEO SAID.
THAT'S NOT …RUE. YOU SAID YOU MADE IT.
I THINK WE ALL MADE OUR …ONSTERS! OUT OF …BAD THINGS THAT HAPPENED TO US WHEN WE WERE KIDS.
BUT YOU WERE THE ONLY ONE WHO WAS ALREADY A MONSTER, ALICE.

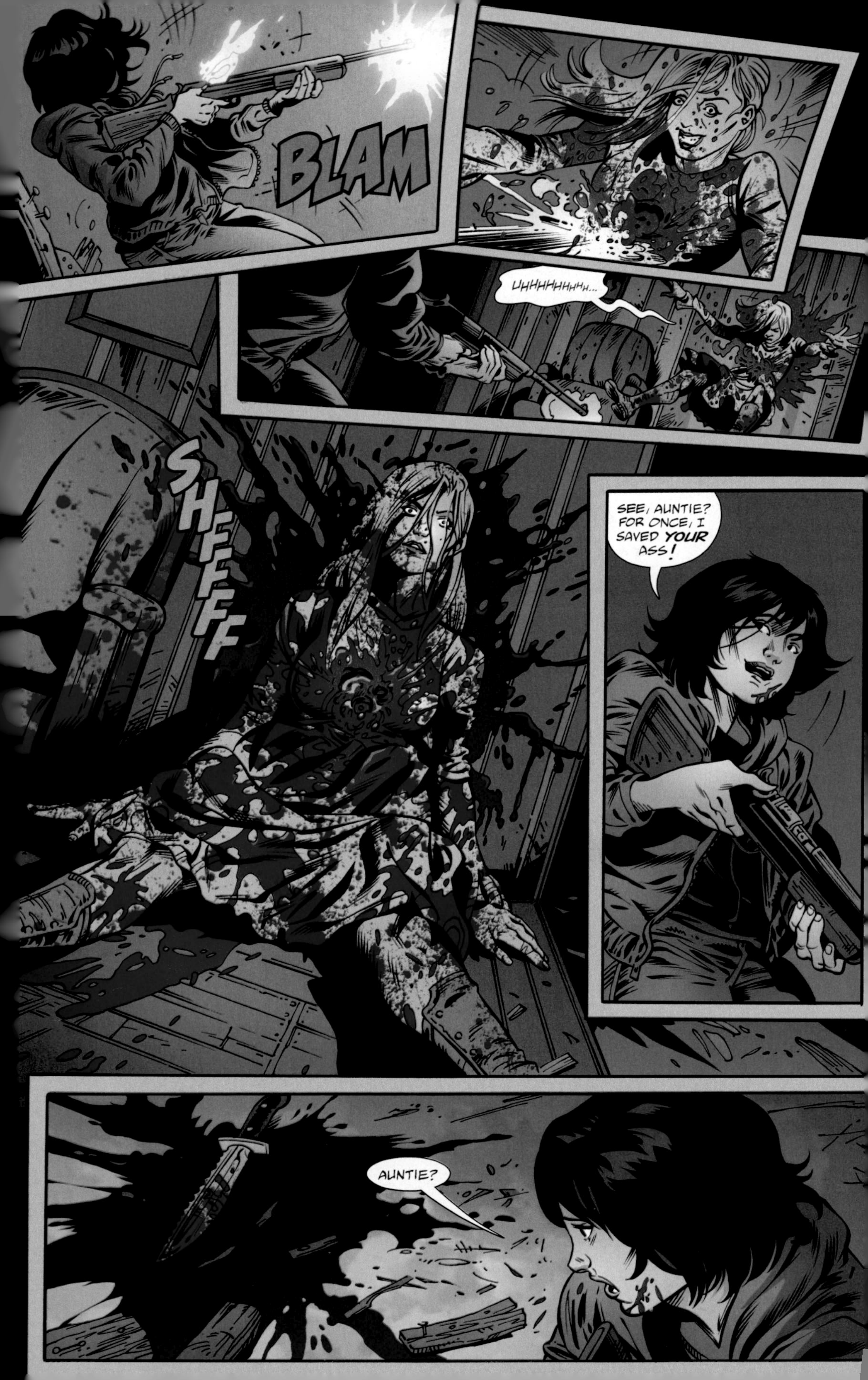
BLAM
UHHHHHHHHH...
SHFFFF
SEE, AUNTIE? FOR ONCE, I SAVED YOUR ASS!
AUNTIE?

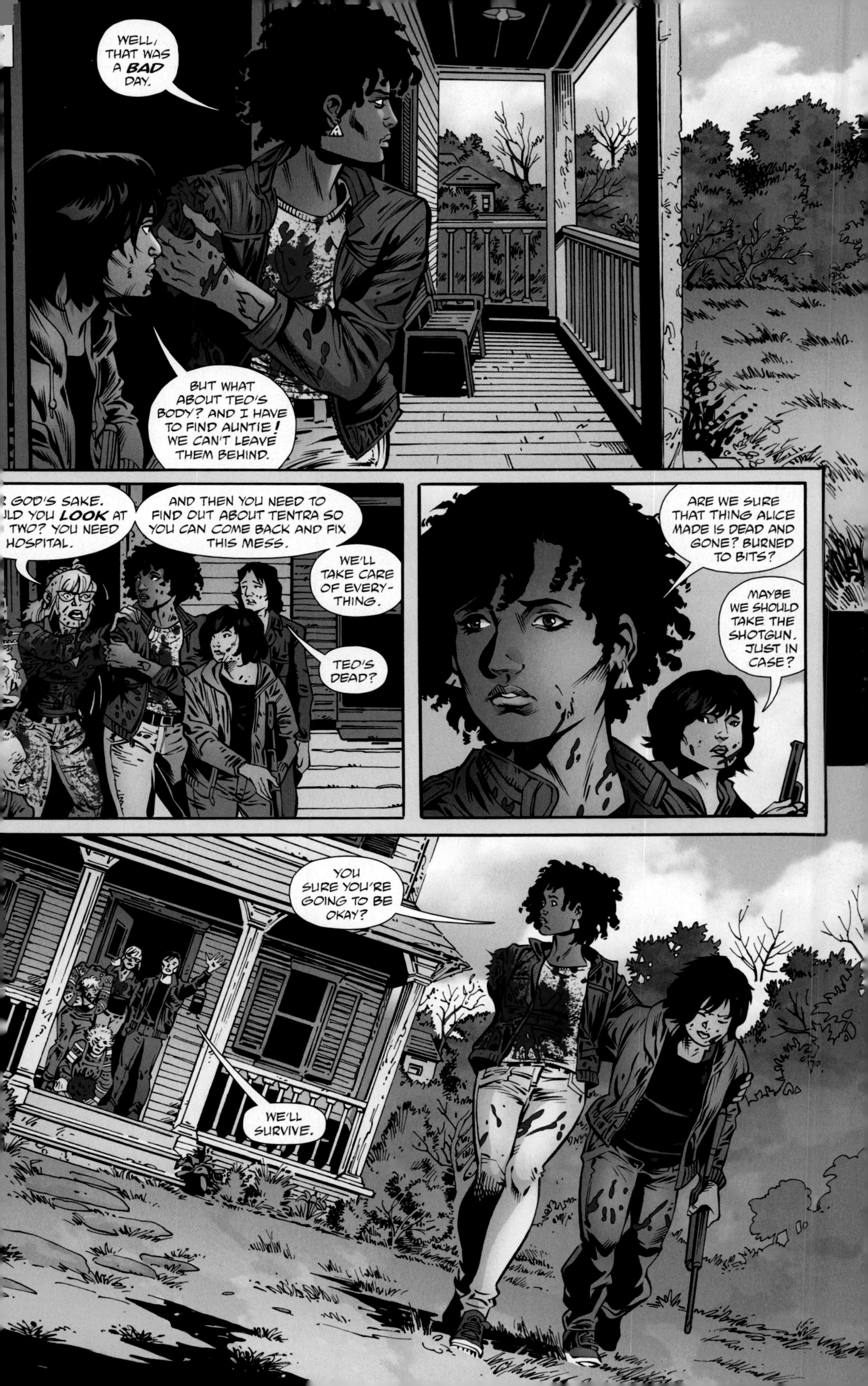
WELL, THAT WAS A **BAD** DAY.
BUT WHAT ABOUT TEO'S BODY? AND I HAVE TO FIND AUNTIE! WE CAN'T LEAVE THEM BEHIND.
GOD'S SAKE. LD YOU **LOOK** AT TWO? YOU NEED HOSPITAL.
AND THEN YOU NEED TO FIND OUT ABOUT TENTRA SO YOU CAN COME BACK AND FIX THIS MESS.
WE'LL TAKE CARE OF EVERY-THING.
TEO'S DEAD?
ARE WE SURE THAT THING ALICE MADE IS DEAD AND GONE? BURNED TO BITS?
MAYBE WE SHOULD TAKE THE SHOTGUN. JUST IN CASE?
YOU SURE YOU'RE GOING TO BE OKAY?
WE'LL SURVIVE.

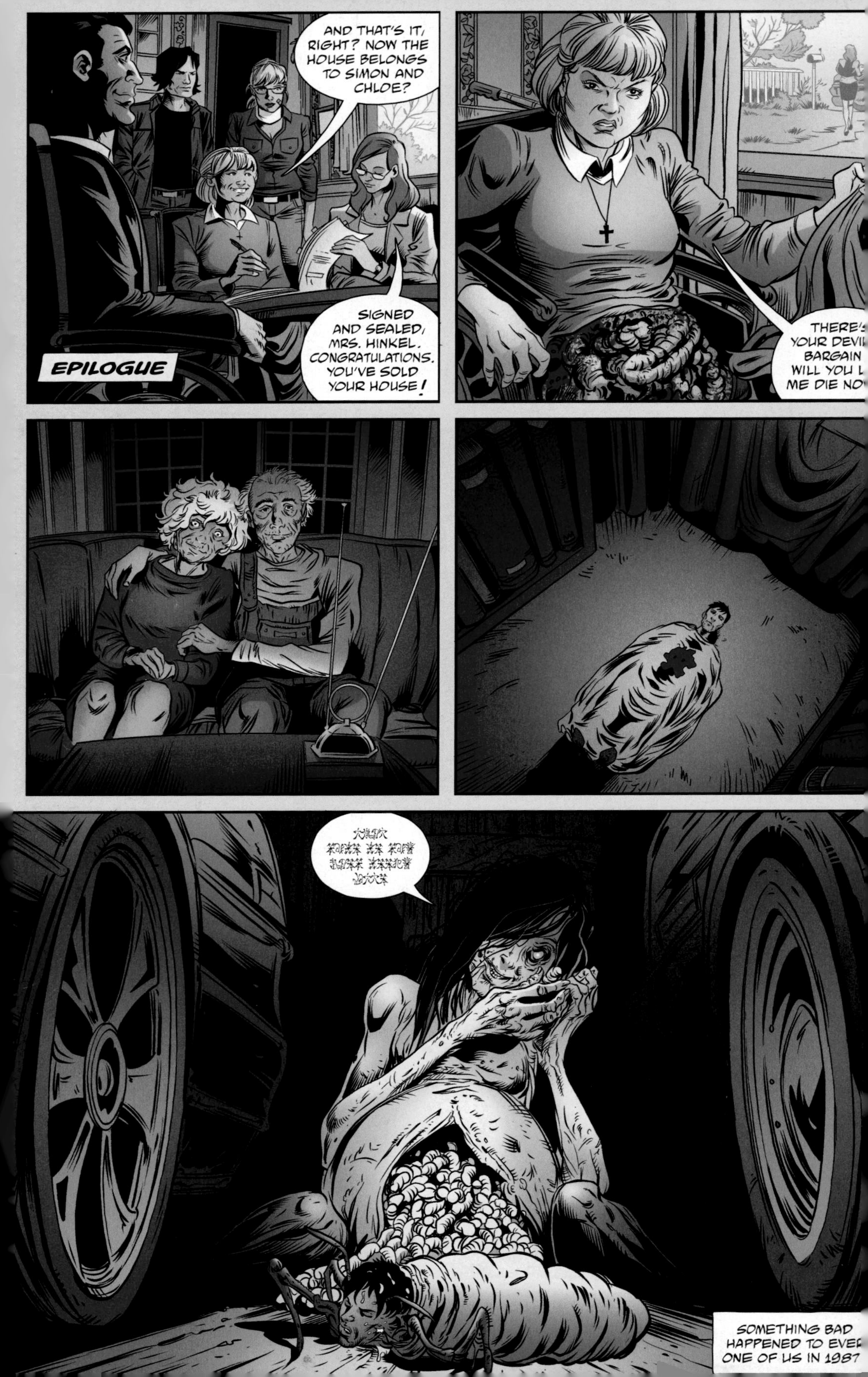
AND THAT'S IT, RIGHT? NOW THE HOUSE BELONGS TO SIMON AND CHLOE?
SIGNED AND SEALED, MRS. HINKEL. CONGRATULATIONS. YOU'VE SOLD YOUR HOUSE!
EPILOGUE
THERE' YOUR DEVI BARGAIN WILL YOU L ME DIE NO
SOMETHING BAD HAPPENED TO EVE ONE OF US IN 1987

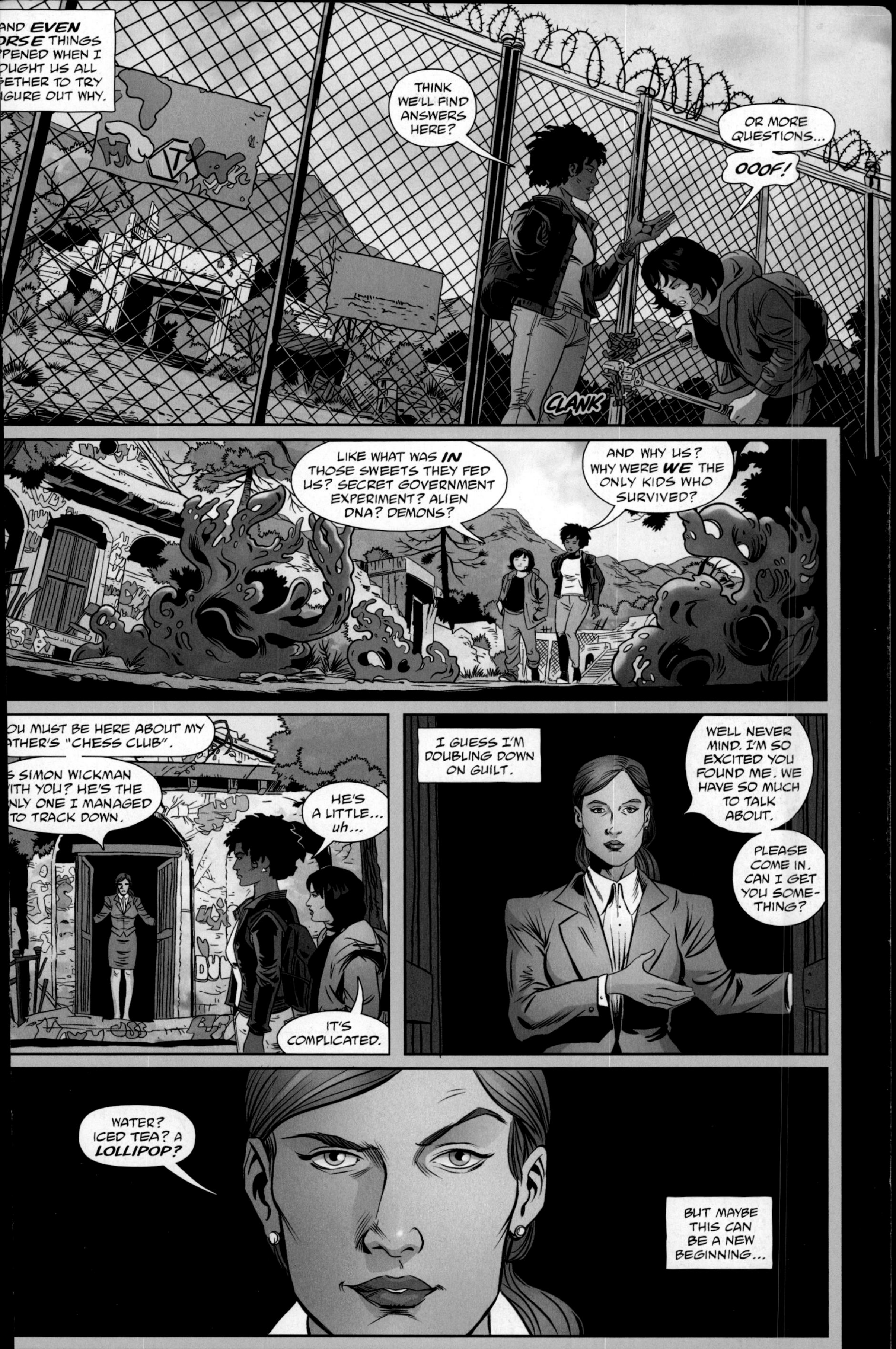
AND EVEN ORSE THINGS PPENED WHEN I OUGHT US ALL GETHER TO TRY IGURE OUT WHY.
THINK WE'LL FIND ANSWERS HERE?
OR MORE QUESTIONS...
OOOF!
CLANK
LIKE WHAT WAS IN THOSE SWEETS THEY FED US? SECRET GOVERNMENT EXPERIMENT? ALIEN DNA? DEMONS?
AND WHY US? WHY WERE WE THE ONLY KIDS WHO SURVIVED?
OU MUST BE HERE ABOUT MY ATHER'S "CHESS CLUB".
S SIMON WICKMAN WITH YOU? HE'S THE NLY ONE I MANAGED TO TRACK DOWN.
HE'S A LITTLE... uh...
IT'S COMPLICATED.
I GUESS I'M DOUBLING DOWN ON GUILT.
WELL NEVER MIND. I'M SO EXCITED YOU FOUND ME. WE HAVE SO MUCH TO TALK ABOUT.
PLEASE COME IN. CAN I GET YOU SOME-THING?
WATER? ICED TEA? A LOLLIPOP?
BUT MAYBE THIS CAN BE A NEW BEGINNING...

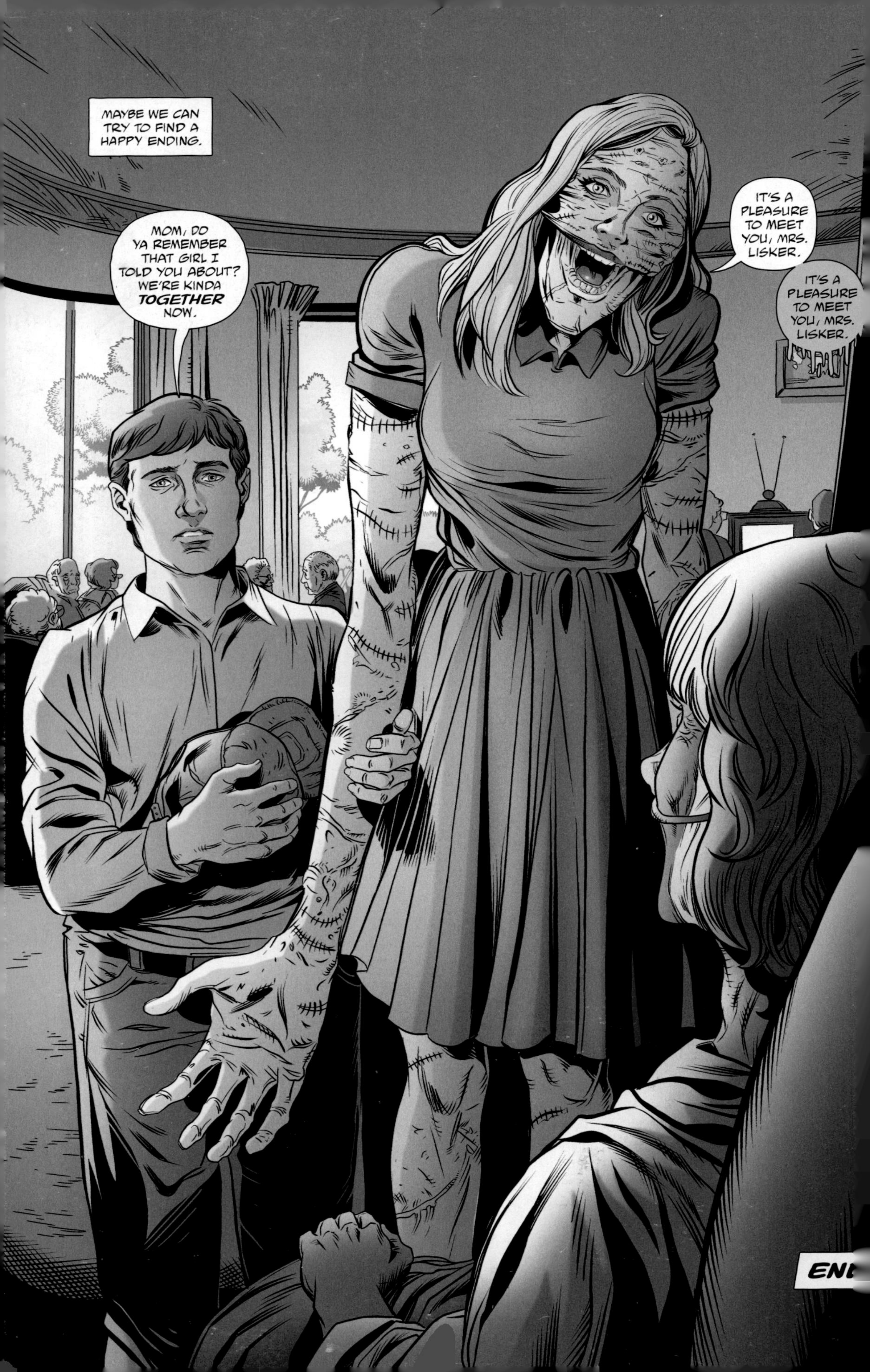
MAYBE WE CAN TRY TO FIND A HAPPY ENDING.
MOM, DO YA REMEMBER THAT GIRL I TOLD YOU ABOUT? WE'RE KINDA **TOGETHER** NOW.
IT'S A PLEASURE TO MEET YOU, MRS. LISKER.
IT'S A PLEASURE TO MEET YOU, MRS. LISKER.